Modern Healthcare Marketing in the Digital Era

Kakhaber Djakeli
University of Georgia, Georgia

A volume in the Advances in Healthcare Information Systems and Administration (AHISA) Book Series

IGI Global
PUBLISHER of TIMELY KNOWLEDGE

Published in the United States of America by
IGI Global
Medical Information Science Reference (an imprint of IGI Global)
701 E. Chocolate Avenue
Hershey PA, USA 17033
Tel: 717-533-8845
Fax: 717-533-8661
E-mail: cust@igi-global.com
Web site: http://www.igi-global.com

Library of Congress Cataloging-in-Publication Data

Names: Djakeli, Kakhaber, 1967- editor.
Title: Modern healthcare marketing in the digital era / edited by Kakhaber Djakeli.
Description: Hershey, PA : Medical Information Science Reference, [2024] | Includes bibliographical references and index. | Summary: "The book will provide relevant theoretical frameworks and the latest empirical research findings in the area of healthcare marketing, big data analytics, artificial intelligence, augmented reality, block chain, mobile technologies, etc"-- Provided by publisher.
Identifiers: LCCN 2023039042 (print) | LCCN 2023039043 (ebook) | ISBN 9798369306796 (hardcover) | ISBN 9798369306802 (ebook)
Subjects: MESH: Marketing of Health Services | Big Data | Artificial Intelligence | Digital Technology
Classification: LCC RA410.56 (print) | LCC RA410.56 (ebook) | NLM W 74.1 | DDC 362.1068/80285--dc23/eng/20231027
LC record available at https://lccn.loc.gov/2023039042
LC ebook record available at https://lccn.loc.gov/2023039043

This book is published in the IGI Global book series Advances in Healthcare Information Systems and Administration (AHISA) (ISSN: 2328-1243; eISSN: 2328-126X)

British Cataloguing in Publication Data
A Cataloguing in Publication record for this book is available from the British Library.

For electronic access to this publication, please contact: eresources@igi-global.com.

Advances in Healthcare Information Systems and Administration (AHISA) Book Series

Anastasius Moumtzoglou
Hellenic Society for Quality & Safety in Healthcare and P. & A. Kyriakou Children's Hospital, Greece

ISSN:2328-1243
EISSN:2328-126X

Mission

The **Advances in Healthcare Information Systems and Administration (AHISA) Book Series** aims to provide a channel for international researchers to progress the field of study on technology and its implications on healthcare and health information systems. With the growing focus on healthcare and the importance of enhancing this industry to tend to the expanding population, the book series seeks to accelerate the awareness of technological advancements of health information systems and expand awareness and implementation.

Driven by advancing technologies and their clinical applications, the emerging field of health information systems and informatics is still searching for coherent directing frameworks to advance health care and clinical practices and research. Conducting research in these areas is both promising and challenging due to a host of factors, including rapidly evolving technologies and their application complexity. At the same time, organizational issues, including technology adoption, diffusion and acceptance as well as cost benefits and cost effectiveness of advancing health information systems and informatics applications as innovative forms of investment in healthcare are gaining attention as well. **AHISA** addresses these concepts and critical issues.

Coverage

- Measurements and Impact of HISA on Public and Social Policy
- IT Applications in Health Organizations and Practices
- IT Applications in Physical Therapeutic Treatments
- Nursing Expert Systems
- Rehabilitative Technologies
- E-Health and M-Health
- Virtual health technologies
- IT security and privacy issues
- Pharmaceutical and Home Healthcare Informatics
- IS in Healthcare

IGI Global is currently accepting manuscripts for publication within this series. To submit a proposal for a volume in this series, please contact our Acquisition Editors at Acquisitions@igi-global.com or visit: http://www.igi-global.com/publish/.

The Advances in Healthcare Information Systems and Administration (AHISA) Book Series (ISSN 2328-1243) is published by IGI Global, 701 E. Chocolate Avenue, Hershey, PA 17033-1240, USA, www.igi-global.com. This series is composed of titles available for purchase individually; each title is edited to be contextually exclusive from any other title within the series. For pricing and ordering information please visit http://www.igi-global.com/book-series/advances-healthcare-information-systems-administration/37156. Postmaster: Send all address changes to above address.

Titles in this Series

For a list of additional titles in this series, please visit: www.igi-global.com/book-series

Pioneering Smart Healthcare 5.0 with IoT, Federated Learning, and Cloud Security
Ahdi Hassan (Global Institute for Research Education and Scholarship, Amsterdam, The Netherlands) Vivek Kumar Prasad (Nirma University, India) Pronaya Bhattacharya (Amity University Kolkata, India) Pushan Kumar Dutta (Amity University Kolkata, India) and Robertas Damaševičius (Center of Real Time Computer Systems, Kaunas University of Technology, Lithuania)
Medical Information Science Reference • © 2024 • 370pp • H/C (ISBN: 9798369326398) • US $375.00

Contemporary Applications of Data Fusion for Advanced Healthcare Informatics
G.S. Karthick (PSG College of Arts and Science, India) and Sathishkumar Karupusamy (Gobi Arts and Science College, India)
Medical Information Science Reference • © 2023 • 514pp • H/C (ISBN: 9781668489130) • US $325.00

Dynamics of Swarm Intelligence Health Analysis for the Next Generation
Arumugam Suresh Kumar (Jain University (Deemed), India) Utku Kose (Suleyman Demirel University, Turkey) Sachin Sharma (Graphic Era University (Deemed), India) and S. Jerald Nirmal Kumar (Sharda University, India)
Medical Information Science Reference • © 2023 • 273pp • H/C (ISBN: 9781668468944) • US $345.00

Revolutionizing Healthcare Through Artificial Intelligence and Internet of Things Applications
Keshav Kaushik (University of Petroleum and Energy Studies, India) Susheela Dahiya (Graphic Era Hill University, Dehradun, India) Shilpi Aggarwal (State University of New York, USA) and Ashutosh Dhar Dwivedi (Copenhagen Business School, Denmark)
Medical Information Science Reference • © 2023 • 277pp • H/C (ISBN: 9781668454220) • US $345.00

Global Perspectives on Probing Narratives in Healthcare
Teresa Casal (University of Lisbon, Portugal) and Maria de Jesus Cabral (University of Minho, Portugal)
Medical Information Science Reference • © 2023 • 349pp • H/C (ISBN: 9781668480649) • US $325.00

Integrating Digital Health Strategies for Effective Administration
Ahmed Chemseddine Bouarar (University of Medea, Algeria) Kamel Mouloudj (University of Medea, Algeria) and Dachel Martínez Asanza (University of Medical Sciences of Havana, Cuba)
Medical Information Science Reference • © 2023 • 450pp • H/C (ISBN: 9781668483374) • US $325.00

IGI Global
PUBLISHER of TIMELY KNOWLEDGE

701 East Chocolate Avenue, Hershey, PA 17033, USA
Tel: 717-533-8845 x100 • Fax: 717-533-8661
E-Mail: cust@igi-global.com • www.igi-global.com

Table of Contents

Detailed Table of Contents

Artificial intelligence with virtual reality and the overwhelming digitalization in the next 10 years will change the role of healthcare marketing from managing to creation of new health. The dynamic of digital force development and the disruptive technological jump to high competitiveness of healthcare providers will make the role of marketing as the core. The functionality of healthcare and its advantages with professional medical manipulations and diagnosis will relay of modern marketing function to flourish the preventive and active healthcare for everyone to bring the health manipulations to the home of patients and make health the daily substance, utilizing deepest digitalization of relation to patients, insurers, health providers, controllers, and to the new health quality systems into one big, branded family. All this innovative development is today under construction, and they rely on healthcare marketing. The chapter includes the evolution of healthcare marketing from the beginning to advanced stages and the future of healthcare marketing development.

The chapter discusses the features of using social media in the healthcare industry. It is emphasized that the role of social media in the era of digital technologies is especially increasing in the market of medical services, which leads to greater involvement of consumers in the field of healthcare. Digital technologies are gradually being introduced in the field of healthcare in Georgia, and an increasing number of medical organizations are using social media marketing to communicate with patients. Nevertheless, the use of social media by healthcare organizations is insufficient. One of the reasons for this is the lack of research in this field. With this in mind, this chapter presents a study that considers the impact of social media marketing activities on healthcare consumer behavior. Social media marketing activities, consumer engagement, consumer trust, and behavioral intention are selected as the main variables of the research. A conceptual model of the research has been developed, and relevant hypotheses have been formulated.

Focusing on China's distinct market, this chapter delves into how healthcare marketing has evolved in the digital age. It analyzes how developments in AI, big data analytics, augmented reality, blockchain, and mobile technologies are fueling a transition toward a consumer-centric health culture. This chapter explores the changing demands and preferences of the Chinese healthcare market, the importance of value-driven marketing tactics, and the function of customer relationship management. Ethical concerns, pricing concerns, and success metrics are also discussed. This chapter is a must-read for anybody with even a passing interest in the rapidly growing field of digital healthcare, since it provides a thorough overview of the history, current applications, and future directions of digital healthcare in China.

The main purpose of the chapter is to review medical systems and their financing, and to popularize these systems through various marketing tools. Within the different approaches to healthcare financing, particular attention has been given to the method of individual medical accounts. According to the authors, this method is conducive to the development of various other methods of treatment due to the availability of funds from one's own therapeutic account and the patient's personal choice of the center and treatment method. In this way, it allows the strengthening of a specific supply of medical services, including alternative treatment methods from the point of view of classical medicine.

There has been a significant rise in the prices of medicines in the recent past. Major pharmaceutical companies, 'Big Pharma', argue in favor of this development as it takes a lot of research and resources to bring a drug to market. Once in the market, the primary source of revenue generation for the companies is through sale of prescription drugs. Companies also have to spend a lot of their income on various marketing communication programs to convince their prescribers, even if it comes at costs that are difficult to ignore. This chapter studies the array of marketing strategies that are adopted by Big Pharma in developing and expanding their businesses. It also places these strategies within the context of the fast-growing generics market with its consequent changes to the marketing mix of the industry. While doing so, the chapter also explores and appreciates the various aspects of the pharmaceutical industry, as it presents features distinct from any other.

Healthcare as a dynamic and complex industry requires marketing to achieve business goals and improve the well-being of society. Transformations in the environment, increased competition, changes in consumer behavior force organizations to adapt to the altered landscape. In this regard, marketing plays a pivotal role in defining consumers' attitudes, motivations, and perceptions, building relationships with stakeholders, developing a strategy, and creating value. Moreover, the aging population, chronic diseases, prolonged pains and disabilities, poverty and poor health conditions, and lack of reliable medical services cause an increased burden not only on the healthcare system but also on the economy and society in all counties. Sustainable Development Goals aim to solve the pressing challenges facing the world. The objectives of this chapter are to discuss healthcare marketing in light of the twin transition: sustainability and digitalization. The chapter illustrates sustainable healthcare marketing opportunities in relation to digital advancements including ChatGPT.

Artificial intelligence (AI) technologies have made enormous strides recently and are already pervasive in many aspects of our daily life. Numerous efforts are being undertaken in the healthcare industry to apply AI technology for useful medical treatments. With the quick advancements in hardware performance and machine learning algorithms, it is anticipated that AI technology would be crucial in efficiently processing and utilizing vast amounts of health and medical data. However, the AI technology differs from the current medical technology in a number of distinctive ways. There are still few medical professionals and members of the general public that accept AI in healthcare, and there are several challenges about the security and dependability of AI technology applications. This chapter describes the state of current AI research and application in the healthcare industry and identifies the various challenges that need to be addressed and suggest how to resolve them.

This chapter represents a significant effort to understand and present a comprehensive overview of telemedicine and digital literacy in the context of healthcare in contemporary society. To achieve this, a thorough review of the most relevant and current studies conducted in the last five years has been carried out. One of the crucial aspects addressed in this chapter is the identification of barriers that hinder the adoption of telemedicine. Additionally, it examines the drivers that promote the adoption of telemedicine. These may include convenience, time and money savings, accessibility to quality healthcare services, and the ability to continuously monitor medical conditions from the comfort of one's home.

This chapter, of a descriptive nature, aims to highlight the challenges that the Colombian healthcare system is facing. The widespread discontent and protests of society over the last few years have led to the proposal that the current government of Colombia presented to the Congress of the Republic for its reform. Bill 339 of 2023 seeks to improve access conditions for the most vulnerable households while also reducing the administrative barriers causing delays in payments to hospitals and specialist appointments. However, it should be stated that the healthcare system is a truly broad and complex ecosystem, so it is not an easy task to assess the outcomes of the potential reforms. Besides, Colombia brings together highly relevant heterogeneous factors, almost like no other country in Latin America, a complex geography, interculturality, unemployment, and social inequality, among many others. Consequently, this work presents and brings together the social, political, economic, and academic perceptions of this new scenario that arises in the potential change.

The aim of this chapter is to assess the potential of fairy tale therapy as a comprehensive relationship marketing tool in the context of cross-sectoral partnerships. The chapter enriches the existing literature on the increasing importance of cross-sectoral collaboration in addressing important social problems, with an emphasis on the use of fairy tale therapy. It also contributes to the debate on the role of fairy tale therapy in building relationships in the health sector. The chapter characterises the issues of relationship marketing, cross-sector partnerships, and one method of bibliotherapy such as fairy tale therapy. Among the factors influencing intersectoral partnerships, those that foster them and those that hinder collaboration will be identified and analysed. The publication uses the case study method as a research method. The chapter will present and analyse a cross-sector partnership between hospitals, businesses, and an NGO that created a fairy-tale therapy programme in children's wards of selected hospitals in Poland.

For this chapter, the systematic review was selected to allow a deep dive and exploration of application design thinking in marketing for healthcare organizations. Moreover, there needs to be more literature that highlights using design thinking in healthcare as a major tool to create awareness and promotion of developed models that enhance the patient experience. This systematic review explores the use and impact of design thinking in healthcare marketing. By synthesizing existing literature, the current study provides comprehension of the theoretical bases, methodologies, and effects of employing design thinking principles in healthcare marketing strategies. Particularly today, technological advancements oblige organizations to be technologically savvy and provide the best future solutions to the customers, in our case, to the patients.

Artificial intelligence (AI) is now becoming an integral part of human life. It is finding applications in almost all domains, such as healthcare, marketing, business development, manufacturing, transportation, etc. This chapter explores the applications of AI in enhancing hospital service quality and presents a framework for its development. The chapter begins by providing an overview of hospital service quality and highlighting the role of AI in healthcare. It emphasizes the importance of enhancing hospital service quality and introduces the need for an AI-driven framework. The foundations of AI in healthcare are then discussed, including its evolution and different types of AI technologies. The challenges in implementing AI in healthcare are also addressed. The chapter also includes applications that illustrate the successful application of AI. The framework development section focuses on understanding the current hospital service landscape and defining key metrics for hospital service quality.

The work aims to characterize and analyze the economic policy of healthcare development in Georgia and, in particular, the policy of digitalization of healthcare. The healthcare system in Georgia has been characterized as a mixture of Bismarck and Beveridge models, with the government's universal healthcare program recently expanding, the goal of which is to increase the affordability of health services for the population. The work describes the goals, tools, institutions, and problems of Georgia's development policy and digitalization of healthcare. In conclusion, the authors consider those areas that should be maximally strengthened in the policy for digitalizing healthcare in Georgia to achieve the goals successfully.

The healthcare field is full of various challenges, such as implementing new technologies, not enough skilled workforce, stress, and anxiety. Patients' ability to communicate effectively may also be affected by their condition, medication, pain, and/or anxiety. Therefore, what is needed for the healthcare professionals is good strategic communication skills and maintaining positivity and simplicity to ensure patient safety, wellbeing, and the overall efficiency of busy healthcare organizations. Besides, serious problems may arise from poor quality communication. If professional communication skills vary in quality, then a patient's understanding of their health status may lack context, completeness, and accuracy – often causing confusion and potential harm. Communication failures in hospitals and medical practices are responsible for malpractice claims, resulting in deaths and high costs.

Preface

In recent times, Health Marketing has undergone a gigantic shift due to the skyrocketing development of online and mobile technologies as a means of communication. Healthcare digitalization is a technical process that has a revolutionary impact on society because it rationalizes the demand for healthcare services from one side and the distribution of health from another into virtual areas (Mihailescu et al., 2017).

Health providers have different meanings, and the patients, consumers of health, playing the role of Rational Man, expect more digitalization of health services with better quality and convenience. With marketing leadership, middle management strategies are decisive in improving the satisfaction of patients, insurers, state regulators, and society. That is why marketing managers and other health administrators must create learning organizations to understand e-health capacities and encourage growth (Gjellebæk et al., 2020). Because consumers increasingly behave virtually and spend more time online, the New Patient Behavior can soon evolve in Healthcare Markets. Health marketers must study the logic of New Patient Behavior to develop their health companies to a new level of consumer centrism. There are many cases in which hospitals run telemedicine. For example, Florida Hospital launched virtual visits with penetration prices to attract patients and retain them well and long. E-visits to hospitals happen for colds, rashes, bladder infections, eye pain, ear pain, and sinus problems, but the circle of diseases will increase soon. Digital healthcare platforms can be understood as a technology-enabled healthcare model, which easily connects healthcare companies, health providers, insurers, and public and private foundations to create healthcare value in distribution (Moro & Morea, 2020). The digitalized healthcare supply chains are patient-centric. Because healthcare is not simply based on demand and supply and healthcare innovation can create new demand, digitalization, versus some physical healthcare action, is cheaper and challenges cost reduction. Healthcare marketing, if it is used fully, strongly affects the healthcare systems of some countries, and healthcare markets as well. Once as a Marketing tool, direct-to-consumer advertising stimulated patients to talk to doctors, increasing their deep interest in new treatments (Kay, 2007); now, Healthcare Marketing stimulates healthcare organizations to rationalize their service distribution via digital, virtual, and mobile channels.

The digitalization of healthcare opens new horizons for its development (Menvielle et al., 2017). Healthcare goes to its semi-privatization in the way of patient empowerment and education. New and old health facilities will use online channels with exercise power. Patients' role will grow in healthcare (Hillestad & Berkowitz,2018). The fantastic movies when heroes do their surgery operation themselves will be accurate. The health education has no frames. The healthcare professionalism of patients, learning their diseases, participating in diagnoses, and taking their part in self-healthcare is already a question of well-organized healthcare marketing and management, leadership, and intelligent education. Marketing is critical for healthcare and its strategic and tactical organization (Berkowitz, 2021).

THE CHALLENGING QUESTIONS

- The critical challenge of modern healthcare marketing is how marketing will plan, organize, influence, and energize the shift of healthcare distribution from physical to digital, from doctor to patient, and from person to artificial intelligence.
- What will be the effective marketing strategy for well-digitized healthcare organizations or organizations that still need to finish or start their digital migration?
- How will the rules of healthcare marketing strategy and tactics be changed and challenged in active digitalization?
- What will adequate insurance and financing strategies be when healthcare markets finish their digital migration?
- What will patients feel and think, and how will patients act in these evolutionary developments in the healthcare market and industry?

SEARCHING FOR A SOLUTION

This book was organized to answer those challenging questions with a research-based, long-term view of healthcare marketing adaptation for the new, challenging, technologically innovative realities and leadership-oriented healthcare marketing perspectives.

Kakhaber Djakeli
University of Georgia, Georgia

REFERENCES

Berkowitz, E. N. (2021). *Essentials of health care marketing*. Jones & Bartlett Learning.

Gjellebæk, C., Svensson, A., Bjørkquist, C., Fladeby, N., & Grundén, K. (2020). Management challenges for future digitalization of healthcare services. *Futures*, *124*, 102636. doi:10.1016/j.futures.2020.102636

Hillestad, S. G., & Berkowitz, E. N. (2018). *Health care market strategy*. Jones & Bartlett Learning.

Kay, M. J. (2007). Healthcare marketing: What is salient? *International Journal of Pharmaceutical and Healthcare Marketing*, *1*(3), 247–263. doi:10.1108/17506120710818256

Menvielle, L., Audrain-Pontevia, A. F., & Menvielle, W. (Eds.). (2017). *The digitization of healthcare: new challenges and opportunities*. doi:10.1057/978-1-349-95173-4

Mihailescu, M., Mihailescu, D., & Carlsson, S. (2017). *Understanding healthcare digitalization: A critical realist approach*. Academic Press.

Moro Visconti, R., & Morea, D. (2020). Healthcare digitalization and pay-for-performance incentives in smart hospital project financing. *International Journal of Environmental Research and Public Health*, *17*(7), 2318. doi:10.3390/ijerph17072318 PMID:32235517

Chapter 1
Healthcare Marketing, Meaning, Historical Development, Applications, and Current Status

Kakhaber Djakeli
University of Georgia, Georgia

ABSTRACT

Artificial intelligence with virtual reality and the overwhelming digitalization in the next 10 years will change the role of healthcare marketing from managing to creation of new health. The dynamic of digital force development and the disruptive technological jump to high competitiveness of healthcare providers will make the role of marketing as the core. The functionality of healthcare and its advantages with professional medical manipulations and diagnosis will relay of modern marketing function to flourish the preventive and active healthcare for everyone to bring the health manipulations to the home of patients and make health the daily substance, utilizing deepest digitalization of relation to patients, insurers, health providers, controllers, and to the new health quality systems into one big, branded family. All this innovative development is today under construction, and they rely on healthcare marketing. The chapter includes the evolution of healthcare marketing from the beginning to advanced stages and the future of healthcare marketing development.

1. INTRODUCTION

We live in a period of disruptive technologies, especially in such an innovative market what is Health Care. Healthcare is established not only by the market but by the Country too, which tries to win in the peaceful competition against some other countries (Gigauri & Djakeli, 2021). Healthcare marketing is a phenomenon with having long history, started with the first outdoor ads, banners, and city walls, engraved or written, sometimes found by archeologists in ancient cities like Pompey, or seen by tourists, glancing at the walls of rare retained taverns in Old Western Europe (Berkowitz,2021). This is the time

DOI: 10.4018/979-8-3693-0679-6.ch001

that we can entitle as Marketing before Marketing, in which, Health Elites, sacredly retain their medical wisdom and give knowledge of Medicine only to their family members, trying to hold the Profession of a physician in scarcity as something alike the premium brand. In recent years, healthcare marketing has increasingly focused on personalization and data-driven approaches. Healthcare organizations use patient data to tailor marketing messages, offer personalized health recommendations, and improve patient engagement. Modern healthcare marketing prioritizes patient-centric approaches, focusing on improving patient experiences and engagement. Content marketing, patient testimonials, and educational materials are used to empower patients to make informed decisions about their healthcare. One study suggests that physicians according to marketing, are divided into very interesting segments: a) rule-bound doctors, b) high flyers, c) skeptical experimenters, d) selective majority, and e) conservators. This segmentation mirrors the readiness of some segments to participate in marketing-based and innovative healthcare with clinical trials (Spielmans & Parry, 2010). Even this understanding shows that marketing implementation made clinics more entrepreneurial. The importance of healthcare marketing is growing and as some researchers claim, from evidence-based medicine, companies turned to marketing-based medicine. Now healthcare fully using the concept of marketing, turning the marketing instruments into healthcare ones, but what was the past?

2. THE HISTORICAL STAGES OF HEALTHCARE MARKETING

The use of marketing in the healthcare industry can be divided into some relevant stages.

a) before the 20th century stage can be named the early healthcare marketing period. In this timeframe, the primitive forms of word-of-mouth communications were very relevant marketing instruments, that could be used well in the rural or urban healthcare business. In this period clinics and hospitals, doctors, and nurses were assessed by aperture of reputation. As we know reputation is a time-consuming business and can be achieved through a hardworking process, via awareness and image. At the same time, the awareness of the health organization, doctor, or nurse must be category-based. This type of awareness is called recall. If a doctor, nurse, hospital, or clinic is immediately recalled by the patient having a category need for healthcare, then this is strong awareness, which leads to a positive image and good reputation. About the use of advertising in healthcare and especially in pharmacy, there is historical evidence engraved on the walls of old cities. Especially interesting are the first newspapers advertising some medicaments. It can be said that European pharmaceutical ads had their origins in the 16th - 17th centuries, especially in the first newspapers. But how can we say that this was marketing if the word marketing only appeared in 1910? Can be signs of marketing before marketing? Logically not, but advertising what now is the part of marketing concept itself is much older than marketing. So we can emphasize that signs of marketing in healthcare appeared before conceptualization of the marketing sciences (Thomas,2008).
b) because the USA was and remains as a classical marketing country the modern healthcare marketing started there, but with complications. In 1950s marketing was already popular among various industries, but in healthcare it was adopted only in retail and supplier sectors. Until 1980 marketing in healthcare was only promotion concept. Some hospitals in the USA already had departments of marketing but the encouraging point for all nonprofit healthcare organizations was the famous article of Philip Kotler entitled as Marketing for Nonprofit Organizations (Kotler,1975). This ar-

ticle energized the use of marketing into health. In 1977 appeared a new Book: Marketing health care, written by MacStravic (MacStravic, 1977). In 1980 appeared one interesting scientific study, about consumers of healthcare services (Berkowitz & Flexner,1980). During 1980s the role of marketing grew in healthcare organizations. Having segmented their patients, organized marketing budget, differentiated their healthcare products and services for patients, targeting customers and promoting the health services – some innovative hospitals and clinics became more competitive. The Society for Healthcare Strategy & Market Development was established. The academic discipline the Healthcare Marketing in 80s was adopted by many academic programs of healthcare administration at universities. In 60s the growing role of electronic media increased the relevance of communication to patient, what emphasized the professional use of public relation. In 1970s the communities as a customers of healthcare became under focus of hospitals and all their communication activities were direct to communities. In 80s healthcare markets became buyer markets, the role of marketing research grew with this issue. The direct to consumer relationship marketing was under demand. The invention and development of Diagnostic Related Grouping model in the late sixties at Yale University was the marketing type of innovation into healthcare management as well (Averill, et al., 1998).

c) In 2000s not only healthcare but also healthcare management and marketing methods became already adopted by many health organizations. The countries reforming their health sector, especially in post-soviet peace, being struggling to turn into new, market driven healthcare, had a lot of problems (Djakeli,2013). Even some countries tried to adopt social insurance healthcare models, then the same countries, turned to market driven, liberal and libertarian models of health financing, encouraged by works of famous American economist Milton Friedman (Friedman,1982). The reform policy and the disasters happened to those countries made some researchers to think that either healthcare, or healthcare financing reforms, must be backed by solid healthcare marketing research, with great role of segmentation, targeting, differentiation and positioning (Djakeli, 2023). The ideas of Milton Friedman and some other liberal economists energized the use of full concept of marketing into health.

d) The exploding power of social media embarrassing the healthcare and the prospect and current patients became one of mainstreams in healthcare marketing of 2010 with the patient engagement and experiential marketing.

e) The Digital Revolution challenged old healthcare market and the focus on Empowered Patient, Telemedicine and virtual healthcare started. The internet enabled healthcare providers to have an online presence through websites, social media, and online advertisements. Patients could now research healthcare options and access information more easily. With advancements in technology, patients could receive medical consultations, diagnoses, and treatment remotely through video calls and online platforms. Personalization and Data-Driven Marketing has great role to empower the patient.

The total spending for healthcare marketing and advertisement was growing. From 1996 to 2017, the USA healthcare marketing grew fast. The promotional learning campaigns for different health services, drugs, disease and laboratory testing increased up from $17 billion to more than $29 billion. The marketers of healthcare were using sharpest type of marketing approaches known as direct-to-consumer (DTC) advertising. The share of Direct to consumer ads in healthcare in above mentioned timeframe increased from 2 billion to more than 9 billion USD in 2017. The same approach was used by pharmacy marketers and the DTCs Also increased from $1.3 billion to $6 billion" in America (Schwartz & Woloshin,2019).

Health service marketing was slowly moving to current indicators. As we know that 20 years ago healthcare ads were banned by American Marketing Association, but American Hospital Association destroyed this ban and ads started regularly. When we speak about Advertising we know that this is not full marketing but, if advertisement in planned by marketers and health administrators, that means that they work on full marketing program, segmenting population to find with whom their message must speak, differentiating the health services to show unique advantages, targeting the selected segment of patients and referrals for better impact and position their brands for long term advantages. So that means that when world started the advertising of health services, it started the cycle of marketing what is unchangeable for any health company, because of rules and experiences. Some marketing approaches in the advertisements have were directed to fear and then hope without emphasizing the methods of the treatment, in cancer clinics for example (Schwartz & Woloshin, 2019). The fourth industrial revolution created better chances for any type of manufacturers to be integrated with Internet of Things (IoT). This revolutionizing approaches affected the healthcare, establishing Healthcare 4.0. henceforth also "HC4.0" (Aceto, et al., 2020).

3. THE DIFFERENCE BETWEEN HEALTH MARKETING AND HEALTHCARE MARKETING

The difference between health marketing and healthcare marketing is obvious, health marketing is defined as a creator and communicator, and a deliverer of health information using consumer-centered and scientific methods to protect and widespread the health for all (Bernhardt, 2006), in the case than healthcare marketing is trying to deal with customer choice, attract and retain customers, work for customer satisfaction and loyalty, like any other service industry, with one exclusion, healthcare is dealing with destiny, health and life and also the continuation of the life, possible death and death avoidance (Corbin et al., 2001). So health marketing is more about great healthy life style and prevention from the possible health related risks, than healthcare marketing is the process organizer for entire healthcare service industry with financiers, insurers, healthcare policy makers, health providers and controllers.

Healthcare is just a technology market, where consumers like hospitals pay huge money for prestigious and competitive equipment (Thimbleby, 2013). Health marketing is defined as combination of realities from marketing of the life sciences, social marketing and marketing of health services (Crié & Chebat, 2013). Sometimes the discussions are about the fact that patients are not regular customers and health is not a good. The study of healthcare marketing has vital objects, the establishment, delivery, promotion and consumption of healthcare services, which are urgent, according the knowledge of customers. Not providing those services what are expected by customers are lethal either in long term or immediately. Customers and patients of health frequently are co-producers of the health. The demand for personalization of healthcare services and even customization is growing and marketing plays here the great role. Environmental changes have great influence on marketing. For example, the COVID-19 has changed many approaches and methods, and made healthcare marketers to digitize (Gigauri & Djakeli, 2021b).

Healthcare marketing for modern digital era is the process what creates needs and predicts wants of patients, insurers, financiers, state funds, controllers, regulators, on the wave of technological inventions, not only in the medical organizations but also among financiers, closely working with digital channels making the health financing more smart and easy. In any process the digitalization will bring a lot of innovations, what will blur the borders between healthcare providing and financing, controlling and periodical market researches.

The old concepts of healthcare marketing were emphasizing that this is a process of understanding the needs and wants of a target market (Cooper, 1994). The purpose of healthcare marketing was understood as some viewpoint about how to integrate health organization, its analysis, management functions and control it in the process of healthcare delivery. This was old view. The digital world will do all these parts in the synchronized way.

The modern healthcare marketing can be defined as a process by which healthcare organizations either create new customers, and engage them to build strong mass customized relationship to create healthcare value and receive the value from customers in exchange. Accordingly, 44% of the marketing costs for healthcare products and services will be dedicated to mobile and digital platforms and this is the future we embrace (Purcarea, 2019). The healthcare is regulated business, that's why the way of health reforms and the philosophy of health of the country emphasizes not only the competitiveness of the system but its actors (Djakeli, 2013).

4. THE MAIN GOALS OF HEALTHCARE MARKETING

Several goals can be differentiated from those what is seen upon healthcare marketing in the digital era:

- The reduction of information asymmetry on healthcare market and Increasing Awareness, Image and Reputation of Healthcare Providers, financiers, insurers, state policy makers, pharmacy stakeholders, medical associations, doctors and nurses: Healthcare marketing is aiming to raise awareness, image and reputation of patients, prospect patients about medical services, healthcare facilities, treatment options, insurers, financiers, state policies, best cases, the empowering patient-clinic engagements and health-related issues among the target audience. By increasing awareness, positive images and strong reputation and via digitalization, healthcare organizations can attract, educate, retain, empower current and potential patients worldwide.
- Patient Acquisition: One of the primary goals of healthcare marketing is to attract new patients or customers to healthcare providers, hospitals, clinics, pharmaceutical companies, and other healthcare organizations. By increasing patient acquisition, healthcare providers can grow their patient base and revenue.
- Enable Provider-Patient Communication: Digital tools facilitate direct communication between patients and healthcare providers, allowing patients to schedule appointments, receive test results, and ask questions conveniently.
- patient empowerment, what means the personalization of healthcare for the patient, education of patient, enabling patients to participate in the process of self-healthcare, train patient, remotely monitoring the patient, controlling the systems for the better results of care, improving the conditions of self-care and comfortability for patients.
- Retention: Healthcare marketing also focuses on retaining existing patients and customers. Satisfied and loyal patients are more likely to return for future healthcare needs and recommend the services to others, contributing to long-term success.

- Brand Building: Building a strong and positive brand image is crucial in healthcare marketing. A well-established brand creates trust challenges strong credibility among potential patients and customers, leading to increased patient loyalty and the Strategic Competitive Advantage (SCA) on the market.
- long term Educating of Patients and prospect patients: Healthcare marketing aims to educate patients and the general public about health conditions, preventive care, treatment options, and overall health and wellness. Informed patients are more likely to make better healthcare decisions and take proactive steps in managing their health.
- Promoting Preventive Care and health life style: Healthcare marketing campaigns often emphasize preventive care and healthy behaviors to encourage individuals to take a proactive approach to their health. Promoting preventive care can lead to better health outcomes and reduced healthcare costs in the long run.
- Supporting Patient Adherence: Marketing efforts can play a role in promoting medication adherence and treatment compliance among patients. By providing information and reminders, healthcare organizations can improve patient outcomes and the effectiveness of treatments.
- Community Engagement: Healthcare marketing often involves engaging with the local community to address specific health concerns, promote health-related events or initiatives, and foster a sense of trust and support.
- Enhancing Reputation and Trust: Healthcare marketing endeavors to enhance the reputation and credibility of healthcare providers and organizations. Positive patient testimonials, high-quality services, and patient satisfaction are vital for building trust within the community.
- Adapting to Market Changes: In a rapidly evolving healthcare landscape, marketing efforts need to be flexible and adaptable. Healthcare marketing must respond to changes in patient preferences, advancements in technology, and shifts in the regulatory environment.
- Supporting New Services and Technologies: When healthcare providers introduce new services or technologies, marketing plays a crucial role in informing the target audience about these innovations and highlighting their benefits.
- Strengthening the ethical principles of health: Healthcare marketers must adhere to strict ethical guidelines and patient privacy regulations when conducting digital marketing campaigns.

5. THE NEEDS AND WANTS OF CUSTOMERS

Some disturbance in health and wellbeing is a need for healthcare services (Donabedian, 1974). The healthcare need must be confirmed either by professional healthcare organization or healthcare worker during medical intervention. A need defined as something like a tension in organism, mostly directed to addiction to alcohol or heroin, must be ignored, to understand the need for healthiness and healthcare (Gustavsson, 2014). Needs can be divided into basic and category needs. Sometimes basic needs called as dispositional ones. The need to healthiness can be understood as basic, but the need for beauty smile is category oriented. For example, if someone has the category need for healthy, pretty smile, what means the beautifulness of lips with healthiness and whiteness of teeth, then this person easily converts this need into want and makes selections among dentist saloons for the best choice, what turns the want into demand. The notion of healthcare need is also characterized by gap between actual state of health and its desired condition. Need in health can be divided into strongly healthcare related needs and those what are directed to quality of life.

The structure of needs well describes some unusual character of Healthcare Marketing. The humanitarian and realistic models of needs in health, emphasizes the fact that needs are supported by resources what must be equivalent for services.

In the Model of Donabedian, it is described two approaches, humanitarian and realistic, to the definition of the need for health care (Acheson, 1978).

The Humanitarian Approach describes the logical flow of the model like this: humanitarian approach is considering the need in harmony to service equivalence of needs, what is linked to services and the services are dependent from resources themselves.

The realistic approach describes the logical flow model like this: realistic approach is considering the need in harmony to Resources what must be equivalent to services and what is linking the service equivalence of resources to the needs.

What customers wants from healthcare? The wants of patients can be divided either to the healthcare system or to their condition. Generally, to say patients want a healthcare system that responds when its needed (Detsky, 2011). Patients already know the concepts of preventive medicine. Well-informed patients want more preventive medicine like cancer screening programs that will prevent the terrible illnesses. But still patients more relay on factual immediate medicine than to preventive. The digital healthcare will be disruptive, bringing more preventive medical manipulations to the home of the healthcare customer, making prevention a lot of diseases, using the healthier lifestyle, genetically oriented preventive medicine, and many other interesting things, backed by medical Artificial Intelligence.

Most innovative health labs and research organizations try to find the unmet healthcare needs and create the new wants for final users (Agatemor et al., 2018). Either the disorders of physical health and mental health, societal problems or the degree of health-related knowledge of society, culture, traditions, social groups and family, together with the knowledge of individual is forming the health need (Stanley et al., 2016). Many residents in many countries are underserved by healthcare and for those who are in this category, the state does some special offerings. For example, in the USA, the community-based organizations called as Federally Qualified Health Centers (FQHC) try to study unmet needs and provide healthcare for underserved American populations. Such centers investigate and describe the underserved population's perceptions, beliefs and practices that impact them in the process of healthcare utilization (Pieh-Holder et al., 2012).

What is healthcare customer's desire? Their desires and wants can be divided into some aspects:

a) patients desire access to healthcare and if they do not procrastinate they want the care soon!
b) Patients want and desire empathy, kindness, and respect, especially to their privacy!
c) Patients want no pain by the treatment!
d) Patients desire more hope!
e) Patients want more options to be well!
f) Patients does not like uncertainty about the diagnoses and they want certainty!
g) Patients and their family members feel guilty if they don't fight for health and don't try to be better!
h) Patients frequently want not to know about the possible near finish of their life!
i) Patients desire continuity and choice among methods of healthcare!
j) Patients desire friendly relationships with health professionals!

k) Patients want their healthcare team to discuss their health conditions and communicate for better decisions in healthcare!
l) Patients want private, comfortable rooms during hospitalization
m) If digital monitoring systems afford them to stay home, patients want to stay home and be under professional systems of Patient Digital Monitoring!
n) Patients don't like out of pocket payment, that's why they desire some financial systems paying for their health costs!
o) Patients want to know that medical team treating them is the best!
p) Patients want persuasive testimonials about high quality of the healthcare brand and the team treating them!
q) Patients want reliable information about many other patients, who are now healthy from the same sickness they had!
r) People perceive healthcare as interaction with their doctor and they want their doctor to listen well, discuss their problems clearly, be attentive (Wen & Tucker, 2015).

We know that only patients are not customers of healthcare systems and organizations. There are institutions, like financiers, insurers, state, patient and medical associations, country and state regulators, policy makers, law makers and so on. Accordingly, they want:

a) Effectiveness and Efficiency of healthcare,
b) Positive indicators about healthcare,
c) New disruptive and innovative healthcare methodologies and products improving the healthcare,
d) Social stability and positive view to healthcare systems,
e) More healthcare providers making healthcare as a buyer's market (Detsky, 2011).

The healthcare providers want to refer their patients easily to other providers, they want more clear and detailed protocols, professional trainings and meeting, transfer of knowledge and easy access to the new knowledge (Learmonth et al., 2018).

6. MARKETING MIX FOR MODERN HEALTHCARE

Marketing mix concept can be very beneficial to manage healthcare organizations in digital age. Some period ago researchers were arguing that marketing mix variables could not easily fit health (Crié, et al., 2013), but now informational revolution and the digitalization made health services to be more flexible in delivery, what made place to be movable. The same changes we see in product and the service of Healthcare, the concept of the levels of the product can be as useful in healthcare as in any other categories. The pricing varies according the strategy of healthcare organization. The promotion is relevant and must be managed well to develop the positive awareness of healthcare unit, health provider and turning this awareness firstly into strong image of the organization and after that develop the reputation, what is achieved by strong healthcare branding stages. But are the four P-s enough? The healthcare marketing practice shows that the 7-P-s concept will add some relevant views to marketing management, improving the stamina of health workers.

6.1. Product/Service

Healthcare products are loosely defined as services (France & Grover,1992). There are product lines and products mixes in healthcare. Healthcare products/services can be divided into levels, like:

- Core level of the product or service, something like a level where the functional product is done by physicians, technology, doctors and nurses, by telemedicine or artificial intelligence in modern healthcare. The core level of the product frequently regulated by some guidelines, having issued by national health systems of the countries;
- The actual level of the product/service, has many components, like a price, brand, design, place, shape, relationship to patient, payment and delivery methodology and popularity. The actual level of the healthcare product/service can be differentiated by marketing, because it has big opportunity to achieve product differentiation on this level of the healthcare business.
- The expected level of the product/service has many components as well. This level is created by education of patients and prospect patients. In proper healthcare marketing cycle, expectations must be managed by marketing department of the hospital and not by the gossips of the street. The real, actual knowledge about the healthcare product/service delivered by special healthcare marketing team and controlled after that, is the effective instrument for the creation of expected product.
- The perspective product makes healthcare more interesting and attractive. Every human tries to find the continuation especially in healthcare. Through referrals or independently if we have good doctor, great nurse, well organized clinic, thus we have not only current but perspective product increasing our safety and good mood in the life.
- The augmented product combines everything to one effective healthcare marketing with guarantees or warranties of implant, results of diagnose, the outcomes of surgery operation, the mechanisms of the healthcare product/service life after utilization in the time.

Products and services of healthcare are very dependent to the form of their delivery. As we see much digitalization in healthcare channels and delivery systems, we can predict the much challenged hybrid and semi digitalized services in healthcare what will be soon or coming years already on the market. The products and services are also linked to the actual topic of empowered and digitally engaged patient, what was discussed earlier. The healthcare services will be platform based what can also encourage the direct to customer type of delivery (Maier et al., 2021). The service and product areas of healthcare will be drivers of technical development. In this new environment tech companies can help healthcare providers to create the product and services in two ways: a) doing healthcare business with health providers to create digital healthcare products and services, b) establish new platforms were healthcare product and services can be created and delivered.

The Virtual treatment and virtual clinical trial, monitoring patients at home is already very interesting for marketing. Especially if we use the marketing knowledge and divide healthcare product or service into levels, we will find that in many cases the core product, either fully or in some partial way can be done in remotely working digital channels, implementing patients diagnostic or patient trial via monitoring approaches (Maier et al., 2021). For product development important is the big data, if Artificial Intellect and Computerized approaches collect data, this makes patient care easier and more efficient.

6.2. Place And the Channels of Distribution

Most revolutionary processes going not only into the new healthcare product/service development where innovations and disruptive marketing has great stake, but into healthcare delivery (Salvini et al., 2022). According long tradition healthcare product or service domestically was delivered in health care providing organization, this was classical understanding of healthcare distribution during a lot of centuries, but all changed when world started its digital migration (Senbekov et al.,2020). The health 2.0. will be on innovative development patch. Stopping people to visit hospitals and empowering them by accredited and high quality information to participate in self-healthcare using approved ways of new healthcare (Thimbleby, 2013).

All digital systems providing patients with healthcare products and services, sometimes entitled as smart product-service systems (SSP) integrate intelligent connected products and digital services into solution bringing smart health care, what desires strong marketing understanding (Negash & Sarmiento, 2023). The healthcare services need the guideline of sustainable marketing, what emphasizing the importance of behavior change from ordinary to healthy, the green marketing and consumer centrism (Djakeli, 2023). In science literature the provision of remotely delivered clinical services via electronic, audio and visual tools, is entitled as Telemedicine. It can be delivered into two forms: a) real time consultation and real time care entitled as synchronous model and b) store and the forward approach entitled as asynchronous model. The development of telemedicine gives doctors chances to develop some new services, alike tele mentoring and even tele surgery. Among channels were health products and services can be created are various channels combined under umbrella – digital health, which contains: e-health, mobile health (m-health), telehealth or telemedicine. Digital health is the new industry and the new market, where healthcare provision conceived and delivered to patients, via digital channels, with the empowering of patients in the management of their health. This is something very new. In digital health, the healthcare product and service is built by empowered patients, who is guided by healthcare providers via digital healthcare channels.

6.3. Promotion And IMC Concept

For healthcare marketing different type of promotion activities are in relevance. The importance of Advertising, Promotion, Sales Promotion, Direct Marketing and the Public Relation is very high for the successful health care business. The healthcare Advertising can be divided into a) old media advertising for healthcare and b) new media advertising for healthcare. Moral, ethical and legal scenario use in healthcare advertising suggests us that this theme must be regulated either by state or horizontal independent systems of physician-patient associations for health and safety (Jalali & Pareek, 2010).

The healthcare promotion - For better health Behavior change campaigns on social media are now very effective. For example, tobacco counter marketing, almost change the behavior and reduced the Tobacco use worldwide (Robinson et al., 2014).

The healthcare sales promotion- is the instrument what involves, healthcare conferences, seminars, publicity, exhibitions and special television, video blogs about innovations. If company is famous, the sales promotion is easy because it already has earned media. The earned media what is used to promote the news of great hospitals, clinics, sanatoriums, doctors, medical associations is very interesting medium connecting, those who are prospect buyers of healthcare and healthcare providers (Balogun,& Ogunnaike, 2017).

Direct marketing for healthcare is vital for success. All times the direct marketing plays great role in new healthcare because it is based on data. The data in new healthcare analyze is the key to open the new markets, to solve old problems by new solutions and direct offerings.

Public Relation for healthcare all times urgent instrument, works for healthcare providers and patients. Public relation must be devoting to improve the attitude of the people, first of all, to the national health system of the country, to vital reforms and trending events, to public and private hospitals, to associations of nurses and medical associations. The Public Relation is also anti-crisis policy of health care market, it is vital as a behavioral change from worst to good, making prevention of the diseases as a very relevant goal either for the society and for the healthcare provider.

6.3.1. Social Media Marketing

Important is the role of social media for healthcare promotion and education (Gupta et al., 2013). The trust what is very relevant in healthcare industry must be communicated by social media networking and the access to word of mouth information in different type of social media. The types of social media are also very important. Kaplan and Haenlein (2009) found important six different types of social media: a) collaborative, b) blogs and microblogs, c) content communities, d) social networking sites, e) virtual game worlds, f) virtual social worlds (Kaplan & Haenlein, 2009). Healthcare organizations with help of social media create user generated content on the internet based applications, having some, practical, useful, even ideological and marketing meaning for them and their customers. Because in 2023, as it is estimated, already 4.9 billion people use social media, this is greatest talking and mind exchanging space for healthcare providers and their patients either to work for image building or learn to have best possible choice. Healthcare providers using social media promptly achieve good results. For example, Mayo Clinic, make patients to tell their own stories about the medical treatment and their happiness to be healthy after that. These videos on different type of social media channels attract other patients and make them to ask questions directly to the organization. That makes the process to be customer centered through social media marketing. The power of word of mouth communication is very valuable, and the Mayo clinic encourages the Blogs where patients write their daily experience about their diseases and the treatment methods. Through the podcasts special healthcare education is offered (Kaplan & Haenlein, 2012). The case of the attraction of customers by the social media can be the following:

- The collaborative social media: coordinates the data management and the data flow among clinics, hospitals, physicians and nurses. Such collaborative sites are: OnPage, Symplr, BuzzMedical Messenger, TigerConnect Clinical Collaboration Platform, Vocera Platform and others. Very important OnPage is working on search engine optimization opportunities to different clinics and healthcare organizations. As one happy customer wrote: "OnPage is the perfect product to be sure that critical alerts are never missed and it works perfectly with ConnectWise. You can create custom schedules to alert on any service ticket you choose and setup escalations as well. This allows for an immediate response from your technicians" (OnPage, 2023). The system is built to increase the capacity for response teams, such as, those in healthcare and IT support. The number of such systems will only grow, what will make the remote healthcare progressive and comfortable.
- Blogs and microblogs, developed by patients, prospect patients, doctors, hospitals are relevant medium, impacting customer behavior in healthcare market.

- Content communities: they provide patients with some information about the illnesses and the possible treatment (Johnson, et al., 2009). Patients connect with others with the same diagnoses to exchange their opinion and start the curation. The online health communities became very popular during COVID -19. The examples for Online Health Communities are: Smart Patients, PatientsLikeMe, HealthBoards, MedHelp, DailyStrength, WebMD, GiveForward, HealthUnlocked, Inspire and others. For example, the Online Community entitled as Smart Patients, works as a search engine optimizer for cancer patients and cases, helping patients to find others with similar cases for conversation, experience sharing, suggestions and advises.
- The social networking sites, the Health Platforms like Sermo, Doximity, DailyRounds, WeMedUp, Figure1, Student Doctors Network, Doctors Hangout and others do their job in best way. Let us discuss the advantage what they bring to the healthcare customers:

for example, famous Sermo, is the most advanced website among healthcare providers is connecting to verified and credentialed physicians from the globe. This site works in 150 countries and entitled as virtual lounge of physicians. Here professionals ask questions to their peers anonymously. In 2023 the number of members of Sermo is more than 800000. The Doximity - this collaborative social media site units US based physicians where they interact to each other and the scientific articles, some innovative works are discussed by members of this site, what makes many physicians to use this site regularly. The half millions of doctors on this site stay innovative and more professional through information they gather from their peers about many pivotal discoveries in healthcare technologies and human nature. The DailyRounds is very interesting online community of Doctors, every physician who seeks expertise are coming here for advise, some suggestion and knowledge based word. It is available on desktop, Android and iOS for daily use. Very innovative WeMedUp is wonderful online community of physicians who looks for information on healthcare job, healthcare related events and health technologies, innovations. The Figure1 is the invaluable tool for saving the lives, collecting physicians working with rare disorders from around the world, sharing anonymous X-ray photos about this rare diseases, making virtual online meetings of doctors to find the solution. But the Student Doctors Network is offering to students the conversations to experienced doctors, for idea exchanges and advises. This site already works from 1999 and encourages young medical staff. Is very interesting to analyze the role of DoctorsHangout where every specialization of medical profession finds here some discussions among peers. The MomMD is social site connecting page of female doctors and nurses. Very challenging is AmongDoctors, where the experienced physicians can open their groups where doctors and nurses exchange their opinions and suggestions. And finally AllNurses what is professional nurses virtual conference where all seek here needed information and some advises, job opportunities, discussing salaries, employers, different cases and give recommendations.

Very challenging virtual worlds will be useful for healthcare, not only for promotion but for medical education, conferences, where something relevant must be shown, discussions and expert advises (Ghanbarzadeh et al., 2014). In this area many relevant discoveries and innovations will be in next five years, what will change the delivery model of healthcare (Liaw et al.,2018). Even this was predicted by the first wave of internet technology development, especially in healthcare education (Johnson et al., 2009). The staff meetings, especially the invitation of foreign located healthcare experts can be done in normal way via virtual worlds (Taylor el al., 2020). Smartness of decision making and the united mind of all members of healthcare team, is very vital in effectiveness of diagnoses of patients. That's why the ability to gather decision makers immediately, despite their geographical location, is relevant for the saved lives and main ability of healthcare to cure patients, based on knowledge and experience of best doctors and nurses. All these can be achieved by virtual gathering of medical academics and doctors, via virtual world. The medical errors in healthcare frequently bring to death of patients and to reduce the chances of errors, we can do many trainings. The medical trainings improving clinical skills of medical staff can be well done in using the virtual worlds. Healthcare games can be also beneficial to train the staff members (Bredl & Bösche, 2013). For example, the scenario based clinical simulations for emergency health and also the communication learning via well-known Second Life Avatars is already the practice of professional development for clinicians (Holloway, 2012). These avatars are very nice vehicles for Health Behavior change modeling, therapeutic interventions learning and decision making.

virtual social worlds – have great importance for healthcare dialog between the sides. In our time when marketing is improved to the level of experiential marketing, the patient looks for something more than only the service, patients seeks the persuasive dialogue what must be developed between health organization and the customer. This dialogue now more comfortably must be managed via virtual world, what has also social character (Williamson, 2015). The health-tracking technologies, personal analytics and the bio pedagogies of digitized health for society, plays big role in customer satisfaction. The Metaverse will revolutionize the delivery of healthcare too. In this way the Chinese Ophthalmologists already utilize the digital systems for virtual consultations and as they reported more than 10,000 eye-related virtual visits were mediated by an AI chat bot (Tan et al., 2022).

6.4. Pricing

Healthcare service pricing positively related either to patient's information search and review quality (Wu et al., 2020). Mostly digital healthcare can reduce cost of the treatment, that means that hospitals and clinics, managed care organizations and doctors, implementing some digital approaches can use cost leadership strategy model and be competitive (Khanal, et al., 2016). From another side the affordability of healthcare services is growing via their digitalization (Moro & Morea, 2020). The distinctiveness of healthcare marketing is that there are healthcare products and services delivered but not with some money equivalence (Purcarea, 2019). That means that importance of healthy customers is not only business, it is great happiness of the whole country. The COVID-19 inspired countries to price the digitally provided services. The term "Telehealth" refers to delivery of healthcare, health education and health information services remotely. The Federal Medicare Program in the USA for example included telehealth services like a psychotherapy, office visits, what was expanded to other services as well. Traditionally the federal Medicare Program is using fee for service reimbursement. But the Digital Health Solutions still don't have strict coverage rules and guidelines. That's why the reimbursement tactics is using bundled payments. In difference to fee for service, bundled payment means the single process for all type of treatments. To decrease the hospitalization, stay days, such tactics looks effective for American Health Institutions (Gerke, 2020).

6.5. Physical Evidence

In healthcare marketing as a physical evidence can be assumed the internal environment of healthcare organization and its external look, design, color, smell, landscape, gardening around and some flora and fauna in it. All things what patients take with, during the leaving the health organization can be assumed by healthcare marketers as the part of physical evidence (Sheaff et al.,2020). Sometimes the physical evidence is not positive, for example the ugly surgery cut on the nice body of patient is symbol of bad care, this will work against the healthcare organization forever. Accordingly, the physical evidence of healthcare must be managed well (Sreenivas et al, 2013).

6.6. People

The concept of the marketing mix and especially its 6th instrument entitled as a people has wonderful meaning that, healthcare and the health, is not only responsible to direct patients but to whole people in its environment, because the healthcare is very relevant for the success of the country and its citizens, coming tourists, economy, social life and the future. If marketers entirely understanding the meaning of this button, they will do their best to attract the hearts of people by a lot of type of marketing communications discussed by us above. First of all, the marketing vision to people based on the social marketing concepts are effective. Without using the Social Marketing concepts in healthcare, marketers will not be able to work effectively with people. Not only patients but the whole people must be the target of many different type of socially directed communications of healthcare organization. The social marketing has mission to change the wrong behavior of people and the person to the good. Frequently the same mission has the preventive medicine and its tries to change the behavior of prospect patients to make them to avoid the illness. With the same sound mission and the goals, the healthcare organization can plan its long-term influence on population through different type of marketing methodologies and instruments to educate people, to attract them to know more about their health.

6.7. Process

It is important to communicate the healthcare manipulations to final customers with Value maintenance and Superior Value, with persuasive communication and brand building process, to increase the image of the process and establish high reputation on the market. Accordingly, the process and effective performance of medical organization, based on the standards of superior quality, if it is allowed by ethical and moral assumptions can be transparent, especially in Digital Era, where telemedicine and mobile health, with some special healthcare technologies are expressing the union of best intellectual and experienced human and AI sources, for final health of the patient. About the process developed by healthcare marketers we speak in next paragraph.

7. THE PROCESS OF HEALTHCARE MARKETING

The process of healthcare marketing either is the satisfaction of needs, wants and demand of customers or establishing new needs, wants and demand through innovative offerings via new medical solutions. The changes in healthcare marketing we can take into account. In the physical healthcare market period, healthcare marketing was trying to satisfy the customer. In first period of healthcare market digitalization, the satisfaction of remote customer could be a target, but in the period of full digitalization of healthcare market and use the modern healthcare marketing concept by clinics, the goal of the healthcare company is the creation of empowered customer, or empowered patient, who will be much different than simple customer of healthcare in the period of physical healthcare market (Robinson, 2013). But some researchers think the enabling digital health companionship can be better than empowerment (Morley & Floridi, 2019).

The process of Healthcare Marketing in Digital Era is already different. We can divide the healthcare marketing into traditional and digital. The traditional process includes:

- Understanding the marketplace, patient's needs, wants desires, their expectations. All these combined into patient's expectation are very relevant to study. What influencing expectations? Personal expectations are driven by needs, values, roles, experience, information, intentions, attributions, interests, moods and emotions, perceived consequences of customers. But there are also social expectations of customers, for example socio demography, social norms, group pressures, tasks, conditions, restrictions, equity and the economic indicators of wealth (Thompson & Sunol, 1995). The healthcare is individual. There are no same health diagnoses. All patients are different and as healthcare marketing professionalizes it achieves more customer orientations. The digitalization gives new methods and methodologies to health organizations to be fully customer focused (Ford & Fottler, 2000).
- To design the customer/Patient driven marketing strategy for healthcare. The customers of healthcare are individuals as a patient, individuals as an non direct patients but those who want to prevent some diseases, also organizations, like insurers, employees, medical associations, patient associations, professional unions, and public organizations like a Parliament office, state healthcare regulators, ministries and municipalities. Accordingly, the strategy of healthcare must feet patients as B2C and B2B customers. The paradox is that not all customers are the same "desirable" for the clinics. If we look from business perspective and have either regulated or limited strict prices looking like a capitation – as light health diagnosis patient has as more desirable this patient is. To avoid all these externalities in healthcare we need customer driven marketing strategy, what is shaped according the mission, vision and goals of healthcare organization (Wu et al., 2020). The healthcare moving from mass marketing to personalization, from low-tech to high-tech points and this must be the trends in future, backing by cost leadership, differentiation and cost focus strategies what are common also in non-healthcare markets. The main role of strategies in healthcare can be the identification of Strategic Competitive Advantage, to build high reputation of the company, to exceed the expectation of customers, be persuasive and build strong healthcare brands.
- Construct the integrated offline and online, marketing program to deliver to patients the superior healthcare value.
- Engage the customers build long lasting relationships and inspire customer delight.
- Exchange values with customers and win mutually, supporting healthiness and wellbeing.

Patients and all customers of Healthcare can find the rational healthcare without borders by some new technologies and methods what are already here. If in the beginning of Health Tourism patients were seeking the new opportunities abroad, relay on health tourism (Cortez, 2008), now they can find them by health tech companies. The Remote Patient Monitoring (RPM) process as the process what is going in the clinic physically has already two main delivery channels of healthcare. Accordingly, Remote Patient Monitoring (RPM) will soon make unprecedented number of countries to restructure their healthcare and be ready for remotely healthcare challenges. The remote working challenges improve and increase the flexibility of healthcare services delivered remotely (Gigauri & Djakeli,2021 A).

The Remote Patient Monitoring (RPM) can be defined as a digital system, transmitting patient's health related data to health care provider (Hayes et al., 2023) to improve patient's wellbeing and decrease the days of hospitalization, physical contact to health organization. Several clinical trials and researches show that the Remote Patient Monitoring (RPM) improve patient health outcomes. The Remote Patient Monitoring needs right segmentation. Which segment of patients are more rational to be with remotely delivery health channels is the topic of healthcare marketing (Mecklai et al., 2021). This is the empowering of patients as well.

Some countries already succeed to Health Digitalization. Germans started Digital Health Reforms in the period of COVID – 19. They prepared special Digital Healthcare Act – "Digitale–Versorgung–Gesetz - DVG", what can be the example for many other countries, because Germany has multi payer health care system, with many insurance companies and social funding agency (Gerke et al., 2020).

8. CUSTOMER BEHAVIOR

The main principle of patient centered healthcare is that the voice of final patient, who is the user of healthcare products and services with other, B2B customers of healthcare, like insurance companies, state, and pharmacy, must be heard well everywhere in company (Djakeli, 2018). But the healthcare is regulated market and the state policy is very relevant to understand the customer behavior on this market. In 1990s, European National Health Systems were transformed into market way (Sheaff et al.,2020). The social insurance healthcare and high solidarity was born in Germany. Taxation based universal coverage healthcare was established in England, France, Italy, Spain. But at the end of 20th century, the US Healthcare mind leadership exploded the old world, when Yale Professors developed the Diagnostic Related Group model challenged everybody. For example, in 1992 Italy introduced as a system of remuneration of prospective hospitals, the model, very alike of marketing segmentation, entitled as the Diagnosis Related Groups (DRG), with entire experience of American health (Nonis et al.,2018). Either Bismarck or Beveridge models were exporting its experience, systems and findings to other countries the behavior of customers became dependent from those (Nuti et al., 2012).

The customer behavior in Healthcare is more linked to healthcare financing and delivery systems established by different countries. For example, the implementation of Diagnostic Related Groups in Italy, decreased Hospital admission rate of patients, especially among Diabetics, but increased the severity of illness. So called "DRG Creep" phenomena, shows terrible moral hazard when patients seem sicker and the system has high ethical problems (Lous,1999).

The hypothesis, that patients and prevention healthcare customers tend to be more consumptive in the era of digitalization is worthy for great marketing research, but also without it any observation of customer behavior, watching digital healthcare platform about current or preventive medicine, gives us more conformation to this hypothesis. According the strengthening the digital healthcare the consumptiveness of consumers will only grow (Fahmi et al., 2022).

If customers of ordinary healthcare had been developing the self-leadership for patients to well organize their healthy skills and habits, through digital health we face new marketing leadership, entitled as IT based leadership, what can combine, e-health, telemedicine, artificial intelligence technologies, virtual monitoring and trial systems, mobile health, cloud computing and others.

What is the customer empowering process in healthcare market? The adoption process by digitalized healthcare customers will be the following: the patients willing to know more about the benefits of digital health, they learn and healthcare providers educate them. The patients have maturity stage in empowering and they start to use the digital healthcare fully, these patients will be the innovators. According the Rogers Diffusion model innovators will be followed by early adopters of Remotely Health. The other cluster who will follow the early adopters are three groups of healthcare customers: early majority, late majority and laggards (Ward, 2013). To satisfy the needs wants and desires of customers' healthcare institutions now use an Artificial Intelligence and healthcare marketing must be very attentive to the skills of its properly use. The AI can be used well in biomedicine, analyzing the healthcare diagnosis, optimization of healthcare treatment for the patient, turn healthcare process into value based healthcare. Important is the role of AI in Medical Educational process.

The process of healthcare is long period driven by different type of quality management standards and the healthcare management rules (Gigauri, & Djakeli, 2021 C). The Empowering Patient concept, what is now much relevant vehicle towards remotely delivered healthcare, is also vital part of the process. The patient empowerment concept can guarantee an effective self-management to improve health and well-being of patients, after their education in self-health-care what answers the theoretical and practical requirements of modern healthcare marketing (Ben Ayed & El Aoud, 2017).

9. FINDINGS AND RECOMMENDATIONS

The discussion about health and healthcare uniqueness is well known. Itself healthcare as an industry doing products and services can be much differentiated from any other industry for several reasons (World Health Organization, 2021):

Firstly, we see strong informational asymmetry in Healthcare Markets. What is seen and knowledge able by doctor cannot easily be understood by patients.

Secondly the healthcare is not only creating products and services according the needs wants and desires of patients by this very innovative and challenging industry creates either the new technologies, methodologies of healthcare, fresh new solutions of old problems with the healthcare products and services, what inspire new needs, wants and demands from the patients. Even it can be the creation of new customers through development of new demand.

Thirdly, the healthcare is frequently involved into life and death matters of the customers and its products and services proved by happiness and the life status of their patients, measured by different indicators. These indicators can be grouped as Quality Adjusted Life years(QUALY), some social and behavioral indicators in Electronic Health Records(EHR), the 29 indicators, divided into five subscales (Lavinia & Elena, 2015). There are also health risks and behavior related eight additional indicators: healthcare immunization, vaccination, insured health and personal care needs, personal care providing supply, blood tests and physical exams and more socially oriented indicators about self-related health status, air quality index, high school diploma, health literacy rate, employment status and others (Sokoya,2022). All these indicators healthcare marketer must use in the process of healthcare market segmentation, targeting, differentiation and positioning.

Fourthly patients, the direct customers of healthcare, either cannot decide themselves from which health provider to choose the healthcare service, or patients are totally unable to manage their needs, wants and healthcare desires, because they are in the hands of referrals. The referral relationship is common on health. Sometimes called as refugees of healthcare systems, referral relationship is under a fierce critic (Enumah, 2022).

The clinics and hospitals need to realize their health strategies according their mission and choose either cost leadership, differentiation or cost focus strategies. The niche health companies try to develop cost focus strategies emphasizing organizations having minimal costs where they differentiate much and are experts of the niche (Djakeli, 2018). Interesting is that some healthcare systems motivate the high role of the state but others give only minimum role to the state interventions. Because the good health is the happiness and bad health is a mortal, the quality of healthcare never can be sacrificed to some other goals. If Patients in traditional physical healthcare delivery markets were less able to discuss the quality of health, in fully digitalized healthcare, well engaged and empowered patients can easily understand the determinants of healthcare service values they received (Kay, 2007).

Modern healthcare marketing in digital age creating the phenomenon of new healthcare. During COVID-19 pandemic developments, new wave of digitalization started in various industries and especially in healthcare, where most interesting digital devices started to work to increase the social capital (Kim & Lee, 2021). The social capital of the general publics is created by healthcare and the role of Marketing in this process is high. The digital devices and digitalization with its abilities to increase connectedness of people and healthcare organizations is working well for improving social capital (Hawe & Shiell, 2000). There are different types of digital applications what can help to healthcare. The smart devices, block chains, virtual clinical trials, telemedicine and 3D printers, organized by the Artificial Intelligence (AI), machine learning (ML), with huge importance of informational clouds, the big data and the different types of remotely delivered medical services, will be big climb of success for entire health.

Something what looks like science fiction today will be routine tomorrow (Thimbleby, 2013). Implementation of digital technologies establish new possibilities in healthcare markets. The revolution of information technologies, challenging the digital migration and creation of Artificial Intelligence made Healthcare to be:

- More accessible and affordable,
- Flexible to access,
- Available and comparable to other similar solutions,
- Better as a medical treatment,
- Smart for customers/patients to write their feedbacks about their satisfaction by healthcare organizations,
- Better to inspire biomedical researches in internet,
- Accurate to diagnostic and consulting,
- Improving equality of urban and rural patients to give them better consultation and a equal treatment,
- Empowering the patients in self – healthcare,
- Popularize the prevention,
- Receive the exceptional patient care with AI, telemedicine, for example the situation when the doctors could see inside the body of the patient and treat her or him precisely than ever before, even from remote.

10. CONCLUSION

The concept of healthcare marketing firstly appeared as a promoter of clinics, their services and happy faces of healed ones, but high competition on the market of healthcare products and services, in the period than this market turned as a market of buyers, demanded cleverer marketing. Because healthcare industry mostly is inflation oriented, with high cost of the medical technologies and the treatments, it is obvious that the stakeholders of big clinics and health hubs, were thinking to use much strategic planning, knowledge of management and smart methods of financing to try to save the markets and the purchasing ability of healthcare service customers, finally fully adopted the marketing concept.

In the end of 90s the old and traditional concept of advertising was senseless, because of high prices of broadcasting television giant companies in America. This was inspiratory of the Integrated Marketing Communication Concepts, complaining the different type of media into one great persuasive marketing instrument. The healthcare companies started to use the social media channels but soon the fourth industrial revolution, creating more chances for healthcare providers to be integrated with Internet of Things (IoT), cloud computing, Artificial Intelligence, Machine Learning, big data and analytics, completely challenged the healthcare market. This revolutionizing type of challenge, entitled as digital migration, affected the healthcare, establishing the telemedicine, mobile medicine, channels to deliver not only the information but the healthcare product to final user. So the new Healthcare 4.0. henceforth known as "HC4.0" was created.

Because the healthcare marketing is very comprehensive in contenting institutions and meaning and it is assumed as the process organizer for entire healthcare service industry, with financiers, insurers, healthcare policy makers, health providers and controllers, it is becoming the scene for the new ways to create a customer. With AI it can change the design and nature of healthcare forever. The Artificial Intelligence, Virtual Reality and fast digitalization, changing the healthcare Marketing from managing concept to creation one. The medicine with its great minds, innovations, genial solutions, data based inventions and discoveries, with the concept of modern marketing is knocking the doors of any current or prospective patient, offering them comfort and solution.

The modern healthcare marketing goals started from patient engagement, education, patient empowerment and the new self-health-care able customer creation, increasing the role of healthcare platforms, their promotion, branding and patient satisfaction, is finalized by the intellectual power of empowered patient as a co-creator of its own health.

REFERENCES

Aceto, G., Persico, V., & Pescapé, A. (2020). Industry 4.0 and Health: Internet of Things, Big Data, and Cloud Computing for Healthcare 4.0. *Journal of Industrial Information Integration, 18*. doi:10.1016/j.jii.2020.100129

Acheson, R. M. (1978). The definition and identification of need for health care. *Journal of Epidemiology and Community Health, 32*(1), 10–15. doi:10.1136/jech.32.1.10 PMID:262581

Agatemor, C., Ibsen, K. N., Tanner, E. E., & Mitragotri, S. (2018). Ionic liquids for addressing unmet needs in healthcare. *Bioengineering & Translational Medicine, 3*(1), 7–25. doi:10.1002/btm2.10083 PMID:29376130

Averill, R. F., Muldoon, J. H., Vertrees, J. C., Goldfield, N. I., Mullin, R. L., Fineran, E. C., Mona Z. Zhang, B.S., SteinbeckB., & Grant, T. (1998). *The evolution of casemix measurement using diagnosis related groups (DRGs).* Wallingford: 3M Health Information Systems.

Balogun, B., & Ogunnaike, O. (2017). Healthcare Organisations in a global marketplace: A systematic Review of the literature on healthcare marketing. *SSRN*, *1*(5). Advance online publication. doi:10.2139srn.3047747

Ben Ayed, M., & El Aoud, N. (2017). The patient empowerment: A promising concept in healthcare marketing. *International Journal of Healthcare Management*, *10*(1), 42–48. doi:10.1080/20479700.2016.1268326

Berkowitz, E. N. (2021). *Essentials of health care marketing*. Jones & Bartlett Learning.

Berkowitz, E. N., & Flexner, W. (1980). The market for health services: Is there a non-traditional consumer? *Journal of Health Care Marketing*, *1*(1). PMID:10251474

Bernhardt, J. M. (2006). Improving health through health marketing. *Preventing Chronic Disease*, *3*(3). PMID:16776874

Bredl, K., & Bösche, W. (Eds.). (2013). *Serious games and virtual worlds in education, professional development, and healthcare*. IGI Global. doi:10.4018/978-1-4666-3673-6

Cooper, P. D. (Ed.). (1994). *Health care marketing: A foundation for managed quality*. Jones & Bartlett Learning.

Corbin, C. L., Kelley, S. W., & Schwartz, R. W. (2001). Concepts in service marketing for healthcare professionals. *American Journal of Surgery*, *181*(1), 1–7. doi:10.1016/S0002-9610(00)00535-3 PMID:11248166

Cortez, N. (2008). Patients without borders: The emerging global market for patients and the evolution of modern health care. *Industrial Law Journal*, *83*, 71.

Crié, D., & Chebat, J. C. (2013). Health marketing: Toward an integrative perspective. *Journal of Business Research*, *66*(1), 123–126. doi:10.1016/j.jbusres.2012.09.002

Detsky, A. S. (2011). What patients really want from health care. *Journal of the American Medical Association*, *306*(22), 2500–2501. doi:10.1001/jama.2011.1819 PMID:22166610

Djakeli, K. (2018). From disruptive marketing to the new model of prestigious branding. Quality - Access to Success, 19(166), 71-76.

Djakeli, K. (2023). Sustainable Healthcare Reforming Model Based on Marketing: Case of Georgia. In I. Gigauri, M. Palazzo, & M. Ferri (Eds.), *Handbook of Research on Achieving Sustainable Development Goals With Sustainable Marketing* (pp. 271–287). IGI Global. doi:10.4018/978-1-6684-8681-8.ch014

Djakeli. (2013). Analyzing Success and Failure of Two Health Reforms in Independent Georgia. *Journal of Business, 2*(2), 5-14. https://jb.ibsu.edu.ge/jms/index.php/jb/article/view/56

Donabedian, A. (1974). *Aspects of Medical Care Administration*. Harvard University Press.

Enumah, Z. O. (2022). Therapeutic citizens or therapeutic refugees? An examination of triage, refugeehood, and referral health care in Tanzania. *Social Science & Medicine, 298*, 114837. doi:10.1016/j.socscimed.2022.114837 PMID:35247780

Fahmi, K., Sihotang, M., Hadinegoro, R. H., Sulastri, E., Cahyono, Y., & Megah, S. I. (2022). Health Care SMEs Products Marketing Strategy: How the Role of Digital Marketing Technology through Social Media? *UJoST-Universal Journal of Science and Technology, 1*(1), 16–22.

Ford, R. C., & Fottler, M. D. (2000). Creating customer-focused health care organizations. *Health Care Management Review, 25*(4), 18–33. doi:10.1097/00004010-200010000-00003 PMID:11072629

France, K. R., & Grover, R. (1992). What is the health care product? *Marketing Health Services, 12*(2), 31. PMID:10119211

Friedman, M. (1982). *Capitalism and freedom (1962). Whether government control over the provision of education through public schools is also efficient is a quite different matter.* Academic Press.

Gerke, S., Stern, A. D., & Minssen, T. (2020). Germany's digital health reforms in the COVID-19 era: Lessons and opportunities for other countries. *NPJ Digital Medicine, 3*(1), 94. doi:10.103841746-020-0306-7 PMID:32685700

Ghanbarzadeh, R., Ghapanchi, A. H., Blumenstein, M., & Talaei-Khoei, A. (2014). A decade of research on the use of three-dimensional virtual worlds in health care: A systematic literature review. *Journal of Medical Internet Research, 16*(2), e47. doi:10.2196/jmir.3097 PMID:24550130

Gigauri, I., & Djakeli, K. (2021a). Expecting Transformation of Marketing During the Post-Pandemic New Normal: Qualitative Research of Marketing Managers in Georgia. *International Journal of Sustainable Economies Management, 10*(2), 1–18. doi:10.4018/IJSEM.2021040101

Gigauri, I., & Djakeli, K. (2021b). Remote working challenges for Georgian social enterprises in the context of the current pandemic. *HOLISTICA – Journal of Business and Public Administration, 12*(3), 39-53. doi:10.2478/hjbpa-2021-0021

Gigauri, I., & Djakeli, K. (2021c). National Health Reforms in Georgia during 1994-2021 and their Success. *HOLISTICA – Journal of Business and Public Administration, 12*(2), 102-108. doi:10.2478/hjbpa-2021-0017

Gupta, A., Tyagi, M., & Sharma, D. (2013). Use of social media marketing in healthcare. *Journal of Health Management, 15*(2), 293–302. doi:10.1177/0972063413489058

Gustavsson, E. (2014). From needs to health care needs. *Health Care Analysis, 22*(1), 22–35. doi:10.100710728-013-0241-8 PMID:23344674

Hawe, P., & Shiell, A. (2000). Social capital and health promotion: A review. *Social Science & Medicine, 51*(6), 871–885. doi:10.1016/S0277-9536(00)00067-8 PMID:10972431

Hayes, C. J., Dawson, L., McCoy, H., Hernandez, M., Andersen, J., Ali, M. M., Bogulski, C. A., & Eswaran, H. (2023). Utilization of remote patient monitoring within the United States health care system: A scoping review. *Telemedicine Journal and e-Health, 29*(3), 384–394. doi:10.1089/tmj.2022.0111 PMID:35819861

Holloway, D. (2012). Virtual worlds and health: Healthcare delivery and simulation opportunities. In *Virtual worlds and metaverse platforms: New communication and identity paradigms* (pp. 251–270). IGI Global. doi:10.4018/978-1-60960-854-5.ch017

Jalali, R., & Pareek, P. (2010). Is there a need to regulate health care advertisement for lay public? *Journal of Cancer Research and Therapeutics*, *6*(2), 131–133. doi:10.4103/0973-1482.65228 PMID:20622357

Johnson, C. M., Vorderstrasse, A. A., & Shaw, R. (2009). Virtual worlds in health care higher education. *Journal of Virtual Worlds Research*, *2*(2). Advance online publication. doi:10.4101/jvwr.v2i2.699

Kaplan, A., & Haenlien, M. (2009). *Users of the world, unite! The challenges and opportunities of Social Media*. Academic Press.

Kaplan, A. M., & Haenlein, M. (2012). Social media: Back to the roots and back to the future. *Journal of Systems and Information Technology*, *14*(2), 101–104. doi:10.1108/13287261211232126

Kay, M. J. (2007). Healthcare marketing: What is salient? *International Journal of Pharmaceutical and Healthcare Marketing*, *1*(3), 247–263. doi:10.1108/17506120710818256

Khanal, P., Gupta, A., & Smith, M. (2016). Virtual worlds in healthcare. *Advances in Healthcare Informatics and Analytics*, 233-248.

Kim, H. K., & Lee, C. W. (2021). Relationships among healthcare digitalization, social capital, and supply chain performance in the healthcare manufacturing industry. *International Journal of Environmental Research and Public Health*, *18*(4), 1417. doi:10.3390/ijerph18041417 PMID:33546393

Kotler, Ph. (1975). *Marketing for Nonprofit Organizations*. Prentice-Hall, Inc.

Lavinia, C. A. Z. A. C. U., & Elena, O. A. (2015). Healthcare Marketing-A Relational Approach. *Revista Economica*, *67*(5), 59–72.

Learmonth, Y. C., Adamson, B. C., Balto, J. M., Chiu, C. Y., Molina-Guzman, I. M., Finlayson, M., Barstow, E. A., & Motl, R. W. (2018). Investigating the needs and wants of healthcare providers for promoting exercise in persons with multiple sclerosis: A qualitative study. *Disability and Rehabilitation*, *40*(18), 2172–2180. doi:10.1080/09638288.2017.1327989 PMID:28524732

Liaw, S. Y., Carpio, G. A. C., Lau, Y., Tan, S. C., Lim, W. S., & Goh, P. S. (2018). Multiuser virtual worlds in healthcare education: A systematic review. *Nurse Education Today*, *65*, 136–149. doi:10.1016/j.nedt.2018.01.006 PMID:29571002

Louis, D. Z., Yuen, E. J., Braga, M., Cicchetti, A., Rabinowitz, C., Laine, C., & Gonnella, J. S. (1999). Impact of a DRG-based hospital financing system on quality and outcomes of care in Italy. *Health Services Research*, *34*(1 Pt 2), 405. PMID:10199684

MacStravic, R. E. (1977). *Marketing health care*. Aspen Systems Corporation. doi:10.1097/00004010-197702040-00017

Maier, E., Reimer, U., & Wickramasinghe, N. (2021). Digital healthcare services. *Electronic Markets*, 1–4. PMID:35602115

Mecklai, K., Smith, N., Stern, A., & Kramer, D. B. (2021). Remote patient monitoring—Overdue or overused? *The New England Journal of Medicine, 384*(15), 1384–1386. doi:10.1056/NEJMp2033275 PMID:33853209

Morley, J., & Floridi, L. (2019). Enabling digital health companionship is better than empowerment. *The Lancet. Digital Health, 1*(4), e155–e156. doi:10.1016/S2589-7500(19)30079-2 PMID:33323183

Moro, V. R., & Morea, D. (2020). Healthcare digitalization and pay-for-performance incentives in smart hospital project financing. *International Journal of Environmental Research and Public Health, 17*(7), 2318. doi:10.3390/ijerph17072318 PMID:32235517

Negash, Y. T., & Sarmiento, L. S. C. (2023). Smart product-service systems in the healthcare industry: Intelligent connected products and stakeholder communication drive digital health service adoption. *Heliyon, 9*(2), e13137. doi:10.1016/j.heliyon.2023.e13137 PMID:36820023

Nonis, M., Bertinato, L., Arcangeli, L., Cadeddu, C., Palinuro, A., Frattura, L., Merlino, G. L., Verdini, E., Lispi, L., & Ricciardi, W. (2018). The evolution of DRG system in Italy: The it-drg project. *European Journal of Public Health, 28*(suppl_4), cky218–cky095. doi:10.1093/eurpub/cky218.095

Nuti, S., Seghieri, C., Vainieri, M., & Zett, S. (2012). Assessment and improvement of the Italian healthcare system: First evidence from a pilot national performance evaluation system. *Journal of Healthcare Management, 57*(3), 182–199. doi:10.1097/00115514-201205000-00008 PMID:22724376

Onpage. (2023). https://marketplace.connectwise.com/onpage#reviews

Pieh-Holder, K. L., Callahan, C., & Young, P. (2012). Qualitative needs assessment: Healthcare experiences of underserved populations in Montgomery County, Virginia, USA. *Rural and Remote Health, 12*(3), 1–11. doi:10.22605/RRH1816 PMID:22812680

Purcarea, E. V. L. (2019). The impact of marketing strategies in healthcare systems. *Journal of Medicine and Life, 12*(2), 93–96. doi:10.25122/jml-2019-1003 PMID:31406509

Robinson, L. (2013). Is digital health technology empowering patients? *Journal of Medical Radiation Sciences, 60*(3), 79–80. doi:10.1002/jmrs.20 PMID:26229613

Robinson, M. N., Tansil, K. A., Elder, R. W., Soler, R. E., Labre, M. P., Mercer, S. L., Eroglu, D., Baur, C., Lyon-Daniel, K., Fridinger, F., Sokler, L. A., Green, L. W., Miller, T., Dearing, J. W., Evans, W. D., Snyder, L. B., Kasisomayajula Viswanath, K., Beistle, D. M., Chervin, D. D., ... Rimer, B. K. (2014). Mass media health communication campaigns combined with health-related product distribution: A community guide systematic review. *American Journal of Preventive Medicine, 47*(3), 360–371. doi:10.1016/j.amepre.2014.05.034 PMID:25145620

Salvini, G., Hofstede, G. J., Verdouw, C. N., Rijswijk, K., & Klerkx, L. (2022). Enhancing digital transformation towards virtual supply chains: A simulation game for Dutch floriculture. *Production Planning and Control, 33*(13), 1252–1269. doi:10.1080/09537287.2020.1858361

Schwartz, L. M., & Woloshin, S. (2019). Medical marketing in the United States, 1997-2016. *Journal of the American Medical Association, 321*(1), 80–96. doi:10.1001/jama.2018.19320 PMID:30620375

Senbekov, M., Saliev, T., Bukeyeva, Z., Almabayeva, A., Zhanaliyeva, M., Aitenova, N., Toishibekov, Y., & Fakhradiyev, I. (2020). The recent progress and applications of digital technologies in healthcare: A review. *International Journal of Telemedicine and Applications*, *2020*, 2020. doi:10.1155/2020/8830200 PMID:33343657

Sheaff, R., Morando, V., Chambers, N., Exworthy, M., Mahon, A., Byng, R., & Mannion, R. (2020). Managerial workarounds in three European DRG systems. *Journal of Health Organization and Management*, *34*(3), 295–311. doi:10.1108/JHOM-10-2019-0295 PMID:32364346

Sokoya, T., Zhou, Y., Diaz, S., Law, T., Himawan, L., Lekey, F., Shi, L., Gimbel, R. W., & Jing, X. (2022). Health Indicators as Measures of Individual Health Status and Their Public Perspectives: Cross-sectional Survey Study. *Journal of Medical Internet Research*, *24*(6), e38099. doi:10.2196/38099 PMID:35623051

Spielmans, G. I., & Parry, P. I. (2010). From evidence-based medicine to marketing-based medicine: Evidence from internal industry documents. *Journal of Bioethical Inquiry*, *7*(1), 13–29. doi:10.100711673-010-9208-8

Sreenivas, T., Srinivasarao, B., Srinivasa Rao, U., & India, A. (2013). An analysis on marketing mix in hospitals. *International Journal of Advanced Research in Management and Social Sciences*, *2*(4), 187–207.

Stanley, N., Oram, S., Jakobowitz, S., Westwood, J., Borschmann, R., Zimmerman, C., & Howard, L. M. (2016). The health needs and healthcare experiences of young people trafficked into the UK. *Child Abuse & Neglect*, *59*, 100–110. doi:10.1016/j.chiabu.2016.08.001 PMID:27552002

Tan, T. F., Li, Y., Lim, J. S., Gunasekeran, D. V., Teo, Z. L., Ng, W. Y., & Ting, D. S. (2022). Metaverse and virtual health care in ophthalmology: Opportunities and challenges. *Asia-Pacific Journal of Ophthalmology*, *11*(3), 237–246. doi:10.1097/APO.0000000000000537 PMID:35772084

Taylor, M. J., Shikaislami, C., McNicholas, C., Taylor, D., Reed, J., & Vlaev, I. (2020). Using virtual worlds as a platform for collaborative meetings in healthcare: A feasibility study. *BMC Health Services Research*, *20*(1), 1–10. doi:10.118612913-020-05290-7 PMID:32429971

Thimbleby, H. (2013). Technology and the future of healthcare. *Journal of Public Health Research, 2*(3).

Thomas, R. K. (2008). *Health services marketing: A practitioner's guide*. Springer Science & Business Media. doi:10.1007/978-0-387-73606-8

Thompson, A. G., & Sunol, R. (1995). Expectations as determinants of patient satisfaction: Concepts, theory and evidence. *International Journal for Quality in Health Care : Journal of the International Society for Quality in Health Care*, *7*(2), 127–141. doi:10.1093/intqhc/7.2.127 PMID:7655809

Ward, R. (2013). The application of technology acceptance and diffusion of innovation models in healthcare informatics. *Health Policy and Technology, 2*(4), 222-228.

Wen, L. S., & Tucker, S. (2015). What do people want from their health care? A qualitative study. *Journal of Participatory Medicine*, *7*, e10.

Williamson, B. (2015). Algorithmic skin: Health-tracking technologies, personal analytics and the biopedagogies of digitized health and physical education. *Sport Education and Society*, *20*(1), 133–151. doi:10.1080/13573322.2014.962494

World Health Organization. (2021). *Global strategy on digital health 2020-2025*. Author.

Wu, H., Deng, Z., Wang, B., & Gupta, S. (2021). How does service price influence patients' decisions? An examination of the free-market pricing mechanism in online health communities. *Electronic Markets*, *31*(4), 877–893. doi:10.100712525-020-00453-0

Chapter 2
The Role of Social Media in Healthcare Marketing

Nugzar Todua
https://orcid.org/0000-0002-1486-2141
Ivane Javakhishvili Tbilisi State University, Georgia

Charita Jashi
Ivane Javakhishvili Tbilisi State University, Georgia

Nia Todua
Ivane Javakhishvili Tbilisi State University, Georgia

ABSTRACT

The chapter discusses the features of using social media in the healthcare industry. It is emphasized that the role of social media in the era of digital technologies is especially increasing in the market of medical services, which leads to greater involvement of consumers in the field of healthcare. Digital technologies are gradually being introduced in the field of healthcare in Georgia, and an increasing number of medical organizations are using social media marketing to communicate with patients. Nevertheless, the use of social media by healthcare organizations is insufficient. One of the reasons for this is the lack of research in this field. With this in mind, this chapter presents a study that considers the impact of social media marketing activities on healthcare consumer behavior. Social media marketing activities, consumer engagement, consumer trust, and behavioral intention are selected as the main variables of the research. A conceptual model of the research has been developed, and relevant hypotheses have been formulated.

1. INTRODUCTION

Social media is an integral part of modern society and is gradually becoming a significant marketing tool that provides companies with ample opportunities to interact with their consumers (Abid *et al.*, 2023). Social media has become a perfect platform for companies to popularize and sell their product, find new information, and useful products, and communicate with their friends (Jacobson *et al.*, 2020).

DOI: 10.4018/979-8-3693-0679-6.ch002

Social media has become a valuable tool for healthcare knowledge management (Khan *et al.,* 2021). New technologies and ways of treatment as well as the growth of expectations in society that they are going to have access to high-quality healthcare create the need for new efficient strategies that will lower the cost of treatment (Kulkov *et al.,* 2021; Çağlıyor *et al.,* 2022). Social media in the public health agenda is another player in the marketing world that inspires and influences potential customers with the usage of social media platforms (Kostigina *et al.,* 2020; Carlsson-Szlezak *et al.,* 2020). Healthcare professionals use social media to build professional relationships with their colleagues and to share information (Rolls *et al.,* 2016). In the era of digital communication, healthcare providers recognize that social media with its diverse programs is the best tool for public health communications (Rolls *et al.,* 2016). Social media is the most effective way of sharing new information in the healthcare sphere as it can reach the widest and most diverse audience (Swan *et al.,* 2019).

Healthcare providers use social media to promote their organizations, also to establish strong relationships with existing and potential customers, and raise awareness of their own brand (Mondal *et al.,* 2022). As for patients, they receive information about their health condition through social media (Kamarudin *et al.,* 2022; Freire *et al.,* 2023).

Nowadays, healthcare organizations face many challenges. First of all, consumers move from a passive state to an active participant in the process of providing medical services (Crie & Chebat, 2013; Osei-Frimpong, 2017; Hung *et al.,* 2023). They are increasingly using digital applications and various technologies that help them to be directly involved in protecting their well-being. Accordingly, healthcare organizations try not to stay behind and improve the methods of providing medical services, in which marketing approaches play a special role. Scholars emphasize the fact that one of the tools for success in the field of healthcare is marketing skills (Anderson *et al.,* 2018; Chaves *et al.,* 2021). That is why healthcare providers increasingly use patient-oriented approaches (Crie & Chebat, 2013; Pilon *et al.,* 2023).

Practice shows that social media is an essential part of the marketing and communication strategies of many medical organizations. The use of social media gives health systems a lot of opportunities. It helps healthcare organizations and physicians build relationships with patients, Openly share their opinions and get feedback from them, strengthen customer confidence, and enhance the attractiveness of their brands. Through online communication, patients, hospitals, and physicians form the foundation of positive relationships. Also, audience-targeting advertising through social media platforms helps healthcare organizations work individually with patients. Users are actively utilizing the Internet and social networks to seek health information (Zhou *et al.,* 2018). It is also notable that 60% of social media users, compared to other groups, trust doctors' posts more (Chen *et al.,* 2018). We should also note the fact that today's doctors, due to their busy work schedules, have less time to post relevant posts on social media. That is why marketers help doctors regularly post messages with original and quality content on their social networks. As we can see, social media, when used wisely, can be a supportive tool for the development of the health care system as well as for the care of patients by raising their awareness and promoting health programs. Social media can make a significant contribution to improving the quality of medical services; however, we must also consider the risks associated with the protection of personal data and the accuracy of information (Alshakhs & Alanzi, 2018; Liu *et al.,* 2021).

Social media changes the nature and speed of communication between healthcare organizations and physicians. Today, a significant number of doctors and patients use social media to raise knowledge about healthcare and disease. In turn, the use of social media is quite effective for healthcare promotion and behavior change (Korda & Itani, 2013). Hospitals and physicians actively involved in social media can identify and solve patients' problems in a timely manner, leading to increased customer satisfaction and loyalty (Jackson *et al.,* 2021). The introduction of innovations in the Internet space contributes to the development of digital health technologies. Under the influence of social media marketing, consumer access to digital healthcare tools is expanding (Swan *et al.,* 2019).

Websites can help patients get more involved with treatment phases by educating and helping them consistently manage their disease. Social media utilization in knowledge sharing can be considered a vitally important issue not only on a personal level but also for organizations. Some hospitals even have websites and apps where people can get free consultations from doctors or even book an online treatment procedure (Koumpouros *et al.,* 2015). Many researchers pay attention to social media and Knowledge Sharing because they play a huge role in decision-making regarding health services. Knowledge Sharing through social media is beneficial for all stakeholders in healthcare to identify existing challenges and find out how to resolve them. Good communication and knowledge sharing renew trust and good relationships, which are particularly important between participants with the same healthcare roles and interests (Aghdam *et al.,* 2021). Providing health knowledge management, particularly for doctors and patients, is significant for increasing their awareness, obtaining new technologies abilities, and skills, and empowering medical infrastructure to guarantee effective healthcare policy (Ghalavand *et al.,* 2020). Such an approach was especially important in the context of the COVID-19 pandemic (Renu, 2021; Prasetya *et al.,* 2023).

Digital technologies are being used by a number of Georgian medical organizations to advertise their services and foster better client interactions. Patients and the general public in Georgia should be willing to give healthcare institutions that use social media marketing their trust and gratitude. This was particularly noticeable during the COVID-19 outbreak. Georgia's government has implemented a unified electronic healthcare system, and it has worked very hard to adjust the healthcare system and bring in cutting-edge medical technologies in response to the continuous changes in the world economy (Healthcare and Social Issues Committee of the Parliament of Georgia, 2017). However, these actions are insufficient. Regretfully, Georgian digital marketing in the medical field is still in its infancy. We may conclude that in the Georgian healthcare sector, using social media marketing techniques is still seen as innovative. As a result, in the Georgian medical services sector, customer awareness and satisfaction with demands are often poor (Todua & Jashi, 2018). The majority of Georgian customers do not get timely or sufficient information on the latest advancements in the healthcare industry. This is due, in part, to the fact that less research has been done on the effects of social media marketing on local customers' behavior in the healthcare industry in Georgian reality (Mladenović *et.al.,*2023). The following, in our opinion, is the most crucial of these issues: The impact of Social Media Marketing activities provided by healthcare organizations on Georgian consumer's engagement, and trust, as well as the impact of engagement and trust on purchase intention. All of this necessitates precise scientific investigation. The course of pertinent research was conditioned by the significance of the problem, the issues in this field, and the need for their scientific investigation. With this in mind, the study's goal is to determine how social media marketing activities impact consumer behavior in the healthcare sector. The following Research Questions (RQ) are presented in light of the foregoing:

RQ 1: How Social Media Marketing activities conducted by health care organizations impact on Georgian consumers engagement in social media?

RQ 2: How Social Media Marketing activities conducted by health care organizations impact on Georgian consumers trust in social media?

RQ 3: How Georgian consumers engagement in social media impact on their behavioral intention regarding healthcare?
RQ 4: How Georgian consumers trust in social media impact on their behavioral intention regarding healthcare?

2. LITERATURE REVIEW AND DEVELOPMENT OF RESEARCH HYPOTHESES

These days, the organization's most valuable intangible asset is seen to be the creation of a customer relations vision (Pansari & Kumar, 2017). According to recent studies, client participation on social media makes it easier for businesses to co-create market characteristics for new products and corporate values (Hollebeek *et al.,* 2019). According to research, client interaction enhances social identification, good attitudes, emotional benefits, and cognitive functions. Accordingly, a certain mental state that consumers develop throughout their interactions with brands and companies is referred to as customer engagement (Hollebeek *et al.,* 2014).

In the healthcare industry, social media consumer interaction is very crucial. For instance, client communication is facilitated via hospital-sponsored activities including online forums, health postings, and preventative webinars. As a result, these initiatives guarantee that patrons adopt a positive outlook and enhance their overall experience (Kumar & Pansari, 2016). Social media platforms are transforming consumer interaction in a number of ways. First, social media platforms have the power to incite client participation by compelling businesses to examine customer interaction data in order to provide better customer service (Carlson *et al.,* 2018). Conversely, social media makes it feasible to get excellent levels of client interaction. Users of social media platforms can establish connections with a wide range of people and organizations (Schivinski *et al.,* 2016). Third, location-based services are now available on social media platforms to assist draw in new users and cultivate relationships with them (Wang & Stefanone, 2013).

Engaging with clients on social media is essential in the healthcare sector. For example, hospital-sponsored initiatives like health posters, preventative webinars, and online chats make it easier to interact with patients. Thus, these programs ensure that customers have a favorable attitude and improve their experience (Kumar & Pansari, 2016). Research shows that patient engagement in the online activities of medical organizations has a significant impact on the effectiveness of their healthcare (Mirzaei & Esmaeilzadeh, 2021). The literature review mentioned above provides support for the following hypothesis (H):

H1: Social Media marketing activities conducted by health care organizations has a positive impact on consumers engagement in social media.

When people are engaged in online activities, the trust issue becomes even more crucial (Kwortnik Jr & Han, 2011). The marketing literature defines "trust" in a variety of ways, but honesty, capacity, competence, and recognition are the foundations for each definition (Pirson *et al.,* 2017). The internet world is characterized by danger and unpredictability. Reputation is built through persuasion-based trust. Benevolence relates to the relationship between the seller and the buyer, while it involves the belief that the other party to the transaction merits confidence (Chiu *et al.,* 2012). Online community perceptions of trust are connected to online behavior. In the context of an online community, trust provides a means for each member to cultivate personal connections with others and encourage them to draw others into the network. Thus, confidence plays a crucial role in shaping customers' intentions as well as their purchase behavior (Asti *et al.,* 2021). It is noteworthy that the online activities of healthcare organizations are an important factor that encourages patients to seek high-tech medical services (Ahmed *et al.*, 2023). Drawing on the aforementioned literature assessment, the subsequent hypothesis is posited:

H2: Social media marketing activities conducted by health care organizations has a positive impact on consumers trust in social media.

Examining the intention to buy is a crucial aspect of researching customer behavior on the internet. One of the main features of consumer behavior is purchase intention, which is connected to it (Oosthuizen *et al.,* 2015). Businesses must exercise caution when evaluating purchase intentions since anticipating customer behavior is crucial to their success (Baabdullah *et al.,* 2019). Simultaneously, it should be mentioned that customers' attractiveness and/or loyalty to items is mostly determined by their positive purchase intentions (Hong & Cho, 2011). According to Farah (2017) and Kahraman & Kazançoğlu (2019), intention indicates the subjective likelihood that customers would purchase the goods and carry out a particular activity. Based on the aforementioned, we may ascertain which products consumers should buy and when they will go shopping by using their purchase intention (Hajli *et al.*, 2017).

Social media, which allows for a two-way dialogue between the company and its clients, has proved ideal for the development of buying intentions. A connection like this strengthens a favorable opinion of the brand and influences purchase intention favorably (Hutter *et al.,* 2013). Furthermore, research has shown that social media marketing initiatives have an impact on consumers' intentions to make purchases (Yadav & Rahman, 2017). Consumer engagement in social media plays an important role in shaping their healthcare awareness and behavioral intention (Khan *et al.,* 2021). Many studies show that trust influences patients' intention to use the technologies offered by healthcare organizations (Zulman *et al.,* 2011; Liu *et al.,* 2023). In light of the literature review mentioned above, the following Hypotheses are presented:

H3: Consumers engagement in social media has a positive impact on their behavioral intention regarding healthcare;

H4: Consumers trust in social media has a positive impact on their behavioral intention regarding healthcare.

3. RESEARCH METHODOLOGY

In order to generalizations about ideas, we employed the deductive approach (Bryman & Bell, 2011). The ideas were then examined by testing the hypotheses (Bryman & Bell, 2011; Malhotra, 2010; Saunders *et al.,* 2019). The following were covered in our study design: determining the information required; choosing research methods; creating a questionnaire and identifying its measuring characteristics; calculating sample size; and data analysis. The study's design required gathering both primary and secondary data. We collected secondary data from public sources, including statistics reports from Georgian government agencies. In this study, primary data are being collected using the quantitative research approach, which offers the use of unified data collection tools (Saunders *et al.,* 2019). In response, we conducted a consumer survey using a specially created questionnaire and descriptive methods.

The variables in this study are developed using quantitative and deductive methods. Our objective is to assess the regression and correlation relationships between the independent variables (social media marketing activities) and the dependent variables (social media engagement, trust, and purchase intention). We can create a conceptual research model that graphically illustrates the influence of social media marketing activities by healthcare organizations on customer behavior based on the above-described structure and literature review (Figure 1).

The primary means of data collection in our study was an internet questionnaire. Furthermore, a self-administered survey was used in this investigation. Because of this strategy, the self-administration technique of directly gathering data from respondents is easy, quick, and affordable (Saunders *et al.*, 2019). The questionnaire's questions were derived from the authors' viewpoints as stated in this paper's literature review section. Based on a deductive methodology, the variables and measuring items in this study were developed using pertinent literature (see table 1). Multiple-choice questions are utilized to provide the responses, and a 5-point Likert scale is employed (1=strongly disagree, 2=disagree, 3=neutral, 4=agree, and 5=strongly agree). The questionnaire took about fifteen to twenty minutes to complete because to its design.

We studied the general population using the probability sampling approach. Georgia was the research area, and it was chosen in a way that made it representative. To get the sample size, we applied a formula from statistics (Krejcie & Morgan, 1970):

$$S = \frac{x^2 N P\left(1-P\right)}{d^2\left(N-1\right)+x^2 P\left(1-P\right)}, \quad (1)$$

Where: S = required sample size; x^2= the table value of chi-square for 1 degree of freedom (df) at the desired confidence level; N = the population size; P = the population proportion (assumed to be .50 since this would provide the maximum sample size); d = the degree of accuracy expressed as a proportion (.05). Value of chi-square for 95% confidence level is 3,8416 (1,96 X 1,96).

Figure 1. Research model

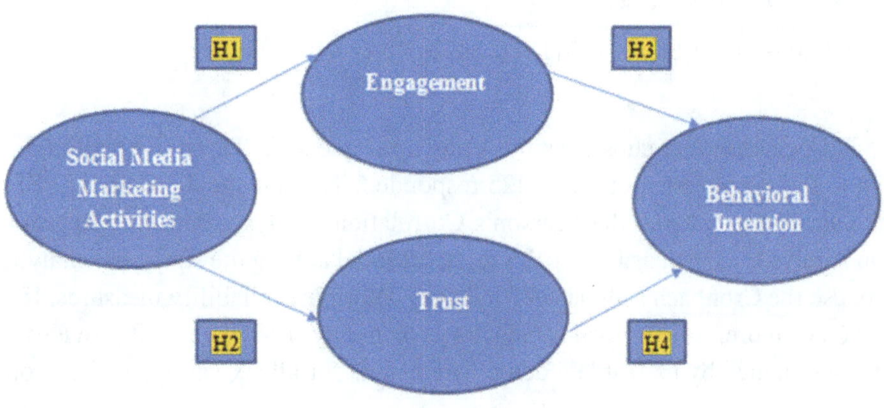

Table 1. Research construct

Variables	Measurement Items	Adopted From
Social Media Marketing Activities (conducted by healthcare organizations)	• *Social media is used by healthcare organizations to advertise their activities* • *Healthcare organizations use social media to build relationships with their customers* • *Healthcare organizations use social media to gain positive customers feedback* • *Healthcare organizations use customers comments on social media to make improvements to the quality of their services* • *Healthcare organizations use different social media marketing strategies* • *Healthcare organizations use innovative strategies to market their services on social media* • *Healthcare organizations use social media to obtain a competitive edge* • *Healthcare organizations use new and creative ways to advertise their services*	Dodokh, & Al-Maaitah, 2019; Swan *et al.*, 2019; Ghalavand *et al.*, 2020
Engagement (Patients engagement on social media regarding healthcare)	• *I frequently browse the social media pages of healthcare organizations* • *I frequently peruse social media posts from healthcare organizations* • *I frequently follow the pages of healthcare organizations on social media to obtain fascinating information* • *I frequently utilize the "like" option on posts made by healthcare organizations* • *I frequently leave comments on the pages of healthcare organizations on social media*	Toor *et al.*, 2017; Rahman, 2017; Kostigina *et al.*, 2020; Mirzaei & Esmaeilzadeh, 2021
Trust (Patients Trust of Social Media Marketing Activities conducted by healthcare organizations)	• *In my opinion, healthcare organizations' social media activity is reliable* • *I would use healthcare organizations' services because I trust their social media marketing activities* • *In my opinion, healthcare organizations are capable of using social media.* • *In my opinion, healthcare organizations will honor the commitments and pledges they make on social media*	Chiu *et al.*, 2012; Hong & Cho, 2013; Ahmed *et al.*, 2023
Behavioral Intention	• *Social media activities conducted by health care organizations use improves my decision-making before I pay for medical services* • *When healthcare organizations use social media, it makes me more interested in purchasing medical services* • *If healthcare organizations recommended medical services on social media, I'm highly inclined to purchase them* • *I would want to suggest to my friends and family that they purchase the services that healthcare organizations advertise on social media* • *When I need in the future, I'll use the social media services provided by healthcare organizations*	Chiu et al. 2012; Wang & Chang, 2013; Toor *et al.*, 2017

Georgia's population as of the 2023 census is 3726400, of which 229400 are Internet users over the age of 18, which is the population our study is aimed at (National Statistics Office of Georgia, 2023). Using formula (1) and the aforementioned data, the sampling size will be:

$$S = \frac{1,96^2 \ x \ 2294000 \ x \ 0,5x\left(1-0,5\right)}{0,05^2\left(2294000-1\right)+1,96^2 \ x \ 0,5\left(1-0,5\right)} = 373,2$$

Therefore, 374 persons were chosen as the study's sample size. Through email and social media, we reached out to 572 responders; of them, 425 responded. The statistical program SPSS 27 was used to process the data. We employed the Pearson's Correlation Analysis, Multiple Regression Analysis and Dispersion Analysis, as well as Linear Regression Model among the statistical analytic techniques.

Researchers use the Cronbach's alpha coefficient to determine reliability measures. If the reliability coefficient is 0.60 or more, it is deemed satisfactory (Nunnally, 1967). Table 2 provides the reliability data that we were obtained by us. Table 4 demonstrates that for all six variables, the Cronbach's alpha coefficient was 0.945, and for each variable, it was greater than 0.8, indicating a much higher reliable coefficient.

4. MAIN FINDINGS AND DISCUSSION

The sample of respondents were uncovered by our marketing study, which was categorized by several criteria. Table 3 displays the sampling characteristics based on the number of respondents and the percentage. According to the poll, the majority of participants (47.1%) are between the ages of 18 and 24, with 1.6% being 65 or older. Women make up 63.5% of the responders, while males make up 36.5%.

Next, we explored whether there is a connection between social media marketing activities and customer engagement. As it turned out, such a connection is statistically reliable (P <0.001), and the correlation coefficient is positive (r = 0.267) (Table 4). As mentioned above, the first hypothesis relates to the impact of social media marketing activities on consumers engagement. Regression analysis is used to test the H1 hypothesis. Table 4 shows that the model we developed is reliable. (P<0.001);

Table 2. Reliability statistics

Variables	Cronbach's Alfa	Number of Items
All	0.945	21
Activity	0.894	7
Engagement	0.855	5
Trust	0.882	4
Behavioral Intension	0.877	5

Source: SPSS output based on own data

Table 3. Demographic profile of a sample (N=425)

Variable	Frequency (Percentage)	Variable	Frequency (Percentage)
Age		Gender	
18-24	200 (47,1%)	Male	155 (36,5%)
25-35	138 (32,5%)	Female	270 (63,5%)
36-45	29 (6,8%)	**Occupation**	
46-55	30 (7,1%)	Student	134 (31,5%)
56 and older	28 (6,5%)	Owner/Entrepreneur	27 (6,4%)
Education		Government Employee	73 (17,2%)
Pre high school	39 (9,2%)	Private Employee	174 (40,9%)
Vocational	26 (6,1%)	Other	17 (4%)
Bachelor's degree	164 (38,6%)		
Master's degree	150 (35,3%)		
Ph.D	46 (10,8%)		

Source: Authors' elaboration

$F=32.581>F_{critical}=3.84$. The H1 hypothesis is supported. Consequently, social media marketing activities have a positive impact on consumers engagement. In addition, R square =0.072, which allows us to say that 7.2% of the activities are caused by engagement, which is quietly low. Accordingly, the rest is due to other factors.

In the next step, we explored whether there is a connection between social media marketing activities and Trust. As it turned out, the result of the study is statistically acceptable (P <0.001), and the correlation coefficient is positive (r = 0.389) (Table 5). As mentioned above, the third hypothesis relates to the impact of social media activities on Trust. With this in mind, we used regression analysis to test the H2 hypothesis. As can be seen from Table 5, the model we developed is reliable (P <0.001; $F = 75.490> F_{critical} = 3.84$). The H2 hypothesis is supported. Therefore, social media activities have a positive impact on Trust. Also, R square = 0.151, which allows us to say that 15.1% of the social media marketing activity is caused by Trust, while the rest is due to other factors.

To explore of the impact of consumers engagement and Trust on Behavioral Intention in social media, we first examined whether there is a connection between consumer engagement in social media marketing activities and behavioral intention. As it turned out, such a relationship is statistically reliable (P <0.001), and the correlation coefficient is positive (r = 0.571) (Table 6). As noted above, the

Table 4. Regression analysis of the impact of social media activity on consumers engagement

R	R²	Adjusted R²	Standard Error of Estimate		Sum of Squares	df	Mean Square	F	Significance Level
0.267	**0.072**	**0.069**	**4.222**	**Regression**	**580.65**	**1**	**580.6**	**32.581**	**0.000**
				Residual	**7538.47**	**423**	**17.8**		
				Total	**8119.12**	**424**			
	Unstandardized Coeficients			Standardized Coeficients			t	Significance level	
	B	Standard Error		Beta					
Activity (Constant)	7.440 0.213	0.895 0.037		0.267			8.310 5.708	0.000 0.000	
Notes: Dependent Variable:Engagement; Predictors: Activity									

Source: SPSS output based on own data

Table 5. Regression analysis of the impact of consumers social media activity on the Trust

R	R²	Adjusted R²	Standard Error of Estimate		Sum of Squares	df	Mean Square	F	Significance Level
0.389	0.151	0.149	2.9674	Regression	664.83	1	664.83	75.490	0.000
				Residual	3725.29	423	8.81		
				Total	4390.12	424			
	Unstandardized Coeficients			Standardized Coeficients			t	Significance level	
	B	Standard Error		Beta					
Activity (Constant)	6.595 0.228	0.629 0.026		0.389			10.479 8.688	0.000 0.000	
Notes: Dependent Variable: Trust; Predictors: Activity									

Source: SPSS output based on own data

5th hypotheses relate to consumers engagement's impact on behavioral intension. We used regression analysis to test the H4 hypothesis. As can be seen from Table 6, the model we developed is reliable (P <0.001 F=204.83>$F_{critical}$ =3.84. The H3 hypothesis is supported. Consequently, consumers engagement affects behavioral Intention. R square = 0.326, which allows us to say that 32.6% of Behavioral Intention is caused by Engagement while the rest is due to other factors.

As mentioned above, the 5th hypotheses reflect the impact of Trust on Behavioral Intention. With this in mind, we used regression analysis to test the H4 hypothesis. As Table 7 shows the model we developed is reliable (P<0.001; F=325.80>$F_{critical}$ =3.84). The H5 hypothesis is supported. Consequently, the Trust affects Behavioral Intention. Also, R square = 0.435, which allows us to say that 43.5% of Behavioral Intention is caused by the Trust while the rest is due to other factors.

5. CONCLUSION

This survey indicates that social media are now an important aspect of Georgian consumers' lives, and they are used often. Consumers in Georgia are increasingly turning to the Internet for medical information,

Table 6. Regression analysis of the impact of consumers engagement on behavioral intention

R	R^2	Adjusted R^2	Standard Error of Estimate		Sum of Squares	df	Mean Square	F	Significance Level
0.571	0.326	0.325	3.4382	Regression	2421.31	1	2421.31	204.830	0.000
				Residual	5000.30	423	11.821		
				Total	7421.61	424			
	Unstandardized Coeficients			Standardized Coeficients			t	Significance level	
	B	Standard Error		Beta					
Engagement **(Constant)**	7.682 0.546	0.502 0.038		0.571			15.297 14.312	0.000 0.000	
Notes: Dependent Variable: Behavioral Intension; Predictors: Engagement									

Source: SPSS output based on own data

Table 7. Regression analysis of trust impact on behavioral intention

R	R^2	Adjusted R^2	Standard Error of Estimate		Sum of Squares	df	Mean Square	F	Significance Level
0.660	0.435	0.434	3.1482	Regression	3229.14	1	3229.14	325.804	0.000
				Residual	4192.47	423	9.91		
				Total	7421.61	424			
	Unstandardized Coeficients			Standardized Coeficients			t	Significance level	
	B	Standard Error		Beta					
Trust **(Constant)**	4.240 0.858	0.586 .048		0.660			7.230 18.050	0.000 0.000	
Notes: Dependent Variable: Behavioral Intension; Predictors: Trust									

Source: SPSS output based on own data

and they are particularly interested in health-related content. According to our study, Georgian customers are still acting in a somewhat passive manner. Furthermore, there is a notable lack of confidence among Georgian customers about the material disseminated on social media. The regression study produced statistically significant values that illustrate the relationships between the social media activities provided by healthcare organizations and consumer engagement, trust, and behavioral intentions. Furthermore, linear regression models that take into consideration the relationships between the aforementioned variables are obtained. By using these models, we may ascertain the extent to which a rise in social media activities provided by healthcare organizations endeavors could influence customer conduct.

6. THEORETICAL AND PRACTICAL IMPLICATIONS

This study has several theoretical ramifications for how social media marketing is used in the healthcare sector. First of all, it's critical to acknowledge that there are still glaring gaps in the field of social media marketing, even if the topic is quite wide and has been the focus of much research. This indicates that fewer studies have been conducted to determine a relationship between the social media marketing strategies employed by healthcare organizations and factors that influence consumer behavior, such as customer engagement, trust, and behavioral intention. This work contributes to the understanding of the link between these factors. A wealth of information from this study may be used in future research to gain a deeper comprehension of how social media marketing affects consumer behavior.

The following are the main contributions made by this study from a managerial perspective: First, the study's conclusions will help managers in the healthcare sector better understand how social media marketing campaigns may be an effective means of establishing connections with both present and potential clients. Second, healthcare organizations may use the study findings to guide the creation of their business plans. Third, health care providers will be able to develop marketing strategies that will help them accomplish their goals by having a deeper grasp of the purchasing perspectives of their clients.

7. RESEARCH LIMITATIONS AND DIRECTION FOR FUTURE RESEARCH

The study took into account certain limitations. First of all, the study's required sample size of responders was constrained by pragmatic considerations. To be more precise, the study's sample is not entirely typical of the population, particularly when it comes to all age categories. The over-24 age group needs to get special attention. The research was primarily focused on the 18–24 age bracket, which makes up the bulk of Internet and social media users in Georgia even if it cannot be considered a whole population. The poll was mostly based on a survey of Georgian consumers in Tbilisi, the capital of Georgia. Since most Georgians reside in Tbilisi and are thus Internet users, the limitation was placed in place.

Future studies into social media marketing activities and associated customer behavior in the Georgian healthcare sector will build upon the findings of this study. This work presents a number of intriguing avenues for further research. It first has to do with how social media marketing campaigns for healthcare organizations affect consumers happiness and loyalty. The creation and execution of such marketing initiatives are unaccustomed to Georgian reality, which offers fascinating research opportunities. Future studies should examine the ways in which consumer loyalty and satisfaction with healthcare organizations social media marketing campaigns influence their buying decisions.

REFERENCES

Abid, A., Roy, S. K., Lees-Marshment, J., Dey, B. L., Muhammad, S. S., & Kumar, S. (2023). Political social media marketing: A systematic literature review and agenda for future research. *Electronic Commerce Research*, 1–36. doi:10.100710660-022-09636-7

Aghdam, Z. N., Rahmani, A. M., & Hosseinzadeh, M. (2021). The role of the Internet of Things in healthcare: Future trends and challenges. *Computer Methods and Programs in Biomedicine*, *199*, 105903. doi:10.1016/j.cmpb.2020.105903 PMID:33348073

Ahmed, S., Alqasmi, I., Ashrafi, D. M., Choudhury, M. M., Rahman, M. K., & Mohiuddin, M. (2023). Determining the intention to use app-based medicine service in an emerging economy. *International Journal of Healthcare Management*, 1–15. doi:10.1080/20479700.2023.2198186

Alshakhs, F., & Alanzi, T. (2018). The evolving role of social media in health-care delivery measuring the perception of health-care professionals in Eastern Saudi Arabia. *Journal of Multidisciplinary Healthcare*, *11*, 473–479. doi:10.2147/JMDH.S171538 PMID:30275699

Anderson, S. T., Nasr, L., & Rayburn, S. W. (2018). Transformative service research and service design: Synergistic effects in healthcare. *Service Industries Journal*, *38*(1-2), 99–113. doi:10.1080/02642069.2017.1404579

Asti, W. P., Handayani, P. W., & Azzahro, F. (2021). Influence of trust, perceived value, and attitude on customers' repurchase intention for e-grocery. *Journal of Food Products Marketing*, *27*(3), 157–171. doi:10.1080/10454446.2021.1922325

Baabdullah, A. M., Alalwan, A. A., Rana, N. P., Kizgin, H., & Patil, P. (2019). Consumer use of mobile banking (M-Banking) in Saudi Arabia: Towards an integrated model. *International Journal of Information Management*, *44*, 38–52. doi:10.1016/j.ijinfomgt.2018.09.002

Bryman, A., & Bell, E. (2011). *Business Research Methods* (3rd ed.). Oxford University Press.

Çağlıyor, S., Tosun, P., & Uray, N. (2022). Communicating value in healthcare marketing from a social media perspective. In *New Perspectives in Operations Research and Management Science: Essays in Honor of Fusun Ulengin* (pp. 143–170). Springer International Publishing. doi:10.1007/978-3-030-91851-4_6

Carlsson-Szlezak, P., Reeves, M., & Swartz, P. (2020). What coronavirus could mean for the global economy. *Harvard Business Review*, 3.

Chaves Prasetya, T. A. E., & Wardani, R. W. K. (2023). Systematic review of social media addiction among health workers during the pandemic Covid-19. *Heliyon*, *9*(6), e16784. doi:10.1016/j.heliyon.2023.e16784 PMID:37274718

Chen, Y. Y., Li, C. M., Liang, J. C., & Tsai, C. C. (2018). Health Information Obtained From the Internet and Changes in Medical Decision Making: Questionnaire Development and Cross-Sectional Survey. *Journal of Medical Internet Research*, *20*(2), e47. doi:10.2196/jmir.9370 PMID:29434017

Chiu, C. M., Hsu, M. H., Lai, H., & Chang, C. M. (2012). Re-examining the influence of trust on online repeat purchase intention: The moderating role of habit and its antecedents. *Decision Support Systems*, *53*(4), 835–845. doi:10.1016/j.dss.2012.05.021

Crie, D., & Chebat, J.-C. (2013). Health marketing: Toward an integrative perspective. *Journal of Business Research*, *66*(1), 123–126. doi:10.1016/j.jbusres.2012.09.002

Dodokh, A., & Al-Maaitah, M. A. (2019). Impact of social media usage on organizational performance in the Jordanian dead sea cosmetic sector. *European Journal of Business and Management*, *11*(2), 75–91.

Farah, M. F. (2017). Application of the theory of planned behavior to customer switching intentions in the context of bank consolidations. *International Journal of Bank Marketing*, *35*(1), 147–172. doi:10.1108/IJBM-01-2016-0003

Freire, Y., Sánchez, M. G., Suárez, A., Joves, G., Nowak, M., & Díaz-Flores García, V. (2023). Influence of the use of social media on patients changing dental practice: A web-based questionnaire study. *BMC Oral Health*, *23*(1), 365. doi:10.118612903-023-03078-9 PMID:37277765

Ghalavand, H., Panahi, S., & Sedghi, S. (2020). Opportunities and challenges of social media for health knowledge management: A narrative review. *Journal of Education and Health Promotion*, *9*, 1–5. PMID:32766329

Hajli, N., Sims, J., Zadeh, A. H., & Richard, M. O. (2017). A social commerce investigation of the role of trust in a social networking site on purchase intentions. *Journal of Business Research*, *71*, 133–141. doi:10.1016/j.jbusres.2016.10.004

Healthcare and Social Issues Committee of the Parliament of Georgia. (2017). *Vision for developing the healthcare system in Georgia by 2030*. Parliament of Georgia. Retrieved October 20, 2023, from https://georgia.un.org/sites/default/files/2020-08/Georgia%205.pdf

Hollebeek, L. D., Glynn, M. S., & Brodie, R. J. (2014). Consumer brand engagement in social media: Conceptualization, scale development and validation. *Journal of Interactive Marketing*, *28*(2), 149–165. doi:10.1016/j.intmar.2013.12.002

Hollebeek, L. D., Srivastava, R. K., & Chen, T. (2019). SD logic–informed customer engagement: Integrative framework, revised fundamental propositions, and application to CRM. *Journal of the Academy of Marketing Science*, *47*(1), 161–185. doi:10.100711747-016-0494-5

Hong, I. B., & Cho, H. (2011). The impact of consumer trust on attitudinal loyalty and purchase intentions in B2C e-marketplaces: Intermediary trust vs. seller trust. *International Journal of Information Management*, *31*(5), 469–479. doi:10.1016/j.ijinfomgt.2011.02.001

Hung, C. L., Wu, J. H., Chen, P. Y., Xu, X., Hsu, W. L., Lin, L. M., & Hsieh, M. C. (2023). Enhancing healthcare services and brand engagement through social media marketing: Integration of Kotler's 5A framework with IDEA process. *Information Processing & Management*, *60*(4), 103379. doi:10.1016/j.ipm.2023.103379

Hutter, K., Hautz, J., Dennhardt, S., & Füller, J. (2013). The impact of user interactions in social media on brand awareness and purchase intention: The case of MINI on Facebook. *Journal of Product and Brand Management*, *22*(5-6), 342–351. doi:10.1108/JPBM-05-2013-0299

Jackson, M., Brennan, L., & Parker, L. (2021). The public health community's use of social media for policy advocacy: A scoping review and suggestions to advance the field. *Public Health*, *198*, 146–155. doi:10.1016/j.puhe.2021.07.015 PMID:34428607

Jacobson, J., Gruzd, A., & Hernández-García, Á. (2020). Social media marketing: Who is watching the watchers? *Journal of Retailing and Consumer Services*, *53*, 1–12. doi:10.1016/j.jretconser.2019.03.001

Kamarudin, Y., Low, D. F. F., Sulaiman, A., Zulhusmi, A. M., & Zakaria, N. N. (2022). Social Media Use and Marketing within the Orthodontic Practice in Malaysia. *Archives of Orofacial Science*, *17*(1), 87–100. doi:10.21315/aos2022.1701.OA05

Khan, I., Saleh, M. A., Quazi, A., & Johns, R. (2021). Health consumers' social media adoption behaviours in Australia. *Health Informatics Journal*, *27*(2), 14604582211009917. doi:10.1177/14604582211009917 PMID:33887968

Korda, H., & Itani, Z. (2013). Harnessing Social Media for Health Promotion and Behavior Change. *Health Promotion Practice*, *14*(1), 15–23. doi:10.1177/1524839911405850 PMID:21558472

Kostygina, G., Tran, H., Binns, S., Szczypka, G., Emery, S., Vallone, D., & Hair, E. (2020). Boosting Health Campaign Reach and Engagement Through Use of Social Media Influencers and Memes. *Social Media + Society*, *6*(2), 1–12. doi:10.1177/2056305120912475

Koumpouros, Y., Toulias, T. L., & Koumpouros, N. (2015). The importance of patient engagement and the use of social media marketing in healthcare. *Technology and Health Care*, *23*(4), 495–507. doi:10.3233/THC-150918 PMID:26409912

Krejcie, R. V., & Morgan, D. W. (1970). Determining sample size for research activities. *Educational and Psychological Measurement*, *30*(3), 607–610. doi:10.1177/001316447003000308

Kulkov, I., Tsvetkova, A., & Ivanova-Gongne, M. (2021). Identifying institutional barriers when implementing new technologies in the healthcare industry. *European Journal of Innovation Management*, *26*(4), 909–932. doi:10.1108/EJIM-02-2021-0093

Kumar, V., & Pansari, A. (2016). Competitive advantage through engagement. *JMR, Journal of Marketing Research*, *53*(4), 497–514. doi:10.1509/jmr.15.0044

Kwortnik, R. J. Jr, & Han, X. (2011). The influence of guest perceptions of service fairness on lodging loyalty in China. *Cornell Hospitality Quarterly*, *52*(3), 321–332. doi:10.1177/1938965511409005

Liu, J. Y. W., Sorwar, G., Rahman, M. S., & Hoque, M. R. (2023). The role of trust and habit in the adoption of mHealth by older adults in Hong Kong: A healthcare technology service acceptance (HTSA) model. *BMC Geriatrics*, *23*(1), 73. doi:10.118612877-023-03779-4 PMID:36737712

Liu, R., Gupta, S., & Patel, P. (2021). The application of the principles of responsible AI on social media marketing for digital health. *Information Systems Frontiers*, 1–25. PMID:34539226

Malhotra, N. (2010). *Marketing research: An applied orientation* (6th ed.). Pearson Education.

Mirzaei, T., & Esmaeilzadeh, P. (2021). Engagement in online health communities: Channel expansion and social exchanges. *Information & Management, 58*(1), 103404. doi:10.1016/j.im.2020.103404

Mladenović, D., Todua, N., & Pavlović-Höck, N. (2023). Understanding individual psychological and behavioral responses during COVID-19: Application of stimulus-organism-response model. *Telematics and Informatics, 79*, 101966. doi:10.1016/j.tele.2023.101966 PMID:36910674

Mondal, T., Jayadeva, S. M., Pani, R., Subramanian, M., & Sumana, B. (2022). E marketing strategy in health care using IoT and Machine Learning. *Materials Today: Proceedings, 56*, 2087–2091. doi:10.1016/j.matpr.2021.11.417

National Statistics Office of Georgia. (2023). Retrieved October 20, 2023, from https://www.geostat.ge/en

Nunnally, J. C. (1967). *Psychometric Theory*. McGraw-Hill Book Company.

Oosthuizen, D., Spowart, J., & De Meyer-Heydenrych, C. F. (2015). The relationship between perceived price and consumers' purchase intentions of private label wine brands. *African Journal of Hospitality, Tourism and Leisure, 4*(2), 1–17.

Osei-Frimpong, K. (2017). Patient participatory behaviours in healthcare service delivery. *Journal of Service Theory and Practice, 27*(2), 453–474. doi:10.1108/JSTP-02-2016-0038

Pansari, A., & Kumar, V. (2017). Customer engagement: The construct, antecedents, and consequences. *Journal of the Academy of Marketing Science, 45*(3), 294–311. doi:10.100711747-016-0485-6

Pilon, L., Foster, A., Zimmerman, P. A., & Macbeth, D. (2023). The role of online marketing to engage healthcare workers with infection prevention and control information and resources: A pilot study. *Infection, Disease & Health, 28*(3), 28. doi:10.1016/j.idh.2023.02.002 PMID:36868992

Pirson, M., Martin, K., & Parmar, B. (2017). Formation of stakeholder trust in business and the role of personal values. *Journal of Business Ethics, 145*(1), 1–20. doi:10.100710551-015-2839-2

Prasetya, T. A. E., & Wardani, R. W. K. (2023). Systematic review of social media addiction among health workers during the pandemic Covid-19. *Heliyon, 9*(6), e16784. doi:10.1016/j.heliyon.2023.e16784 PMID:37274718

Rahman, Z. (2017). The Impact of Social Media Engagement Metrics on Purchase Intention: A Study on Brand Fan Page Followers. *LUMEN Proceedings, 1*, 665-681.

Renu, N. (2021). Innovative Healthcare Marketing Strategies during COVID-19. *Journal of Marketing Management, 9*(2), 45–49.

Rolls, K., Hansen, M., Jackson, D., & Elliott, D. (2016). How health care professionals use social media to create virtual communities: An integrative review. *Journal of Medical Internet Research, 18*(6), e166. doi:10.2196/jmir.5312 PMID:27328967

Saunders, M., Lewis, P., & Thornhill, A. (2019). *Research methods for business students* (8th ed.). Pearson Education Ltd.

Schivinski, B., Christodoulides, G., & Dabrowski, D. (2016). Measuring consumers' engagement with brand-related social-media content: Development and validation of a scale that identifies levels of social-media engagement with brands. *Journal of Advertising Research, 56*(1), 64–80. doi:10.2501/JAR-2016-004

Swan, E. L., Dahl, A. J., & Peltier, J. W. (2019). Health-care marketing in an omni-channel environment: Exploring telemedicine and other digital touchpoints. *Journal of Research in Interactive Marketing, 13*(4), 602–618. doi:10.1108/JRIM-03-2019-0039

Todua, N., & Jashi, Ch. (2018). Influence of Social Marketing on the Behavior of Georgian Consumers Regarding Healthy Nutrition. *Soobshcheniia Akademii Nauk Gruzinskoi SSR, 12*(2), 183–190.

Toor, A., Husnain, M., & Hussain, T. (2017). The impact of social network marketing on consumer purchase intention in Pakistan: Consumer engagement as a mediator. *AJBA, 10*(1), 167–199.

Wang, J. C., & Chang, C. H. (2013). How online social ties and product-related risks influence purchase intentions: A Facebook experiment. *Electronic Commerce Research and Applications, 12*(5), 337–346. doi:10.1016/j.elerap.2013.03.003

Wang, S. S., & Stefanone, M. A. (2013). Showing off? Human mobility and the interplay of traits, self-disclosure, and Facebook check-ins. *Social Science Computer Review, 31*(4), 437–457. doi:10.1177/0894439313481424

Yadav, M., & Rahman, Z. (2017). Measuring consumer perception of social media marketing activities in e-commerce industry: Scale development & validation. *Telematics and Informatics, 34*(7), 1294–1307. doi:10.1016/j.tele.2017.06.001

Zhou, L., Zhang, D., Yang, C. C., & Wang, Y. (2018). Harnessing social media for health information management. *Electronic Commerce Research and Applications, 27*, 139–151. doi:10.1016/j.elerap.2017.12.003 PMID:30147636

Zulman, D. M., Kirch, M., Zheng, K., & An, L. C. (2011). Trust in the internet as a health resource among older adults: Analysis of data from a nationally representative survey. *Journal of Medical Internet Research, 13*(1), e1552. doi:10.2196/jmir.1552 PMID:21324832

Chapter 3
The Transformation of Healthcare Marketing in the New Digital Era:
A Comprehensive Analysis With Reference to China

Mohamad Zreik
https://orcid.org/0000-0002-6812-6529
Sun Yat-sen University, China

ABSTRACT

Focusing on China's distinct market, this chapter delves into how healthcare marketing has evolved in the digital age. It analyzes how developments in AI, big data analytics, augmented reality, blockchain, and mobile technologies are fueling a transition toward a consumer-centric health culture. This chapter explores the changing demands and preferences of the Chinese healthcare market, the importance of value-driven marketing tactics, and the function of customer relationship management. Ethical concerns, pricing concerns, and success metrics are also discussed. This chapter is a must-read for anybody with even a passing interest in the rapidly growing field of digital healthcare, since it provides a thorough overview of the history, current applications, and future directions of digital healthcare in China.

1. INTRODUCTION

Marketing in the healthcare business is a multifaceted profession that draws from a wide range of disciplines to advertise and sell goods and services. Since the middle of the twentieth century, this field has expanded at an exponential rate, paralleling the rise of healthcare consumerism. Promoting medical items and drugs was an early focus of healthcare marketing, with doctors frequently serving as the intended audience (Gunjan et al., 2015).

As the industry developed, however, attention turned from marketing products to marketing services like those offered by hospitals, clinics, and wellness centers. Marketing strategies were implemented

DOI: 10.4018/979-8-3693-0679-6.ch003

by hospitals in an effort to improve their standing in the eyes of patients, healthcare professionals, and insurance companies. The key goals were to increase the number of new patients, keep the current patients happy, and boost the hospital's standing in the community.

The digital revolution has brought about even more radical changes in healthcare advertising. While there is still a place for more traditional types of advertising, digital channels have begun to supplement and even supplant them. In order to connect with patients, healthcare organizations now need to implement digital marketing methods such as search engine optimization (SEO), social media marketing, content marketing, email marketing, and online reputation management (Desai & Vidyapeeth, 2019).

In addition, the widespread availability of the internet and cellphones has given consumers greater access to healthcare information, allowing them to become more involved, knowledgeable, and engaged in their own healthcare decisions (Carrera & Dalton, 2014). Patient-centric marketing, which puts patients' wants, needs, and values first, emerged as a result of the rise in consumer activism (Hernandez, 2009). Therefore, current healthcare marketing takes a more comprehensive strategy, emphasizing not just the promotion of healthcare products and services but also consumer education and awareness.

As a result, healthcare marketing's history is one of constant change, as new technologies and preferences have shaped the industry. Engaging patients, educating them, and promoting health products and services ethically are now at the center of the business, which once focused on the product.

The introduction of the digital age has significantly modified the promotion and distribution of healthcare services. Thanks to globalization and technological progress, there is now a generation of healthcare customers that are well-versed in their options and take an active role in making decisions about their care.

The widespread adoption of the Internet and smartphones has forced a change from conventional to digital healthcare marketing strategies. The term "digital marketing" encompasses a wide range of techniques, such as search engine optimization (SEO), content marketing, social media engagement, email marketing, and online reputation management (Bala & Verma, 2018). Improved patient satisfaction can result from the use of these methods because healthcare professionals can communicate with a wider audience, interact with customers on a more human level, and offer timely information or support.

Information is the driving force behind this shift. The use of artificial intelligence (AI) and big data analytics has helped healthcare professionals learn more about their patients' habits, preferences, and requirements (Chattu, 2021). These findings can be used to build individualized health promotion campaigns that better meet the needs of each patient.

Healthcare services are now more accessible than ever thanks to innovations like telehealth and mobile health (mHealth) apps. Patients are able to schedule appointments, monitor their health, and learn more about their problems through the use of these online systems. Telehealth's ability to reach underprivileged areas has been crucial to expanding access to quality healthcare (Haleem et al., 2021).

In addition, AR and VR have broken through in the healthcare marketing sphere by presenting fresh methods of showcasing products and services and of educating healthcare professionals. Blockchain technology also has great potential to protect patient information and strengthen the credibility of healthcare advertising (Chakraborty, 2022).

Another major shift brought on by the information age is the expansion of value-based healthcare (Da Silva Etges et al., 2020). It has transformed healthcare marketing techniques to place greater emphasis on quality of care and the patient experience rather than service volume.

There are many reasons why China is a focal point in the international conversation on how healthcare marketing will evolve in the digital age. As the world's most populous country, it offers a massive opportunity for medical tourism. High-quality, conveniently accessible healthcare is in high demand due to rising middle-class populations and an aging population.

China has made great achievements in the field of digital healthcare during the past several years. Due to technological developments and government initiatives, its healthcare market is becoming increasingly digitized. As part of its "Healthy China 2030" goal, the Chinese government has promoted digital innovation in the healthcare sector to increase healthcare's availability and affordability (Tan, Liu, & Shao, 2017).

Tech giants like Alibaba and Tencent in China are making significant investments in digital healthcare by building platforms that link millions of people with healthcare providers. Millions of people use sites like Tencent's WeDoctor and Alibaba's AliHealth, which allow them to consult with doctors, get prescriptions, and schedule appointments online (Harrison, 2021).

China also actively employs cutting-edge technologies in healthcare, including artificial intelligence, big data, and mobile technology. Disease diagnosis, medication research, patient monitoring, and predictive analytics are just some of the many uses of artificial intelligence and big data in China (Chattu, 2021). A large number of people in the country now own smartphones, which has stimulated the development of mobile health apps.

In addition, China's hybrid public-private healthcare system can teach us a lot about how to advertise healthcare services in other countries. The country's healthcare market is as varied as its population, ranging from huge urban hospitals to rural clinics, providing valuable insight into the ways in which healthcare marketing strategies can be adapted to serve a wide variety of populations and settings (Reynolds & McKee, 2011).

As such, the development and trajectory of healthcare marketing in the digital age can be studied effectively by looking at China as a case study. Other countries attempting to digitally modernize their healthcare systems should learn from its experiences and strategies.

2. A BRIEF HISTORY OF HEALTHCARE MARKETING IN CHINA

2.1. Overview of the Evolution

Over the past few decades, healthcare advertising in China has seen significant changes in response to the country's rapid economic and social development. Before the late 20th century, the Chinese government had a significant role in providing and overseeing the country's healthcare system (Yu et al., 2010). As a result, conventional healthcare marketing was essentially nonexistent at the time.

Market liberalization and economic reforms ushered in a new era in the 1980s. As the private sector became more involved in healthcare, competition grew (Wagstaff, 2009). Because of this, marketing tactics were required to win over clients and set apart from competitors. However, early healthcare marketing efforts were limited to more conceptually straightforward forms of promotion, and healthcare consumerism was still in its infancy (Wang, 2010).

The arrival of the digital age in the latter part of the 2000s marked a watershed moment. Consumers' access to information and services was revolutionized by the widespread use of the internet and the smartphone. The promise of digital platforms to connect with and engage consumers has slowly dawned on tech businesses, startups, and traditional healthcare providers. There was a tipping point in healthcare marketing when the popularity of mobile health apps, online consultations, and health information platforms skyrocketed.

There has been a dramatic increase in the number of digital healthcare projects in China during the past decade. Alibaba and Tencent, two major tech businesses, have launched healthcare portals, AliHealth and WeDoctor, respectively. Millions of people across the country benefit from the services offered by these websites, which range from virtual doctor visits to the distribution of pharmaceuticals (Harrison, 2021). At the same time, healthcare facilities have become avid users of digital marketing tools like websites, social media, and online advertising to draw in new customers and keep existing ones coming back.

Healthcare marketing using cutting-edge tools such as AI and big data has also been pioneered in China. By analyzing patient behavior, predicting health trends, and tailoring marketing strategies, these technologies improve the involvement and pleasure of patients.

2.2. Current Status and Role of Technology

At the present time, China is a world leader in the digital health sector, having made extensive use of technology in healthcare advertising (Wang et al., 2021). A vibrant digital health ecosystem has emerged thanks to the growing use of internet services and mobile device usage. The convergence of shifting demographics, rising healthcare expenditures, and innovative technologies has created a fertile environment for growth in China's digital health business.

China's healthcare advertising is being revolutionized by tech giants like Alibaba, Tencent, and Baidu. They've developed websites that offer a wide range of digital medical services like virtual doctor visits, patient records storage, appointment scheduling, and medication management (Yip & McKern, 2016). These sites double as advertising avenues, connecting healthcare professionals with vast pools of prospective patients.

Healthcare advertising in China now relies heavily on AI and big data. In order to better understand patient habits, preferences, and industry health trends, healthcare providers and tech firms use AI algorithms and big data analytics (Thomason, 2021). Insights like this are priceless for tailoring marketing strategies to each individual client and for using in healthcare to boost efficiency and effectiveness.

Healthcare marketers are finding uses for not only AI and big data, but also augmented reality (AR), virtual reality (VR), and blockchain. By providing patients with realistic simulations of medical procedures or the inner workings of a medicine, AR and VR can empower them to make more educated healthcare decisions (Haleem et al., 2022). However, blockchain technology can improve healthcare transaction security and transparency, which will increase patient and customer confidence.

The COVID-19 pandemic has contributed to China's already rapid expansion of telemedicine (Zreik, 2023). It's a great way to get the word out about your practice while also helping patients, especially those in outlying locations, get the care they need more easily and quickly. Healthcare professionals and patients can market their services and develop trusting connections through the use of telemedicine platforms that allow for direct communication.

There is a plethora of fitness tracking and chronic disease management apps available on mobile devices. These apps amass huge troves of user information, which can be used for personalized advertising and in-app purchases.

3. THE EVOLUTION OF NEEDS, WANTS, AND DEMANDS IN CHINA'S HEALTHCARE MARKET

3.1. Understanding the Changing Healthcare Consumer

Successful healthcare marketing requires an in-depth familiarity with the ever-evolving requirements of healthcare consumers. Rapid economic development, population shifts, urbanization, increasing digital access, and a shifting illness burden are all factors that have affected these aspects in China.

The growing middle class in China is a direct result of the country's rapid economic development over the past few decades. The rising middle class in China has brought with it higher standards for medical care. In addition to cost-effective treatment, they prioritize individualized attention (Azam et al., 2019). Consumers in China's modern healthcare market value speed, price transparency, and ease of access above everything else.

The rising aging of China's population is another big shift. An estimated 24% of the Chinese population will be 60 or older by the year 2025 (Tan et al., 2020). Because of this change in the population's make-up, more people are in need of geriatric care services such long-term care, rehabilitation, and management of chronic diseases.

Consumers in China have become increasingly active participants in their healthcare decisions as internet availability and smartphone usage have increased. The wealth of resources available to them online in the realm of health care allows people to make well-informed decisions about their treatment (Thapa et al., 2021). Due to this change, digital health services including telemedicine, online pharmacies, and mobile health apps have become increasingly popular (Wang et al., 2022).

As Chinese society has changed, so too has the composition of its diseases. Urbanization, sedentary lifestyles, and bad diets have all contributed to the rise in the prevalence of non-communicable diseases (NCDs) like diabetes, heart disease, and cancer (Reubi et al., 2016). The importance of preventative treatment, early diagnosis, and ongoing management of many illnesses has grown as a result of this trend.

Healthcare marketers in China, in response to these shifting demands, have adjusted their approaches. Value-based, patient-centered care has become a priority for them. Personalized, convenient, and effective healthcare delivery has become possible thanks in large part to the widespread adoption of digital technologies.

3.2. Implications for Healthcare Marketing

For healthcare providers, governments, IT companies, and other players in the healthcare sector, the digital transformation of healthcare marketing in the era of China has far-reaching ramifications.

To begin, it is essential for healthcare providers to have a strong online presence in light of the growing importance of digital platforms. For this reason, it's important to have a search engine optimization (SEO) plan, an active social media presence, and a user-friendly website. To expand their customer base, service providers could also promote their offerings through internet ads and email campaigns. Given the proliferation of mobile devices, it is essential that content and services be optimized for them.

Second, there is a great potential for more targeted advertising thanks to the availability of big data and AI. Healthcare providers can increase consumer participation and happiness by conducting in-depth analyses of patients' habits, interests, and needs in order to create segmented marketing campaigns and individualized services. Proactive healthcare marketing is made possible by the ability to foresee and respond to emerging health trends, made possible by the predictive analytics made possible by these technologies (Wang et al., 2018).

Third, new strategies for advertising healthcare services are needed to accommodate the growth of value-based care. Advertising should stress the excellent quality of care and the positive outcomes achieved for patients rather than the sheer number of services offered. Examples of such marketing methods could include highlighting positive feedback from patients, high success rates, and the knowledge and experience of doctors.

Fourthly, the shift toward patient-centered treatment means that consumers must be the focus of healthcare marketing. Transparency in healthcare delivery and pricing, as well as consideration of patient preferences and input, are all part of this process.

Healthcare providers will need to adjust their services to match the growing demand for digital health options like telemedicine and mobile health apps. For instance, telemedicine not only increases access to care but also presents new possibilities for healthcare advertising because doctors and other medical professionals can talk to consumers face-to-face and pitch their services.

Finally, as digital health expands, concerns about patient privacy and data security emerge as crucial ethical issues. In order to keep their patients' confidence, healthcare professionals must ensure that their advertising strategies are compliant with all applicable laws and codes of ethics.

4. DIGITAL HEALTHCARE LANDSCAPE IN CHINA

4.1. Past Development

Recognizing the significant progress made over the past couple of decades is crucial to comprehending China's digital healthcare sector. China's digital healthcare business has grown tremendously in recent years, thanks to the country's booming economy, substantial healthcare investments, and widespread acceptance of digital technologies.

Information technology was singled out by the Chinese government as a primary factor in healthcare reform in the early 2000s (Mei, 2020). As a result, they started a program to create a digital health infrastructure across the country. Electronic health records, better hospital information systems, and the expansion of telemedicine to remote areas were the initial targets of these initiatives. During this time period, many Chinese hospitals began using electronic systems for patient intake, appointment scheduling, and billing (Song et al., 2022).

The late 2000s was a watershed moment for China's digital healthcare when the country launched its 3G network. Online health platforms providing health information, online doctor consultations, and digital health services have proliferated in tandem with the expansion of high-speed, widely available internet (Keane et al., 2020).

Mobile health apps and wearable health gadgets have emerged during the past decade, significantly improving patient participation and individualized treatment. Fitness monitoring, chronic disease management, mental health, and women's health are just a few of the many areas that have thousands of specialized applications in China today.

Furthermore, AI applications in healthcare, ranging from predictive analytics to intelligent medical imaging, have proliferated in China as a result of the government's encouraging policies and substantial investment in artificial intelligence research (Arenal et al., 2020).

Disease prediction, data security, patient education, and immersive health experiences are just some of the areas that have benefited from the combination of big data analytics, blockchain, and augmented reality in healthcare.

4.2. Current Applications

Telemedicine, AI-driven diagnostics, and individualized health management are only some of the existing digital healthcare uses in China. Telemedicine is one of the most well-known uses, and it's been increasingly important since the COVID-19 pandemic (Rush et al., 2021). Healthcare is now more accessible than ever in China, even for patients in remote areas or who are isolated, thanks to the proliferation of digital platforms that provide virtual consultations, remote patient monitoring, and digital health records.

The use of mobile health apps is now commonplace. Apps that keep tabs on a person's exercise, food intake, sleep patterns, and mental wellness give people the tools they need to take charge of their health. Patient convenience is further increased by the fact that certain apps provide services like as online medical consultations, medication reminders, and appointment booking.

Disease prediction, individualized treatment, medication development, and medical image analysis are just some of the applications of AI and big data analytics that are seeing widespread use in China (Bhattacharya et al., 2021). By analyzing massive amounts of medical data, AI algorithms can, for instance, foretell the likelihood of disease, provide individualized treatment regimens, and speed up the discovery of new pharmaceuticals. AI can help doctors better understand medical images like CAT scans, MRIs, and X-rays (Siddiq, 2020).

The medical field is increasingly making use of AR and VR systems for teaching, informing, and treating patients. For instance, VR can be used to treat diseases like phobias and post-traumatic stress disorder (PTSD), while AR can assist medical students perceive complex anatomical systems (Zreik & Abunamous, 2020).

Secure data interchange, patient consent management, and the elimination of fake pharmaceuticals are all possible thanks to blockchain technology. Blockchain has the potential to boost data security and patient trust in digital health services by providing a transparent, immutable record of transactions.

4.3. Future Research Directions

China's digital healthcare landscape is constantly changing, opening up a wealth of new research opportunities. The expansion of digital healthcare's accessibility and equity is a priority. Despite great strides, there is still a huge gap between urban and rural communities in terms of access to digital healthcare. Research in the future could examine how to develop and evaluate novel approaches to increasing the availability of digital healthcare for underserved communities.

Data security and privacy is another important field for study. Concerns regarding data security and privacy are growing in tandem with the adoption of digital health devices. Research in the future should look into ways to deal with these issues, such as the creation and evaluation of reliable data encryption technologies, data anonymization techniques, and user consent management systems. Regulatory and policy considerations, such as how China's legal system might be improved to better protect patient data, should also be investigated.

The role of the patient is another vital one that needs more research. The need for successful methods of patient engagement with digital health technologies is growing in tandem with the field itself. Strategies for improving digital health literacy among patients and healthcare professionals can be developed after we learn more about the factors that affect patient uptake and utilization of digital health technologies.

Furthermore, there is still a lot of room for exploration into the possibilities of emerging technology in healthcare. The medical field requires research into the benefits of emerging technologies including AI, blockchain, AR, and VR. It's not just the technical details that matter; the effects on patients, healthcare expenditures, and the industry as a whole must be considered, too.

Finally, studies need to investigate how well various digital health solutions can communicate with one another. With so many digital health platforms and apps out now, it can be difficult to ensure compatibility between them. A more unified and effective digital healthcare environment may result from this line of inquiry.

5. CUSTOMER RELATIONSHIP MANAGEMENT IN HEALTHCARE

5.1. Understanding Patient Loyalty in China

Chinese customer relationship management (CRM) in healthcare focuses on patient loyalty and retention through better communication and relationship management. Loyal patients are an important part of CRM in healthcare, and in China's specific setting, doing so requires an in-depth grasp of both cultural and market-driven elements. Due to cultural beliefs emphasizing respect for authority, Chinese patients have historically shown their doctors great deference. However, the democratization of medical information via digital media is changing the nature of this respect. Patients are becoming more active participants in their healthcare, learning about their options, and advocating for the care they receive (Bridges et al., 2018).

The level of satisfaction with the care provided is another factor that can affect patient loyalty in China. Chinese patients now have access to more healthcare options, such as digital platforms providing remote consultations and AI-powered health advice, as a result of the rise of digital healthcare (Guo & Li, 2022). Therefore, in order to keep their patients satisfied, healthcare professionals must guarantee that both their digital and traditional services adhere to the highest standards of care.

CRM would not be possible without technology. As digital health apps and platforms gain popularity, they will soon give healthcare providers with a wealth of information about their patients' habits, preferences, and health. With the use of AI, CRM systems may evaluate this information to spot trends, anticipate patient requirements, and tailor care to each individual.

It's also important to talk to each other. Keeping patients informed, engaged, and connected through tailored communication on a regular basis has been shown to boost loyalty. In China, this usually means using social media like WeChat to disseminate health information, remind people of appointments, and educate the public (Liu, 2021).

5.2. Tools and Strategies

When considering the digital healthcare environment in China, a wide variety of CRM solutions and tactics have proven particularly beneficial.

Data Analytics: Modern customer relationship management relies heavily on gathering and analyzing patient information. Advanced data analytics techniques are being used by the healthcare industry to better understand patient habits, requirements, and preferences. This can help with strategic planning, tailor care to each individual patient. Patients at risk of health issues or non-compliance can be identified, for example, with the aid of predictive analytics, allowing for timely treatments.

Personalized Communications: The success of customer relationship management hinges on the ability to personalize interactions. Using customer relationship management solutions, medical professionals can routinely send out tailored messages to their patient populations. Personalized health advice, prescription or appointment reminders, and niche advertising are all examples. In China, this usually means combining customer relationship management software with social media apps like WeChat (Hong et al., 2021).

Telemedicine Platforms: Due to the rapid development of digital healthcare in China, telemedicine systems are now integral components of healthcare customer relationship management. Patients place a premium on the accessibility and ease of use that can be provided by these platforms. Additionally, they facilitate continuous monitoring and serve as community hubs for patient mentoring and guidance.

AI-Driven CRM Systems: Artificial intelligence is used by modern customer relationship management systems to enhance operational efficiency and deliver individualized patient experiences. To allow for greater attention to be paid to the more difficult aspects of patient care, AI can be utilized to do things like predict patient requirements, personalize marketing communications, and automate routine tasks.

Patient Portals: Healthcare customer relationship management relies heavily on patient portals. Patients can use these to get in touch with their doctors, view their medical records, request prescription refills, and schedule appointments. User-friendliness and mobile optimization are particularly important for patient portals in China's digital healthcare setting, as the vast majority of Chinese consumers utilize smartphones to access digital services (Tan et al., 2022).

Feedback Systems: Including patient feedback in regular system updates is an important CRM tactic. It aids healthcare providers in learning from patients' perspectives, figuring out where they can make changes, and addressing issues as soon as possible. This could be as straightforward as a survey emailed after a hospital visit or as intricate as a system that allows for constant communication and participation.

Patient Education and Engagement: Another useful customer relationship management tactic is encouraging patient participation by giving them access to up-to-date health information. This could include providing health education programs, holding patient support groups, or writing useful content for a healthcare provider's website.

Loyalty Programs: Patient retention can be boosted by loyalty schemes. Some examples of such perks are price reductions, referral bonuses, and early access to new offerings (Zineldin, 2006).

6. B2B HEALTH MARKETING IN CHINA

When doing business in the health care industry in China, it's important to understand the many players and factors at play, from government agencies to regulators to financiers. These groups have considerable sway on healthcare policy and marketing methods.

Healthcare policies, standards, and regulations are heavily influenced by state institutions like the National Health Commission. They are in charge of establishing norms, enacting changes, and keeping an eye on the healthcare system as a whole (Wang et al., 2023). In order to remain compliant and adapt their marketing tactics accordingly, business-to-business (B2B) health marketers must keep up with the norms and regulations imposed by these bodies.

Compliance with healthcare norms and standards relies heavily on the work of regulators. They are in charge of issuing licenses to medical professionals, keeping tabs on the standard of treatment provided, and upholding ethical standards. B2B health marketers need the guidance of authorities to ensure their practices are legal and ethical.

B2B health marketing in China is significantly impacted by both public and private financiers. They have an effect on the accessibility and affordability of healthcare services because of the money and resources they give to healthcare institutions. Insurance firms and other healthcare financiers set the reimbursement policies and pricing structures for medical supplies and services (Li & Wang, 2022). In order to create successful pricing and marketing strategies that fit into the financial ecosystem, B2B health marketers must first understand their impact.

B2B health marketing involves a wide variety of stakeholders, including governmental agencies, regulators, and financiers, as well as medical societies and professional organizations. These organizations speak for the concerns of the medical community. B2B health marketing campaigns can benefit from the alliances, endorsements, and networking opportunities made possible by collaboration with medical groups.

7. PRICING OF HEALTH SERVICES IN THE DIGITAL ERA

7.1. Understanding the Chinese Context

Considerations specific to China must be taken into account when setting prices for digital health services. The public and private sectors, insurance programs, and government restrictions all play a role in setting prices in China's healthcare system.

The Chinese government has a major impact on the cost of healthcare, especially for basic medical procedures (Li et al., 2017). To make healthcare more accessible and affordable, governments have instituted price limits and reimbursement systems. To strike a fair balance between the price of healthcare and the demand for high-quality care, the government routinely revises pricing legislation and publishes recommendations (Long et al., 2013). To guarantee their pricing plans are in compliance with government guidelines and regulatory obligations, healthcare marketers need to manage these regulations.

The cost of medical care in China is affected by both the government and private sectors. Price setting may be affected by reimbursement rates and policies as a result of the proliferation of insurance programs including government-sponsored basic medical insurance and commercial insurance options. When setting prices for their services, healthcare providers must account for the rates at which insurers compensate them.

Pricing dynamics in the digital era are further influenced by the Chinese consumer market and patient expectations. Consumers in China are becoming picky and demanding when it comes to the quality of their healthcare. They look for affordable treatment, clear pricing, and easy accessibility (Miao, 2016). Thanks to the clear pricing information and comparison features on digital health platforms, consumers now have a greater ability to make informed choices (Huang et., 2017). As a result, healthcare marketers need to think carefully about customer expectations before settling on a pricing strategy.

Pricing healthcare in the digital age presents both opportunities and challenges. Providers can now offer services at a wider range of prices and experiment with new pricing structures because to the proliferation of telemedicine and digital health platforms. Concerns about data privacy, security, and quality assurance are legitimate in digital healthcare, and marketers in this space must address them.

7.2. Implications for Marketing Management

Marketing managers in China need to give serious thought to how they set prices for digital health services. In order to maximize their marketing strategies and successfully compete in today's healthcare market, companies in the healthcare industry must take into account a number of critical factors.

First, it's important to have a firm grasp of healthcare costs and availability. Pricing strategies in China need to take into account the purchasing power of the intended consumer base. Healthcare providers can expand their customer base and increase their market share by providing affordable services. To reach budget-conscious customers, marketers must stress the benefits and low price of their services.

Second, dynamic pricing methods can be implemented with the help of digital technologies and platforms. Healthcare marketers can adapt their pricing strategies to meet the needs of their customers by utilizing real-time data and market insights. Individual health histories, service consumption patterns, and bundled service packages can all play a role in this type of tailor-made pricing. In order to adapt to market shifts and maximize revenue, healthcare businesses should implement digital technologies for price optimization (Elton & O'Riordan, 2016).

Third, it is critical that pricing strategies be communicated clearly. Trust can be established and patient expectations can be managed by open discussion of costs. Marketers in the healthcare industry need to make sure that all of their digital channels, including their websites, make it simple for customers to find and understand price details. Justifying prices and assuaging customer worries can be aided by providing specific examples of the value customers would receive from the services.

Marketers must also ensure that their pricing strategies are consistent with other marketing initiatives (Davidson & Simonetto, 2005). The pricing plan should align with the company's values, its target market, and the perceived worth of its offerings. This congruence enables a unified strategy for advertising the healthcare services' advantages over the competition.

Furthermore, pricing methods must be constantly monitored and evaluated. Marketers in the healthcare industry must regularly evaluate their pricing strategies, determine how they are performing in terms of market share and profitability, and make data-driven adjustments as necessary. By conducting regular market research and analyzing the strategies of competitors, marketers can gain insight into price trends, consumer preferences, and market dynamics and adjust their plans accordingly.

8. ASSESSING THE SUCCESS OF HEALTHCARE MARKETING IN CHINA

8.1. Metrics and Measures

Metrics and criteria that accurately assess the impact and efficacy of marketing tactics are essential for gauging the success of healthcare marketing operations in China (Marzuki et al., 2023). Healthcare marketers can evaluate their campaigns' efficacy using a number of different measures.

Patient acquisition is a key indicator since it quantifies the number of new patients attained as a direct result of advertising efforts. Measuring the success of marketing efforts to acquire new patients is made possible through tracking patient acquisition. Successful acquisition methods can be uncovered by segmenting this number further by demographics, referral sources, or individual marketing channels (Berkowitz, 2021).

Patient loyalty and retention rates are also important indicators of a campaign's success. Patients' loyalty and pleasure can be gauged by their frequency of return visits. Effective marketing methods for establishing and maintaining positive relationships with and inspiring loyalty from patients can be assessed by tracking retention rates and assessing patient satisfaction through surveys or feedback systems.

The success of a healthcare brand relies heavily on the strength of its name recognition and reputation. Metrics like brand recognition, brand recall, and brand sentiment tracking can give healthcare providers valuable insight into how their brands are perceived by their target audiences. The efficacy of campaigns to cultivate a favorable impression of a brand can be measured, in part, by keeping tabs on brand mentions, sentiment, and engagement using online reputation management tools and social media analytics.

Success of online marketing efforts may be measured with digital marketing indicators including website traffic, click-through rates, and conversion rates. These measures are useful for gauging the ROI of digital advertising, SEO, and other forms of online promotion (Bala & Verma, 2018). Marketers may improve their plans and budget allocation with the help of data collected through digital campaign analytics.

Return on investment (ROI) and cost per acquisition (CPA) are two of the most important financial measures for gauging the success of marketing campaigns (Weideman & Kritzinger, 2017). Healthcare marketers can evaluate the efficacy and profitability of their marketing efforts by comparing the costs paid in marketing activities to the income earned.

Finally, qualitative metrics like patient feedback, online reviews, and testimonials can shed light on the whole scope of patients' experiences and satisfaction. These intangibles are useful for gauging how people feel about healthcare advertising and how much they value it.

8.2. Evaluation of Existing Initiatives

In order to establish the efficacy of current healthcare marketing campaigns in China, to locate areas for improvement, and to make data-driven decisions for future plans, evaluation is essential. The success of advertising campaigns in China's healthcare sector can be measured in a number of ways.

Key performance indicator (KPI) analysis is a typical way of assessment. These metrics may change based on the nature of the marketing effort being undertaken. KPIs may include the number of planned appointments, conversion rates, or shifts in patient volume if the objective is to increase patient appointments (Woodcock et al., 2017). Healthcare marketers can gauge the efficacy of their efforts by comparing actual results to arbitrary targets.

Patient happiness and experience can be better understood with the help of surveys and feedback systems. It is possible to evaluate the full scope of the effect on patients' attitudes and actions by collecting feedback from those who have participated in the marketing efforts. Patient feedback surveys can also be used to examine how well various channels of communication are performing. Online reviews and patient testimonials are two examples of feedback systems that provide timely qualitative feedback to supplement quantitative data (Schlesinger et al., 2015).

The success of a marketing campaign can be gauged in large part by conducting market research and analyzing the performance of competitors. Healthcare marketers can evaluate their efforts in relation to industry standards by looking at market developments, consumer preferences, and rival strategies. To fully grasp the dynamics of a market, market researchers may use qualitative interviews, focus groups, or quantitative data analysis.

A financial perspective on the success of marketing campaigns can be gained through calculating their return on investment (ROI). Healthcare marketers can evaluate the efficacy and profitability of their efforts by estimating the ROI based on the expenditures paid and the revenue earned from the marketing activity. The results of a return on investment analysis can be used to better plan future marketing campaigns (Farris et al., 2015).

The success of a digital marketing campaign can be better understood with the use of data analytics and tracking tools. Healthcare marketers can monitor their websites' traffic, engagement levels, click-through rates, and conversion rates with the help of web analytics, social media analytics, and other digital tracking technologies. This information can be used to fine-tune digital advertising approaches and boost the effectiveness of campaigns.

9. FUTURE TRENDS IN HEALTHCARE MARKETING

9.1. Emerging Developments

Several new trends are emerging in the Chinese healthcare marketing sector that will significantly alter the way healthcare businesses interact with their intended audience in the near future. An important new trend is the widespread adoption of AI and ML tools in the healthcare industry's advertising efforts. Chatbots and virtual assistants driven by artificial intelligence are being utilized to improve customer service and provide more one-on-one encounters between doctors and patients (Ahuja et al., 2023). Massive volumes of patient data are analyzed using ML algorithms to facilitate predictive analytics and individualized healthcare suggestions. Healthcare marketers may take advantage of AI and ML as these technologies evolve to reach specific audiences with relevant messages and better patients' overall experiences.

The widespread implementation of telehealth and remote patient monitoring is yet another developing pattern. The need for online medical treatment has increased since the COVID-19 pandemic, and this pattern is likely to continue (Pandey & Pal, 2020). Consultations, tracking of chronic illnesses, and prompt interventions are all made possible by telehealth technologies. Marketers in the healthcare industry can reach tech-savvy customers who prefer the privacy and comfort of their own homes by emphasizing the many advantages of telehealth services.

Marketing in the healthcare industry will also increasingly emphasize individualization. Healthcare marketers may learn more about their patients' individual tastes, habits, and requirements thanks to the abundance of data and sophisticated analytics at their disposal. Because of this, relevant content, suggestions, and marketing efforts may be sent to specific patients. Improved patient engagement, loyalty, and good brand perception can result from personalized messaging and experiences.

Another emerging direction in healthcare advertising is the use of social media and influencer marketing. Healthcare conversations, patient support groups, and information sharing have all found a powerful new home on social media. Marketers in the healthcare industry may use social media to reach out to patients, disseminate helpful information, foster two-way dialogue, and team up with other experts in the field to boost their visibility and credibility (Park et al., 2016).

Concerns about data privacy and ethical implications will remain high priorities for healthcare marketers. Transparency, data security, and compliance with data protection legislation are all duties of healthcare businesses. The development and maintenance of patient confidence will rely heavily on privacy-enhancing technology, consent management systems, and strong data security measures.

9.2. Case Study of China

China's distinctive healthcare environment and rapid digital development make the country an intriguing case study in the field of healthcare marketing. Amazing developments in digital health technologies have taken place in the country, as have novel methods to advertising and patient interaction.

The widespread use of digital platforms and mobile technology is a standout feature of the Chinese healthcare market. Despite having the world's largest population of smartphone users, China has been an early adopter of telemedicine, health apps, and wearable medical technology (Zreik, 2022). With so many people using digital media, healthcare marketers may more effectively reach and interact with a large audience through specific campaigns and tailored communications.

In addition, the Chinese government has been instrumental in developing the country's healthcare system. The government of China has made it a top priority to use data-driven decision making and provide patient-centered care through policies and programs such as the Healthy China 2030 policy (Tan et al., 2017). Healthcare marketers now have access to a very dynamic environment as a result of these programs' stimulation of innovation and investment in digital health solutions.

The sheer size and variety of the Chinese people creates both distinct marketing opportunities and challenges. Marketers in the healthcare industry need to be sensitive to geographical and demographic variances as well as cultural norms and preferences. It is essential to employ localization and segmentation tactics when catering to the requirements, interests, and habits of geographically dispersed populations.

There has also been a shift toward value-based care and patient agency in China's healthcare market. More and more people want healthcare that is better, easier, and more tailored to their own needs. To keep up with the changing needs and preferences of Chinese patients, healthcare marketers must employ customer-centric tactics including patient education, collaborative decision-making, and enhanced patient engagement.

10. CONCLUSION

Significant shifts and new openings have resulted from the digital era's impact on healthcare marketing in China. We've covered a lot of ground in this chapter, from the history of healthcare marketing to its current state, from the changing nature of the industry's goals and needs to the concept of a value-driven healthcare marketing strategy, from the current digital healthcare landscape to projected future developments. Let us now review what has been covered, consider how different groups may be affected, and propose some avenues for future study.

Rapid change can be seen in China's healthcare marketing as a direct result of the advent of the digital era. Patients now demand more individualized and convenient healthcare than ever before, signaling a move toward putting the consumer first. Enhancing patient involvement, bettering care delivery, and optimizing marketing tactics are all possible because to technological advancements like AI, big data analytics, AR, blockchain, and mobile technologies. The delivery of high-quality and patient-centered care has become more dependent on value-driven healthcare marketing strategies that put an emphasis on patient-centricity, co-creation of healthcare, and partnerships between stakeholders. New avenues for patient participation and healthcare delivery have opened up thanks to the proliferation of digital health platforms, telehealth services, and health applications in China. Metrics such as patient acquisition, retention, brand awareness, digital marketing analytics, financial indicators, and qualitative feedback are essential for gauging the performance of healthcare marketing in China. Integrating AI and ML technologies, growing telehealth and remote patient monitoring, emphasizing personalization, leveraging social media and influencer marketing, and stressing the importance of ethical considerations and data privacy are all predicted to become more prominent in the near future in China's healthcare marketing.

The digital era's impact on healthcare marketing has far-reaching consequences for many parties involved. To keep up with patients' ever-shifting wants and demands, healthcare providers must put patients first, adopt digital technology, and personalize their marketing efforts. Healthcare policymakers and regulators have a significant impact on the industry and should promote the use of creative marketing approaches while protecting patients' personal information and adhering to ethical standards. Reimbursement policies from insurers and investors should reflect the shifting landscape of healthcare marketing and encourage the adoption of digital tools proven to enhance both patient care and satisfaction. Patient care that is more tailored to each individual, easily accessible, and focused on their needs is what healthcare marketers strive for. They should have access to up-to-date information, chances for meaningful participation, and the autonomy to make their own healthcare choices.

Several crucial aspects need to be explored further in future studies on healthcare marketing in China. First, healthcare practitioners and policymakers would benefit greatly from research into the efficacy and influence of digital health technologies like AI, big data analytics, and telemedicine on patient involvement, care results, and marketing tactics. Optimizing marketing tactics and enhancing patient-centered care requires an in-depth understanding of patients' experiences and happiness in the digital era, as well as the elements that influence patients' loyalty and engagement. It would also be helpful to investigate the effects of social media and influencer marketing on patient attitudes, knowledge, and choices regarding medical treatment. Effective pricing models that strike a balance between cost, accessibility, and quality of care can be developed with the help of research on pricing strategies in the digital era, including the effects of government laws, insurance coverage, and patient expectations. More research is needed into the ethical considerations of healthcare marketing, such as patient privacy, data security, and informed consent. Patient co-creation and public-private partnerships are two examples of value-driven healthcare marketing techniques that may be analyzed for their effectiveness in improving healthcare delivery and patient satisfaction.

REFERENCES

Ahuja, A. S., Polascik, B. W., Doddapaneni, D., Byrnes, E. S., & Sridhar, J. (2023). The digital metaverse: Applications in artificial intelligence, medical education, and integrative health. *Integrative Medicine Research, 12*(1), 100917. doi:10.1016/j.imr.2022.100917 PMID:36691642

Arenal, A., Armuna, C., Feijoo, C., Ramos, S., Xu, Z., & Moreno, A. (2020). Innovation ecosystems theory revisited: The case of artificial intelligence in China. *Telecommunications Policy, 44*(6), 101960. doi:10.1016/j.telpol.2020.101960

Azam, M., Khan, A. Q., & Ozturk, I. (2019). The effects of energy on investment, human health, environment and economic growth: Empirical evidence from China. *Environmental Science and Pollution Research International*, *26*(11), 10816–10825. doi:10.100711356-019-04497-4 PMID:30778925

Bala, M., & Verma, D. (2018). A critical review of digital marketing. *International Journal of Management, IT & Engineering*, *8*(10), 321–339.

Berkowitz, E. N. (2021). *Essentials of health care marketing*. Jones & Bartlett Learning.

Bhattacharya, S., Maddikunta, P. K. R., Pham, Q. V., Gadekallu, T. R., Chowdhary, C. L., Alazab, M., & Piran, M. J. (2021). Deep learning and medical image processing for coronavirus (COVID-19) pandemic: A survey. *Sustainable Cities and Society*, *65*, 102589. doi:10.1016/j.scs.2020.102589 PMID:33169099

Bridges, J. F., Janssen, E. M., Ferris, A., & Dy, S. M. (2018). Project Transform: Engaging patient advocates to share their perspectives on improving research, treatment and policy. *Current Medical Research and Opinion*, *34*(10), 1755–1762. doi:10.1080/03007995.2018.1440199 PMID:29429378

Carrera, P. M., & Dalton, A. R. (2014). Do-it-yourself healthcare: The current landscape, prospects and consequences. *Maturitas*, *77*(1), 37–40. doi:10.1016/j.maturitas.2013.10.022 PMID:24287177

Chakraborty, C. (Ed.). (2022). *Digital Health Transformation with Blockchain and Artificial Intelligence*. CRC Press. doi:10.1201/9781003247128

Chattu, V. K. (2021). A review of artificial intelligence, big data, and blockchain technology applications in medicine and global health. *Big Data and Cognitive Computing*, *5*(3), 41. doi:10.3390/bdcc5030041

Da Silva Etges, A. P. B., Ruschel, K. B., Polanczyk, C. A., & Urman, R. D. (2020). Advances in value-based healthcare by the application of time-driven activity-based costing for inpatient management: A systematic review. *Value in Health*, *23*(6), 812–823. doi:10.1016/j.jval.2020.02.004 PMID:32540239

Davidson, A., & Simonetto, M. (2005). Pricing strategy and execution: An overlooked way to increase revenues and profits. *Strategy and Leadership*, *33*(6), 25–33. doi:10.1108/10878570510631639

Desai, V., & Vidyapeeth, B. (2019). Digital marketing: A review. *International Journal of Trend in Scientific Research and Development*, *5*(5), 196–200. doi:10.31142/ijtsrd23100

Elton, J., & O'Riordan, A. (2016). *Healthcare disrupted: Next generation business models and strategies*. John Wiley & Sons.

Farris, P. W., Hanssens, D. M., Lenskold, J. D., & Reibstein, D. J. (2015). Marketing return on investment: Seeking clarity for concept and measurement. *Applied Marketing Analytics*, *1*(3), 267–282.

Gunjan, M., Naing, T. W., Saini, R. S., Ahmad, A., Naidu, J. R., & Kumar, I. (2015). Marketing trends & future prospects of herbal medicine in the treatment of various disease. *World Journal of Pharmaceutical Research*, *4*(9), 132–155.

Guo, C., & Li, H. (2022). Application of 5G network combined with AI robots in personalized nursing in China: A literature review. *Frontiers in Public Health*, *10*, 948303. doi:10.3389/fpubh.2022.948303 PMID:36091551

Haleem, A., Javaid, M., Singh, R. P., & Suman, R. (2021). Telemedicine for healthcare: Capabilities, features, barriers, and applications. *Sensors International*, *2*, 100117. doi:10.1016/j.sintl.2021.100117 PMID:34806053

Haleem, A., Javaid, M., Singh, R. P., & Suman, R. (2022). Medical 4.0 technologies for healthcare: Features, capabilities, and applications. *Internet of Things and Cyber-Physical Systems*, *2*, 12–30. doi:10.1016/j.iotcps.2022.04.001

Harrison, V. J. (2021). *Leveraging Pharma, Digital Innovation, and Partnerships to Increase Healthcare Access in China: A COVID-19 Case Study* [Doctoral dissertation]. Harvard University.

Hernandez, L. M. (Ed.). (2009). *Health literacy, eHealth, and communication: putting the consumer first: workshop summary*. National Academies Press.

Hong, Y., Wan, M., & Li, Z. (2021). Understanding the health information sharing behavior of social media users: An empirical study on WeChat. *Journal of Organizational and End User Computing*, *33*(5), 180–203. doi:10.4018/JOEUC.20210901.oa9

Huang, F., Blaschke, S., & Lucas, H. (2017). Beyond pilotitis: Taking digital health interventions to the national level in China and Uganda. *Globalization and Health*, *13*(1), 1–11. doi:10.118612992-017-0275-z PMID:28756767

Keane, M., Yu, H., Zhao, E. J., & Leong, S. (2020). *Chinas digital presence in the asia-pacific: Culture, technology and platforms*. Anthem Press. doi:10.2307/j.ctv20pxxzt

Li, H., Liu, K., Gu, J., Zhang, Y., Qiao, Y., & Sun, X. (2017). The development and impact of primary health care in China from 1949 to 2015: A focused review. *The International Journal of Health Planning and Management*, *32*(3), 339–350. doi:10.1002/hpm.2435 PMID:28670754

Li, J., & Wang, X. (2020). Does VAT have higher tax compliance than a turnover tax? Evidence from China. *International Tax and Public Finance*, *27*(2), 280–311. doi:10.100710797-019-09567-4

Liu, C. (2021). Health information systems amid COVID-19 outbreak: Lessons from China. *The HIM Journal*, *50*(1-2), 99–100. doi:10.1177/1833358320947557 PMID:32806959

Long, Q., Xu, L., Bekedam, H., & Tang, S. (2013). Changes in health expenditures in China in 2000s: Has the health system reform improved affordability. *International Journal for Equity in Health*, *12*(1), 1–8. doi:10.1186/1475-9276-12-40 PMID:23764104

Marzuki, S. Z., Zreik, M., Buyong, S. Z., Goyipnazarov, S., Mirzaliev, S., & Bakhramovna, I. A. (2023). An Importance Satisfaction Analysis of Hosting Events in Hangzhou, China: A Pilot Study. *Advances in Social Sciences Research Journal, 10*(6.2), 107-117.

Mei, C. (2020). Policy style, consistency and the effectiveness of the policy mix in China's fight against COVID-19. *Policy and Society*, *39*(3), 309–325. doi:10.1080/14494035.2020.1787627 PMID:35039723

Miao, Y. (2016). *Being middle class in China: Identity, attitudes and behaviour*. Taylor & Francis. doi:10.4324/9781315643014

Pandey, N., & Pal, A. (2020). Impact of digital surge during Covid-19 pandemic: A viewpoint on research and practice. *International Journal of Information Management*, *55*, 102171. doi:10.1016/j.ijinfomgt.2020.102171 PMID:32836633

Park, H., Reber, B. H., & Chon, M. G. (2016). Tweeting as health communication: Health organizations' use of Twitter for health promotion and public engagement. *Journal of Health Communication*, *21*(2), 188–198. doi:10.1080/10810730.2015.1058435 PMID:26716546

Reubi, D., Herrick, C., & Brown, T. (2016). The politics of non-communicable diseases in the global South. *Health & Place*, *39*, 179–187. doi:10.1016/j.healthplace.2015.09.001 PMID:26365886

Reynolds, L., & McKee, M. (2011). Serve the people or close the sale? Profit-driven overuse of injections and infusions in China's market-based healthcare system. *The International Journal of Health Planning and Management*, *26*(4), 449–470. doi:10.1002/hpm.1112 PMID:22213261

Rush, K. L., Seaton, C., Li, E., Oelke, N. D., & Pesut, B. (2021). Rural use of health service and telemedicine during COVID-19: The role of access and eHealth literacy. *Health Informatics Journal*, *27*(2), 14604582211020064. doi:10.1177/14604582211020064 PMID:34041936

Schlesinger, M., Grob, R., & Shaller, D. (2015). Using patient-reported information to improve clinical practice. *Health Services Research*, *50*(S2), 2116–2154. doi:10.1111/1475-6773.12420 PMID:26573890

Siddiq, M. (2020). ML-based Medical Image Analysis for Anomaly Detection in CT Scans, X-rays, and MRIs. *Devotion Journal of Community Service*, *2*(1), 53–64.

Song, M., Zheng, C., & Wang, J. (2022). The role of digital economy in China's sustainable development in a post-pandemic environment. *Journal of Enterprise Information Management*, *35*(1), 58–77. doi:10.1108/JEIM-03-2021-0153

Tan, H., Zhao, F., Hao, H., & Liu, Z. (2020). Estimate of safety impact of lane keeping assistant system on fatalities and injuries reduction for China: Scenarios through 2030. *Traffic Injury Prevention*, *21*(2), 156–162. doi:10.1080/15389588.2020.1711518 PMID:32023126

Tan, T. F., Li, Y., Lim, J. S., Gunasekeran, D. V., Teo, Z. L., Ng, W. Y., & Ting, D. S. (2022). Metaverse and virtual health care in ophthalmology: Opportunities and challenges. *Asia-Pacific Journal of Ophthalmology*, *11*(3), 237–246. doi:10.1097/APO.0000000000000537 PMID:35772084

Tan, X., Liu, X., & Shao, H. (2017). Healthy China 2030: A vision for health care. *Value in Health Regional Issues*, *12*, 112–114. doi:10.1016/j.vhri.2017.04.001 PMID:28648308

Thapa, D. K., Visentin, D. C., Kornhaber, R., West, S., & Cleary, M. (2021). The influence of online health information on health decisions: A systematic review. *Patient Education and Counseling*, *104*(4), 770–784. doi:10.1016/j.pec.2020.11.016 PMID:33358253

Thomason, J. (2021). Big tech, big data and the new world of digital health. *Global Health Journal (Amsterdam, Netherlands)*, *5*(4), 165–168. doi:10.1016/j.glohj.2021.11.003

Wagstaff, A. (2009). *Reforming China's rural health system*. World Bank Publications. doi:10.1596/978-0-8213-7982-0

Wang, J. (2010). *Brand new China: Advertising, media, and commercial culture*. Harvard University Press. doi:10.4159/9780674044821

Wang, Q., Su, M., Zhang, M., & Li, R. (2021). Integrating digital technologies and public health to fight Covid-19 pandemic: Key technologies, applications, challenges and outlook of digital healthcare. *International Journal of Environmental Research and Public Health*, *18*(11), 6053. doi:10.3390/ijerph18116053 PMID:34199831

Wang, W., Sun, L., Liu, T., & Lai, T. (2022). The use of E-health during the COVID-19 pandemic: A case study in China's Hubei province. *Health Sociology Review*, *31*(3), 215–231. doi:10.1080/14461242.2021.1941184 PMID:34161186

Wang, Y., Kung, L., & Byrd, T. A. (2018). Big data analytics: Understanding its capabilities and potential benefits for healthcare organizations. *Technological Forecasting and Social Change*, *126*, 3–13. doi:10.1016/j.techfore.2015.12.019

Wang, Z., Xu, R., Liu, Y., & Li, Y. (2023). Licensing policy and platform models of telemedicine: A multi-case study from China. *Frontiers in Public Health*, *11*, 1108621. doi:10.3389/fpubh.2023.1108621 PMID:36817879

Weideman, M., & Kritzinger, W. (2017). Parallel search engine optimisation and pay-per-click campaigns: A comparison of cost per acquisition. *South African Journal of Information Management*, *19*(1), 1–13.

Woodcock, E., Kier, S., & Zhao, V. (2017). Patient access metrics in the ambulatory enterprise. *Management in Healthcare*, *2*(2), 153–164.

Yip, G. S., & McKern, B. (2016). *China's next strategic advantage: From imitation to innovation*. MIT press.

Yu, X., Li, C., Shi, Y., & Yu, M. (2010). Pharmaceutical supply chain in China: Current issues and implications for health system reform. *Health Policy (Amsterdam)*, *97*(1), 8–15. doi:10.1016/j.healthpol.2010.02.010 PMID:20307912

Zineldin, M. (2006). The royalty of loyalty: CRM, quality and retention. *Journal of Consumer Marketing*, *23*(7), 430–437. doi:10.1108/07363760610712975

Zreik, M. (2022). US-China Relations in The Era of Multi-Polarism: Trade War Between the Two Economic Giants. *Eurasian Research Journal*, *4*(2), 43–65. doi:10.53277/2519-2442-2022.2-03

Zreik, M. (2023). From Boom to Bust: A Study of China's Economy in the Wake of COVID-19 Outbreak in H1 2020. *BRICS Journal of Economics*, *4*(1), 147–171. doi:10.3897/brics-econ.4.e101050

Zreik, M., & Abunamous, M. O. (2020). Human thinking at the time of Covid-19 and the role of swot analysis: A case study on the Chinese and Palestinian societies. *Psychology Research on Education and Social Sciences*, *2*(1), 31–40.

Chapter 4
Marketing of the Healthcare System in the Light of Sources of Its Financing and Tools for Building a Competitive Advantage

Agnieszka Jadwiga Wójcik-Czerniawska
https://orcid.org/0000-0002-9612-1952
SGH-Warsaw School of Economics, Poland

Zbigniew Grzymała
SGH-Warsaw School of Economics, Poland

ABSTRACT

The main purpose of the chapter is to review medical systems and their financing, and to popularize these systems through various marketing tools. Within the different approaches to healthcare financing, particular attention has been given to the method of individual medical accounts. According to the authors, this method is conducive to the development of various other methods of treatment due to the availability of funds from one's own therapeutic account and the patient's personal choice of the center and treatment method. In this way, it allows the strengthening of a specific supply of medical services, including alternative treatment methods from the point of view of classical medicine.

These physicists dealt not only with healing but also with education and broadly understood prophylaxis for the subjects, the feudal family and the army. Next, the institution of physicists developed in royal and private towns, which marked the beginning of public health care. (Public health). The financing of such health care was either the responsibility of the rulers or the private payment of medical services. Healthcare funding has always been balanced between a private and a public fee. For example, in the eighteenth-century Polish-Lithuanian Commonwealth (now Poland, Lithuania, Belarus and Ukraine),

DOI: 10.4018/979-8-3693-0679-6.ch004

the Hospital Constitution was adopted in 1775 by the Warsaw Extraordinary Sejm, in which provincial physicists were appointed whose task was to supervise all medics in the state, and then in The Polish-Lithuanian Police Commission assumed the creation of the institution of district and district doctors .(Public health) These doctors were to provide free medical services to the poor and paid to the wealthy. This meant partially cross-financing the treatment of the poor by the wealthy and by public institutions. Balancing between the commercial and public model of providing medical services continues to this day. Between these two separate approaches, the possibilities of financing health care through voluntary or compulsory health insurance entered.

The basic research method is a literature review on the financing of health care systems in the world, especially in those countries where individual medical account solutions are used. The Polish proposal of individual medical accounts proposed by the former Minister of Health, Dr. Zygmunt Hortmanowicz, with whom one of the authors interviewed during his lifetime, is also described.

LITERATURE REVIEW

Health Care Financing Models

In practice, financing for healthcare around the world relies on several sources. A particular source may dominate in the treatment financing structure, for example, public health care facilities financed from the state budget or from health insurance, etc. Nevertheless, several basic models of financing medical services are distinguished in the literature:

1) Bismarck Model (Germany) – health insurance,
2) Semashko Model (Soviet Model) - centrally planned system,
3) Beveridge (British) - the system of the national health service,
4) free market (American) - treating health as a free market commodity.

The literature also distinguishes four other normative models of health care corresponding to the above division:

1) a moral model based on the principle of the sanctity of life and health, absolutizing the rights of the patient and disregarding economic conditions, in which medical professions are missionary professions,
2) bureaucratic, paternalistic model, centrally managed and supervised according to established procedures,
3) a free-market model in which the patient is responsible for his own health, and the scope of medical services is governed solely by the principle of their supply and demand,
4) an insurance model in which the scope of health services is the result of agreements between three parties: the patient, the doctor and the insurer.

The Bismarck model developed at the turn of the 19th and 20th centuries. Its creation was largely a political movement aimed at improving the living conditions of workers and nipping in the bud the growing socialist movements. The system later became a role model for other countries, including France,

Belgium, Austria, the Netherlands, Japan and Poland. Most Central and Eastern European countries introduced systems based on the German model before World War I. The Bismarck Model was characterized by elements such as:

- establishment of insurance institutions - sickness funds;
- creating funds from insurance premiums to finance health services;
- co-payment of contributions partly by the employee and partly by the employer;
- management of funds independent of the state administration;
- financing consisting in concluding contracts with service providers;
- development of subjective entitlements (ie covering also the family or dependents of the insured person with the insurance) and objective entitlements (ie gradual increase in the scope of guaranteed health services) (Karłowska, 2017).

Funds financing this model were also supplemented from the state budget. In essence, the Bismarck Model referred to solutions also inscribed in the bureaucratic model and, to some extent, in the moral model.

In the Soviet Semashko Model which in its assumptions also corresponds to the moral model, health care is financed through the state budget, which thus assumes full control of a given state over health care, including the policy of employing employees. This, therefore, determines the rather centralized management and financing of this model. In practice, this means that marketing tools promoting given solutions are basically not needed. A patient who has full access to health care, of course, uses what is offered to him. This also applies to the adopted methods of treatment, the waiting period for an appointment, etc. In general, the patient's influence on the choice of treatment method is limited.

In the Beveridge system, it was assumed that health care would be financed also through the state budget from general taxes, similarly to the Soviet Model. In this way, the government or field agencies would exercise control over the system. However, this system allowed the participation of patients in financing the costs and the participation of private services. In the part financed by the state budget and patients, there was full access to medical services. Health care workers received a salary depending, among other things, on the number of patients. In this system, you can see elements of the bureaucratic, insurance and moral model. Some solutions of Beveridge's system are similar to those of Semashko or Bismarck's models.

In the free market model, which is most effective in the United States, it is assumed that a health service is a kind of commercial transaction. Attention is also paid to the financial efficiency of this system. Healthcare financing in this model is mainly based on insurance packages or individual payment for the service if someone is not insured. In the United States alone, the health care financing system is a complex institutional system dominated by the private sector - one of its elements are medical savings accounts (MKO), which are a supplementary mechanism protecting against excessive financial burden during illness and old age.

In the USA in 2020, over 66 percent. of the insured had private insurance plans, while 35 percent. was covered by public plans (Medicare, Medicaid and VHA). In addition, about 9 percent. (28 million people) had no health insurance, despite the efforts of recent years to popularize this type of protection. Most working Americans and their families are insured by their employers, some pay contributions themselves (Kozierkiewicz, Gilewski, 2023).

Individual Medical Accounts

Individual medical accounts function, among others, in the USA, as already mentioned, Singapore and China. In the USA, there is also a solution consisting in setting up Health Savings Accounts - HSA. These accounts were created under the Medicare Prescription Drug, Improvement and Modernization Act (Public Law No: 108-173 (12/08/2003)) signed by President George W. Bush on December 8, 2003, replacing existing medical accounts savings account (Medical Savings Account (MSA). Currently, no financial institution in the US is opening new MSA accounts, although there are still accounts launched in the past (*Archer MSA. investopedia.com. 2008-08-25. Retrieved 2016-09-03).* Of course, the discussion about individual medical accounts in the US has been going on for a long time. This concept was, for example, combined with catastrophic health insurance established in conjunction with individual health accounts (IHAs). This was to ensure, on the one hand, the reduction of health care costs, and, on the other hand, to encourage saving. Under this plan, the employer establishes both a high-deductible health insurance plan and an IHA. Annual contributions to the IHA are equal to a substantial fraction of the deductible. Employee health care costs below the deductible are then paid out of the IHA; Costs above the deductible are paid by the insurance plan. Assets remaining in the account when the employee retires, or becomes Medicare eligible, are then available for other purposes. The motivation for the parallel saving and insurance plans, of course, is that each employee is spending his or her "own" money for medical care, except in the event of serious illness. The plan thus combines the desirable features of catastrophic coverage for reducing medical expenditures, with a mechanism that creates a reserve from which individual expenses can be paid (Eichner, McClellan, Wise 1998; Feldstein 1971, Feldstein and Gruber 1994).

This discussion was intertwined with the concept of an acceptable national health plan. According to (Stano, 1981) the plan should meet the following objectives:

- Provide all with access to care;
- Eliminate financial hardships;
- Control or limit increases in costs;
- Be administratively simple; and
- Be widely accepted by the public and providers of care.

At first glance, it appears impossible to achieve the first two goals without extensive insurance coverage for all regardless of ability to pay. This in turn would aggravate the cost and efficiency problems unless substantially more cost sharing is included. Such measures, though, would be politically unpopular and meet strong public opposition.

However, the apparent need for insurance, and for first-dollar coverage if out-of-pocket costs are to be avoided, rests on the false premise that insurance (defined narrowly as third-party coverage) is the only device which can reduce the kinds of financial risk which most individuals clearly wish to avoid. Under current methods of insurance, no relationship exists between an individual's consumption of health services and premiums received by the insurer from that individual. Only for the group of insureds will premiums be sufficient to cover expected claims and other costs. This is an inevitable outcome of uncertainty and the pooling of risks in the conventional way. Consequently, there are large redistributions from healthy to sick persons, with no special financial rewards for avoiding the use of services, as well as the major faults of overconsumption of health services and inefficiencies arising from a minimum of cost participation by patients.

It is possible, though, to provide the security associated with insurance, but with substantial reductions in insurance as measured by third-party payments while, at the same time, creating significant rewards for efficient and cost saving behavior by both patients and providers. To achieve these conditions, our proposal would abandon current methods of financing health care in favor of a system with the following three basic elements (specific details will be discussed later in this paper) (Stano, 1981).

This is where the concept of individual health accounts came in. Rather than contributing premiums into an insurance pool, employers and individuals would be required to contribute, subject to both minimum and maximum amounts, into individual (interpreted as an appropriately defined family unit) health accounts handled by a qualified administrative organization. The functions of the administrator are: to credit the individual's account for contributions received; to invest the balance in suitable assets; and to debit the account for claims for services received by the individual at terms agreed to by the individual and the provider (Stano, 1981).

Currently, HSA funds are basically a savings account where funds are pooled for medical purposes. In this way, they can be used to pay for medical services and products specified in the regulations without being burdened with federal tax liabilities. Withdrawals other than for medical services and products are treated similarly to Individual Retirement Account (IRA) withdrawals, which may be tax-exempt if used after retirement age . The accounts listed above are part of Consumer-Driven Healthcare. HSA funds can be used to pay for regulated medical services and products without being subject to federal tax liability. Withdrawals other than for medical services and products are treated similarly to Individual Retirement Account (IRA) withdrawals, which may be tax-exempt if used after retirement age. The accounts listed above are part of Consumer-Driven Healthcare. (Kozierkiewicz, Gilewski, 2023).

Insured persons do not need the consent of their account manager or their insurer for the withdrawal of accumulated funds, which are not subject to income tax if they are intended for qualified medical expenses. These expenses include the costs of services and products covered by health insurance, which are co-financed by the insured person (co-pay), as well as many other expenses not covered by the health plan, such as dental, eye and chiropractic care ; medical equipment such as glasses and hearing aids; in addition, transport costs related to healthcare (*IRS outlines changes to health care spending available under CARES Act.* www.irs.gov).

The country whose healthcare system is generally viewed positively and which has implemented the concept of medical savings accounts is Singapore. This system has been specifically described. Singapore's medical system is part of the social security system . It was built on three principles: the principle of supporting health protection and promoting a healthy lifestyle, the principle of private responsibility (implemented by the 3M system - Medisave, Medishield and Medifund), and the principle of controlling the supply of medical services in order to ensure an appropriate level of prices. The system is co-created by three institutions:

-Ministry of Health, which is responsible for the regulation of the medical services sector, the distribution of budget funds and all health programs conducted at the central level, etc.;

- the Central Supply Fund (CPF), which is the central financing institution;
- Central Bank responsible for regulating the entire insurance sector (Karłowska, 2017 p. 37-38).

MediSave is a savings account that's part of a set of CPF accounts. It is compulsory for you and your employer to contribute to your MediSave account. For employees, this money is set aside automatically from your monthly salary. All Singaporeans and PRs residing and working in Singapore are required to make MediSave contributions. Singaporeans residing and working overseas do not have to make compulsory MediSave contributions, but they are free to make voluntary contributions. Money in your MediSave account can be used for your healthcare needs such as medical treatments, dental care, MediShield Life, Integrated Shield Plans and ElderShield or CareShield Life with certain limits. MediSave can be used to pay for your personal or approved dependents' healthcare needs. It is meant to help you save for future medical expenses in your later years. It can only be used for certain healthcare and medical expenses like: (1) Hospitalization and surgery (including wisdom tooth surgery), (2) Palliative care, (3) Outpatient treatments, (4) Chronic disease management, (5) Health screenings, (6) Vaccinations, (7) Having a baby, (8) Health insurance (MediShield + Integrated Shield) premiums, (9) Disability insurance (CareShield + ElderShield) premiums. However, there are limits to how much you can withdraw. Here is a quick snapshot of what you can withdraw for different purposes:

- inpatient care:
    - Minimum 8-hour admission - up to $550 for first 2 days, $400 per day from third day onwards
    - Psychiatric episodes - up to $150 per day, maximum of $5,000 per year
    - Day surgeries - up to $300 per day including surgical limit ($250-$7,550)
    - Approved community hospital – up to $250 per day, maximum of $5,000 per year
    - MediSave Maternity Package – up to $550 for first 2 days and $400 per day from third day onwards + $900 for pre-delivery medical expenses
- outpatient care:
    - MediSave500/MediSave700 Scheme – simple chronic conditions: up to $500; complex chronic conditions: up to $700 per patient
    - Selected childhood and adult vaccinations
    - Health screenings – mammograms for women over 50 years old and newborn screening tests in outpatient setting
    - Patients above 60 years old + spouse - $300 per patient per year
    - Renal dialysis treatment - $450 per month
    - Radiotherapy – $80-$2,800 per treatment
    - Radiosurgery treatment – Up to $7,500 per course
    - Chemotherapy – Up to $1,200 per month with MediShield Life claim limit above $5,400. Up to $600 per month for other treatments
    - Anti-retroviral treatment for HIV – up to $550 per month per patient
    - Immuno-suppressants after organ transplants - $300 per month per patient
    - Autologous bone marrow transplant – up to $2,800 per year per patient
- long-term care:
    - Inpatient hospice palliative care services – up to $250 per day (general palliative care) and up to $350 per day (specialized palliative care)
    - Home palliative and day hospice care – combined lifetime withdrawal limit of $2,500 per patient
    - MediSave Care – withdraw up to $200 per month for long-term care needs (Poh).

MediSave is a savings account funded by CPF contributions. It helps all Singaporeans and Permanent Residents (PR) save for their and also their dependents' future healthcare needs. MediShield Life is a personal health insurance plan that covers all Singaporeans and PRs from birth. It boosts your MediSave account's coverage and helps you pay less for expensive hospital bills in B2/C class wards (6-8 beds in a room). MediShield Life can also be used to help pay for expensive outpatient treatments like chemotherapy or dialysis.The savings in your MediSave account can eventually be depleted while MediShield Life covers you for life. There's also no limit on how much you can claim in your lifetime (with annual limits). MediShield Life provides coverage for pre-existing medical conditions such as cancer, blood disorders, heart diseases and more. There's also the potential for coverage to include treatment for attempted suicide, substance abuse and alcoholism in the future - traditional health insurance plans usually exclude these conditions.You can pay for your MediShield Life premiums with MediSave. MediSave can also be used to pay for a portion of your Integrated Shield Plans, a type of private hospitalization insurance that helps to reduce your out-of-pocket healthcare expenses. The MediShield Life portion of your Integrated Shield Plan is fully payable by MediSave. The additional private insurance portion is also payable by MediSave and any excess is paid in cash: $300 per year - 40 years and below aged on their next birthday; $600 per year – aged 41-70 years on their next birthday; $900 per year – aged 71 years and above on their next birthday (Poh).

MediSave account contributions vary depending on your monthly salary, business or work income, and whether you're an employee or self-employed. A percentage of your salary is set aside and deposited into your CPF accounts – employee CPF contribution (table 1).

The MediSave account had an interest rate of 4 percent in 2022. Depending on the accumulated amount and age, the interest rate is increased (Poh). The experiences of thc last period in the world concerning inflation put a question mark over the protection against inflation of these accounts. Inflation in health care significantly exceeds general inflation. From 2002 to 2022, the CPI All-Items increased 44.7%, while the CPI-Healthcare rose by 53.6%. During that same period, the average headline inflation rate was 1.86%, while the average healthcare inflation rate was 2.17% (Lim).

Moreover, according to the data provided by the Ministry of Health, in the period 2007-2017, the cost of private hospital care in Singapore increased at an annual rate of 9%, while in the case of public hospitals it was about 4.5%. This led to attempts to limit the increase in costs, eg by introducing co-payments to private IP health plans (Jasiński, 2022) described earlier. Another reason for the increase in government spending on health care is, among others, the aging of the population. The older generation

Table 1. CPF contribution rates in 2022

Age	By Employer (Calculated as % of Your Wage)	By Employee (Calculated as % of Your Wage and Set Aside From Your Salary)	Total (Calculated as % of Your Wage)
55 and below	17%	20%	37%
Above 55-60	14%	14%	28%
Above 60-65	10%	8.5%	18.5%
Above 65-70	8%	6%	14%
Over 70	7.5%	5%	12.5%

Source: CPFContributionRatesTable_1Jan2022.pdf , accessed 7/17/2023; from: Everything You Need to Know about Your MediSave Account in 2021 I The Income Blog

forces more spending on medical care. Figure 1 shows the share of government spending on healthcare in selected countries.

Chart 1. Domestic general government health expenditure (% of current health expenditure) – Singapore, Poland, United States, China, Hungary, South Africa

Among the countries presented, the share of government spending in the period 2000-2022 was increasing, except for China. In other countries, this increase took place regardless of whether they had medical savings accounts or not.

In Singapore, in the first place, the main emphasis was placed on accumulating own savings (MediSave) and insurance, eg from serious illnesses requiring expensive hospitalization (MediShield Plus). Only in the next stages, when the amount of collected funds becomes insufficient, support by MediFund is launched. In contrast, other countries are trying to give their citizens access to a range of benefits "right away". The only condition is that you pay for government medical "insurance". This often results in shortages, queues to doctors and low quality of services provided. In Singapore, citizens' own savings are the backbone of the system, not an addition. Secondly, in addition to own savings, an important element of the Singaporean system are additional direct payments to be made by insured persons under MediShield Plus: deductible and co-payment, which partially reduces moral hazard. Thanks to this, the basis is direct payments, and not universal health insurance "for everything". What's more, MediShield Plus finances the most expensive services, and the less expensive or routine ones are financed from MediSave, which well illustrates the purpose and meaning of health insurance. What's more, the funds collected on MediSave bear interest, and overpayments entitle to tax reliefs. Thirdly, the above solutions make the structure of financing access to medical services more rational, and the insured/account holders have a lot of time to adequately protect themselves against future medical expenses. An additional advantage is the general prosperity of Singaporeans, which is possible thanks to the liberal nature of their economy (Jasiński, 2022).

Another country that introduced medical savings accounts was China, where the MKO project was launched in two cities, Jiujiang and Zhenjiang. In 1994, the existing universal insurance was replaced by individual medical accounts supplemented by an insurance policy with a franchise. Since 1998, the changes have affected all Chinese cities. During this period, there was a change in the use of inpatient care in favor of outpatient care, which also contributed to a decrease in total expenditure by 8%. There was also a reduction in the number of hospitalizations and their length. Between 1993 and 1998, expenditure growth slowed down. This is attributed to a reduction in the use of expensive diagnostic services and medications. On the other hand, research indicated a deterioration in access to care (this concerned the poor, unemployed - mainly for financial reasons) and an increase in health expenditure among people without MKO (Jurkiewicz-Świętek, 2014).

Based on almost twenty years of Chinese experience, the most important problems related to their functioning have been identified in MKO:

- small savings accumulated on MKO (mainly among patients with chronic diseases), which results in poor implementation of the accumulation function;
- the complicated method of capitalization of the funds accumulated on MKO does not sufficiently protect them against inflation and the increase in the cost of medical services over time. Therefore, MKO holders see no point in keeping funds in the account (and spend them on an ongoing basis). In addition, the sooner the funds for MKO run out, the sooner they will be able to benefit from financing by the insurance policy;

- IOCs do not sufficiently limit moral hazard. A huge asymmetry of information between the patient and the doctor has been noticed, where the other party is not sufficiently controlled, which results in abuse/inappropriate use of services;
- setting the same amount of the franchise (after which the insurance can be used) for all MKO holders seems to be unfair. People with high incomes can reach this limit very quickly, while those with less income will have difficulties (resulting from the simple fact of limited financial resources). This means remaining in the phase of direct financing of medical services and a negligible chance to take advantage of the insurance;
- incorrect/misuse of funds collected for the MKO (eg medical supplies, foodstuffs) resulting from the lack of faith that the MKO will actually cover the costs of benefits in old age. In addition, there was a lack of understanding, especially among young people, of the purpose of accumulating funds in an individual account (Kong, Yang, Gong, Zhao).

Medical savings accounts have also been introduced in South Africa. This took place in 1994. These accounts became part of private health insurance. As a result, there has been a reduction in health spending in this country. Of the European countries, the only country that decided to apply the idea of MKO was Hungary. There, together with the private health insurance policy, the patient accumulates funds in a separate account in order to cover the costs of co-payment or purchase medical services on the private market. Unfortunately (Jurkiewicz-Świętek, 2014). Unfortunately, the authors failed to collect more information about the MKO in Hungary.

In Poland, the concept of introducing MKO was promoted by Zygmunt Hortmanowicz [1]. This doctor, together with the team (Jarosław Góra, Bogusław Dembiński, Waldemar Flisiński, Anna Bielawka-Hortmanowicz, Sebastian Kamiński, Sławomir Krystosiak, Włodzimierz Kucharski, Krzysztof Słoński, Krzysztof Teodorowicz and consultant Janusz Kołodziejczyk) promoted the idea of such accounts . This resulted in the creation of assumptions for the draft act on financing medical care in Poland by the senator of the 2nd term of office of the Republic of Poland and the main author, Zygmunt Hortmanowicz, together with the aforementioned team, dated December 17, 1992.

The preamble to this bill mentions that healthcare financing reform should be based on four pillars:

- liberal profession of a doctor,
- free choice of doctor,
- free market of medical services,
- free use of means of payment by every citizen who has an account in the so-called Health Protection Bank (BOZ).

This model was moving towards a market approach, even more so than the Singapore model. In any case, it was an innovative approach to financing healthcare in Poland. The aforementioned Bank Ochrony Zdrowia would replace the National Health Protection Fund and take over its assets and organizational structure. In this bank, funds would be accumulated on family (individual) bank accounts of working people, pensioners, and would only be used for health purposes, as in Singapore or even the United States. From such an account, transfers for medical services would be made. It would also be possible to provide subsidies and loans to people in the event of severe and chronic illnesses and to save lives. These loans would be redeemable in 50-80%. This bank would also co-finance the activities of scientific and research institutes and medical education from its own developed funds.

Such family accounts in BOZ would consist of amounts from various sources, including:

– 7% of the health insurance premium,
– 5% from Treasury bonds, stock exchange operations, investment income, etc.,
– 5-10% from insurance companies (reimbursement of road accident costs), from KRUS (10% on agricultural contributions),
– 10% on funds accumulated in the National and Provincial Funds for Environmental Protection,
– 10% on funds obtained from the privatization of State Medical Care Institutions,
– 10% on the income of plants with harmful workplaces,
– 20% of the funds awarded for medical malpractice,
– 3% on the sale of drugs to finance independent research on their effectiveness,
– 1% on the sale of alcoholic products, high-proof alcohol products (except for spirit for medical purposes), tobacco products, non-organic fuels, chemical plant protection products and chemical detergents and cosmetics, food produced using non-organic methods (containing synthetic ingredients that have a harmful effect on health),
– from the part of the state budget allocated to health care (1% of GDP),
– from possible subsidies from the EU,
– from funds allocated for revaluation due to inflation,
– from voluntary contributions from citizens (Assumptions).

The funds would be administered by the account owner or a family member authorized by him. Funds accumulated in these family individual accounts after the death of the owner would be transferred to the account of the heirs or the person indicated in the last will of the deceased. The funds accumulated on the family (individual) account in BOZ would give individuals and their families the opportunity to, among others:

- making any choice of the place of medical service - in doctor's, dental, nursing, midwifery, physiotherapy and therapeutic massage, outpatient clinics, specialist clinics, laboratories and diagnostic laboratories, sanatoriums and preventoria (this type of possibility would be conducive to the promotion of various treatment methods and the use of marketing tools by companies medical,
- purchase of medicine, dressings, ophthalmological, orthopedic and dental equipment and hearing aids,
- coverage of account management costs by BOZ, up to 2% per annum of the value of accumulated funds,
- serving up to 15-29% as help to people who have exhausted funds from their account and have health needs (so-called mutual assistance),
- free choice of the place of using the medical service (in doctor's, dental, nursing, midwifery, physiotherapy, therapeutic massage, clinics, including specialist clinics, laboratories and diagnostic laboratories, sanatoriums and preventoria,
- purchase of medicines, dressings, ophthalmological, orthopedic and dental equipment and hearing aids,
- covering the costs of servicing the BOZ account up to 0.03%,
- mutual aid to 15-20% for people who have exhausted these funds from their account, and would have health needs (Assumptions).

For people under supervision, for example, the unemployed, homeless and others who are dependent on social welfare, the costs of medical services provided would be covered by the Local Social Welfare Facility. Funds accumulated on the family (individual) account (account) in the bank, after the death of the account owner, would be transferred to the account of the closest family (spouse, children) or to the account of the person indicated in the last will of the deceased (will).

The essence of the idea of Z. Hortmanowicz and his team also referred to the promotion of a healthy lifestyle, which would promote not only physical activity, but also nutrition, animal husbandry and plant cultivation. There is a view propagated by an increasing number of doctors that many diseases of modern societies are caused by the conditions of the natural environment in which we live and the quality of the products we eat. Poisoned air and food chemically stimulated to grow and some chemical plant protection products cause an increase in the amount of toxins in our bodies. These, in turn, contribute to many diseases, especially chronic diseases. Improving the condition of the environment in which we live and the quality of the products we consume should, on the one hand, reduce the number of cases and, on the other hand, facilitate the recovery of people who are already ill. In this way, Poland as a country would stand out against the background of Europe and the world and would gain a new valuable specialization, also of an economic nature. As in Singapore, financial support from the state budget was envisaged, which would cover in full:

- costs of treatment and rehabilitation in provincial, clinical (university, academic) and infectious diseases hospitals,
- medical rescue services,
- activities of Sanitary Inspectors, - activities of blood donation stations,
- operation of dialysis laboratories, banks of organs for transplantation.

Payment to individual medical accounts would be made by bank transfer to the accounts of facilities providing services or a health credit card or in other selected form. The Ministry of Health would be responsible for the transfer. Substantive supervision over medical care facilities would also be exercised by the Ministry of Health through the voivodeship and poviat health departments. According to the originators, this reform does not require additional funds from the state budget and additional taxes. Pursuant to the constitutional provision, the Polish state does not renounce financing the health care of its citizens. The Minister of Health will be allowed to deal with the issues of health security of citizens, and not with the financing of medical facilities, as has been the case so far. It does not divide citizens into rich and poor. There is no need to maintain special medical facilities for the poor - all subjects are treated equally. The introduction of this solution should cause a beneficial phenomenon of universal self-discipline in taking care of one's own health. In addition, compared to the currently applicable solutions in Poland in the field of health care, the citizen will stop paying 3 times for the same services. Implementation of this system as soon as possible will prevent further pathology in medical care. It will improve working conditions and prevent unnecessary protests of medical staff on a national scale. Free use by citizens of means of payment for medical services will make citizens independent of the whims of the rulers. Everyone will benefit from medical services under the 4 x BEST formula (most effective, best, cheapest, closest). The market mechanism will contribute to improving the motivation of both the healers and the treated. It will also contribute to the self-education of medical staff. BOZ is not threatened with bankruptcy due to the large number of sources of financing the accounts. Most of the medical staff is insured against civil liability in insurance companies. The Insurance Company pays for errors made by the medical staff, proven in court, which will facilitate the collection of receipts. The system provides opportunities for mutual assistance in the event of exhaustion of the health account in BOZ. Funds accumulated on the BOZ account (they are not lost) after the death of its owner. They are transferred to the account of the person indicated in the last will of the deceased or to the account of the closest family (spouse, children) (Assumptions).

This proposal is clearly conducive to the use of various marketing mechanisms and tools of medical facilities that will seek patients. With this proposal, the originator, Dr. Zygmunt Hortmanowicz, wanted to support and promote medical centers whose treatment methods go beyond classical medicine. He himself admitted patients with chronic diseases, including cancer, and treated them, among others, with the use of an ecological diet, dietary supplements or climate. For many years he ran an outpost in the mountains. At the same time, he did not give up diagnostic tests provided in the public health service. He was one of the originators of the so-called integrated medicine. In an interview with one of the authors, he claimed to have cured the so-called solid tumors in more than 80% of patients with such a disease. Using these methods, he cured himself of cancer. He applied the principle of experimenting with healing methods first on himself. However, the costs of staying in the mountains and purchasing supplements were relatively high for Polish patients. Unfortunately, many of them could not afford the full choice of the method promoted by Dr. Z. Hortmanowicz. Individual medical accounts (MKO) would facilitate the financing of treatment stays in the mountains or other places with a favorable climate for treatment.

Besides, in a system based on the Semashko Model, moral or even Bismarck Model, where the state predominantly finances health care, the patient is dependent on the solutions adopted in this country. For example, in Poland, a very effective and minimally invasive method of treating leukemia, the so-called Car-T is not financed by the state budget for adults. This condemns such patients to accept the cheaper methods offered by the state. Sometimes the sick are influenced by people without medical education who offer unconventional methods of treatment. The effects of treatment vary. Individual medical accounts could help in the selection and promotion of various treatment methods, even the so-called unconventional. The condition would be that the specialist had a medical education and was able to equip his center with the necessary tools to provide diagnostic and preventive care, including modern methods, such as the aforementioned Car-T.

The authors have also encountered practices of lobbying by pharmaceutical corporations for a specific drug or treatment method. One representative of the Polish parliament responsible for shaping health policy in Poland blocked the development of drugs obtained, for example, from medicinal marijuana. This was probably the result of lobbying activities of certain pharmaceutical corporations. If treatment is financed from the state budget, patients must accept the treatment methods proposed by the state health policy. Not every patient can afford to use private medical centers that may offer other treatment methods. It seems that MKO would make it easier for patients to choose a given treatment method from the pool proposed by representatives of integrated medicine. The choices made by patients would also transform public healthcare.

TOOLS FOR BUILDING A COMPETITIVE ADVANTAGE IN MEDICINE

The basic tools for building a competitive advantage include, among others, increasing the quality of the service or medical product offered, reducing the costs of production or service provision, or appropriate promotion being part of broadly understood marketing. Medical marketing is a set of activities aimed at the emergence of, for example, a medical facility in the minds of the consumer, ie a potential patient. Polish law prohibits advertising of medical services, which is also part of marketing. According to Article 14 pt. 1 of the Act of 15 April 2011 on medical activity, an entity performing medical activity may disclose to the public information about the scope and types of health services provided, provided that the content and form of this information do not bear the characteristics of advertising. In other words, doctor's offices cannot directly persuade patients to use their services or purchase treatments. However, they can inform potential customers, eg about the advantages of disease prevention, or even educate them in the field of pro-health behaviors. It is also allowed to provide information about the types, methods and scope of services provided in the facility. Medical marketing focuses on such activities, and their goal is to build a positive image of the office, doctor or clinic and increase their visibility on the web (Rzetecki, 2020).

Comparing the creativity of the public and private medical market, it should be stated that the market of private services is the most dynamic. In Poland, the dental services market itself was privatized the fastest and almost in 100%. In practice, public institutions are marginal, and if they exist, access to them is very difficult, and the quality of services offered is far from the level of services provided by private institutions. As a result of this situation, patients almost always choose a private clinic for highly specialized services (Olewniczak, 2022). Dental services are not cheap, hence MKO accounts would probably be conducive to financing the dental service.

Due to the growing social demand and the inefficiency of the public health sector, the share of private service providers in the provision of rehabilitation services is also increasing. The aging of the society is the main reason that generates the demand for, among others, therapy services after spine or joint surgery: knee, hip, ankle or shoulder. Treatment of postural defects (especially in adolescents) and broadly understood physiotherapy services are also of interest to private entities. These entities, providing the above-mentioned services, have modern medical and diagnostic equipment and the current best medical knowledge (Olewiczak, 2022). The demand for such services will increase. You can even find information about it on social networks. Demand is limited by the costs of providing this type of service. If individual medical accounts were introduced in Poland, this demand would transform from potential to actual and would probably allow for increasing the digitization of medical services.

Digitization of medical services, such as teleconsultations, consultations via chat, video advice, e-prescriptions, etc., has gained a permanent place on the medical market, especially during and after the pandemic. Also, the results of pharmaceutical research conducted by transnational corporations confirm the introduction of permanent digitization of medical services, although it was not easy.

Managers of pharmaceutical companies also pointed out to various effects of changing the ways of providing services. For example, the aforementioned directors and managers of these corporations in free interviews pointed to the negative effects of remote work, in the form of isolation from teams or clients, which is particularly difficult for people working in teams that have direct contact with the client. This aspect was also noticed by the respondents, who indicated that the form of hybrid work would be the most optimal for them in the future, as it would provide them with the possibility of both conceptual work at home and direct contact in the office with the team and supervisor (Bartosiak). Attention was also drawn to the advantages of remote work. The need to further develop methods related to hybrid work was noticed - based on the research results, it should be concluded that in the post-pandemic period some tasks will be carried out remotely, taking into account the hitherto achievements related to this form of work . Due to the advantages associated with the provision of remote work, it is recommended to further improve the solutions developed by enterprises in the field of tools and methods used to enable the indicated form of remote work. Implementation of the above solutions, even to a limited extent, will allow enterprises to prepare for possible turbulences in the immediate environment and, as a result, to make them more resistant to the effects of potential crises and turbulences in the future (Bartosiak).

The competitive advantage of private medical entities is currently also built by the fact that they also have a developed diagnostic base, ranging from ordinary laboratory analyzes to highly specialized diagnostics using the latest medical equipment and devices. In addition, in some areas, aesthetic medicine services are provided exclusively by private entities. The purpose of these services is to remove health problems (e.g., excessive adipose tissue) or to make corrections, such as: reduction of cellulite and stretch marks, removal of wrinkles, etc. A separate phenomenon - going beyond health aspects - is, for example, lip modeling and enlargement or nose correction. However, here too the private sector meets social expectations (Olewniczak, 2022).

Patients look for doctors on the Internet, so information about medical services must also be visible there. According to Gemius/PBI data from September 2019, as many as 15 million Poles searched the Internet for information on treating diseases, proper nutrition and a healthy lifestyle. In 2019, an average of 57% of Polish Internet users searched for health information online (Rzetecki, 2020) . Social media, in which medical facilities are promoted, have also turned out to be very popular. The profile of a given medical facility on Facebook or Instagram has now become a necessity. Professional companies have specialized in building such an image. Social media is a great way to communicate with patients. Today, marketing and communication in the medical industry is carried out in the omnichannel formula. The patient asks for advice on his problem via Facebook, asks additional questions via Whatsapp to finally arrange an appointment by phone. The solutions proposed by such companies are:

- running a Facebook profile for doctors,
- paid social media campaign on social networks for the medical industry (eg Facebook Ads, Instagram Ads),
- preparation and maintenance of a Google business card visible in Google Maps,
- lead generation: acquiring new clients for a medical office in social media,
- social media posts : static (eg photos, graphics) & video (eg Instagram Stories, animations),
- social media moderation : building engagement and establishing good relationships with recipients for efficient brand activity in social media comments,
- doctors - copywriters : experts who will take care of the quality and content of publications on your profiles instead of interns who will be provided by the competition (Social Media for doctors and veterinarians (doctortarget.pl)

It is likely that the digitization of medical services will develop even more in the future. Perhaps it will be possible to install an application on a mobile phone that will allow, among other things, to measure blood pressure, perform a simple blood analysis, etc. Such results can then be sent electronically to a doctor's consultation. The medical consultant will then be able to make a preliminary diagnosis and recommend certain further actions, including, for example, taking a drug.

SUMMARY

Healthcare is one of the most important aspects of our lives. In a changing and turbulent environment, such as the increase in the incidence of cancer, pandemics, etc., it must keep up with these changes. An important issue is its financing. Observing the experience of different countries, the most effective solution is the choice of an individual treatment method by the patient. In the palette of various models of medical care, ranging from more centralized – Semashko, Beveridge, moral or bureaucratic to free-market, the most creative solutions include private medical services open to many different treatment methods supported by the private choice of the patient of a given medical facility. Centralized models, which in their assumptions allow all citizens on equal terms to public health care, also have their drawbacks. One of these disadvantages is the constant lack of funds to finance all medical procedures in a relatively reasonable time, as well as various other treatments, including the use of modern more expensive drugs. This results in long waiting periods for a doctor's appointment or hospital treatment and premature deaths. It also fosters corruption and a certain social passivity in terms of responsibility for one's health. The inclusion of private medical services, accompanied by the promotion of certain medical methods, meets the demand for medical services. In order for patients to be able to use such solutions more easily, they should be able to decide on the direction of their treatment and financing. Having individual medical accounts with the possibility of inheritance, etc., they choose the path of medical care development. In this way, they stimulate service providers to create new ways of treatment and use tools such as digitization of medical services.

Accounts also have their drawbacks related to the relatively higher inflation of medical services compared to other goods or services. One of the methods of limiting inflation is the introduction of greater competition in the broadly understood healthcare market. Centralist models of health care do not favor the consolidation of a competitive market for medical services. Such a market will be strengthened by individual medical accounts and the possibility for patients to choose the use and financing of various treatment methods from these accounts, which in the long run may reduce the inflationary pressure on medical services.

The proposed model for Poland was a draft. In a conversation with the authors, Z. Hortmanowicz maintained that Polish individual medical accounts should not be perceived as instruments diversifying society. Through the mutual possibility of sharing their accounts in the event of exhaustion of funds accumulated on them, they were to support the financing of treatment. Hence, they were not connected with the function of the pension fund. Polish health accounts were also intended to allow patients to choose which method they wanted to be treated, whether a more traditional one or an alternative one under the supervision of an educated doctor. Discussions over these accounts have been suspended in Poland. This article is an attempt to resume this interrupted discussion.

REFERENCES

Archer MSA. (2008). investopedia.com

Assumptions for the Draft Act on Financing Medical Care in Poland Based on the legislative initiative of the Senator of the Second Term of the Republic of Poland, Zygmunt Hortmanowicz of 17 December 1991.

Bartosiak, N. (2021). *Human Resources Management during a Pandemic in Selected Corporations in the Pharmaceutical Industry. Dissertation.* Academy of War Art.

Cianciara, D. (Ed.). (2010). *Public Health - a Review of Issues.* Medical Center for Postgraduate Education – School of Public Health.

Eichner, M. J., McClellan, M. B., & Wise, D. A. (1998). *Insurance or Self-Insurance? Variation, Persistence, and Individual Health Accounts.* University of Chicago Press.

Feldstein, M. (1971). A New Approach to National Health Insurance. *The Public Interest, 23*, 93–105.

Feldstein, M., & Gruber, J. (1994). *A Major Risk Approach to Health Insurance Reform.* NBER Working Paper no. 4852. National Bureau of Economic Research.

Health Savings Accounts in the US – Structure and Role in the System. (2023). *Health Manager – Termedia.*

IRS Outlines Changes to Health Care Spending Available under CARES Act. (n.d.). www.irs.gov

Jasiński, Ł. (2023). *Singapore – is it a Good Example of a Market-Based Healthcare System.* Mises Institute.

Jurkiewicz-Świątek, I. (2014). Medical Savings Accounts as a Method of Financing Health Services. The Results of their Financing so Far in the World and the Perspective for Europe. *Public Health Management, 12*(3), 248–257.

Karłowska, J. (2017). *Analysis of the Polish Health Care System – a Proposal for Changes on the Example of Other Countries* [Master's thesis]. Warsaw School of Economics.

Kong, X., Yang, Y., Gong, F., & Zhao, M. (2012). Problems and the Potential Direction of Reforms for the Current Individual Medical Savings Accounts in the Chinese Health Care System. *The Journal of Medicine and Philosophy, 37*(6), 556–567. doi:10.1093/jmp/jhs049 PMID:23192456

Kozierkiewicz, A., Gilewski, D. (2023). Health Savings Accounts in the USA – Structure and Role in the System. *Health Manager – Termedia.*

Leowski, J. (2010). Health Policy and Public Health. CeDeWu.

Lim, A. (n.d.). *The Average Healthcare (Medical) Inflation Rate in Singapore.* https://smartwealth.sg/medical-inflation-rate-singapore

Musielak, M. (2012). *Ethical Aspects of Health Care Management in Poland.* Nowiny Lekarskie, No. 4, OECD Health Statistics.

Olewniczak, A. (2022). *Impact of the Coronavirus (Covid 19) Pandemic on the Financial Results and Development Prospects of the Private Medical Services Sector in Poland* [Master's thesis]. Warsaw School of Economics.

Poh, J. (2021). *Everything You Need to Know about Your MediSave Account in 2021.* Academic Press.

Poh, J. (2022). *Guide to Your MediSave Account in 2022: Its Uses.* Contributions, Limits & More.

Public Law No: 108-173 (08/12/2003).

Rzetecki, M. (2020). *Marketing of Medical Services – what is it?* mrzetecki.com

Stano, M. (1981, September). Individual Health Accounts: An Alternative Health Care Financing Approach. *Health Care Financing Review*, *3*(1), 117–125. PMID:10309471

ENDNOTES

1 Zygmunt Hortmanowicz, b. September 5 1938 in Pacanów - Polish doctor, politician, minister of environmental protection, natural resources and forestry from July 11, 1992 to May 4, 1993. In 1968, he graduated from the Medical Academy in Warsaw. He obtained the academic degree of Doctor of Medical Sciences. He worked in the public health service, after being released for political reasons, he took up farming. Later he started his own medical practice. He was the vice-chairman of NSZZ RI "Solidarity" . In the years 1991–1993, he was a senator of the second term on behalf of the People's Agreement, representing the Krosno Voivodeship . He held the position of Minister of Environmental Protection, Natural Resources and Forestry in the government of Hanna Suchocka . He later retired from politics. Wikipedia, https://pl.wikipedia.org/wiki/Zygmunt_Hortmanowicz (July 17, 2023). He died in 2023.

Chapter 5
Marketing Strategies of Big Pharma and Impact of Generics in Healthcare

Aditya Prasad
https://orcid.org/0000-0001-5790-5247
Lovely Professional University, India

Ashwani Panesar
Lovely Professional University, India

ABSTRACT

There has been a significant rise in the prices of medicines in the recent past. Major pharmaceutical companies, 'Big Pharma', argue in favor of this development as it takes a lot of research and resources to bring a drug to market. Once in the market, the primary source of revenue generation for the companies is through sale of prescription drugs. Companies also have to spend a lot of their income on various marketing communication programs to convince their prescribers, even if it comes at costs that are difficult to ignore. This chapter studies the array of marketing strategies that are adopted by Big Pharma in developing and expanding their businesses. It also places these strategies within the context of the fast-growing generics market with its consequent changes to the marketing mix of the industry. While doing so, the chapter also explores and appreciates the various aspects of the pharmaceutical industry, as it presents features distinct from any other.

1. INTRODUCTION

While India is very distant in terms of having a robust health infrastructure, it certainly stands tall in supplying pharmaceutical products to the entire world. The Indian pharmaceutical market ranks among the top three markets globally, in terms of volume, and 14th globally in terms of value (Invest India, 2022). It also accounts for 8% of the global API market, with more than 500 different APIs are manufactured in the country, while contributing more than half of APIs to prequalified list of the WHO (Department of

DOI: 10.4018/979-8-3693-0679-6.ch005

Figure 1.

India's per capita health spending increased by 74% since the last Health Estimates in 2013-14.

Source: National Health Accounts Estimates India 2018-19

Pharmaceuticals, Annual Report 2022-23). Lately, Indian pharmaceutical companies have become the global leaders in the production of generic medicines and vaccines. Indian pharmaceutical companies meet more than half of the global vaccine demand, more than $1/3^{rd}$ of the US's generic medicine demand and one-fourth of all of the UK's medicine demand (Invest India, 2022). As some of the indicators are changing, these producers need to play more pivotal role on the global stage. Further, with India's epidemiological profile rapidly changing, healthcare is becoming a priority for the government as outlay for the sector is being progressively increased in every budget. With the change in the lifestyle and rapid urbanization, a host of diseases are on the rise - cardio-vascular problems, neurological disorders, and other form of chronic diseases like diabetes, hypertension etc. All these factors together combine to make India a very promising market for the global pharmaceutical manufacturers.

The pharmaceutical marketplace is shifting quite dramatically, with enormous implications for the entire industry. Like every industry in the recent past, the Pharma industry too is experiencing labor shortages, supply chain snags and higher input costs due to inflationary pressure. Lot of factors are responsible for the launch of new efficacious drugs in the market, even if companies are burdened with very high costs of R&D, enhanced competition and growing pressure from various stakeholders to reduce their healthcare costs without compromising profitability. The industry has made some structural changes and found more novel ways to augment their drug discovery potential, reducing time from the ideation to commercialization, and controlling their cost along the whole value chain. The goal is to stay profitable and lead the market, all while keeping the social and economic value of treatments for chronic diseases low and accessible.

While keeping with this overall goal, deeper penetration of branded generics and growing government initiatives for encouraging branded generics have emerged as a definite trend globally, due to the immense potential that generics hold to bring about substantial financial savings for governmental healthcare systems and out of pocket saving (OOPS) for individuals; thus, making healthcare more cost effective and accessible to its peoples.

Food and Drug Administration (FDA) defines a generic drug to be,

Identical or bioequivalent to a brand-name drug in dosage form, safety, and strength, route of administration, quality, performance characteristics and intended use.

Figure 2.

Global branded generics market is projected to reach $414.99 billion by 2028, from $235.86 billion in 2022.

Source: Research and Markets, 2022

Thus, the main point of contention remains to make these generic drugs as effective and safer as its counterparts, but pricing them much lower competitively. The low costs of generics are majorly on account of negligible R&D to be undertaken and minimal expenditure on marketing, advertising and sales promotion. According to Association for Accessible Medicines (AAM), Generics constituted 91% of drug prescriptions dispensed in the US in 2021, while these prescriptions accounted for only 18.2% of the total drug spend of the country. In the previous decade, US government healthcare system saved around $1.67 trillion largely due to better availability of generic medicine (Association of Accessible Medicines, 2017).

It has also been found that, generics have played significant role in lowering the prices of off-patent original drugs and other equivalents through introduction of price competition in the market (Yina et al., 2023). In the European Union, the entrance of generic drugs has brought down the price of off-patent medicines by 61% (Cameron et al., 2012). Taking into account the above-mentioned reasons, the generics market has given them a new lease of life, with industry experts expecting the global generics market size to expand at a CAGR (Compound annual growth rate) of 8.3% this decade until 2030 (Grand View Research, 2023).

2. PHARMA PRODUCT DIFFERENT FROM CONSUMER PRODUCTS

Pharmaceutical companies supply drugs or medicinal products that are used for diagnosis, prevention and treatment when specific medical conditions occur. Consumer products like tooth paste, snacks, stationery items, etc., are used more routinely. The pharmaceutical products differ from consumer products of other industries in that it has longer stages in its product life cycle. A new pharmaceutical product's development has a high price tag and a number of hazards. On an average only .0002% of the drugs get into the stage of commercialization among the 5000 molecules in the pipeline and were eventually approved for the patient use. Studies reported that only 30% of the approved drugs in the US were able to meet or exceed their average R&D cost, which are being projected at anything in the range of US $500 million to US $2 billion per molecule (DiMasi et al., 2003; Admas et al., 2006; Kraljevic et al., 2013).

Figure 3.

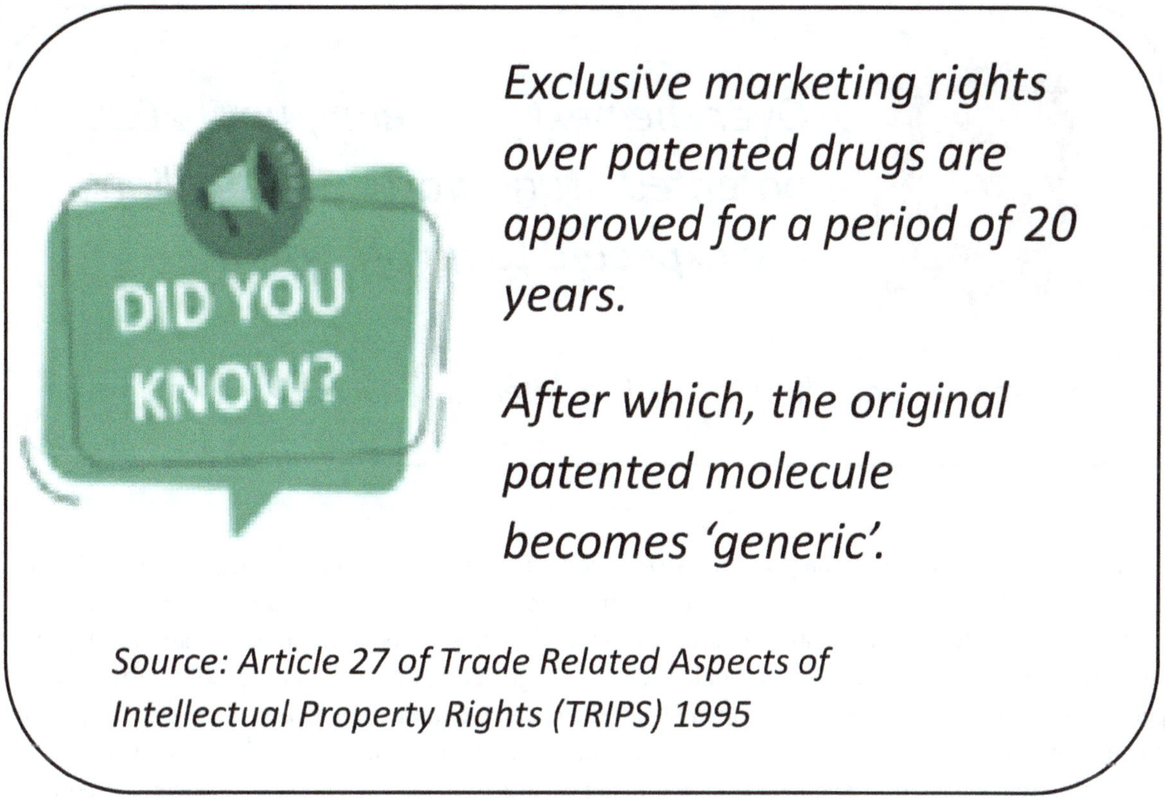

Pharmaceutical industry bank on new patented drugs to exploit its income from a novel pharmaceutical product. Since recent years, the average lead time between receiving marketing authorization and patenting a new chemical entity has decreased to 6.4 years (Keyhani et al., 2006).

Pharmaceutical industry is quite distinct from other industries in number of ways. Firstly, the company uses various communication strategies to make their prescriber aware and these prescribers prescribe their patients medicines, who are the ultimate customer or consumer in the entire chain. These health care professionals also take the choice about whether the patient requires a drug to be prescribed or not, and, if yes, what type of drug and in what dosage and its affordability; the druggist/pharmacist, who might be actively encouraged to sell the branded drugs by their generic counterparts of what was prescribed by the health care provider (Generic Substitution).

Companies adopt rapid penetration strategies in the introduction stage with the launch of a new pharmaceutical drug and segment the market to target early adopters who will be among the majority of the prescribers. Pharmaceutical companies use very intense marketing communication strategies like continuing medical education (CME), drug samples, sales promotional tools etc. to leave mark in the chamber of the health care prescriber.

The next phase in the life cycle of drug being the growth phase which is aimed at augmenting the perceived value and loyalty among its users and targeting new set of prescribers to expand their prescriber base. In the maturity phase, company might bring some line extension of the drug to target another set

Figure 4.

Over the next few years, until 2026, patented drugs worth $240 billion are expected to go off-patent.

Source: Deccan Chronicle article dated 28th Aug, 2021

of customers as the competition gets intensified seeing the progress in the size of the market. But the company still keeps its drug on the active promotion and the new prescribers are called laggards.

Finally, in all the above-mentioned strategies involving product penetration & market development supported by intense marketing communication campaigns and personnel selling skills of their sales-people, the stage comes when the company loses the exclusive marketing rights of the drug as product patent is no more valid, which results in a significant drop in sales and generic drugs enter the market and exploit the pre-established market but marketing of drug remains a grave area of concern. In addition to the product life cycle, some of the major differences between pharmaceutical products and consumer products have been summarized in Table 1.

All the pharmaceutical companies' intent to produce effective and efficient drugs, but the same needs to be done proficiently by balancing the profitability and the market share. This can also lead to an anxious situation with the respective governments of countries as they may be otherwise trying to cover budgets of healthcare, specifically of prescription drugs. This conflict was recently apparent, during the COVID-19 pandemic, when many life-saving drugs, like albuterol inhalers, azithromycin, hydroxychloroquine and sedation drugs, were in huge demand and pharma companies made millions by charging exorbitant prices (Christina, 2021).

The first reason for high pricing is the unique way the consumer surplus functions in the asymmetric health care market; it is so odd that we can call it patient surplus. The number of patients tends to infinity as a disease's severity rises. When one's health or, worse yet, life is in danger, how much will they be willing to spend for it or how much pressure can they put on the payer?

A monopoly is the second. The drug patent is defended in this context as the sole way to generate revenues to fund the future R&D in the entire pharmaceutical industry. Pharmaceutical drugs are primarily used to treat acute and chronic conditions. Acute illnesses generally develop suddenly and last for less than a month, like common cold, influenza, and gastroenteritis. Chronic illnesses are more persistent health conditions that develop gradually over time and lasts for longer periods of time, sometimes entire lifetime. Chronic conditions are often hereditary, but can also be linked to age, lifestyle choices and environmental factors. Examples include, Type 2 diabetes, asthma, epilepsy, hypertension (increased blood pressure), hyperlipidemia (high level of LDL-cholesterol) and thyroid disease.

Table 1. Major differences between pharmaceutical products and consumer products

Target Customer	
Primarily, the target customer is the doctor prescribing the drugs. In some cases, the pharmacist is the target customer. The patient is considered the consumer.	In consumer market, the buyer is the target customer. Invariably, there is no difference between customer and consumer.
Advertisement	
Advertisements of pharma drugs are regulated by authorities. Prescription drugs cannot be advertised.	No regulations subject to adherence to basic guidelines for advertisement of consumer products.
Distribution	
Can be sold only through registered pharmacists.	Can be sold in any general store.
Demand Creation	
Demand of the drug is created by medical sales representatives through generating prescription - 'Demand Pull'.	Demand for consumer products is created by advertising and point of purchase visibility - 'Demand Push'
Regulation	
Highly regulated market with manufacturing regulations, prescription only by licensed medical practitioners and prices regulated by authorities.	Comparatively unregulated. No regulation on price of consumer products.
Focus Strategy	
Here product is the asset and huge effort goes into R&D to create the product. R&D and sales management is vital.	Huge investment and marketing effort goes into creating and maintaining the brand over time. Marketing strategy and brand management is vital.
Images source: Freepik.com I Content source: Memisoglu, 2018.	

Figure 5.

Micro Labs has been accused of bribing doctors to the tune of Rs. 1000 crores to push up sales of its drug 'Dolo-650'.

Source: Federation of Medical & Sales Representatives Association of India (FMRAI) vs Union of India, 2022

Figure 6.

Definition: Consumer Surplus

In economics, consumer surplus is the difference between the price a consumer pays for an item and the price he/she would be willing to pay rather than do without it.

Source: Encyclopaedia Britannica

Figure 7. Indian pharma drug market

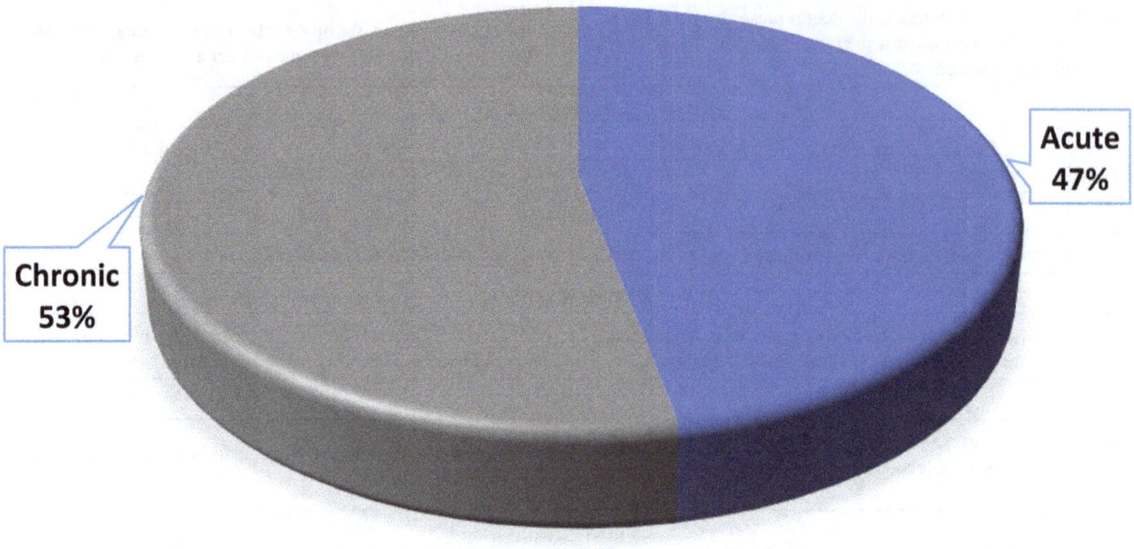

Data Source: AIOCD-AWACS 2022 data

As per recent insight from AIOCD projected that the acute drugs segment is growing at 5.3% year-on-year, while accounting for 47% of the Indian pharma market. The chronic drugs segment while accounting for 53% of the market, has a year-on-year growth of about 9% (Figure 1). Since the 2000s, as per India Infoline (IIFL) analysts, the chronic drug segment has been growing faster than the acute drug segment due to product introductions, improving diagnosis rates for lifestyle diseases and better drug compliance by patients.

3. BIG PHARMA

As per the Merriam-Webster dictionary, the term "Big Pharma" is used quite often to describe large and successful pharmaceutical businesses that generate literally billions of dollars and exert considerable economic, political and social influence. These leading pharmaceutical firms, also referred to as "big pharma," are mostly of American and European origin. Half of the top 10 pharmaceutical companies in the world belong to United States, while the other half are headquartered in Europe. Even these businesses and the entire pharmaceutical sector rely heavily on international supply chains, with China and India playing crucial roles in the supply of both active pharmaceutical ingredients (APIs) and finished pharmaceuticals. Figure.2 gives the top 10 pharma companies with sales revenue and % increase in sales in 2022.

After the Trade-Related Aspects of Intellectual Property Rights (TRIPS) agreement of the World Trade Organization (WTO) entered into force in 2005, Big Pharma effectively received exclusive patents in all markets. In third world countries, the patent regime amounted to merely the granting of 'private

Figure 8. Top 10 global pharma companies (2022)

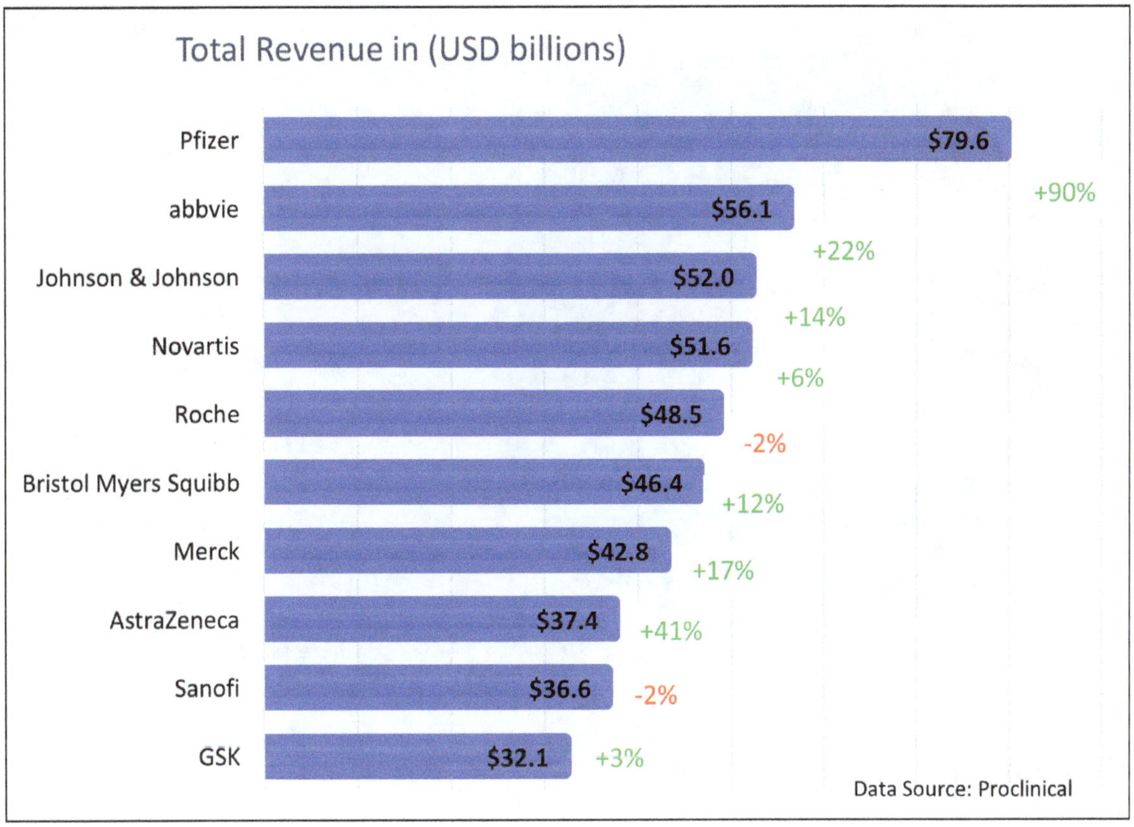

rights of exclusion' to foreign patent-holders. India, a nation better renowned for its services sector in the global economy, developed a distinctive and prosperous manufacturing industry as a result of the lack of product patents in the pharmaceutical business from 1972 to 2005 and limits on foreign investment in the 1970s and 1980s.

India being one of the fastest growing pharmaceutical markets among the "Emerging Markets -7", also called 'EM7' - (Brazil, Russia, India, China and South Africa + Mexico, Turkey and Indonesia), and growing at 13%, is also the third major producer of pharmaceuticals in the world by volume. The country's Department of Pharmaceuticals reported that India accounted for one-fifth of the total global exports of "generic" drugs. India, also has the 2nd highest number of FDA approved facilities outside the US and it is further estimated that in future this will rise to 40% of its generic formulations supply to the US markets (Department of Pharmaceuticals, Annual Report 2022-23). Indian companies, led by the likes of Sun Pharma, Aurobindo, Cipla, Dr. Reddy's Laboratories Ltd, Emcure, Hetero, Macleods, Matrix and Strides have played a massive part in supplying numerous life-saving medicines globally.

From the above chart (Figure 3), it is quite evident that patented / over-the-counter drugs / generic drugs constitute the combined revenue of all the companies. Lately, off-patented drugs like Lipitor (Pfizer), Metformin (Eli-lily), etc., have given lot of opportunities for big Indian pharma companies to establish their footprint of being the most efficient and leading players in entire global pharmaceutical industry.

Figure 9. Indian pharma sub-segment revenue share %, 2021

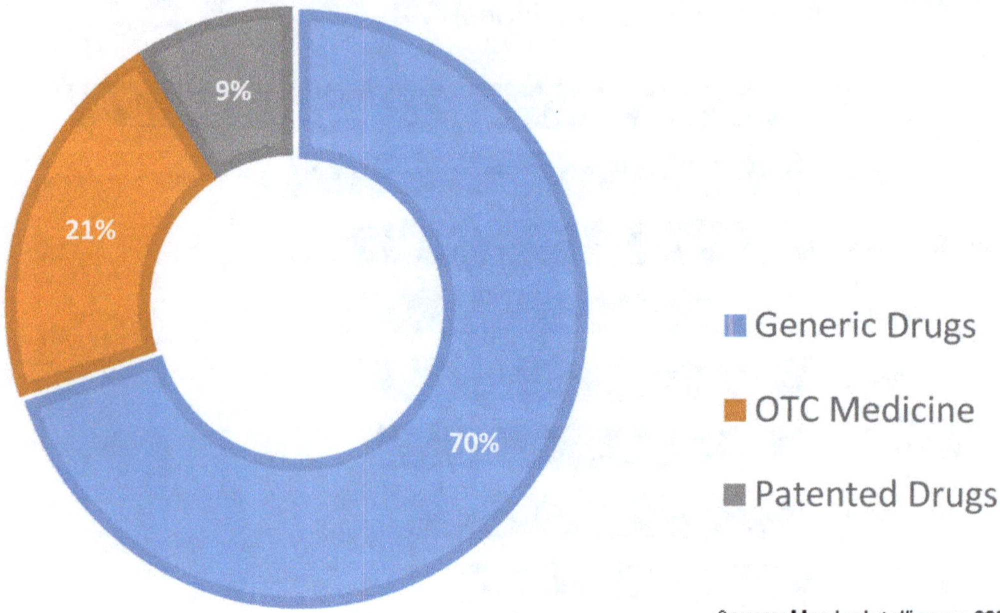

Source: Mordor Intelligence, 2022

4. PHARMACEUTICAL MARKETING

The structure of pharmaceutical market is quite complex and is a highly controlled industry. In addition to the statutory regulations, the Food and Drug Administration (FDA) officials consistently assess medicines (Dyer, 2004 and Grey, 2015) on the aspects of their

(a) efficacy, safety, and conditions of their manufacturing quality as to whether they comply with the good manufacturing practices as a condition of market access;
(b) promotion; and
(c) prices of drugs

The definition of pharmaceutical marketing, according to WHO and Health Action International (HAI), is the "activities focused on making physicians as well as the general public aware of new and existing pharmaceutical brands; it can include giveaway samples, detailed product literature, disease management programs, and support material for patients, and events/meetings for physicians". There are several factors that influence the success in marketing efforts, such as – drug affordability, illness prevalence and severity, new breakthroughs and medical technologies, public attitude, and supply chain related factors. Marketing strategies have traditionally been built around the four 'Ps' i.e., Product, Price, Place, Promotion, popularly called the 'Pharmaceutical marketing mix', first introduced by Borden in 1964 (Hailu, 2021). Figure 4 shows the main elements constituting the 4 Ps of marketing.

Moreover, James (2004) identified that two new 'Ps' are also relevant to pharmaceutical marketing, thus making it 'the 6 Ps of Marketing'. The two new Ps are,

Figure 10. Marketing's 4Ps

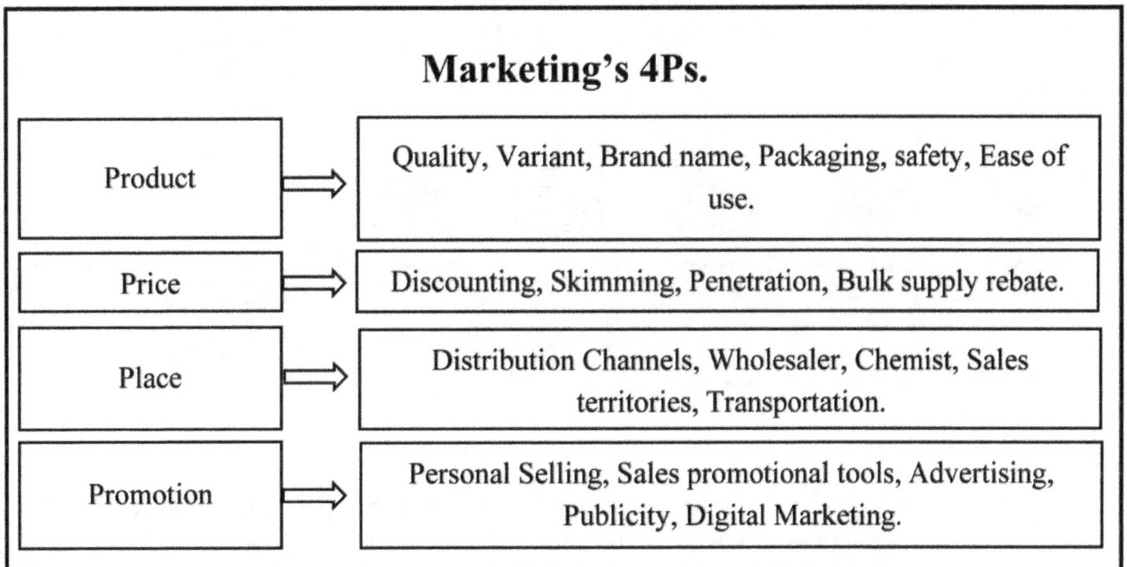

Source: Pharmaceutical Marketing – A Practical Guide

a) Political relationships with those organizations responsible for payment and
b) Patients, who have access to information and an increasing economic oversight into their care.

Patients are the final consumers of the pharmaceutical drugs being prescribed by the doctors and retailers / chemist / druggist honor these prescriptions which are supported by pharma company appointed Wholesalers / distributors supplied by carrying and forwarding agents (CFA). Figure 5 shows the entire pharmaceutical supply chain.

The pharmaceutical industry has gone under paradigm shift in honoring the prescriptions of the doctors, with the use of various marketing strategies. Marketing strategies help the companies to build competitive advantage over its peers, which can be take the form of the below mentioned.

I. Innovate Strategies
II. Differentiate Strategies
III. Focus strategies
IV. Defense strategies
V. Strategic alliances

4.1. Innovate Strategies

Majority of the drugs being launched in the market by the multi-national corporations belong to the category of innovative drugs also called as patented drugs. Innovation in the industry involves new drug

Figure 11. Pharmaceutical supply chain

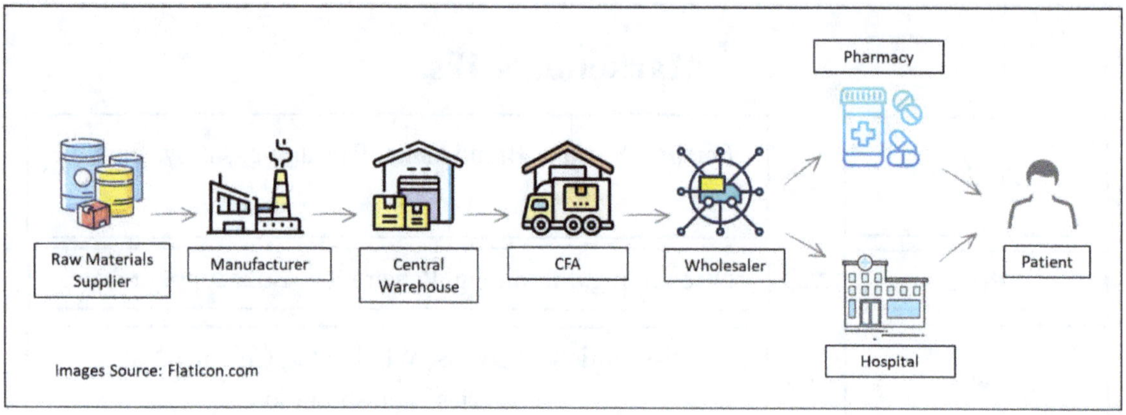

development and bringing next generation drugs. But, in India as the spending on the R&D is low in contrast to the developed nations which lowers the scope of bringing new drugs for providing efficacious

Figure 12. Marketing strategies in pharma

Figure 13.

Top global pharma companies spend roughly 25% of their sales revenue on R&D, while top Indian pharma companies spend less than 13% of their revenue on the same.

Source: Drug Discovery and Development, 2021

drugs with less side effects. But the time taken from the ideation to formally launching the drug take around more than a decade well supported by more than billion in dollars and you never know in the end you will get the required results but use of blockchain & cloud technologies, artificial intelligence, and machine learning has helped them to get better results.

Companies bring new drugs or focus on improving the existing product line as patients start developing resistance to older drug molecules. The major reasons for which companies need to innovate include

1. Improve the existing business revenue
2. To stay relevant to the competitive market place
3. Some therapeutic area has become more attractive
4. Some drugs have become off-patented in developed nations
5. The existing drugs have come under price regulation

Rusu et al. (2011) stressed the importance of implementing better drug pipeline strategies, including the ongoing development and introduction of new compounds, as well as the time of entry into the market, to make up for losses incurred as a consequence of the fierce rivalry of established or developed markets. The growth in the business revenue of pharmaceutical companies has also been helped by support from the availability at the chemist/druggists. Once the new drug has been invented, companies ensure to have the product patent (IPR) so as to commercially exploit the market and have exclusive market rights for the next 10/ 20 years depending on the country. Essentially, the grant of exclusive market rights has further helped the companies to get a state of temporary monopoly situation so that they can recover the hefty costs incurred in discovery of drug and its development. The reports indicate that grant of patents to the companies and their charging of hefty pricing does not guarantee that their entire input cost of developing new drugs can be recovered in a decade; with about 90% of patented drugs are having direct competitors in the same therapeutic category (Australian Academy of Science, 1995).

According to Bain and Company, the competition in the pharmaceutical industry is becoming more intense:

The average window of time in which a drug remains on the market before competing products arrive has fallen to 4 years, down from 8 years between 2000 and 2004.

In March 2022, Drug Controller General of India (DCGI) announced the approval of its antiviral drug VIRALEX to Themis Medicare Ltd. (Themis). Sun Pharmaceuticals Limited; India's largest drug maker has also floated its R&D arm called Sun pharmaceuticals advanced research centre (SPARC) as it expects to augments its revenue by $1.5 billion in sales in the forthcoming period of 3-4 years. Lately, technology can also play a decisive role in bringing more value across the entire value chain starting from diagnostics to treatment and drug delivery. This is further helped the companies reduce their cost of acquiring new customers, improve quality of treatment of their patients that too with better accessibility of services round the clock. The intervention of government has ensured that the time taken to take regulatory approval of drugs and Ayushman Bharat to make drugs more accessible to the length and breadth of India. Developing new chemical entities (NCEs) has also put Indian pharmaceutical players in direct competition with global innovators. About 30% (400 out of 1,200) of the scientists in Zydus are involved in NCE research under its dedicated research arm, Zydus Research Center. Sitagliptin is a new drug, Metformin OD once a day delivery, is a drug with improved delivery system. Single shot DPT vaccine.

4.2. Differentiate Strategies

The consistent ever-growing competition has forced the companies to adopt novel strategies to stay better off than their competitors. Pharmaceutical companies themselves or when the drug regular brings the drugs in the pricing control ensure that the prices of the drugs fall. This also helps the companies to target the larger market who otherwise might not able to consumer due to its cost. This strategy of reducing their profit margins by lowering their prices and maximize the reach is called as market penetration.

But sometimes the companies adopt a strategy of reformulating the innovative patented drug to target it for different therapeutic indication or for promote the same drug with different dosage regimen, or it being an improved version that can demonstrate better therapeutic superiority (e.g., tolerability, greater safety, or improved convenience of administration), an additional 3 years of exclusivity rights may be granted. But the grant of this type of extension is largely dependent on sanction of a new application by the competent authority like FDA in U.S, which requires data from new clinical trials aimed to establish their superiority in new indications, formulation, or dosage.

4.2.1. Evergreening

A primary patent, which completely covers a novel molecular or chemical entity, grants the inventor a free right to all sales of that entity in the market for 20 years, which being the full life of the patent. But this looks to a pretty short period in context of their investment and sales.

The best strategic alternative for these companies would be to get their pre-existing exclusivity extended in the market or enter in those global markets where they can still reap the fruits of patenting. This will help the corporations to keep the competition from the generics at a distance. Since, it is practically not desirable to get the term of their preliminary filed patent extended, but a few of the creative alternatives can help these corporations. Some innovators instead used other strategic alternatives which included subsequent filing of patents that were only the improved variations of their parent compound called as

Figure 14.

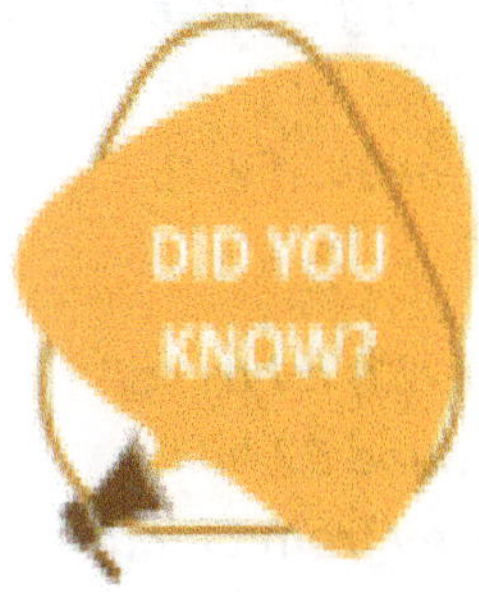

Recently diabetes molecule 'Sitagliptin' had got off-patented, with its price dropping over 50%. It has clocked a 54% jump in volume and 12.7% in value growth thereafter.

Source: Business Standard article dated 28th Aug, 2022

secondary patents. This practice, is defined as evergreening, which allowed an extended monopoly which denies the public at large an accessibility of drugs at fair and equitable prices unfairly.

The statute as per Sec 3(d) of the Patents Act, 1970 clearly defined the standard for follow-on patents on drugs, "as one of therapeutic efficacy, where applicants may need to supply some clinical evidence". But this standard was tested and upheld by the Supreme Court in one of its landmark decision in 2013 while hearing for the patent application of Novartis' anti-cancer drug Gleevec (imatinib mesylate), or Glivec. Novartis had claimed that the drug gets absorbed more easily into the bloodstream and will help to fight leukemia, that was enough evidence of an upgrading to warrant patent protection. Enormous examples are there in the history of India whereby the timely Indian government intervention has curbed the evergreening, ensuring that the interests of its citizens are safeguarded and the drugs are accessible to them at economical prices. But India's trade and industry ministry held it as "absolutely justified under the law" and reiterated that India's patent law "does not accept evergreening."

According to a 2018 study published in the Journal of Law and the Biosciences, more than two thirds of new drug patents granted in the previous 10 years were for products that were previously available on

Figure 15.

Ranbaxy entered into a marketing alliance with Zydus Cadilla to market the once-a day formulation of ofloxacin. Called Zanocin-OD, it uses a novel drug delivery system that provides better convenience.

Source: Business Standard article dated 28th, Jan, 2013

Figure 16.

Source: AXIOS

Lipitor(atorvastatin), the patented drug of Pfizer, was launched in the US back in 1996. Used for lowering of cholesterol, the drug's global sales peaked with around $13 billion in 2006.

Even though its patent expired in 2011, it has still been clocking an annual sale of around $2 billion with large chunks of it coming mostly from China.

the market. The next list of bestselling 100 drugs included with 70% of them got their exclusivity protections extended at least once, and 50% of them got their patents extended on more than once occasions.

The second strategic move was "thicketing," which involves filing numerous patent applications with the U.S. Patent and Trademark authority which makes it harder for other companies to get patents. These tactics further aided pharmaceutical companies in maintaining their monopolies.

4.2.2. Line Extensions

Line extensions, which are often based on the original substance, offer patients an improved medication. Through their communication strategies, brand teams try to convince prescribers to convert their patients to the newly patented drug before the original drug's patent expires under the guise of convenience or lower cost. This strategy helps the companies to minimizes the loss in the market share to its competitors and makes it less striking for the generic players to enter the market thereby raising the barriers of entry because now they will be targeting a very a depleted segment of patient population.

Examples include Alkem Labs putting out the extension for its cefpodoxime-proxetil brand, Swich, or Intas Pharma launching brand extensions for its anti-infective drug-based drug, Ceftas. Even a well-known medication like Voveran has seen brand extension. Similar instances have been witnessed by both Indian and MNC's. across the therapeutic categories.

Brand extension strategy helps the pharmaceutical companies to get better mileage in combination drugs, since they are meticulously in line to the therapeutic areas of the original drug. This methodology is being widely adopted in India and changed the entire landscape of global pharmaceutical market.

Additionally, brand extensions might generate more revenue than the primary brand. As an illustration, sales of Abbott Lab's vitamin B complex medicine Betonin have increased following the debut of its brand extensions.

4.3. Focus Strategies

Companies need to look into those aspects of markets which can be segmented on the basis of product, therapy, or patient wise, and identified those key elements which influenced treatment options for a

Figure 17.

Most of the drugs prescribed to treat diabetes belong to a combination therapy involving metformin, like Gliclazide + Metformin, Glipizide + Metformin, Pioglitazone + Glimepiride + Metformin, etc.

pertinent indication, such as tolerability, safety, efficacy and side effects (Paich et al., 2011). Lately, pharmaceutical companies have started to practice either a highly focused clinical strategy by showing the exclusive features of their drugs that provided value to its prescribers, or build a novel set of therapeutic indications hovering around their brand well supported by promotional tools like continuing medical education (CME), grant for research aimed at creating brand loyalty (James, 2004). Many pharmaceutical businesses practice a "weak" marketing strategy, whereby the weak sales pitch is presented to larger customers, despite the fact that the toughest marketing strategies were intensive on certain client segments that are most likely provide them better profits. The examples of these kind of strategies include launching of sustained/extended formulations of their existing drugs.

When Lilly company confronted the challenge of expiry of product patent of its bestseller antidepressant drug Prozac(brand), the company thereby developed and attained patent protection approval for its once-a-weekly, sustained-release Fluoxetine (generic name). Additionally, Bristol-Myers Squibb received FDA approval and patent protection for their extended-release version of the diabetes medication Glucophage (Metformin hydrochloride). This new formulation, sold under the trade name Glucophage XR, enables type II diabetics to take a dose once daily.

4.4. Defensive Strategies

R&D expenditures in the pharmaceutical business account about 20% of annual revenue. Every time a new drug is introduced with a cutting-edge chemical or a brand-new method of delivery, an established player usually has to protect their market share.

4.4.1. Price cut-off

The Ranbaxy corporation sold medications at "pocket-friendly costs" in an effort to appeal to the rural and small-town populations of the nation. It built up its brands in less expensive, less competitive small towns before catching rivals off guard in the metropolitan market with pharmaceuticals that were just slightly more expensive than the market leaders' offerings. Additionally, it saved money on building infrastructure and had their pharmaceuticals manufactured through contracts, allowing the business to lower the price of their goods and surprise rivals. For instance, compared to GSK and Ranbaxy's brands, which used to cost Rs 40 each, Mankind Pharma launched its flagship antibiotic brand Moxikind CV costing for Rs 11 (a six-tablet box of 500 gm). It goes without saying that both business and consumers have praised this tactic.

4.4.2. Polymorphic Patents

The idea of polymorphism states that a molecule can adopt many crystal forms. The shelf life, solubility, formulation qualities, and processing features of a medicine can all be significantly impacted by polymorphism. One drug polymorph may be more potent than another, easier to make or harder to make, or even harmful. Because a business may decide to patent the molecule's structure, a particular crystalline state, or both, polymorphs create patenting issues. Some businesses have benefited from polymorphism. A business can prolong its window of market exclusivity by patenting a polymorph after the primary medication has been protected by a patent. Ritonavir, an antiretroviral medication sold by Abbott Laboratories under the trade name Norvir® and used to treat HIV infections and AIDS, was the first medicine in which many polymorphic-forms were discovered. The first generic patent for the HMG-CoA inhibitor class was filed in 1986 for atorvastatin, a medication sold by Pfizer Inc. under the trade name Lipitor®. This patent expires in 2010. The business also submitted a particular patent in 1991 for calcium atorvastatin, which gave it an extra year of exclusivity until it expired in 2011. Another patent was filed to further prolong market rights, exposing the medications' unique polymorphs (form-I, -II, and -IV, of which form-I was the most prevalent).

4.4.3. Flanking

Some companies lately have used a strategy of launching a generic version of their patented drug which are on the verge of losing patent either themselves or in exchange of royalty, the "flanking" or "approved" generics strategy enables branded drug companies to manufacture at capacity. Due to the industry's generally low profit margins, it is far less enticing for other generics producers to try to compete when one generic form of the drug gets established in the market before the patent expiration. This method ensured that there existed only one generic form of the drug and preventing loss in market share which could have been there by the introduction of multiple generic drug introductions. An approved generic contains the exact same active and inactive components as the brand-name medication. It is frequently produced in the same location and using the same machinery as the brand-name drug, but is usually offered at a lower cost. Branded generics and authorized generics are frequently confused, but they are not the same. After the patents on branded drugs expire, branded generics go through the same FDA approval procedure as other generics.

However, authorized generics are produced by manufacturers of branded pharmaceuticals and are allowed to be sold prior to the expiration of drug patents under the same NDA (New Drug Approval) permission as the original branded drug. Authorized generics and branded generics typically cost more than regular generics, but less than branded. Only innovator businesses are authorized to sell generics, but both innovator and generic companies may sell branded generics. They both differ from one another and have varied effects on customers, generic medication manufacturers, and brand-name drug manufacturers. However, a generic drug may differ slightly from the name-brand product in some small ways, such as using alternative inactive components.

4.4.4. Pay for Delay Deals

A "reverse payment" or "pay-to-delay" arrangement - Manufacturers of branded medications use a variety of life cycle management techniques to prolong their market exclusivity and postpone the introduction of generic medications. The sale of branded medicine makers declines as generic medications enter the market. Therefore, many innovator businesses occasionally use "pay for delay deals," in which they agree with generic corporations to postpone the release of their generic version on the market, to address this issue and lessen the impact of generic debuts on market share. Consumers pay a price for these pay for delay agreements because they are only given the choice of branded or legal generic medications to purchase. According to Section 3 of the Competition Act of 2002 in India, "pay for delay" behavior can be investigated as an anti-competitive agreement or as a monopoly abuse under Section 4.

4.4.5. Divesting

Also known as 'divestiture strategy', Divesting involves organizations cutting down on the range of their business activities in an effort to obtain higher efficiency, improve financial health and build brand value. Many Indian and foreign businesses sell off their non-core brands, assets, divisions or subsidiaries to concentrate and strengthen their primary portfolios. The divestment strategy reduces expenses associated with inventories, field force, sales, and marketing by liberating resources and freeing up time that can be reassigned to the important brands. It also helps to maintain a low debt-to equity ratio. This strategy also helps in enticing investors, as it brings into sharp focus the company's profitable growth. When adopted during a lean period, the divesting strategy also results in greater returns for its shareholders. All these benefits make it an attractive strategy to build sustainable core competencies, thus eventually leading to gain competitive advantage in the industry. While Pfizer sold its non-core brands to Abbott and Sun Pharma, Sanofi sold its nutraceutical business to Universal Nutriscience. In addition to selling its orthopedic portfolio to Integrace earlier, Glenmark Pharmaceuticals also sold its gynecology division to Integrace Pvt. Ltd.

4.5. Strategic Alliances

Rusu et al. (2011) told that mergers and acquisitions could be used to build the pipeline management well supported by prioritization of R&D projects. Some of the forms of strategic alliances a pharmaceutical company can adopt are given below:

4.5.1. *Licensing Arrangements*

Aside from expanding the portfolio of new products, in-licensing agreements are a less expensive and hazardous option to secure items than buying businesses or investing in R&D, which is far more expensive. The in-licensing model aids Indian businesses in introducing innovative drugs to the nation at fair costs. Additionally, because these drugs have already received commercial approval in other nations, the regulatory processes are also simpler and quicker because they move straight through a bio-equivalence study and phase-III trials.

Eli Lilly and Zydus Cadila have signed a new medication discovery and development agreement to work on potential new treatments for cardiovascular disease. India is likewise becoming as a centre for advanced research. In a recent announcement, Johnson & Johnson (J&J) stated that it would use India as a global hub for the development of its newest medications. As a result of this strategy, J&J will conduct final pre-production testing in India for all upcoming novel medications and chemicals. Such cooperative agreements are becoming more prevalent among domestic enterprises.

Deals involving the licensing of patented goods fall into three categories.

- Acquiring exclusive marketing rights (EMR): Territorial rights to the licensee for a predetermined time. For instance, Boehringer Ingelheim and Lupin announced a contract to co-market Boehringer's diabetes medications Ajaduo and Gibtulio Met in India. Remogliflozin Etabonate, an anti-diabetes medication, to be co-marketed in India by Glenmark Pharmaceuticals and Torrent Pharmaceuticals.
- Non-exclusive agreements: In order to address the increased demand for some pharmaceuticals as a result of the pandemic, businesses have also made non-exclusive agreements. Examples of non-exclusive deals between pharmaceutical corporations include the licensing of Remdesivir by Gilead, Molnupiravir by Merck, and Baricitinib by Eli Lilly.
- Off-patent licensing contracts: Businesses are willing to licence generic, non-patented portfolios as well. A contract was negotiated by Abbott to take over the marketing and distribution of MSD's generic product line in India.

4.5.2. Mergers and Acquisitions

Mergers and Acquisitions (M&A) are very common in the pharmaceutical industry, as well as the tech industry. Due to its immediate strategic implications, M&A has been a 'go to' strategy for the pharma companies to capture market share and augment growth. So much so, it has been quite a regular occurrence. Healthcare companies in India spent $4.32 billion on mergers and acquisitions from January to June 2022 compared to $2.02 billion during the same time last year.

The latest to join the group of Chinese medicine manufacturer Shanghai Fosun Pharmaceutical's acquisitions in India was Hyderabad-based injectables manufacturer Gland Pharma. Company in its effort to grow its contract manufacturing business in Europe, it purchased French Contract Development & Manufacturing Organisation (CDMO), Cenexi Group for a value of about 1,000 crores. The Goa-based bulk pharmaceutical formulations division of Teva Pharma India had been purchased by local company Marksans Pharma.

5. GENERICS

The World Health organization (WHO), defined generic as a drug, "that can be interchangeable with the original one". So, instead of writing branded drug names like 'Allegra' 'Agimfast' or 'Alafree', health care prescribers had to prescribe their patients the same medicine to treat allergy indications with its molecule name, *fexofenadine*. During the term of the patent, pharmaceutical innovators are allowed to forbid rival firms from releasing generic copies of their products before their patents expire (s).

For the medicine Flurazepam Hydrochloride (Brand: Dalmane; Company: Roche), a generic business called Bolar Pharmaceuticals was barred from developing generic versions by the innovator corporation Roche years ago. This incident sparked the landmark legal case of Roche Products v. Bolar Pharmaceutical.

Figure 18. Product market matrix

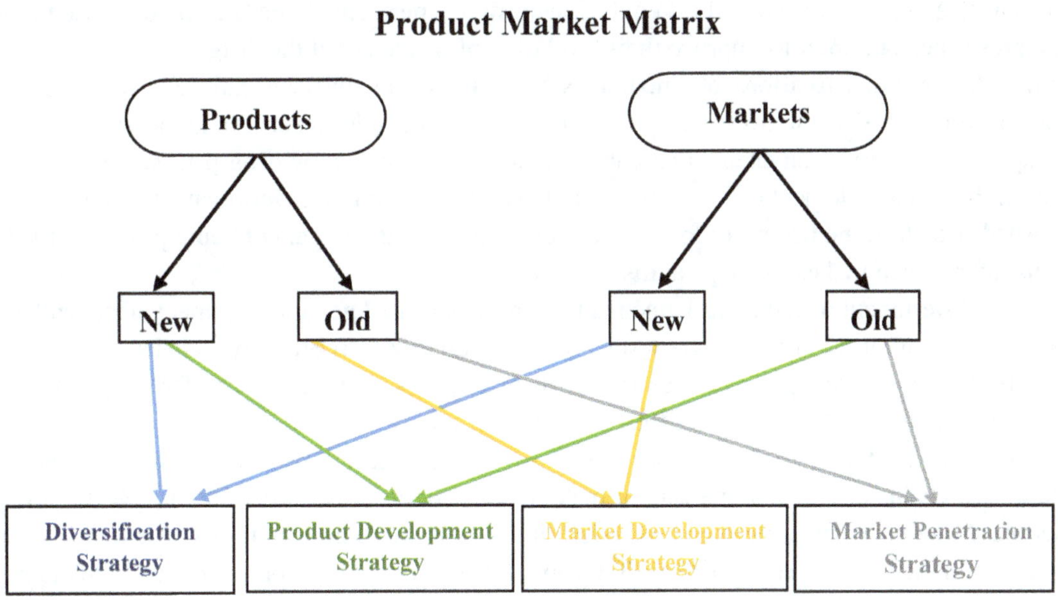

Source: Pharmaceutical Marketing – A Practical Guide

Afterward, the US Congress passed a law allowing the manufacture, use, offering to commercialize, or sale of patented inventions during the patent's term if such actions were solely for uses that were reasonably associated to the development and submission of evidence under laws that govern the production, use, or sale of drugs. The "Bolar" principle came to be known as a result of this reform in patent law. This also goes by the name "early working exception." Through the 2002 Amendment, the Bolar flexibility was incorporated into Indian patent law. Recently, the Indian Bolar provision was put to the test in court cases involving two different medications: one covered the cancer treatment Sorafenib Tosylate (marketed under the Bayer brand name Nexavar), and the other covered the blood-thinning medication Rivaroxaban (Bayer brand: Xarelto).

5.1. Inhibiting Factors for the Penetration of Generics

Taking a cue from the 6 Ps of marketing described earlier, various key elements for the penetration of generic drugs can be discussed. The following are the concerns:

1. Policies - Drugs that are getting off-patented are to be clearly demarcated as ethical drugs or branded drugs. Moreover, the off patented drugs should not be allowed to be sold as ethical branded drugs to improve the R&D in the industry. Also, the government should make a policy whereby the off patented drugs should be notified so that companies are able to augment their presence in those therapeutic categories.
2. Product - The level of acceptance of the generic molecules also needs to improve at the prescriber level. Even though the generic drugs are being made available in India through huge chain of hos-

pitals/ dispensaries/stores, yet still the revenue and the usage of these drugs is dismally low, about 1%. In addition, the pharmacies need to be given quotas for sales of generics to augment their presence. Also, the bioavailability/ equivalence studies performed needs to be discussed among the prescribers, in order to improve their level of confidence about the drug.

3. Price- Accessibility to affordable medicines still remains a significant public health priority for most governments' world over. The government regularly conducts surveys to measure the impact of approved generic equivalents that can have on consumer generic drug prices. The major barrier in the pricing element of generics is that beyond a handful of government stores, namely Jan Aushadi Kendras, the benefit of low cost of generics is, by and large, not being passed to the final consumer, which makes its usage at dismal low.
4. Place - Government of India has launched their much-awaited generic pharmacy chain called Jan Aushadi Scheme in 2008, which is now renamed as Pradhan Mantri Bharatiya Janaushadi Pariyojana (PMBJP), to ensure that generic drugs are largely made accessible to majority of the population with bare minimum cost. Also, in one of the recent developments, One India pharmacy, private generic pharmacy chain, has opened more than 550 store and are looking to expand further. However, just these two chains of stores alone cannot make these generic drugs accessible to 140 billion plus people. More pharmacies need to be brought into operation to be able to help the distribution of generics in the country. However, reach, geography and cost of distribution concerns will present a major bottleneck that they will have to iron out.
5. Promotion - The pharmaceutical industry uses number of marketing communication channels to ensure that their prescribers stay updated to the latest developments in the medicine field. But this is true in the case of ethical branded drugs where the cost of drugs is low and they are being sold at high prices, thus providing better profitability. However, pharma companies are hardly spending on the promotion of generic drugs as the profitability is bare minimum in comparison to it counterpart. Notwithstanding, whatsoever being the profit, most of it gets evaporated in the distribution cost. All the pharmaceutical companies can push for at least one of their generic offerings to be promoted by their sales teams, along with their branded drugs, which can not only improve the level of awareness of generics among the populace, but also help to bring about efficiency in operations. This could also tweak the interest of the pharmacists and druggists in dispensing generics.
6. People - Previous studies carried out in the domain have revealed key strategic insights and have found that the entire research theme could be grouped into three clusters for the better adoption of the generic drugs among the people.
    (i) Improving the attitude towards generic medicine through public awareness programs and public policy.
    (ii) Conducting many more bioequivalence studies to address the safety and risk indications of generic drugs. These could help build confidence among health professionals in their prescription behaviors.
    (iii) Making dispensing of generics economically viable even for pharmacists, through exploration of various business models.

So, from the above discussion it can be gleaned that the habits of doctors and pharmacists are key to adoption and are also apparently very difficult to change. Although laws allow a pharmacist to substitute a generic equivalent for a branded drug (generic substitution), unless the prescription indicates not to, however such substitution was not that common. Additionally, there aren't any generic players in many of the drug segments; for example, the medicine producer Valeant abruptly raised the price of isoproterenol from $440 to around $2,700 each dose, sending the price of a single drug for inpatient use soaring from $300,000 to $1.9 million. Isoproterenol is used as heart medication. The drug helps in the indication of heart attacks and works to keep patient's blood pressure within range.

When the price of isoproterenol suddenly increased, the typical response would have been to stop using it and start looking for alternatives; however, hospitals began stockpiling up in pharmacy backup boxes so they would always have the essential medication on hand. The medication isoproterenol was once patented but is no longer. Therefore, in theory, any pharmaceutical company should be able to produce a generic version and market it at a reasonable price. But the generic version never appeared as it ought to have.

The credibility of independent businesses that produce generic drugs was also damaged by a controversy in 1989. Generic drug producers were accused of fabricating laboratory tests and buying FDA officials to approve their products. This incident made it even more difficult for doctors and pharmacists to switch out branded medications for generic ones. By the beginning of the 1990s, a number of significant pharmaceutical companies stepped up to fill the void by creating their own divisions to sell generics or by acquiring stakes in businesses that supplied generics. In 2015, more than one recall of a generic medication product occurred every other day, totaling 267 product recalls. These product recalls were carried out due to quality problems, such as improper product dissolution, contamination, or even blatant fake products. In another instance, two generic drug producers are accused of forming a cartel to set artificially high pricing for ranitidine, the generic version of the ulcer medication Zantac.

Traditional medicine fills a significant gap in modern medicine in developing nations like India. Industry estimates indicate that 70% of Indians use traditional medicines as a complement to, and occasionally instead of, pharmaceutical medications. All these factors collectively inhibit the adoption of generic medicines and realization of its true potential.

6. CONCLUSION

The usage of generic medicines will provide considerable savings to overall healthcare systems. With the increasing pressure on government budgets and containment of healthcare expenses, the window of opportunity for generics may stay open for long. The promotion of these drugs among the prescribers are quite needed for a country like India where no formal social security system exists. The present business environment, pose the entire generics industry with two opposing forces that complicate their profitability and future growth. On the one hand, demand for generics continues to rise in India. The demand for generics shall remain strong, as the next wave of patent expiries will create additional business opportunities for those companies who will get the license for selling these off-patented drugs. At the same time, there are some global barriers like inflation, supply constraints of generic molecules and deteriorating health of economies. While these macro forces could be beyond the reach of pharmaceutical companies to control, individual marketing strategies are very well in their grasp to mold and augment generic medicine growth. Such strategies will have to adopt a wholistic approach, understanding the concerns of all the stakeholders involved – government agencies, pharma companies, pharmacists and patients. Only then a sustainable adoption of generics can be achieved and thus furthering the cause of universal health coverage and health equity in the country.

REFERENCES

Adams, C. P., & Brantner, V. V. (2006). Estimating the cost of new drug development: Is it really $802 million? *Health Affairs*, *25*(2), 420–428. doi:10.1377/hlthaff.25.2.420 PMID:16522582

Annual Report 2022-23. (n.d.). Department of Pharmaceuticals, Ministry of Chemicals & fertilizers, Government of India. Available at: https://pharmaceuticals.gov.in/sites/default/files/Annual%20Report%202022-23%20Final-3_0.pdf

Association of Accessible Medicines. (2017). *Generic Drug Access and Savings in the U.S.* Available at https://accessiblemeds.org/sites/default/files/2017-07/2017-AAM-Access-Savings-Report-2017-web2.pdf

Figure 19.

Case for discussion

Read the case below and answer the questions after the case.

India has a population of 1.4 billion people. The population is spread geographically across the length and the breadth of nation with some cities being densely populated. But most of the population, around 70%, still resides in rural India which do not have good accessibility to healthcare facilities. In healthcare it includes all the primary healthcare facilities. The Indian Pharmaceutical market has a volume of Rs. 1.8 lakh crores for the financial year 2022. In this market, the ethical drugs and branded drugs constitute around 30% and 70% respectively. Pharmaceutical companies are striving to stay relevant to the needs of their prescribers owing to competition from the multinational corporations.

But lately with the drugs getting off-patented, the healthcare costs have reduced but at the cost of sales of their branded drugs. Many established pharmaceutical companies like Cipla, Cadilla, Merck, GSK, etc., have augmented their presence in the generic drugs market with government announcing the opening of Jan Aushadi stores across the country. But getting a generic form/name of the drug being prescribed still remains a distant dream for majority of the population.

Question 1. How can the companies augment their presence in the generic market?

Question 2. Do you think this increase in sales will come at the cost of loss of revenue in branded drugs?

Question 3. Can you think of a novel distribution channel to make these drugs available to patients? Name few of them and the rationale of your choice.

Barei, F., & Ross, M. (2015). The refinement of the super generic concept: Semantic challenge for product re-innovation? *Generics and Biosimilars Initiative (GaBI) Journal*, *4*(1), 25–32.

Cameron, A., Mantel-Teeuwisse, A. K., Leufkens, H. G., & Laing, R. O. (2012). Switching from originator brand medicines to generic equivalents in selected developing countries: How much could be saved? *Value in Health*, *15*(5), 664–673. doi:10.1016/j.jval.2012.04.004 PMID:22867775

Chandra, P. (2019). Surviving Generics – Top Pharma Brand Marketing Strategies. *Linkedin*. Available at https://www.linkedin.com/pulse/surviving-generics-top-pharma-brand-marketing-phanish-chandra

Chaudhuri, S. (2016). Reverse payment deals in patent disputes and its impact on competition. *ET Healthworld*. Available at https://health.economictimes.indiatimes.com/news/pharma/reverse-payment-deals-in-patent-disputes-and-its-impact-on-competition/52024742

Christina, M. B. (2021). Drugs Shortages Amid the COVID-19 Pandemic. *U. S. Pharmacist*, *46*(2), 25–28.

Ciron Pharma. (2021). *Marketing Strategies of Pharmaceutical Products of India*. Available at https://www.cironpharma.com/blog/pharmaceutical-products-in-india-marketing-strategies/

Cutting Edge Information. (2004). *Combating Generics: Pharmaceutical Brand Defense*. Available at http://www.PharmaGenerics.com

DiMasi, J. A., Hansen, R. W., & Grabowski, H. G. (2003). The price of innovation: New estimates of drug development costs. *Journal of Health Economics*, *22*(2), 151–185. doi:10.1016/S0167-6296(02)00126-1 PMID:12606142

Duflos, G., & Lichtenberg, F. R. (2012). Does competition stimulate drug utilization? The impact of changes in market structure on US drug prices, marketing and utilization. *International Review of Law and Economics*, *32*(1), 95–109. doi:10.1016/j.irle.2011.08.003

Dyer, O. (2004). NHS takes makers of generic drugs to court for price fixing. *BMJ (Clinical Research Ed.)*, *329*(7456), 12. doi:10.1136/bmj.329.7456.12-a PMID:15231602

Fox, E. (2017). How Pharma Companies Game the System to Keep Drugs Expensive. *Harvard Business Review*. Available at https://hbr.org/2017/04/how-pharma-companies-game-the-system-to-keep-drugs-expensive

Galani, V. (2017). Choice of better medicine in India: Branded vs generic medicine. *Pharmacy & Pharmacology International Journal*, *5*(3), 124–125. doi:10.15406/ppij.2017.05.00125

Gilbert, T., Ural, A., & Lopez, M. (2012). Five Branded Generic Strategies to Master for Global Pharmaceutical in Emerging Markets. *Accenture Life Sciences*. Available at https://www.accenture.com/t20161128T001148__w__/us-en/_acnmedia/Accenture/Conversion-Assets/DotCom/Documents/Global/PDF/Industries_1/Accenture-Five-Branded-Generics-Strategies-Pharmaceuticals-in-Emerging-Markets.pdf

Gray, J. V., Siemsen, E., & Vasudeva, G. (2015). Colocation still matters: Conformance quality and the interdependence of R&D and manufacturing in the pharmaceutical industry. *Management Science*, *61*(11), 2760–2781. doi:10.1287/mnsc.2014.2104

Gupta, H., Kumar, S., Roy, S. K., & Gaud, R. S. (2010). Patent protection strategies. *Journal of Pharmacy & Bioallied Sciences*, *2*(7), 2–7. doi:10.4103/0975-7406.62694 PMID:21814422

Hailu, A. D., Workneh, B. D., & Kahissay, M. H. (2021). Influence of pharmaceutical marketing mix strategies on physicians' prescribing behaviors in public and private hospitals, Dessie, Ethiopia: A mixed study design. *BMC Public Health, 21*(1), 65. doi:10.118612889-020-10063-2 PMID:33413248

Hess, J., & Litalien, S. (2004). Battle for the market: Branded drug companies' secret weapons generic drug makers must know. *Journal of Generic Medicines, 3*(1), 20–29. doi:10.1057/palgrave.jgm.4940095

Invest India. (2022). *Pharma industry in India: Invest in Indian Pharma Sector.* Available at https://www.investindia.gov.in/sector/pharmaceuticals

James, B. (2004). The new 6 Ps of pharmaceutical marketing. *Pharmaceutical Marketing, 18*(1), 1–3.

Jishnu, L. (2021). Big pharma and intellectual property: Why is India afraid of compulsory licenses. *Down To Earth.* Available at https://www.downtoearth.org.in/blog/health/big-pharma-and-intellectual-property-why-is-india-afraid-of-compulsory-licences--77470

Kalotra, A. (2014). Marketing Strategies of Different Pharmaceutical Companies. *Journal of Drug Delivery and Therapeutics, 4*(2), 64–71. doi:10.22270/jddt.v4i2.771

Keyhani, S., Diener-West, M., & Powe, N. (2006). Are development times for pharmaceuticals increasing or decreasing? *Health Affairs, 25*(2), 461–468. doi:10.1377/hlthaff.25.2.461 PMID:16522587

Khajuria, A., & Khajuria, V. (2013). Impact of pharmaceutical marketing communication strategies on prescription practices of physicians. *Research Journal of Pharmaceutical, Biological and Chemical Sciences, 4*(3), 882–889.

Kraljevic, S., Stambrook, P. J., & Pavelic, K. (2004, September). Accelerating drug discovery. *EMBO Reports, 5*(9), 837–842. doi:10.1038j.embor.7400236 PMID:15470377

Llamas, M. (2022). Selling Side Effects: Big Pharma's Marketing Machine. *Drugwatch.* Available at https://www.drugwatch.com/featured/big-pharma-marketing/

Masood, I., Hassali, M. A., & Ahmad, M. (2009). Evolution of Marketing Techniques, Adoption In Pharmaceutical Industry And Related Issues: A Review. *Journal of Clinical and Diagnostic Research : JCDR, 3*(6), 1942–1952.

McGahan, A. M. (1994). Industry Structure and Competitive Advantage. *Harvard Business Review.* Available at https://hbr.org/1994/11/industry-structure-and-competitive-advantage

Memisoglu, M. (2018). Branding of Prescription and Non-prescription Drugs. *Acta Pharmaceutica Sciencia, 56*(1), 21. doi:10.23893/1307-2080.APS.05602

Mukherjee, W. (2008). Pharma pops brand-extension pill. *The Economic Times.* Available at https://economictimes.indiatimes.com/industry/healthcare/biotech/pharmaceuticals/pharma-pops-brand-extension-pill/articleshow/3173587.cms?from=mdr

Paich, M., Peck, C., & Valant, J. (2011). Pharmaceutical market dynamics and strategic planning: A system dynamics perspective. *System Dynamics Review, 27*(1), 47–63. doi:10.1002dr.458

Piergentili, P. (2017). Monopoly and public health in the medication market: The case of sofosbuvir. *Journal of Generic Medicines, 13*(3), 131–136. doi:10.1177/1741134317705691

Prajapati, V., Tripathy, S., & Dureja, H. (2013). Product lifecycle management through patents and regulatory strategies. *Journal of Medical Marketing, 13*(3), 171–180. doi:10.1177/1745790413497388

Press Trust of India. (2019). 25 batches of drugs of 18 pharma companies found substandard since Jan 2018 by BPPI. *The Hindu Business Line.* Available at https://www.thehindubusinessline.com/news/25-batches-of-drugs-of-18-pharma-companies-found-substandard-since-jan-2018-by-bppi/article27956298.ece

Rathod, S. K. (2017). The curious case of India's Bolar provision. *Journal of Generic Medicines, 14*(1), 16–21. doi:10.1177/1741134317745351

Rathod, S. K. (2017). Compulsory licences on pharmaceutical patents in India: A short article. *Journal of Generic Medicines, 13*(3), 108–113. doi:10.1177/1741134317691804

Rusu, A., Kuokkanen, K., & Heier, A. (2011, October). Current trends in the pharmaceutical industry—A case study approach. *European Journal of Pharmaceutical Sciences, 44*(3), 437–440. doi:10.1016/j.ejps.2011.07.008 PMID:21782941

Schramm, M. E., & Hu, M. Y. (2013). Perspective: The evolution of R&D conduct in the pharmaceutical industry. *Journal of Product Innovation Management, 30*(S1), 203–213. doi:10.1111/jpim.12072

Singh, K. (2010). Ramesh Juneja: A journey from Medical representative to meteor of India's biggest marketer of ED drugs. *The Economic Times.* Available at https://economictimes.indiatimes.com/ramesh-juneja-a-journey-from-medical-representative-to-meteor-of-indias-biggest-marketer-of-ed-drugs/articleshow/5831020.cms?from=mdr

Sinha, S., & Rajagopal, D. (2017). Max Bupa, Hospital Lobby Group spar over generic drug prescription. *The Economic Times.* Available at https://economictimes.indiatimes.com/industry/healthcare/biotech/healthcare/max-bupa-hospital-lobby-group-spar-over-generic-drug-prescription/articleshow/58634898.cms?utm_source=contentofinterest&utm_medium=text&utm_campaign=cppst

Smedley, T. (2013). Patent wars: has India taken on Big Pharma and won? *The Guardian.* Available at https://www.theguardian.com/sustainable-business/patent-wars-india-takes-on-big-pharma

Song, C. H., & Han, J. W. (2016). Patent cliff and strategic switch: Exploring strategic design possibilities in the pharmaceutical industry. *SpringerPlus, 5*(1), 1–14. doi:10.118640064-016-2323-1 PMID:27347468

Steering Committee of the Climate Change Study, Australian Academy of Science, Australian Academy of Technological Sciences, & Academy of the Social Sciences in Australia. (1995). *Climate Change Science: Current Understanding and Uncertainties.* Australian Academy of Technological Sciences and Engineering.

Yina, C., Pengcheng, L., Haomiao, N., & Yang, C. (2023). An empirical study of the impact of generic drug competition on drug prices in China. *Frontiers in Public Health, 11*, 1146531. doi:10.3389/fpubh.2023.1146531 PMID:37304112

Chapter 6
Sustainability and Healthcare Marketing in the Digital Age

Iza Gigauri
https://orcid.org/0000-0001-6394-6416
St. Andrew the First-Called Georgian University, Georgia

ABSTRACT

Healthcare as a dynamic and complex industry requires marketing to achieve business goals and improve the well-being of society. Transformations in the environment, increased competition, changes in consumer behavior force organizations to adapt to the altered landscape. In this regard, marketing plays a pivotal role in defining consumers' attitudes, motivations, and perceptions, building relationships with stakeholders, developing a strategy, and creating value. Moreover, the aging population, chronic diseases, prolonged pains and disabilities, poverty and poor health conditions, and lack of reliable medical services cause an increased burden not only on the healthcare system but also on the economy and society in all counties. Sustainable Development Goals aim to solve the pressing challenges facing the world. The objectives of this chapter are to discuss healthcare marketing in light of the twin transition: sustainability and digitalization. The chapter illustrates sustainable healthcare marketing opportunities in relation to digital advancements including ChatGPT.

1. INTRODUCTION

Demand for marketing in healthcare organizations is growing to effectively communicate with patients, suppliers, governments, and providers but also to successfully respond to their needs and wants. The consumer for healthcare marketing is not only an individual patient or a physician but also companies purchasing care for their employees as well as insurance companies (Berkowitz, 2021).

Marketing communication is an essential part of health promotion as health marketing relates to health promotion programs. According to the definition of WHO (n.d.), "Health promotion is the process of enabling people to increase control over, and to improve, their health. It moves beyond a focus on individual behavior towards a wide range of social and environmental interventions". Studies demonstrate that health promotion including education prevents diseases, reduces health

DOI: 10.4018/979-8-3693-0679-6.ch006

risks, and stimulates behavior changes (Pham et al., 2020; Basińska-Zych & Springer, 2021). Thus, the integration of health promotion and social marketing can add value to health improvement and increase effectiveness.

Healthcare marketing is characterized by consumers instead of products or services. For this reason, marketing aims to create a long-term relationship with consumers in order to ensure their satisfaction and loyalty. Marketing aims at understanding the health needs of the target population and responding to the demands with accessible products and services. In addition, the reputation and image of healthcare institutions influence patients' choices. Moreover, marketing can improve healthcare quality, gain employee satisfaction, and allocate human, financial, or material resources efficiently. Furthermore, marketing increases awareness of healthcare issues among the population and contributes to sustainability.

A successful marketing strategy should begin with the research of consumers' needs, desires, and opinions based on which new or improved services must be offered by a healthcare organization. It should be taken into account that patients' behaviors and attitudes are affected by families and friends and hence, can change across countries (Syed et al., 2021). Only under such conditions, it is possible to acquire and maintain consumers, earn income, and gain a competitive advantage in the market. Research, based on a systematic review of relevant papers, confirm the significance of marketing strategies and technological progress for healthcare organizations (Syed et al., 2021).

Recently introduced advanced technologies enable healthcare consumers to access various information and special offers through the Internet, evaluate healthcare services, and share their experiences (Berkowitz, 2021). Patients now know their needs and assess alternatives. Consumers are increasingly seeking values whilst transparency and global competition become paramount (Berkowitz, 2021; Syed et al., 2021).

Researchers underline the importance of communication in healthcare marketing which can be performed through electronic means such as television, outdoor billboards, and especially social media (Syed et al., 2021). Studies show that a huge number of people worldwide use social media and even advertisements directing customers to the Facebook page of a company are considered to be reliable and less annoying than those leading visitors to the brand's webpage (Pelet & Ettis, 2022). However, marketing activities promoting health-related issues can be performed with utmost caution given the powerful effect of social media. For this reason, governments tend to pose regulations on advertisements in order to protect patients since they are unable to distinguish the authenticity of messages (Syed et al., 2021).

In order to address the pressing challenges, the world has faced, Sustainable Development Goals (SDGs) have been initiated by the United Nations. Since then, sustainability has become a buzzword. Organizations of all types and sizes are expected to contribute to SDGs. The joint efforts of various agents should ameliorate people's lives on Earth.

Against this background, the purpose of this chapter is to examine healthcare marketing in light of the twin transition - Sustainability and Digitalization. The chapter illustrates sustainable marketing opportunities for healthcare organizations and establishes the links between healthcare marketing, digital transformation, and Sustainability. Social marketing, digital technologies, particularly chat GPT, and ethical considerations are also discussed.

2. SUSTAINABILITY HEALTHCARE MARKETING

2.1. Sustainable Marketing

The importance of sustainable marketing is growing strongly associated with consumer behavior and preferences. Consumers' purchase decisions have changed as they become aware of pressing environmental and social issues demanding that brands integrate responsibility and sustainability aspects in their products and services. Moreover, a new transformative role of marketing has been widely discussed with regard to consumerism and sustainability (Gigauri & Djakeli, 2021). Traditional marketing is often referred to as manipulative, unethical, and irresponsible, causing pollution and excessive consumption problems. For this reason, marketing evolved towards a responsible and ethical direction, adopting a fair, honest, transparent, and stakeholder-oriented approach.

The paradigm shift from traditional to sustainable marketing has induced an expansion of the research agenda in the field. Yet agreement on the definitions and related terms is not reached among scholars. Martin and Schouten (2014) define sustainable marketing as "the process of creating, communicating, and delivering value to customers in such a way that both natural and human capital are preserved or enhanced throughout". Furthermore, Dahlstrom and Crosno (2022) describe sustainable marketing "as the study of all efforts to consume, produce, distribute, promote, package, and reclaim products in a manner to achieve ecological, economic, and social objectives". In this sense, sustainability-oriented marketing considers environmental concerns and tries to decrease the negative impacts of marketing activities on the environment, builds the relationships with all stakeholders of a company, and promotes social equity and ethical behavior (Belz & Peattie, 2012).

Kemper and Ballantine (2019) suggest that sustainability marketing unifies both sustainable marketing and green marketing and hence, sustainability marketing, sustainable marketing, and green marketing are represented under one term of 'Sustainability Marketing'. This perspective proposes that sustainability is incorporated into marketing mix, promotes sustainable consumption, defines the role of marketing in contributing to sustainable development, takes responsibility for social well-being, and leads to consumers' healthy choices.

Thus, sustainable marketing integrates traditional commercial marketing with relationship marketing, environmental or green marketing, ethical marketing, social marketing, and SDGs. Sustainable marketing incorporates sustainability into marketing programs. In this context, sustainable marketing aims to satisfy consumer needs and consider economic, environmental, and social aspects simultaneously (Belz & Peattie, 2012; Lloveras et al., 2022).

The special focus of sustainable marketing on the consumer is a distinctive characteristic of healthcare marketing centering on patient satisfaction. Consumer needs are studied to develop marketing programs and the marketing mix is changed in order to better respond to sustainability goals. Although marketing has put emphasis on customer satisfaction in order to increase profit, the sustainable marketing concept has also addressed ecological and social factors paving the way to ethical, green, and social marketing ultimately merging into the idea of sustainable marketing (Martín-Cervantes et al., 2022; Gigauri, Palazzo & Ferri, 2023). The concept strives to create and maintain long-term relationship instead of short-run profit. Sustainable marketing enables organizational change in favor of sustainability while recognizing and using strategic opportunities.

2.2. Social Marketing for Healthcare Services

Social marketing comes into play to implement healthcare marketing programmes and to find solutions in terms of inclusiveness, of serving customers with diverse needs, of improving quality of life, and participating in value co-creation (Gil Guzman et al., 2021). Effective healthcare project requires stakeholder participation, which can be ensured through social marketing. Successful social marketing includes appropriate products/ services developed in response to community needs, a proper place for them to be delivered, affordable prices, and effective promotion strategies, but social marketing also encompasses financial sustainability, organization sustainability, and market sustainability (Aras, 2011).

Studies show that social marketing aims at reaching different groups of people to improve their behavior in favor of public health while also focusing on the sustainability aspects (Aras, 2011). Moreover, social marketing can identify barriers to behavioral change and design appropriate interventions (Morris & Clarkson, 2009). Since conditions and institutional norms influence individuals' behavior, social marketing can lead to healthy habits and create an enabling environment for informed decisions and better choices.

Scholars advise planning social marketing campaigns to accomplish health goals based on three sets: identifying the social problem, describing the benefits of changed behavior, and developing the marketing mix (Da Silva & Mazzon, 2016). Although social marketing resembles commercial marketing, its objectives are different. Still, social marketing uses commercial marketing tools. Social marketing aims at changing the behavior of individuals to improve life in societies. Consequently, social marketing programmes should be appropriately developed for the country's context, main actors should act coordinately, persuasive communication designed to change behavior should be implemented, benefits should be emphasized, and sustainability should be considered (Donovan, 2011; Marchioli, 2006; Lloveras et al., 2022).

In order to facilitate health and social changes, social marketing can arrange communication and educational campaigns (Weinreich, 2010). Using various communication strategies and marketing tools such as media, healthcare providers, promotion, and community outreach, social marketing encourages healthy behavior.

According to Henley et al. (2011), social marketing for the healthcare industry involves the following aspects:

- Consumer's perspectives - as their interests are considered in the planning process;
- Marketing activities and plans are in agreement with the target audience and management, accomplishment, and assessment are carried out accordingly;
- Communication messages and channels are directed to reach the target audience;
- Public satisfaction is increased due to marketing research activities and healthcare campaign results are achieved;
- Individual behavior is changed as market research determines a specific health problem that needs to be addressed (Henley et al., 2011).

Studies analyzed social marketing programmes from 2005-2017 around the world found that social media including Facebook was mainly used for sharing information, connecting target populations, raising awareness, and reaching disadvantaged groups (Shawky et al., 2019). Moreover, social media marketing impacts brand loyalty, trust, and business sustainability (Veseli-Kurtishi, 2018; Ibrahim &

Aljarah, 2018). Consequently, companies effectively utilizing social and digital marketing can increase sales and improve branding strategies (Dwivedi et al., 2021).

Thus, social marketing using various communication channels can improve public health and society's quality of life. Therefore, healthcare marketing can apply social marketing tools to successfully reach its goals.

2.3. Healthcare Marketing Addressing Sustainable Development Goals

The term 'Sustainable Development' has its roots in the Report of the World Commission on the Environment and Development (WCED). In particular, Norwegian Prime Minister Gro Harlem Brundtland published his report "Our Common Future" in 1987, where he defined the concept as "development that meets the needs of the present without compromising the ability of future generations to meet their own needs" (WCED, 1987).

Since the Brundtland Report, the term has spread around the globe and attracted attention from policymakers, governments, scholars, professionals, and educators. Additionally, 'Sustainable Development' entered the everyday language (Lloveras et al., 2022) and has become a matter of discussion in almost all areas of society. The concept is related to Elkington's Triple Bottom Line (TBL) known for three interconnected dimensions of sustainability - economic, social, and environmental facets (Elkington, 1998).

Later, the United Nations introduced Sustainability Development Goals as a response to Grand Challenges. The 17 SDGs are the most recent global policy to ensure societal welfare and prosperity (Lloveras et al., 2022). This development has been also reflected in the marketing efforts of business enterprises. Marketing has been transforming towards sustainability while taking into consideration all stakeholders and developing innovative products or services (Bocken, 2021). Since health issues impede the quality of life, SDG 3 is dedicated to the target "Ensure healthy lives and promote well-being for all at all ages" (UN, n.d.), nonetheless the rest sixteen goals, directly or indirectly, are related to improving the health of people and promoting healthy lifestyle. In this respect, marketing has a pivotal role to play to promote SDGs and tackle healthcare issues.

Health marketing contains elements from health promotion, commercial marketing, and communication to provide health-related information to the general public. Health marketing campaigns can raise public awareness of health issues, health protection, new treatment opportunities, or a healthy lifestyle. With respect to sustainable development, a healthcare system should develop the infrastructure that manages and ameliorates people's health and educates them about healthy behavior, as well as prevents illnesses (Popa et al., 2022).

The purpose of healthcare marketing is to attract consumers, accompany them throughout healthcare service, and maintain them through public relations and communication efforts. Healthcare marketing strategy encompasses segmentation and targeting activities using both online and offline channels. Accordingly, healthcare Marketing helps organizations to invite prospective patients by increasingly delivering values and advantages as the competition in the industry is high. By the same token, healthcare marketing activities should be engaged in the relationships with patients through multiple channels to keep them long-term and enhance their loyalty to the brand and healthcare company. In order to redesign and strengthen strategy, healthcare marketing also contains performance evaluation and measurement activities.

In addition, digitalization can contribute to SDGs by improving the accessibility of disadvantaged and vulnerable groups of the population to various services they may need (Gigauri et al., 2023). Digital progress stimulates innovation, brings new approaches to processing information, enables digital communication, and facilitates dealing with challenges (Gigauri, Apostu & Popescu, 2023; Pelet, Belda & Arezki, 2023). Digital tools occupy a prominent place as users of online communication channels are growing around the world. For example, the majority of patients tend to search healthcare facilities through search engines (e.g. Google) and book their appointments online. Patients have access to health-related information through digital technologies and use it. However, overwhelming information can confuse patients, a solution of which can be a company's website serving consumers with reliable and accessible information. Moreover, thanks to numerous health and wellness applications and gadgets, patients have greater influence over their health.

Therefore, marketing becomes progressively vital to reach consumers in such a competitive market. An online presence can enhance branding position and increase revenues. Furthermore, data-driven marketing analysis as well as digitalized data enables healthcare organizations to better predict and observe diseases, to improve health management and patient care (Moro Visconti & Morea, 2019).

Currently, there is a considerable lack of studies related to healthcare marketing from the perspective of sustainable development as the scholars were unable to identify any research themes through the comprehensive bibliometric analysis (Popa et al., 2022). Consequently, the examination of healthcare marketing in the context of sustainability is important for the implementation of SDGs but also for society's well-being. Marketing seems to have a part in sustainable healthcare strategies.

3. DIGITAL MARKETING FOR HEALTHCARE AND ETHICAL CONSIDERATIONS

3.1. Digital Technologies, Marketing, and Ethical Concerns

Technologies revolutionized medicine and have shaped the healthcare industry. Trendy technologies expand marketing efforts in healthcare. Technological advancements such as the Internet of Things (IoT), Machine Learning (ML), Robots, AI, cloud computing, etc. are used in the healthcare system to enhance patient satisfaction and assist professionals in medical care and treatment (Mondal et al., 2022; Popescu et al., 2022). Specifically, ML and IOT are applied for healthcare digital marketing in order to target consumers, improve search engine optimization, and make better strategic decisions (Mondal et al., 2022).

Digital marketing enables healthcare professionals to promote their services and disseminate marketing messages around the globe while improving the reputation of healthcare companies (Mondal et al., 2022).

Studies emphasize the positive impact of digital marketing on consumers behaviors concerning healthcare and social media campaigns becoming an effective tool for health promotion, in particular, pain management, health education, mental health awareness, as well as for preventing disease, and adopting healthy attitudes (Rogers et al., 2017; Buchanan et al., 2018; O'Reilly et al., 2019; De Veirman et al., 2019; Murphy et al., 2020; Günther et al., 2021; Alonzo & Popescu, 2021).

On the other hand, or exactly due to its powerful influence, ethical considerations need to be taken into account while applying digital marketing tools. In public health, ethical issues are related to data privacy and patient protection (Clar et al., 2014). While using digital marketing campaigns to provide consumers with health education and self-care benefits, misunderstanding health information can lead to certain risks (Huntsman & Bulaj, 2023). To avoid dangers, scholars indicate that ethical marketing strategy needs to be integrated into health advertising activities (Huntsman & Bulaj, 2023).

Moreover, diversity and inclusion should be incorporated into healthcare marketing. Consumers require diverse products and services and individualized treatment. Inclusive healthcare marketing directs its efforts towards disadvantageous populations and plans marketing strategy in a way to address their needs and wants. In this respect, inclusive marketing aims to conquer inequality in the healthcare domain by embracing inclusiveness and equality and considering underrepresented individuals in marketing communication. Diversity, equity, and inclusion are parts of marketing efforts in healthcare. As a result, marketing effectiveness and consumer well-being can be boosted. Marketing objectives comprise studying target markets, developing tailored products and services, and connecting with target consumers. Through health marketing activities, it is possible to overcome discrimination, stigma, and stereotypical mindset.

Since inclusive marketing is essential in healthcare, the World Wide Web Consortium has published resources for the accessibility of digital marketing platforms (W3C, 2023). As a result, marketers, web designers, and social media professionals can adopt the main principles of accessible digital marketing including seen and heard content, user-friendly navigation from different devices, and understandable content design.

3.2. ChatGPT for Healthcare Marketing

After technological developments comprising digital tools, social media, and Artificial Intelligence (AI), new applications such as ChatGPT are assessing now for healthcare. GPT - Generative Pretrained Transformer that can write like a person based on AI that creates a language model ChatGPT, which can be used in the healthcare system for improving patient care, planning, and evaluating treatment possibilities (Javaid et al., 2023). As a chatbot, it can answer questions, for which it must access to correct and current medical data and without which ChatGPT cannot provide reliable recommendations, existing treatment possibilities, or healthcare solutions (Javaid et al., 2023). Therefore, data should be updated consistently to ensure improved results in ChatGPT responses. Consumer privacy and data security plays also here an important role (Javaid et al., 2023; Mijwil et al., 2023).

In addition to physicians, also patients can use it to retrieve information about their disease or symptoms, support their health education, manage their chronic illnesses or pains, as well as schedule appointments according to their needs (Javaid et al., 2023). Furthermore, ChatGPT can analyze marketing data and segment consumers based on their behavior or needs and hence, ensuring a better experience through targeted marketing campaigns and by responding to questions on various online platforms (Javaid et al., 2023; Kung et al., 2023). A number of patients can be treated simultaneously and hence, improve health service and patient satisfaction as ChatGPT delivers information and gives answers on different subjects (Javaid et al., 2023). It generates text data from various sources rapidly (Alkaissi & McFarlane, 2023), and therefore, can be utilized for social media content. Figure 1 summarizes how ChatGPT can be used in healthcare focusing on its application for marketing.

Yet, ChatGPT lacks emotional support and tone of human responses, is less individualized, and is unable to react or understand users emotionally, which makes it less suitable for mental health services (Javaid et al., 2023).

Thus, digital marketing technologies must be carefully selected for effective healthcare marketing in order to, on the one hand, reach marketing objectives and, on the other hand, engage in ethical conduct.

Figure 1. ChatGPT in healthcare marketing
Source: Author's elaboration based on Javaid et al., 2023.

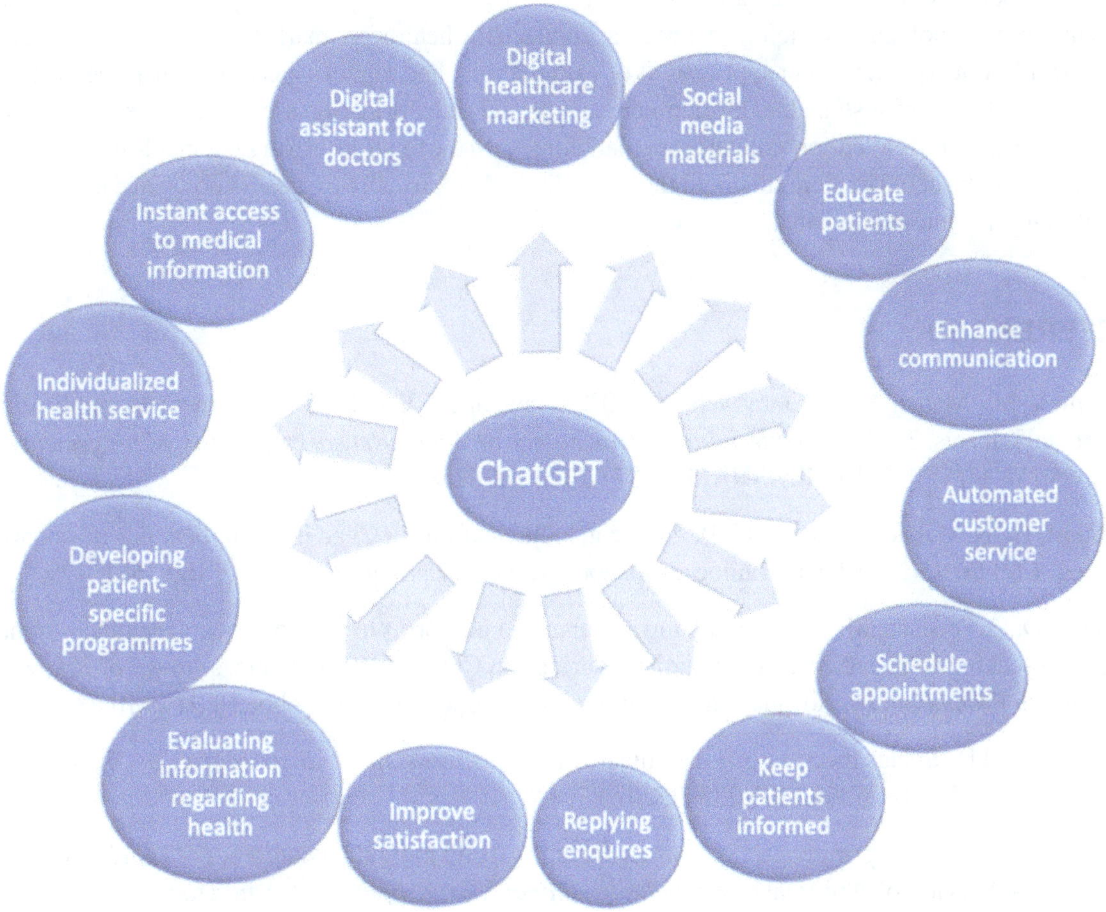

4. CONCLUSION

This chapter has been dedicated to the potential connection between healthcare marketing and sustainable development agenda with an emphasis on digitalization. The relationship between sustainability and healthcare marketing is becoming prevalent in the current digital age. Sustainable marketing is a comprehensive approach to healthcare marketing as it aims to maintain equilibrium in economic, social, and environmental performance while generating value for all stakeholders.

Marketing, especially in the healthcare sector needs to pay attention to privacy and other ethical issues when using digital technologies. Social media can be integrated into social marketing programmes in the healthcare industry to communicate with the target population and encourage their healthy behavior. Health promotion and communication marketing campaigns should be planned and implemented carefully taking into consideration risks of misinterpretation of disseminated information.

Eventually, AI cannot replace humans but can be used to serve humans in automated tasks. ChatGPT is beneficial for healthcare marketing by responding to questions, performing automate processes, and analyzing data leading to enhanced customer experience and ultimately increased sales. This groundbreaking innovation tends to boost AI capacities with a simple and convenient interface creating agreeable customer service expanding patient satisfaction.

Thus, digital tools and technological progress enhance the healthcare marketing domain for achieving better results effectively. Further applications of sustainability and digital aspects as well as the influence of emerging trends of sustainable development and digital transformation are yet to be explored. Since scholars devoted little attention to healthcare marketing with the relationship to sustainable development, further research should explore this field theoretically and empirically to create knowledge and provide insight into this interrelated area.

REFERENCES

Abdullah, M., Madain, A., & Jararweh, Y. (2022, November). ChatGPT: Fundamentals, applications and social impacts. *2022 Ninth International Conference on Social Networks Analysis, Management and Security (SNAMS)*, 1-8. 10.1109/SNAMS58071.2022.10062688

Alkaissi, H., & McFarlane, S. I. (2023). Artificial hallucinations in ChatGPT: Implications in scientific writing. *Cureus*, *15*(2). Advance online publication. doi:10.7759/cureus.35179 PMID:36811129

Alonzo, D., & Popescu, M. (2021). Utilizing social media platforms to promote mental health awareness and help seeking in underserved communities during the COVID-19 pandemic. *Journal of Education and Health Promotion*, *10*. Advance online publication. 1 doi:0.4103/jehp.jehp_21_21 PMID:34222531

Aras, R. (2011). Social marketing in healthcare. *The Australasian Medical Journal*, *4*(8), 418–424. doi:10.4066/AMJ.2011.626 PMID:23393528

Basińska-Zych, A., & Springer, A. (2021). Organizational and individual outcomes of health promotion strategies—A review of empirical research. *International Journal of Environmental Research and Public Health*, *18*(2), 383. doi:10.3390/ijerph18020383 PMID:33419033

Belz, F.-M., & Peattie, K. (2012). *Sustainability Marketing*. Wiley & Sons.

Berkowitz, E. N. (2021). *Essentials of Health Care Marketing* (5th ed.). Jones & Bartlett Learning.

Bocken, N. (2021). Sustainable Business Models. In W. Leal Filho, A. M. Azul, L. Brandli, A. Lange Salvia, & T. Wall (Eds.), *Decent Work and Economic Growth. Encyclopedia of the UN Sustainable Development Goals*. Springer. doi:10.1007/978-3-319-95867-5_48

Buchanan, L., Kelly, B., Yeatman, H., & Kariippanon, K. (2018). The effects of digital marketing of unhealthy commodities on young people: A systematic review. *Nutrients*, *10*(2), 148. doi:10.3390/nu10020148 PMID:29382140

Clar, C., Dyakova, M., Curtis, K., Dawson, C., Donnelly, P., Knifton, L., & Clarke, A. (2014). Just telling and selling: current limitations in the use of digital media in public health: a scoping review. *Public Health*, *128*(12), 1066–1075. doi:10.1016/j.puhe.2014.09.009 PMID:25443388

Da Silva, E. C., & Mazzon, J. A. (2016). Developing social marketing plan for health promotion. *International Journal of Public Administration*, *39*(8), 577–586. doi:10.1080/01900692.2015.1023447

Dahlstrom, R., & Crosno, J. L. (2022). Sustainable Marketing. Chicago Business Press.

De Veirman, M., Hudders, L., & Nelson, M. R. (2019). What is influencer marketing and how does it target children? A review and direction for future research. *Frontiers in Psychology, 10*, 2685. doi:10.3389/fpsyg.2019.02685 PMID:31849783

Donovan, R. J. (2011). The role for marketing in public health change programs. *Australian Review of Public Affairs, 10*(1), 23-40.

Dwivedi, Y. K., Ismagilova, E., Hughes, D. L., Carlson, J., Filieri, R., Jacobson, J., Jain, V., Karjaluoto, H., Kefi, H., Krishen, A. S., Kumar, V., Rahman, M. M., Raman, R., Rauschnabel, P. A., Rowley, J., Salo, J., Tran, G. A., & Wang, Y. (2021). Setting the future of digital and social media marketing research: Perspectives and research propositions. *International Journal of Information Management, 59*, 102168. doi:10.1016/j.ijinfomgt.2020.102168

Elkington, J. (1998). *Cannibals with Forks: The Triple-Bottom Line For 21st Century Business*. New Society Publishers.

Gigauri, I., Apostu, S. A., & Popescu, C. (2023). Digital Transformation: Threats and Opportunities for Social Entrepreneurship. In Two Faces of Digital Transformation: Technological Opportunities versus Social Threats (pp. 1-17). Emerald Publishing Limited.

Gigauri, I., & Djakeli, K. (2021). Expecting Transformation of Marketing During the Post-Pandemic New Normal: Qualitative Research of Marketing Managers in Georgia. *International Journal of Sustainable Economies Management, 10*(2), 1–18. doi:10.4018/IJSEM.2021040101

Gigauri, I., Janjua, L. R., Panait, M., & Guillen, F. P. (2023). Exploring the Nexus Between Financial Inclusion, Poverty, Digitalization and Sustainable Development Goal. *LUMEN Proceedings, 19*, 63-81. 10.18662/lumproc/gekos2022/06

Gigauri, I., Palazzo, M., & Ferri, M. A. (Eds.). (2023). *Handbook of Research on Achieving Sustainable Development Goals With Sustainable Marketing*. IGI Global. doi:10.4018/978-1-6684-8681-8

Gil Guzman, J. M., Hernandez-Fernandez, A., & Canales-Ronda, P. (2021). Bringing social marketing closer to the disability field. *Journal of Social Marketing, 11*(4), 321–341. doi:10.1108/JSOCM-06-2020-0105

Günther, L., Schleberger, S., & Pischke, C. R. (2021). Effectiveness of social media-based interventions for the promotion of physical activity: Scoping review. *International Journal of Environmental Research and Public Health, 18*(24), 13018. doi:10.3390/ijerph182413018 PMID:34948628

Henley, N., Raffin, S., & Caemmerer, B. (2011). The application of marketing principles to a social marketing campaign. *Marketing Intelligence & Planning, 29*(7), 697–706. doi:10.1108/02634501111178712

Huntsman, J. L., & Bulaj, G. (2023). Health education via "empowerment" digital marketing of consumer products and services: Promoting therapeutic benefits of self-care for depression and chronic pain. *Frontiers in Public Health, 10*, 949518. Advance online publication. doi:10.3389/fpubh.2022.949518 PMID:36703812

Ibrahim, B., & Aljarah, A. (2018). Dataset of relationships among social media marketing activities, brand loyalty, revisit intention. Evidence from the hospitality industry in Northern Cyprus. *Data in Brief, 21*, 1823–1828. doi:10.1016/j.dib.2018.11.024 PMID:30519601

Javaid, M., Haleem, A., & Singh, R. P. (2023). ChatGPT for healthcare services: An emerging stage for an innovative perspective. *BenchCouncil Transactions on Benchmarks, Standards and Evaluations*, *3*(1), 100105. doi:10.1016/j.tbench.2023.100105

Kemper, J. A., & Ballantine, P. W. (2019). What do we mean by sustainability marketing? *Journal of Marketing Management*, *35*(3), 277–309. doi:10.1080/0267257X.2019.1573845

Kung, T. H., Cheatham, M., Medenilla, A., Sillos, C., De Leon, L., Elepaño, C., Madriaga, M., Aggabao, R., Diaz-Candido, G., Maningo, J., & Tseng, V. (2023). Performance of ChatGPT on USMLE: Potential for AI-assisted medical education using large language models. *PLOS Digital Health*, *2*(2), e0000198. doi:10.1371/journal.pdig.0000198 PMID:36812645

Lloveras, J., Marshall, A. P., Vandeventer, J. S., & Pansera, M. (2022). Sustainability marketing beyond sustainable development: Towards a degrowth agenda. *Journal of Marketing Management*, *38*(17), 2055–2077. doi:10.1080/0267257X.2022.2084443

Marchioli, A. (2006). Marketing social et efficacité des campagnes de prévention de santé publique: Apports et implications des récents modèles de la communication persuasive. *Market Management*, *6*(1), 17–36. doi:10.3917/mama.031.0017

Martin, D., & Schouten, J. (2014). *Sustainable marketing*. Pearson.

Martín-Cervantes, P. A., del Carmen Valls Martínez, M., & Gigauri, I. (2022). Sustainable Marketing. In *Encyclopedia of Creativity, Invention, Innovation and Entrepreneurship* (pp. 1–8). Springer. doi:10.1007/978-1-4614-6616-1_200101-1

Mijwil, M., Aljanabi, M., & Ali, A. H. (2023). ChatGPT: Exploring the Role of Cybersecurity in the Protection of Medical Information. *Mesopotamian Journal of CyberSecurity*, *18–21*, 18–21. Advance online publication. doi:10.58496/MJCS/2023/004

Mondal, T., Mugaloremutt Jayadeva, S., Pani, R., Subramanian, M., P, A., & Sumana, B. (2022). E marketing strategy in health care using IoT and Machine Learning. *Materials Today: Proceedings*, *56*, 2087–2091. doi:10.1016/j.matpr.2021.11.417

Moro Visconti, R., & Morea, D. (2019). Big Data for the Sustainability of Healthcare Project Financing. *Sustainability (Basel)*, *11*(13), 3748. doi:10.3390u11133748

Morris, Z. S., & Clarkson, P. J. (2009). Does social marketing provide a framework for changing healthcare practice? *Health Policy (Amsterdam)*, *91*(2), 135–141. doi:10.1016/j.healthpol.2008.11.009 PMID:19147249

Murphy, G., Corcoran, C., Tatlow-Golden, M., Boyland, E., & Rooney, B. (2020). See, Like, Share, Remember: Adolescents' Responses to Unhealthy-, Healthy- and Non-Food Advertising in Social Media. *International Journal of Environmental Research and Public Health*, *17*(7), 2181. doi:10.3390/ijerph17072181 PMID:32218252

O'Reilly, M., Dogra, N., Hughes, J., Reilly, P., George, R., & Whiteman, N. (2019). Potential of social media in promoting mental health in adolescents. *Health Promotion International*, *34*(5), 981–991. doi:10.1093/heapro/day056 PMID:30060043

Pelet, J., Belda, S., & Arezki, D. (2023). Use of AI in Predicting Trends in Vegetation Dynamics in Africa. In J. Wang (Ed.), *Encyclopedia of Data Science and Machine Learning* (pp. 31–56). IGI Global. doi:10.4018/978-1-7998-9220-5.ch003

Pelet, J., & Ettis, S. A. (2022). Social Media Advertising Effectiveness: The Role of Perceived Originality, Liking, Credibility, Irritation, Intrusiveness, and Ad Destination. *International Journal of Technology and Human Interaction*, *18*(1), 1–20. doi:10.4018/IJTHI.2022010106

Pham, C. T., Phung, D., Nguyen, T. V., & Chu, C. (2020). The effectiveness of workplace health promotion in low-and middle-income countries. *Health Promotion International*, *35*(5), 1220–1229. doi:10.1093/heapro/daz091 PMID:31495871

Popa, A. L., Ţarcă, N. N., Sasu, D. V., Bodog, S. A., Roşca, R. D., & Tarcza, T. M. (2022). Exploring Marketing Insights for Healthcare: Trends and Perspectives Based on Literature Investigation. *Sustainability (Basel)*, *14*(17), 10499. doi:10.3390u141710499

Popescu, C., El-Chaarani, H., El-Abiad, Z., & Gigauri, I. (2022). Implementation of Health Information Systems to Improve Patient Identification. *International Journal of Environmental Research and Public Health*, *19*(22), 15236. doi:10.3390/ijerph192215236 PMID:36429954

Rogers, M. A., Lemmen, K., Kramer, R., Mann, J., & Chopra, V. (2017). Internet-delivered health interventions that work: Systematic review of meta-analyses and evaluation of website availability. *Journal of Medical Internet Research*, *19*(3), e90. doi:10.2196/jmir.7111 PMID:28341617

Shawky, S., Kubacki, K., Dietrich, T., & Weaven, S. (2019). Using social media to create engagement: A social marketing review. *Journal of Social Marketing*, *9*(2), 204–224. doi:10.1108/JSOCM-05-2018-0046

Syed, M., Ahmed, F., Zahid, N., Khalid, N., & Israr, N. (2021). Essentials of Healthcare Marketing. *Asian Journal of Medicine and Health*, *19*(2), 73–79. doi:10.9734/ajmah/2021/v19i230306

UN. (n.d.). *Sustainable Development Goals*. United Nations. Retrieved July 9, 2023 from https://www.un.org/sustainabledevelopment/

Veseli-Kurtishi, T. (2018). Social media as a tool for the sustainability of small and medium businesses in Macedonia. *European Journal of Sustainable Development*, *7*(4), 262–262. doi:10.14207/ejsd.2018.v7n4p262

W3C. (2023). *Accessibility Fundamentals*. World Wide Web Consortium. Retrieved 5 July 2023 from https://www.w3.org/WAI/fundamentals/

WCED. (1987). Our common future (The Brundtland Report). World Commission on Environment and Development, Oxford University Press.

Weinreich, N. K. (2010). *Hands-on social marketing: a step-by-step guide to designing change for good.* Sage Publications.

WHO. (n.d.). *Health Promotion*. World Health Organization. Retrieved July 3, 2023 from https://www.who.int/westernpacific/about/how-we-work/programmes/health-promotion

Chapter 7
Artificial Intelligence in Medical and Healthcare Service:
Applications and Challenges

V. Sangeetha
Ramaiah Institute of Technology, India

A. Mamatha
Ramaiah Institute of Technology, India

M. Vaneeta
Ramaiah Institute of Technology, India

K. Beena
K.S. Institute of Technology, India

ABSTRACT

Artificial intelligence (AI) technologies have made enormous strides recently and are already pervasive in many aspects of our daily life. Numerous efforts are being undertaken in the healthcare industry to apply AI technology for useful medical treatments. With the quick advancements in hardware performance and machine learning algorithms, it is anticipated that AI technology would be crucial in efficiently processing and utilizing vast amounts of health and medical data. However, the AI technology differs from the current medical technology in a number of distinctive ways. There are still few medical professionals and members of the general public that accept AI in healthcare, and there are several challenges about the security and dependability of AI technology applications. This chapter describes the state of current AI research and application in the healthcare industry and identifies the various challenges that need to be addressed and suggest how to resolve them.

INTRODUCTION

When artificial intelligence (AI) first emerged in the United States in 1956, its main purpose is a task of self-learning algorithm created by studying the data that was already available. Following years of

DOI: 10.4018/979-8-3693-0679-6.ch007

development, AI has made tremendous development in applications such as medical image processing, medical process optimization, medical education, and other domains. It has gradually become a component of standard medical care (Jiang, 2021). Since AI technology has developed so quickly, a variety of problems have arisen, making it less common in clinical and public health settings. Artificial intelligence technology has advanced significantly recently and is now present in many facets of our daily lives.

The health care sector is making several attempts to integrate Artificial Intelligence technology to treatment patient. There are some notable ways in which AI technology is different from contemporary medical technologies. There are a few gaps in the current system that must be filled in order for AI to be employed in healthcare more regularly and successfully.

Future advancements in healthcare technology are anticipated to result from ongoing improvements in artificial intelligence technologies. As a result, lot of research work is done and researchers already published a significant number of research papers with enormous volumes of health related data by applying various technologies for patient diagnosis and treatment.

Furthermore, most of the researchers demonstrated using Artificial Intelligence in the healthcare industry produces superior results to those obtained using current technologies. Encrypting medical data, forecasting patient history of a disease using multiple sources, and analyzing medical photos with Artificial Intelligence technology to categorize images and apply for therapies are some of the studies being conducted in this area.

In this chapter, we outline the present barriers preventing AI from becoming widely accepted as well as the current use of Artificial Intelligence in medicine (Park, 2020). Chapter first section describes the state of current AI research and application in the healthcare industry and analyzes the problems that require fixing. We also discuss about potential approaches to tackling issues.

CURRENT STATE OF AI IN HEALTHCARE

This section describes the related articles published in a crisp manner.

AI Applications in the Healthcare Industry

These days artificial technology is making new advances since it affects additional psychological areas, including judgment, intelligence and knowledge. World Health Organization (Ziglio, 2004) states that 60% of aspects relating to one's health and quality of life are related to one's habits, including exercise, maintaining a healthy diet, reclining, reducing anxiety, using antidepressants, and socializing.

Automation technology with AI is now able to offer lifestyle modifications including daily affirmations based on the psychological signs of the individuals. Artificial Intelligence based methods are anticipated to radically alter the functioning of medical systems, patient interactions and patient care services in order to enhance the patient outcomes. Along with deep learning technology, Machine learning algorithm's capacity for pattern recognition has increased significantly, and for some tasks, AI technology's capacity for deciphering information patterns has surpassed that of a typical human aptitude.

Artificial Intelligence is being employed in diagnostic imaging and with chronic diseases to create precise and useful products that will help treat the sufferers with illnesses and discover treatment at the earliest stage. The former technology has significant advantages over traditional approaches to healthcare decision-making and analytics. AI algorithms understand training data as they process it, improving system accuracy. Humans are now able to gain insights on treatment variability, care procedures, diagnostics, and patient care that were previously impossible.

Forecasts from Acumen conclude the study that by 2026, the worldwide economy for AI in the healthcare sector will be worth US$8 billion.

Let's now examine some of artificial intelligence's current applications in the medical industry.

Accurate Identification of Cancer

Clinicians can make accurate diagnoses with Path AI. As shown in the Figure 1, PathAI which lowers errors in the cancer diagnostic process and provides a variety of newer methods for customized medical care. Numerous lives may be saved if cancer patients were diagnosed more accurately so that the majority of them could be treated or cured before it becomes fatal.

Robot-Assisted Surgery

Robot - assisted surgery has become immensely popular. Robotic technology is being used by certain health facilities helping them to complete activities that call for precision, supervision and versatility. It is used for tasks like cardiac surgery that are beyond the capabilities of humans.

The knowledge, skills, and experience of the surgeons are improved by the use of surgical robots that are furnished with robotic arms, camera, and other necessary tools. Facilitating doctors to control the robot's arms from a computer display while the robot provides a magnified, three-dimensional vision of the surgical site which is impossible through visual inspection as depicted in Figure 2. Artificial intelligence-assisted surgery with robots result in fewer complications, comparatively reduced pain for the patients, and shorter recovery times (Lee, 2020).

The extreme precision, controllability, and flexibility of robotic surgery make it the favored method for surgeons. Doctors can deal with incredibly complex or previously impossible treatments with robotic surgery. During surgery, real-time data coupled with medical records enables specialists to see more patient's information instantly. By doing this, they can benefit from AI systems that have successfully utilized data from comparable procedures with success. (Safari, 2019).

Virtual Nursing Assistants

In the patient rooms of Cedars-Sinai Hospital in Los Angeles, California, Amazon's Alexa robots act as virtual nurse aides (Johnson, 2017). Alexa assists patients with their daily tasks by performing the tedious

Figure 1. AI for pathologists

Figure 2. Robot-assisted surgery

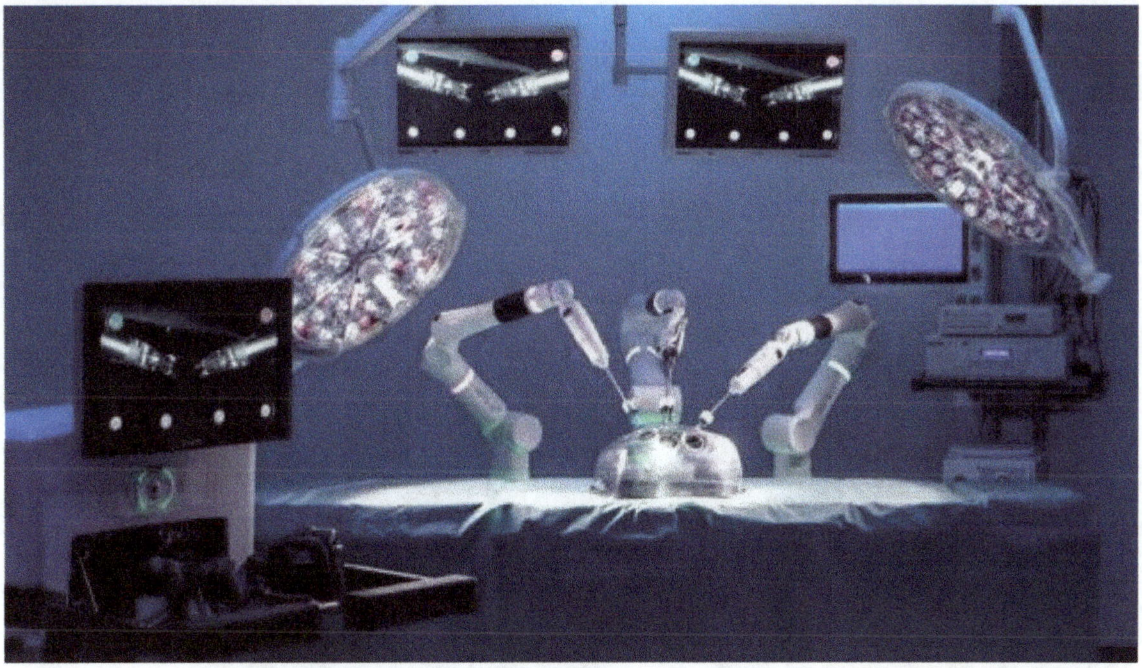

tasks assigned to nurses; other patients will take their medicines and become busy with appointments, and also offer medical advice as shown in the Figure 3.

The robot helps the doctors and nurses with their sessions of patient visits and provides a list of hospitalized patients who need to be addressed and managed by the medical staff (*Uzialko et al, 2020)*. The robot can recognize voices, accompany medical staff to the ward, and translate speech to text to quickly transcribe electronic medical information.

Care for Rare Diseases

A diagnostic and therapeutic AI-based biomedical platform called BERG aims to map illnesses to speed up the discovery and development of cutting-edge breakthrough medicines and vaccines, transforming the way healthcare is delivered. Due to exploratory biology, medical professionals can create durable products for patients with rare illnesses.

Additionally, BERG has emphasised their progress in Parkinson's illness. This neurological disorder causes tightness, shakes, and impairments with movement, balance, and other everyday routines. Parkinson's disease is one of the worst diseases since its signs and symptoms develop gradually and get worse with time. BERG connects previously unconnected chemical relationships in the human body using artificial intelligence.

Automation of Redundant Healthcare Tasks

Administrators can then use their leisure time to work on other crucial and imperative jobs. Olive is a Intelligence platform that automatically perform a variety of tasks, such as detecting the eligibility of

Figure 3. Virtual nursing assistants

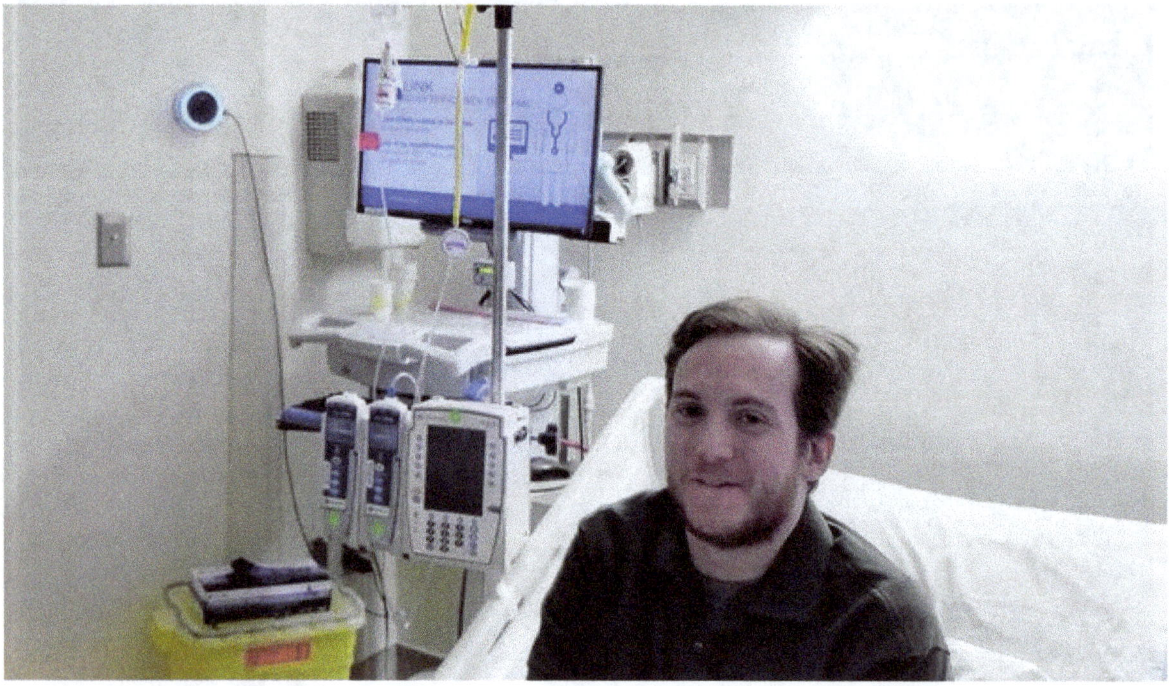

adjudicated medical claims and transmitting the necessary medical data to the right medical professionals. Olive simply interacts with a hospital's existing equipment and software, eliminating the need for pricey downtimes and integrations.

Analysis of Medical Image

Medical disciplines that use images, such as gastrointestinal, ophthalmology, pathology, dermatology and cardiology, use various machine learning algorithms in medical image analysis and significantly increases radiology process. Machine learning methods especially use positron emission tomography (CT), electromagnetic resonance imaging (MRI), ultrasonography, pathological imaging, fundus image, and endoscope data to identify or categories the severity of the disease.

For the benefit of chest CT diagnosis, Siemens Health engineers have created AI-based AI-Rad Companion Chest CT software (Fischer et al, 2020). GE Healthcare is also developing Artificial intelligence technology based medical image analysis.

OPPORTUNITIES INVOLVED IN AI APPLICATIONS IN HEALTHCARE

The current expectation from the market is to construct systems aligned to specific field using machine learning algorithm with training instances that incorporate details of patients in order to improve the AI system diagnosis accuracy. The greater the volume of learning examples, AI systems will become more intelligent. AI medical system offers several novel opportunities to diagnose ailments, offer good care and a righteous patient experience, motivate patients to take part in their own health care routine, decreases medical fallacy and healthcare expenditure, and increases managerial effectiveness by healthcare providers.

But the other perspective of AI brings a lot of new issues. Patient details used for analysis brings in negative impact on job security (Philips, 2018), mistake accountability and confidentiality and safety threats in cyber space (Coventry, 2018). To make sure wise use of AI and successful endorsement in the medical sector, it is very important to traverse major pros and cons involved with AI based applications.

The usage of AI technology in medicine has given rise to a broad spectrum of opportunities. Below are few critical ones discussed.

Better Patient Participation and Interaction

The extensively used fitness training application for smartphones, Noom, is a software diet application program on mobile phones that perform as portable diabetes preventive programme. The objective of this coaching software is to have persistent devotion to the action plan.

Meticulous disease diagnosis and patient safety is dependent on patient involvement in medical treatment process. Patient involvement and participation should be main goal for healthcare professionals in order to enhance service quality while also making the patient experience better.

Most of the patients are not well known about the usage of AI health care systems, more number of participants can be expected, if they are made aware about the strength for faster and correct diagnosis, medical costs reduction while attending the physician. Healthcare systems should establish methods to notify, teach patients and their clan about the gains and hazards of the AI-integrated medical systems (Reardon, 2019). Patients who are cognizant will use AI integrated medical systems universally.

Enhanced Medical Care

The release of IBM Watson made a critical decision-making point in the information-controlled stream of medical investigations and attracted common people in usage of leading-edge technology to enhance patient wellbeing. Dawes et al. (2017) summarized magnetic resonance imaging (MRI) method of circulatory motion supported by Artificial Intelligence algorithm should be employed to diagnose patients suffering from hypertension and lung disorder. Technologies based on AI plays a predominant role are in upgrading health care professionals practically in all facets of patient treatment and increasing the health care services in developing nations.

The task can be completed in short duration with increased accuracy and by AI software. The continuous usage of AI systems helps substantially to supplement medical personnel job, where the system alerts the personnel when blunders are encountered in the treatment process. Systems are capable of intimating minor areas that humans typically skip and help to decrease medical blunders during diagnosis of the patient. With increased collection of data and medical research makes AI medical software smarter.

Better Service Delivery and Medical Error Reduction

An AI medical system can detect early-stage polyps that most of the gastroenterologists leave out when analyzing colonoscopy examinations. Therefore, AI system helps physicians in discovering tiny polyps providing better patient care and decreasing the medical error.

A group of researchers at University of Tokyo Medical School built an Artificial Intelligence system based on optimal algorithms and many other parameters. The usage of novel algorithms resulted in leading accuracy rate when combined with deep-learning approach was 83.5% for the sample group of patients (Sato et al., 2019).

Radiologists are most frequently named medical professionals who are expected to be substituted by AI (Pesapane et al., 2018). AI system's performance exceeded radiologists accuracy, therefore, AI system are good replacements for radiologists. As a result, doctors have time saved which can be used for peaceful conversations with patients which will standardize the treatment.

Enhanced Operational Effectiveness and Lower Medical Costs

Several diagnostic process can be taken care by AI-support systems without the interference of humans. Acute leukaemia can be discovered by latest AI algorithm eliminates cost consuming procedures of analyzing characteristics of the bone marrow structure. The health care treatment procedure with use of AI is cost effective and quicker.

AI solutions are not only used in medical field, but they also assist operational improvements. Maintenance systems, accounting, and information enquiry are examples of mundane tasks of AI systems, which be accomplished effectively than human. The effectiveness of operational mechanism can be elevated by AI-enabled chatbots and robots.

Enhanced Productivity and the Creation of New Jobs

Will robots and Artificial Intelligence eventually replace human work? The first through fourth industrial revolutions in history have seen the development of industrial expansion and the creation of new occupations even if many manual work were replaced by cutting-edge technologies.

For instance, the hard copy printing industry has come to an end, which created the scope for digital editing and typography.

An eye disease diagnosis using AI system for degeneration and diabetic edoema using transfer learning is another excellent illustration of the increased productivity increase. In just 30 seconds, an AI system can finish the diagnosis procedure, recognizing the disease and its stage of progression. Additionally, the diagnosis accuracy rate was over 95% when compared diagnosis of five professional ophthalmologists. These examples show how AI systems can increase productivity by lessening the error rates, shortening treatment and diagnosis times, and looking into ways to expand care offerings that weren't previously available.

Lower Medical Costs

The perfect healthcare system would offer the following: information and proof based illness prevention, best-available automation detection and therapy, patient centric, personal attention, and best quality care from compassionate medical staff. AI system ensures both quality and cost reductions when used to assist such a perfect healthcare. ABI Research, a research marketing company, published a paper claiming that by 2021, the US healthcare sector may save $52 billion as a result of clever applications of artificial intelligence (Lee,2021). Many health centers in US and Israel have implemented AI based illness prevention programmers, according to ABI Research.

In these two nations, it is anticipated that count of AI equipment's to avoid readful ailment (such as diabetes and high blood pressure) will ascent from 53,000 in 2017 to over 3.1 million by 2021, a 176% annual increase. AI applications have capacity to significantly lower medical expenditures for both individual patients and society. Such savings might be used nationally to improve everyone's quality of life through disease prevention.

APPLICATION OF AI IN HEALTHCARE: CHALLENGES

AI applications produces opportunities for enhancing people's day to day life, they also bring in complications that need to be managed successfully. The challenges in the healthcare sector are huge in number because human life is on stake. The below mentioned are few of the difficulties.

System Use Accountability

A human was killed on May 7, 2016, when a Tesla Model S autonomous vehicle malfunctioned. It was necessary to provide an answer to the question of "Who should bear responsibility for the accident?" If medical personnel employed an AI system and an incident or error happened, who is responsible? Human-developed machine learning algorithms are the foundation of how AI-based applications operate. Hospital administration will decide whether to purchase an AI system after considering input from the medical personnel, consultants, and experts in the field. The procured equipment must be used by medical professionals to cater patient needs. So, should the health center, medical professionals or manufactured organization have held responsible for the incident? With various discussion, deliberation with respect to technical and ethical concerns, it is very arduous to answer the question (Lupton, 2018) mentioned the importance of creation of moral and ethical behavioral traits of AI that benefit the society rather than causing harm to it. With increased usage of AI technologies, these systems must be fabricated with accomplishment adhering to social norms and values. Accountability for negative effects of AI system has to be truly grounded on social agreements.

The AI Divide

The fact of patient belief in medical professionals differentiates healthcare from other service industries. This belief can be proven by the placebo effect, which states medical effect happens when a patient blindly believes a doctor's medication will treat her illness. Therefore patient-professional trust is important because it enhances the patient care. The human individual will be part of care delivery process that build a bonding between AI system rather than real personage, if an AI system takes over the job of a medical professional.

Digital technology usage is going to be difficult to individual who has not used before and to trust AI completely. AI divide might be bridged, if doctor provides confidence to patient that AI system will ensure to provide better treatment.

Security and Confidentiality in Cyberspace

AI-based technologies and systems are built on large volume of datasets, this leads to privacy concerns regarding data collection. Medical records for patients contain personal information, making it challenging to transfer disease-related information between various platforms. Therefore, developer must align to the laws which are a major challenge for AI. The distinctive circumstance of patient is ignored because AI technology decision making is dependent on data gathered by machine learning algorithm which is of ethical, moral and legal concern. As a result, it is crucial to concentrate on the morals, regulations, and values that guide people's behaviour in society and which an AI system should uphold.

Managerial Control Loss

Health care industry in recent past was a place where patient illness is treated by doctor and nurses. Now, in addition of receiving treatment, healthy lifestyle gains a important role.AI system are capable of resolving time and space issues. The conventional method of closed health care system is not prevalent. Preventive medicine is of focus that lies between healthy lifestyle and technology assistance in medication. For instance, several smartphone-based apps can assist person's well-being. AI-based apps can remotely access, diagnose, treat, and monitor patients who are living at home.

Care providers are relying on the knowledge of consultants and specialists in healthcare. Therefore, offering individual attention to patients has emerged into team sport including various internal and external experts. As a result, the conventional governance system would be ineffective in hospitals. In the view of this process administrators may sense the loss of management control in hospitals (Lee, 2018).

The Suffering of Transition, Education Needs, and Loss of Employment

AI system will inspect medical pictures more correctly than humans. There is a talk that Radiography may become extinct. Adoption of AI system will result in unemployment and losing the current job.

In future, it is predicted that AI would focus on building stronger relationship between patient and professionals. The curriculum for the medical institute should be revised to include AI knowledge.AI systems are dependent on past dataset of patients (Lupton, 2018). Highly trained professional team is created to cater the patients instantly by adapting to cutting edge technologies.

AI'S SOCIAL AND SAFETY IMPLICATIONS FOR HEALTHCARE

Healthcare AI may present us with a number of unique difficulties. Additionally, non-IT personnel with little to no knowledge of AI can make the ultimate decisions about whether or not to integrate a technology. Increasing public knowledge, dispelling prevalent AI preconceptions, and developing persuasive communication skills with governments are all important to address this problem and convince them of the benefits of integrating the technology (Matheny, 2023).

The issue of information security and privacy presents another obstacle for AI in healthcare.

Since AI learns from data from past disease instances, steps must be taken to stop this data from getting into the hands of unauthorised parties. Additionally, a reliable defence against cyberattacks is required. Although this is a concern across all industries, it is especially important in healthcare because the sector directly impacts people's lives and cyberattacks have the potential to be lethal. Alarmists frequently cite as instances remote hacking of a cardio stimulator andpurposeful"retraining"ofadiagn osticandrecommendationsystemtoproposealethalmedication or operation. This could, in a worst-case scenario, result in mass slaughter.

Wearable technology must therefore be secured from outside threats. However, there are a number of issues that need to be addressed, including who determines what protection is dependable and who will be held accountable in the even to an occurrence (Habli, 2018).

We also need to consider how AI diagnostic systems will impact all of the people who are still working in medicine as specialists in terms of their jobs and personal life. There may be two positioning options (Herrle, 2018).

Therefore, AI serves as a helper, and the doctor is responsible for evaluating and applying the findings of its work. If we choose the second option, we must conduct study to determine how much a doctor can actually be replaced by sophisticated technology. Clearly, there is a concern with the quality of services that AI may offer and their dependability as doctors. There is also the issue of job loss. For instance, The Guardian reports that the Japanese company Fukoku Mutual Life Insurance, which specializes in health insurance, announced the termination of 34 employees in January2017.

Nevertheless, the layoff of 34 employees was justified by the fact that, from a technological standpoint, considerable work remains to be done in the areas of privacy and safety, legal obligations, and health insurance, ethical and psychological concerns. If we build on all of these ideas, AI will develop into a fantastic tool for preserving and improving human life on a daily basis.

AI IN INDIA HEALTHCARE SECTOR: ITS USAGE, BENEFIT AND LEVEL OF ACCEPTANCE BY PROFESSIONALS

By 2025, it is anticipated that India would spend $11.78 billion on AI. By 2035, it is projected to have increased India's economy by $1 trillion. The massive increase in investment, especially in AI, is taking place for a variety of reasons. Compared to the global average of 150 doctors per 100,000 people, India only has 64 doctors available for every 100,000 people. Primary healthcare facilities are underdeveloped in rural areas. Since more than 70% of the country's population lives in rural areas, there is a dearth of high-quality diagnostic services there. The impact of technology has been minimal, even in urban regions. Online medical consultations saw a significant increase during COVID-19, but the effect has not been as revolutionary as anticipated. (Selvaraj, 2023).

Result and Analysis

The Benefits of Using AI in the Indian Healthcare Sector

In India, AI grew by more than 109% in 2018, growing to a $665 million industry. By 2025, it is anticipated to reach $11.78 billion, which will boost India's economy by $1 trillion by 2035. According to estimates, the market for artificial intelligence in healthcare would grow at a CAGR of 37% from 2022 to 2030, from a 2021 value of US$ 11.06 billion to US$ 187.95 billion by 2030 as shown in Figure 4.

Figure 4. AI market for artificial intelligence

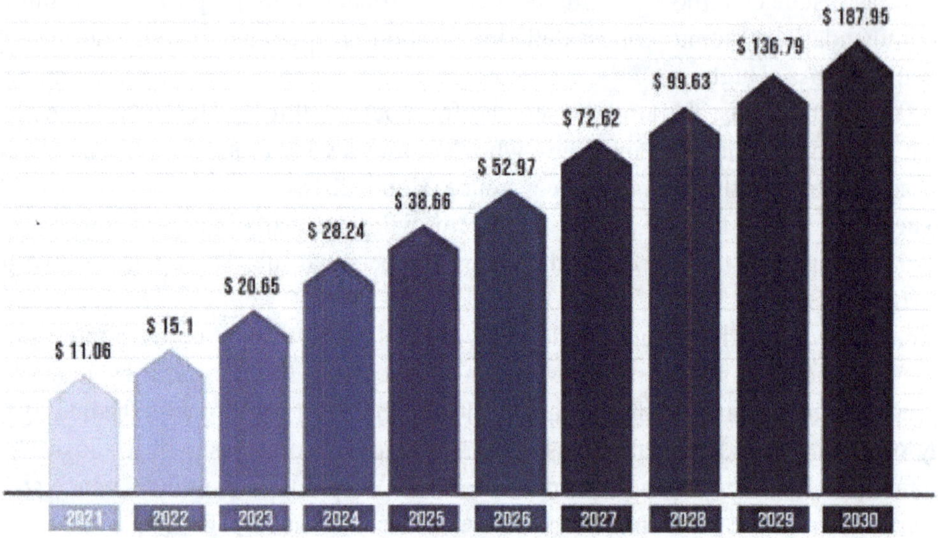

Leading Healthcare Organizations Using Artificial Intelligence in India

Artificial intelligence can't only be a curiosity for India, a nation with over 1.3 billion people and a dire need for medical professionals. India only produces50,000 doctors annually, which is well short of the required minimum. By 2030, India will require 2.3 million doctors in order to reach the WHO-recommended minimum doctor-patient ratio of 1: 100. Some of the leading AI organizations working in the healthcare sector from among the many that are active in the field. The funding received by these organizations and the research they have published are the two factors used to score them.

The organizations shown in Figure 5 are the best according to the criteria, according to research and investigations (Kang, 2023). There is a lot more progress being made in the field of AI, and since the pandemic Covid-19 expanded to India, many businesses, including hospitals like Apollo Hospital and Sawai Man Singh Hospital, are incorporating it into their operations. The potential for AI in India is enormous, making the struggle among different firms to retain or even improve their standing exceedingly difficult.

CONCLUSION AND FUTURE SCOPE

Innovation is much more necessary than ever in the dynamic digital age. The rapidly expanding technology is the primary tool for bringing real worth ideas into practice and connecting them together. Because of the cutting-edge nature of healthcare, the field is especially susceptible to the special application capabilities of AI. AI-based applications are changing not just how healthcare is provided in terms of the treatment and diagnosis processes, but also how patients lead their lives since their well-being demands the full spectrum of healthy living habits. We looked into the ways in which AI technology has permeated the healthcare sector with fresh potential and challenges it has brought. Effective management

Figure 5. Organizations in healthcare in India

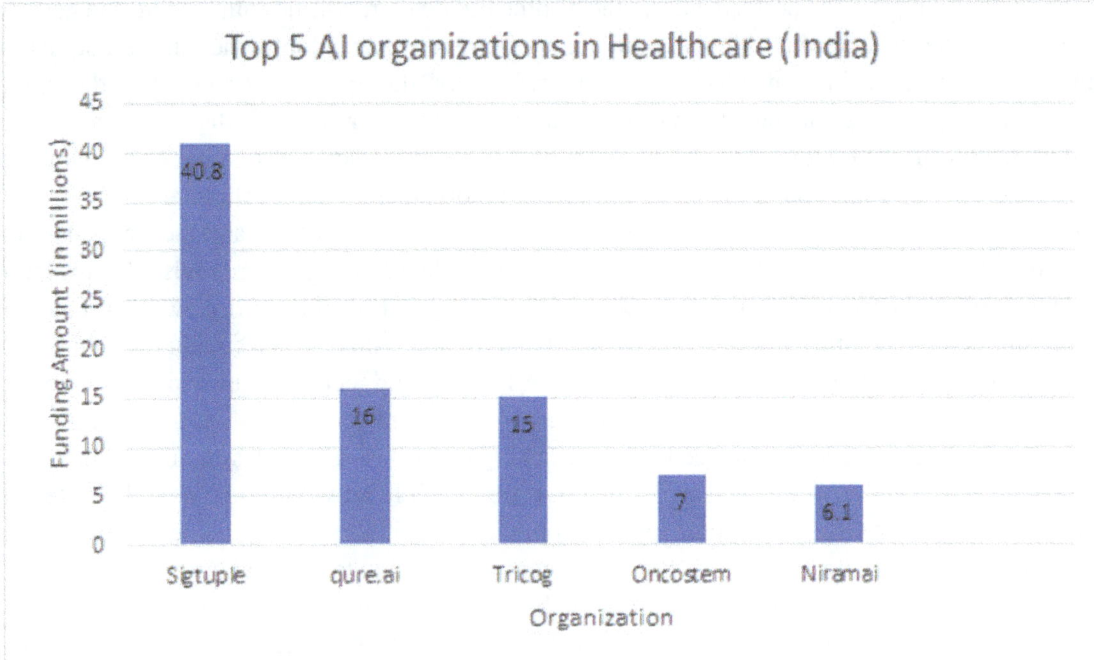

of these opportunities and challenges necessitates the joint knowledge and tenacity of all healthcare industry stakeholders.

Implications of AI Applications in Healthcare

With the medical staff's monopolistic power, health services is no longer delivered in a separate shell. A patient's health is influenced by a variety of factors, including a healthy diet, physical activity, managing physical and mental stress, preventive services, and the treatment of illness (Scherer, 2023). Nowadays, a lot of patients use web resources to conduct their own study into the circumstances affecting their health or ailments. The job of medical practitioners is regularly supported by AI as well as other digital tools. A complete view of the dynamic healthcare environment is needed in order to evaluate the trends of modern technological solutions, as well as the opportunities and issues that these changes bring to bear(Poly,2023).

Before adopting these systems, it is crucial to gather and evaluate records of many kinds (such as patient racial and ethnic traits), as the machine learning technique in AI-based systems necessitates a significant amount of information for an accurate diagnosis. AI has made considerable inroads into the medical sector, and this tendency is projected to accelerate in the future, despite the fact that there are both positive and negative difficulties related to its application and its many elements(Morris, 2023).

Thus, there is a goal to increase AI research, transparency, and pragmatic use in the healthcare industry. Here are a few tactics that, in our opinion, can be used to manage healthcare-related AI applications (Darwiesh, 2023).

Establishing legal regulations for data collection and management for AI applications is the first step in the strategy. To improve AI performance in the healthcare sector, real-time data sharing and gathering information are needed. Because "higher data quality increases users' confidence in the outputs they produce, minimizing risk in the results and boosting efficiency" data quality is crucial. Healthcare organizations should prioritise data quality improvement projects to ensure the reported values are genuine and reliable. Because symptoms vary based on human traits such racial and ethnic background, way of life, and economic condition of the patient's neighbourhood thereby the qualitative accumulation of precise and realistic data is essential. As a result, suitable data access criteria and mechanisms should be designed, taking into account the benefits and hazards of data sharing, to improvise the availability of top-notch information at the national level. Additionally, it is necessary to follow legal guidelines to safeguard the private information of every patient and to only utilize it collectively for public good.

Second, Key AI challenges including data exchange, liability, and secrecy require social agreement. It is important to encourage public participation in order to collect information as it is a vital resource for medical AI. Social agreement is also needed on the quality control of AI-based systems and liability for any potential misdiagnosis or medical errors that may occur while providing treatment. Despite widespread worries about the loss of personal information, there is still no social agreement on who should control the data and how it should be shared, and technology has led to medical mistakes.

Third, the collaboration of professionals in a number of pertinent domains is required for the application of AI-based systems for care services. The medical AI solution's success or failure will depend on how closely collaboration with medical field expertise, nursing staff, physicians, mental health workers, chemists, and patients from the development stage to study and assess the technologies being focused. Therefore, a collaborative environment must be created for the creation, application, and analysis phases of AI application.

Fourth, efforts should be made to make the best use of manpower in innovative value-creating sectors rather than concentrating primarily on the potential job-destroying impacts of AI systems. Automation will create new kinds of work, much as what happened during the Industrial Revolution, even though robots are performing some tasks that humans have previously undertaken. Healthcare businesses ought to seize the chance to reassign displaced workers to better-paying employment. For instance, the number of radiologists may decline if AI-based technologies are employed more frequently for diagnostics and processing medical images. Afterward, radiologists can transition into positions such as medical technicians, who are far more beneficial employees in hospitals. Because they can combine medical science with ICT. To provide a platform for exchanging and analyzing massive amounts of healthcare data, the government, ICT industry, and medical community should work together to do studies on medical informatics.

Limitations and Needs for Future Research

It is projected that the 5G network would accelerate the use of AI in the market for healthcare services in the foreseeable future. For instance, medical imaging equipment, including MRIs, generates files with a very big capacity. Advanced networks can raise the calibre and accessibility of medical services by enabling the quick and precise transport of high-capacity medical picture data. Patients can consult with specialists right away because the 5G network can be utilised for healthcare on networks without a LAN connection. In circumstances where the future is uncertain, quick action is the most efficient method to reduce damage. AI-based technology is removing time and space barriers and reinventing healthcare, wellbeing, and perhaps life itself by going beyond the boundaries of expert knowledge.

In this regard, it is anticipated that the scope of AI-based medical systems would eventually expand from pre-disease through treatment and post-care to daily living, even though they currently focus on patient-centered management of diseases. As a result, every part of our everyday lives and every aspect of healthcare are being impacted by AI-enabled technologies. It should therefore be used from a wide perspective that takes into account all facets of people's daily life.

REFERENCES

Coventry, L., & Branley, D. (2018). Cybersecurity in healthcare: A narrative review of trends, threats and ways forward. *Maturitas, 113*, 48–52. doi:10.1016/j.maturitas.2018.04.008 PMID:29903648

Darwiesh, A., El-Baz, A. H., Abualkishik, A. Z., & Elhoseny, M. (2023). Artificial Intelligence Model for Risk Management in Healthcare Institutions: Towards Sustainable Development. *Sustainability, 15*(1), 420.

Dawes, T. J., de Marvao, A., Shi, W., Fletcher, T., Watson, G. M., Wharton, J., Rhodes, C. J., Howard, L. S. G. E., Gibbs, J. S. R., Rueckert, D., Cook, S. A., Wilkins, M. R., & O'Regan, D. P. (2017). Machine learning of three-dimensional right ventricular motion enables outcome prediction in pulmonary hypertension: A cardiac MR imaging study. *Radiology, 283*(2), 381–390. doi:10.1148/radiol.2016161315 PMID:28092203

Habli, I., Lawton, T., & Porter, Z. (2020). Artificial intelligence in health care: Accountability and safety. *Bulletin of the World Health Organization, 98*(4), 251–256. doi:10.2471/BLT.19.237487 PMID:32284648

Herrle, J. (2018). Artificial Intelligence in Health Care. *CJO : Canadian Journal of Optometry = RCO : Revue Canadienne d'Optométrie, 80*(4), 67–68.

Jiang, L., Wu, Z., Xu, X., Zhan, Y., Jin, X., Wang, L., & Qiu, Y. (2021). Opportunities and challenges of artificial intelligence in the medical field: Current application, emerging problems, and problem-solving strategies. *The Journal of International Medical Research, 49*(3). doi:10.1177/03000605211000157 PMID:33771068

Johnson, S. G., Speedie, S., Simon, G., Kumar, V., & Westra, B. L. (2017). Quantifying the effect of data quality on the validity of an eMeasure. *Applied Clinical Informatics, 8*(04), 1012–1021. doi:10.4338/ACI-2017-03-RA-0042 PMID:29241241

Kang, E. Y. N., Chen, D. R., & Chen, Y. Y. (2023). Associations between literacy and attitudes toward artificial intelligence–assisted medical consultations: The mediating role of perceived distrust and efficiency of artificial intelligence. *Computers in Human Behavior, 139*, 107529. doi:10.1016/j.chb.2022.107529

Lee, D., & Yoon, S. N. (2021). Application of artificial intelligence-based technologies in the healthcare industry: Opportunities and challenges. *International Journal of Environmental Research and Public Health, 18*(1), 271. doi:10.3390/ijerph18010271 PMID:33401373

Lee, S. M., & Lee, D. (2020). Healthcare wearable devices: An analysis of key factors for continuous use intention. *Service Business*, *14*(4), 503–531. doi:10.100711628-020-00428-3

Lupton, M. (2018). Some ethical and legal consequences of the application of artificial intelligence in the field of medicine. *Trends Med*, *18*(4), 100147. doi:10.15761/TiM.1000147

Matheny, M., Israni, S. T., Ahmed, M., & Whicher, D. (2019). *Artificial intelligence in health care: The hope, the hype, the promise, the peril*. National Academy of Medicine. doi:10.17226/27111

Morris, M. X., Song, E. Y., Rajesh, A., Asaad, M., & Phillips, B. T. (2023). Ethical, Legal, and Financial Considerations of Artificial Intelligence in Surgery. *The American Surgeon*, *89*(1), 55–60. doi:10.1177/00031348221117042 PMID:35978473

Park, C. W., Seo, S. W., Kang, N., Ko, B., Choi, B. W., Park, C. M., Chang, D. K., Kim, H., Kim, H., Lee, H., Jang, J., Ye, J. C., Jeon, J. H., Seo, J. B., Kim, K. J., Jung, K.-H., Kim, N., Paek, S., Shin, S.-Y., ... Yoon, H. J. (2020). Artificial intelligence in health care: Current applications and issues. *Journal of Korean Medical Science*, *35*(42), e379. doi:10.3346/jkms.2020.35.e379 PMID:33140591

Pesapane, F., Codari, M., & Sardanelli, F. (2018). Artificial intelligence in medical imaging: Threat or opportunity? Radiologists again at the forefront of innovation in medicine. *European Radiology Experimental*, *2*(1), 1–10. doi:10.118641747-018-0061-6 PMID:30353365

Philips. (n.d.). *IntelliSpace discovery*. Updated 2020. Accessed August 19, 2020. https://www.usa.philips.com/healthcare/product/HC881015/intellispace-discovery

Poly, T. N., Islam, M. M., Walther, B. A., Lin, M. C., & Li, Y. C. J. (2023). Artificial Intelligence in Diabetic Retinopathy: Bibliometric Analysis. *Computer Methods and Programs in Biomedicine*, 107358. doi:10.1016/j.cmpb.2023.107358 PMID:36731310

Reardon, S. (2019). Rise of robot radiologists. *Nature*, *576*(7787), S54–S58. doi:10.1038/d41586-019-03847-z PMID:31853073

Sato, M., Morimoto, K., Kajihara, S., Tateishi, R., Shiina, S., Koike, K., & Yatomi, Y. (2019). Machine-learning approach for the development of a novel predictive model for the diagnosis of hepatocellular carcinoma. *Scientific Reports*, *9*(1), 7704. doi:10.103841598-019-44022-8 PMID:31147560

Scherer, L., Kuss, M., & Nahm, W. (2023). Review of Artificial Intelligence–Based Signal Processing in Dialysis: Challenges for Machine-Embedded and Complementary Applications. *Advances in Kidney Disease and Health*, *30*(1), 40–46. doi:10.1053/j.akdh.2022.11.002 PMID:36723281

Selvaraj, M. S., Rajaprakash, S., & Mariappan, R., & RajeshKumar, M. M. (2023). An Innovation Technique Of Artificial Intelligence Enabled Doctor Assistant In Field Of Health Care. *Journal of Pharmaceutical Negative Results*, 2352–2358.

Uzialko, A. 2019, June 9). Artificial Intelligence Will Change Healthcare as We Know it. Business News Daily.

Ziglio, E., Currie, C., & Rasmussen, V. B. (2004). The WHO cross-national study of health behavior in school aged children from 35 countries: Findings from 2001–2002. *The Journal of School Health*, *74*(6), 204–206. doi:10.1111/j.1746-1561.2004.tb07933.x PMID:15468523

Chapter 8
The Relevance of Literacy in Digital Health for Success of Healthcare and Its Marketing:
Navigating Towards Digital Health Literacy

Mario Sierra Martin
Universidad de Málaga, Spain

Pilar Alarcón Urbistondo
Universidad de Málaga, Spain

ABSTRACT

This chapter represents a significant effort to understand and present a comprehensive overview of telemedicine and digital literacy in the context of healthcare in contemporary society. To achieve this, a thorough review of the most relevant and current studies conducted in the last five years has been carried out. One of the crucial aspects addressed in this chapter is the identification of barriers that hinder the adoption of telemedicine. Additionally, it examines the drivers that promote the adoption of telemedicine. These may include convenience, time and money savings, accessibility to quality healthcare services, and the ability to continuously monitor medical conditions from the comfort of one's home.

1. INTRODUCTION

Digital health is seen as a new possibility to interact with the Health System; it has actually entirely changed the way we communicate with practitioners and handle medical consultations. Internet related topics have been addressed many times by researchers and so have social network issues; their impact on the health sector is of interest for the community because of the drastic changes they represent.

DOI: 10.4018/979-8-3693-0679-6.ch008

Digitalization has invaded all sectors, and healthcare is no exception to that.

For over a decade now, the use of new technologies has emerged into societal manners; these play an increasingly important role and have a deep impact on society itself (Paramio-Pérez et al., 2015). Today, both patients and professionals have changed the way they behave to handle health matters. The health sector is experiencing changes to apprehend, for example, a medical consultation, or some intercommunication between practitioner and patient, or even the tools used to search any kind of health information on the Internet.

In this context, easy access to the internet and, constant information updates are responsible for patients to use this tool as their main source on health matters (Serhrouchni & Malmartel, 2021). This new trend and, the collapse of health systems observed today in many countries, is promoting both the Internet and social networks as the main advertising sources, when trying to get answers on possible health doubts or issues (Serhrouchni & Malmartel, 2021).

This tendency intensified during the COVID-19 pandemic, when the health sector started to make a more intense use of technologies to provide medical information, while respecting social distancing; the health sector had been quite suspicious towards its digitalization needs until then with doctors and patients feeling quite reluctant to attend virtual consultations.

The convergence and integration of Internet and related technologies into the health sector shows in new concepts like the "E-Health" or the "Telemedicine". Today, about 39% of the global audience is making use of telemedicine. These technological advances progress every day by leaps and bounds. There is, however, a digital divide which means that with technology advances, digital health literacy becomes an issue for health equity (Zamora & Clingerman, 2011). It is true that digital health is evolving significantly and provides benefits for all, most particularly in the way certain medical care challenges are addressed; it provides new opportunities to improve patient diagnosis.

Today, we can differentiate seven main large blocks inside the digital health sector:

1. Telemedicine: With the use of ICT tools, medical consultations are carried out remotely.
2. Automation of processes and services: This is contributing to take more efficient and effective decisions, thanks to the existence of automatic controls, continuous updates and improvements that reduce the margin of error in diagnosis.
3. mHealth: These are all kinds of mobile applications used to facilitate the access of patients and practitioners to records, guidelines, or to more secure control means.
4. Wearables: These are electronic devices used to monitor different indicators on individual health like: smart watches, bracelets...
5. Virtual Reality: Patients have access to surgical simulations to reduce their insecurity levels; they get the most precise and updated information with a touch of realism.
6. Augmented Reality: This is used mainly by health professionals, to enrich virtual reality representations with added elements that would remain otherwise hidden. Both the rehabilitation process and remote operations can be improved with this technique.
7. Big Data and Artificial Intelligence: The access to large amounts of real-time and updated information opens new horizons for health researchers. These tools present -altogether or separately- a wide potential to advance and improve in digital health.

Professionals need to carry on improving the level of technological literacy within society and provide new ways to make these tools more available.

According to Paramio et al. (2015), digital health literacy is "the ability to search, find, understand and evaluate, health information derived from electronic sources, and apply the knowledge acquired to address or solve a health problem".

Medical professionals must consider the digital health literacy of their consumers. Developing telemedicine also means practitioners must have sufficient digital knowledge. An assessment of the current digital literacy situation in health and the detection of improvement interventions can ease communication between medical professionals and patients (Baker et al., 2007; DeWalt, Dilling, Rosenthal, & Pignone, 2007; Schillinger, 2002; Yin et al., 2007).

Today, more than ever, there is a wide range of opportunities available to transform the health sector and involve the two fundamental acting parts: doctors and patients. However, the digital divide cannot be radically addressed. This is why it is important to differentiate the two types of literacies entailed: digital literacy and digital health literacy.

2. THE DIGITAL TRANSFORMATION OF HEALTHCARE: LITERACY AND TELEMEDICINE IN TODAY'S SOCIETY

2.1 Digital Literacy

Technology is not inherent to the human being. On the contrary, technology is a transformation process that is to be learned progressively. The great challenge for technology within society is for users to become fully autonomous to then make the most of it. Our modern world has seen Information and Communication Technologies (ICT) rapidly address all layers of society and, transform the way we communicate or share information. Internet is now one of the most popular daily activities for a large part of the population worldwide; its importance is increasingly evident and so are the progressive changes experienced in different sectors.

Currently, the term ICT is defined as the use of digital technologies to improve information and communication in real time (Sarkar, 2012). ICT plays an important role in the daily life of users; it improves their quality of life and has become an indispensable part of society.

All these facts lead to a key question before ICTs can carry on its advances and developments into the community: Is society really prepared to face such rapid digital advances? The use of digital technologies requires of some specific skills and competencies to perform tasks, adapt, and solve problems within digital environments (Fu, 2013; Sarkar, 2012; Martin & Grudziecki, 2006).

The twenty-first century society is multimodal, which means that all contents generated -either educational or informative- are expressed, produced, and distributed using different supports (paper, screens) to do so, different technologies are used (computers, mobiles, internet networks ...) (Salcedo Aparicio et al, 2022). All this is creating a revolution and, for over a decade now, the need to incorporate new means to help develop a good digital literacy is felt as a necessity.

Although these technologies offer different possibilities to improve users 'quality of life, there needs to be an increasing commitment between all organizations to develop good digital literacy. These skills are essential to adapt and reduce the existing digital divide that is present in a large part of our global society.

The 'digital literacy' term was first employed by Paul Glister, in 1997, in his "Digital Literacy" volume. He used elements of the critical literacy by Len Masterman and defined the concept as the 'the ability to understand and use information in multiple formats from a wide range of sources when it is presented via computers". Glister's proposal is based on several skills used to face digitization on the Internet:

- Ability for the user to generate value judgments through all the information provided by the internet.
- Ability to obtain and evaluate their own opinion, avoiding bias.
- Creation of a 'personal information strategy' based on the different sources of information and mechanisms.
- Caution to judge the veracity of the information obtained through internet links.

As technologies advances are produced, the concept of digital literacy is expanding; according to Fu (2013), we can consider digital literacy as a set of skills that is necessary to become competent. It is focused mainly on getting skills for the use of information and communication. To achieve a high level of digital literacy, twenty-first century persons need to get the same starting opportunities, which is, an access to digital tools and to the digital world. Non digitally literate users will therefore confront more limitations when trying to progress, than the literate ones (Burnett et al., 2014). Progression towards digitization has started -to a greater or lesser extent-, with digitization set as a final goal.

The digital revolution, in which we are already immersed, has made the concept of digital literacy very popular in our society and has aroused the interest of researchers; some of them asking for its inclusion in different educational, political or health… programs (Reddy et al., 2020; Ata & Tilirim, 2019; Kumar et al., 2019; Nand & Sharma, 2019).

In short, all people now feel the need to be digitally qualified to face work, service or professional challenges provided by digital communication environments. The digital divide can not only be produced by the lack of equipment and supports that prevent any action in digital environments. It can also be produced by the insufficient capacity to manage the information and communication presented online. A consensus on the subject is that literacy is a very complex process today due to the exponential growth of these digital environments. We present here three types of literacy levels, classified from the most basic to the most complex. Learning how to use technology and then put it into practice or be able to get the most out of it has become a necessity.

-Learning to make use: The user is learning how to employ technological devices and handle the digital tools available. The user acquires practical skills to continue advancing towards good digital literacy. In this way, the user will experience a greater benefit by making use of 100% of the capabilities that these technologies offer.

-Understanding of use: Once the basic knowledge of these tools is acquired, users need to identify and assess how these tools can affect their lives and facilitate that of others. So that they become part of the patient's daily routine.

-Creation of digital contents: Finally, digital literacy should be a hand towards being connected, improve communication, share experiences or, in our case, share diagnoses or medical results -a helping tool for us and for others.

Getting to know the different levels of literacy is important to advance in a more technological society. Limiting oneself to a purely practical purpose is not sufficient, it is also important to understand how technology can improve our quality of life and provide more practical digital solutions in health environments. Currently, the main growth barrier for these digital healthcare tools is the low literacy among a significant portion of society regarding the use and adoption of these tools.

2.2 Telemedicine

When technology was gaining momentum during the last decades, new tools and new digital solutions were created and progressively incorporated into our lives. Technological progress has emerged into all sectors. The health sector, though later than others, is also being drastically altered by the incursion of technologies (Matarín, TM., 2015), this is mainly due to the benefits provided by the use of these technologies (Ekow Arkorful, V. et al.; 2019). As a result, the tendency has boosted and improved health sector outcomes (Chang et al., 2004; Cline & Haynes, 2001; Kreps, 2006; Lorence, Park, & Fox, 2006; Neuhauser & Kreps, 2003; Rippen & Yasnoff, 2004). The health sector has not been able yet, to adapt quickly and develop improvement actions on productivity and patient satisfaction.

The digital evolution in this sector has had a significant impact on the transformation and improvement on the provision of services. Digital transformation should therefore be in constant evolution to present novel products for both patients and physicians to help them provide the most accurate diagnosis, supported by technological progress (Belliger, A., & Krieger, D.J., 2018).

Some research findings evidence the positive impacts of telemedicine, while others report the underlying complexities of such technological uses: social, cultural, financial and legal barriers, lack of knowledge, low telemedicine literacy or evidence deficiency (Ekow Arkorful, V. et al.; 2019); too few government policies regulating a new health system incorporating telemedicine (Ahern, Kreslake, & Phalen, 2006) and lack of technological culture when providing health services (Lee, 2014).

Telemedicine is not a new concept; in fact, it has showed to be quite successful in different health areas. It emerges as an effective fusion of ICTs with health sciences. In this way, digital healthcare tools are experiencing increasing growth due to the technological evolution of society.

The concept of telemedicine was first coined in the 70s (Strehle, E.M., Shabde, N., 2006) when its attractiveness and interest for society lied in the provision of remote health services (Allen, A., Allen, D., 1995). Though before, in 1959, the Nebraska University already had started to use the first doctor to patient telemedicine video consultations to transmit neurological tests performed (Marily, J., 1996).

So, for years, practitioners have offered telemedicine services to their patients to simplify health processes. Currently, due to the COVID-19 pandemic, we were forced to join that digital revolution, when the force majeure completely changed the usual channels to provide health services (Gopal et al., 2018). Physical consultations experienced a complete revolution with the use of telemedicine. And though telemedicine had been existing for years, it was quite a challenge to adapt to these technologies because only a small part of the population had previous experience of virtual consultations.

It is interesting to observe how, in health emergency situations, a greater use of telemedicine technologies is adopted to combat local, national, and international crises (Smith AC, et al., 2020). Telemedicine is sometimes used too by people living in geographically disadvantaged regions (Bashshur, 1995).

In recent years, telemedicine has become a clear alternative to improve healthcare, with doctor / patient social distancing issues. It reduces travel costs and increases access to high quality care in rural areas. Such measures are important, but efforts to describe the added value of telemedicine may be different for the parties involved (Greenhalgh et al., 2017). We can differentiate two types of telemedicine: synchronous telemedicine, that is, both the doctor and the patient perform a consultation in real time (video call, phone call, chats) or asynchronous telemedicine when the consultation is carried out in deferred time (email, remote monitoring platforms, notifications by questionnaires) (Montserrat, J.M, et al., 2021).

2.2.1 Types of Telemedicine

Synchronous: real-time (e.g., video conferencing)
Asynchronous: delayed results
E-mails
Remote monitoring with delayed reception
Transmission and storage of tests
Access to data collected from therapy sessions.
Automated care and self-management systems
Interactive voice response
Web platform access
Notifications via text messages
Questionnaire notifications. App
Source: Montserrat, J.M, et al. (2021)

The constant evolution in medical care has been optimized thanks to technological advancements. This has improved the life expectancy of the population though, to do so, it is fundamental for health centers to develop a protocol based on cutting-edge technologies and to educate their professionals in their uses.

Several authors consider the existence of 3 necessary basic characteristics for the use of telemedicine: 1) A necessary easy and personalized use, because complexity might lead to abandonment; 2) Some gradual implementation in the society to ensure good acceptance, even when not useful in all health areas; and 3) Telemedicine should simplify and facilitate the management of clinical work. (Montserrat, J.M, et al.; 2021).

There are different elements of the mosaic called "Digital Health". Telemedicine -limited to remote health care services- is considered as the biggest revolution ever within health services, not only from a more a technological point of view, but also at cultural and social levels, because it eased the access to some healthcare evolution in the Twenty-first century.

After the problems observed during the COVID-19, Telemedicine is presented as a quick and abrupt solution to expand medical care (Tenforde, AS., et al., 2020).

The population is already prepared to understand the concept of telemedicine, where technology is included to improve medical provision; its uses have become much more ubiquitous in daily care.

With the great acceptance of mobile phones in recent decades, technological applications in health communication have intensified with the firm objective to perform consultations and patient monitoring (Logan et al., 2007). Currently, telemedicine is used in many medical specialties. Some medical centers even offer their own mobile application for patients to use teleconsultation or simply interact with physicians.

The main reason for medical professionals to increasingly use telemedicine is due to the high volume of demand issued by our society.

2.2.2 Benefits of Telemedicine

Telemedicine has the necessary potential to respond the many and current challenges faced by our health systems like rising costs, aging population, increasing loneliness, management of chronic conditions, unequal access, and fragmentation/lack of continuity in care.

- Greater comfort: patients receive medical care without leave their homes. Sometimes a simple virtual consultation is enough to provide a diagnosis, this is time saving and often means less travel hassle.
- Greater accessibility: Especially for those patients with difficulty of access to the nearest medical consultation, because of geographical issues.

2.3 Digital Literacy in Health

Health literacy is broadly defined as the "level of ability one has to obtain, to process, and understand basic health information and services necessary to then make appropriate health decisions" (Seng et al., 2023).

As underlined before, during the last decades, the use of ICTs has intensified progressively, and their there is now a recurrent activity in almost all sectors. Internet is an endless source of information, with millions of people consulting health-related topics every single day. Digital health literacy is presented as a crucial element as far as individual empowering is concerned because it enables them to make informed decisions about their well-being. That's why studying and researching to improve in this field becomes of vital importance so that healthcare technology can continue to evolve and provide increasing benefits to patients.

People with higher levels of digital competence or literacy are empowered to play a more active role in healthcare self-management. However, our society is still lacking good literacy and patients sometimes miss the necessary skills to search, evaluate or apply all health-related information available on the Internet; the management and consultation of medical appointments through mobile devices being quite difficult for them.

Inadequate levels of digital health literacy have proved to be a widespread problem worldwide, despite technological advances in recent decades.

In our modern world, all the information we need is accessible. However, barriers persist within society with the corresponding limit of it uses and benefits.

Different barriers make it complicated for these technologies to be experienced widely. The digital divide means that, on one hand, some do have access to the TCIs and to the corresponding information, while others have not yet stepped proactively towards their use. Technological complexity is sometimes overwhelming for part of our society; some people contemplate that frenzied evolution without being able to adapt and become familiar with these digital tools. The lack of criteria to verify what type of information extracted online might be accurate, is another barrier put forward by reluctant users towards these technologies.

To confront these barriers, health experts work on the need to increase digital health literacy levels. As advanced tools keep progressing towards a more technological world where doctors and patients interact digitally, there is an increased need to help users acquire such skills and adopt these technologies.

Digital health literacy has been discussed, extensively and from different perspectives at the academic level, after Professor Scott K. Simonds first used the concept in 1974. Since then, it has gained importance due to technological advances and is now considered as a global strategy - a strategy that will encourage and improve the health system itself and the coverage of patients 'needs when providing more immediate responses.

The vertiginous diffusion of health information on Internet together with the popular demand for such information has increased progressively. The number of adults with high levels of digital skills to research, understand and evaluate the health information available on the Internet, is still scarce, as are the resources and capacities needed to make good use of these digital technologies to handle health matters. Health literacy is often influenced by other different individual characteristics like for example, age, education levels, digital literacy skills, degree of motivation when seeking information or health status. These variables that can alter the understanding and use of such technological tools.

It has been evidenced that people with higher levels of digital health literacy have better therapeutic compliance, lower capacity for self-management of their disease. That is the main reason for the existence of a global strategy on these issues -where the main objective is to involve and educate the population so as to counteract the existing divide in digital health literacy. To do so, it is fundamental to know more about citizens' competences and to raise awareness on the importance of acquiring such skills. When otherwise, people tend to play a more passive role in the management of their health or that of their relatives. Some of these competences considered as of importance for citizens to acquire a high level of digital literacy in health, are as follows:

- To know the importance of good digital health literacy in society.
- To be able to identify the existing barriers for technological use to then eliminate or reduce them.
- To know which are the reliable sources of information when conducting searches on health prevention or health care.
- To know how to use the different applications available in each health system to get appointments or read diagnosis.

ICTs used for health issues can potentially reduce medical disparities between citizens, regardless of their geographical location, because they provide all people with information access, medical consultations or digital tools that are used for prevention and care.

3. TELEMEDICINE, DIGITAL DIVIDE, AND PATIENTS

The digital transformation of the health sector towards a more technological society should focus, above all, on improving and facilitating health coverage for all and on accelerating the development and implementation of digital solutions. The World Health Organization (WHO) recognized digital health as a key factor to guarantee -the access to universal health systems, -the protection against health emergencies and, -the improvement of well-being for one billion people around the world. To address the importance of the digital divide and to reveal the corresponding digital determinants in health is fundamental to ensure the highest level of digital health literacy.

In 2005, WHO already announced to member states it was about to "consider developing a long-term strategic plan to develop and implement eHealth services and, develop information and communication technology infrastructure for health" (WHO, 2005).

But this plan was set up only in 2020, due to the COVID-19 pandemic -an event that changed completely the global health system- where medical assistance was firstly virtual so as to protect all patients. The COVID-19 served as a driver towards digital transformation in the health sector.

Although there has been changes, it is still quite common to see individuals with great limitations in the use of telemedicine. Its implementation is still limited by the existing digital divide.

The digital divide is defined as the distance between people making daily use of new technologies and, those with still no access to the Internet or with access to it but no know how.

New technologies have played an important part in all these drastic societal changes since they have accelerated this separation (the digital divide). Internet is a powerful binary communication tool that emerged last century, though its benefits have been felt by a quite small portion of the world. Even so, the proportion of poor people with access to an internet connection has increased in the past 5 years, though this is not enough to reduce this digital divide. The accelerated pace of technological innovations accentuates the digital divide and splits populations.

The lack of technological infrastructure -especially in rural areas or less developed countries-, the lack of digital tools and, even the absence or low internet connection levels, in remote areas is reverting likewise into a lack of technological skills and, therefore, in low levels of digital literacy.

Given the situation, we propose an analysis of health technology implementation to apprehend its benefits and limitations for users.

4. METHODOLOGY

The first step to address the digital literacy issue is to identify the barriers blocking or slowing down the implementation of telemedicine. To detect different variables easing the use of telemedicine services and those representing a limitation towards the acceptance of these technologies.

To comply with these objectives, we performed a systematic literature review (RSL), with a qualitative approach, using an inductive analysis based on a non-experimental and cross-sectional design (Barrios et al., 2021). For the research to be as truthful as possible and to ensure its validity and traceability, we focussed on the PRISMA methodology (Preferred Reporting Items for Systematic Reviews and Meta-Analyses), designed by Urrútia and Bonfill (2010). The PRISMA methodology is a statement aiming to be a guide for the preparation of literature reviews (Yepes-Nuñez et al., 2021).

During the first phase, we systematically reviewed the literature to locate previous studies on the subject. We consulted several scientific databases of relevance for our topic with some international results like - Web of Science (WoS) and Scopus. The choice of articles was guided by descriptors like digital literacy, telemedicine, barriers and technological drivers; these were considered as alternate concepts during the analysis.

Please find in Figure 1, the work diagram representing the different phases our selection of articles was submitted to, according to the PRISMA criteria.

During the first RSL phase, a total of 467 articles were gathered as a result of the bibliographic search in the following databases: WoS and Scopus. These searches were performed with the words mentioned above. An extraction of 467 articles was made and they were manually incorporated to the Mendely document manager. Of these documents obtained during the first phase, 84 articles were excluded by search criteria and, 92 articles for being duplicates; the final list of selected articles included 291 items. Of these 291 articles, 154 articles were excluded at the title level and, 76 at the abstract level; only 61 articles were considered valid for full-text evaluation. Finally, we extracted data from these 25 articles that met the chosen inclusion criteria and focused on our object of study.

Figure 1. Article selection flowchart (adaptation PRISMA)

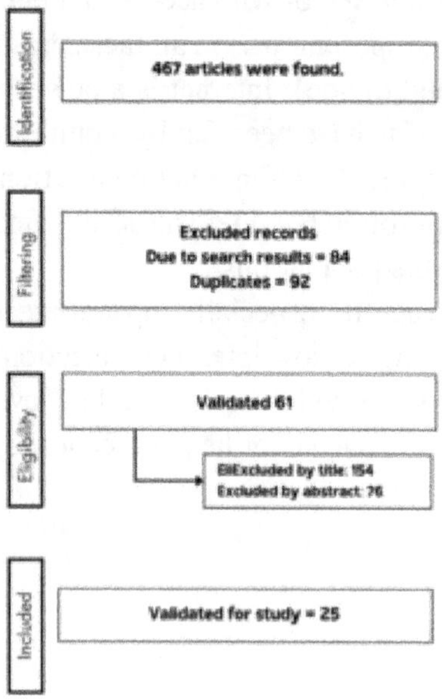

4.1 Telemedicine Drivers

After the bibliographic analysis of the 25 selected articles, we identified 8 factors as drivers that help facilitate the use of digital tools specialized in health.

- Level of health insurance coverage
- Access to internet services
- Access to technological devices
- Savings on travel costs
- Shortage of specialists
- Work-life balance
- Age
- Confidentiality and privacy

Level of health insurance coverage: The level of health insurance coverage is identified as one of the facilitating variables for the use of telemedicine (Lattimore, et al., 2021; Eberly, et al., 2020; Whaley, et al., 2020). Studies show that, a medical coverage including the possibility of a medical consultation by phone, is helping patients adapt much better to these tools, as compared to those who do not have any health insurance.

Access to internet services: The relevance of access to Internet services as a key factor in accessing telemedicine service is highlighted by researchers (Lattimore, et al., 2021). Internet offers the necessary infrastructures to provide telemedicine services between practitioners and patients: it favors real-time communication without interruptions. Internet access creates a digital bridge which urges patients to make use of these technologies.

Access to technological devices: The Internet connection is a key factor because it helps patients adopt digital technologies to respond health demands like telemedicine, though owing technological devices is another key factor in this online communication with practitioners. The ownership of devices that provide the opportunity to make a virtual consultation is a propeller for patients because it pushes them to perform this type of online consultation (Chen, et al., 2022).

Savings in travel costs: Making use of health technology applications also means saving money; an average of $ 147 to $ 186 per consultation, according to data published by the JAMA Network Open journal. But it not only implies financial savings, it also time saving with an average of 2.9 hours (round trip) and, 1.2 hours in the clinic per consultation. This is particularly important as far as work-life balance is concerned. A balance between professional and personal life that is often difficult to obtain -for in person medical appointments for example-. That is when savings and facility of use for patients carrying out a virtual consultation, are seen progressively as necessary measure.

Shortage of specialists: Telemedicine allows patients living in remote geographical areas to make a medical consultation with a wide catalog of available specialists. To attend health problems, many patients travel around -even outside their city- to get a medical consultation with a specialist, or expert, in their condition. Making use of telemedicine helps patients connect remotely with doctors from different geographical areas and receive accurate diagnosis.

Work-life balance: As already mentioned, not only economic savings are important. Time saving matters are too to adopt these technologies. Sometimes, going to a medical appointment and combining it with work life can be a problem, especially for those patients with diseases requiring of some kind of medical routine control. In these cases, telemedicine saves time and travel costs and, helps patients enjoy their medical consultation with no work rhythm alteration.

Age: Age is one of the strongest drivers underlined in the studies we have worked with. Some patients, -especially the young ones-, have grown up with technology are more predisposed to receive a medical consultation online. On the contrary, patients having always attended physical consultation, feel uneasy and limited when making an online consultation. That is why age is for many authors a driver for the implementation of health technologies.

Confidentiality and privacy: Depending on the problem they are attending with their practitioner; some patients feel more protected and given more privacy when having a consultation at home. In this way, the articles studied underline that patients feel less judged in situations that are related to mental health or sexual health issues, among others. In these cases, telemedicine can provide a more discreet and less intimidating environment.

4.2 Telemedicine Barriers

Despite the large number of telemedicine initiatives and the interest in promoting its uses within society, the reality is that its implementation is still scarce. Telemedicine is a health system nourished by technology and, without it, the service would not be realistic. This is why patients need to have a high level of digital literacy to make use of digital health tools.

After the literature review, we established a group of 6 barriers, perceived by society, to be limitative for the implementation of telemedicine.

- Access to technology
- Digital and technological literacy

- Privacy and data security
- Lack of face-to-face interaction
- Limitations in diagnosis and treatment
- Resistance to changes

Access to technology: It is undoubtedly one of the main reasons for part of the society to be prevented from using virtual consultations. This barrier refers to the ability of patients and the availability of access to mobile devices; having the necessary infrastructures to maintain good communication is fundamental. Patients with no access to these devices are currently facing great challenges since the actual trend is to provide a more technological health system. This lack of technology is most particularly present in more rural areas or in marginalized communities. This barrier against technology prevents patients from benefiting all the advantages offered by telemedicine; it also leads to health disparities and increases the digital divide in society. As Greenhalght et al. (2020) points out, the lack of access to technology increases disparities in medical care, because patients not using telemedicine may miss the opportunity to receive a diagnosis with other doctors, or get a closer follow up on their condition, etc.

Digital and technological literacy: Not only is it necessary to access technological devices to get virtual consultations, it is also fundamental to possess an acceptable level of digital literacy to make a good use of telemedicine. This barrier is especially relevant in the context of telemedicine, -where it is necessary for patients to make use of technological applications to attend the medical consultation-; patients need therefore to manage well these technological tools.

A study published in the Journal of Medical Internet Research (Bokolo, 2019), analyzed the link between digital literacy and telemedicine implementation. Results showed that there was a significant relationship between the two concepts. The lack of knowledge on digital technologies and, the lack of skills to navigate online applications or platforms, can be a major obstacle for patients to engage in telemedicine. And this situation is most increasingly noticeable for population groups not having been exposed to these technologies routinely.

In short, digital literacy is presented as a barrier that patients feel and see as a limitation to interact with telemedicine.

Privacy and data security: The privacy of personal data is a major barrier that limits the use of telemedicine, not only for patients but also for health professional; both are concerned about the protection of medical information, especially those specialties too highly sensitive to interact online. A study in the journal Health Affairs underscored the importance of data security when adopting these technologies. (Adler-Milstein et al., 2016)

Lack of face-to-face interaction: Many people value very positively the personal connection and face-to-face relationship with their personal practitioner. Telemedicine providers face here a strong barrier that prevents users from adopting the use of telemedicine. Such barrier is characterized mostly by patients' perception of online medical consultations lacking key elements that are usually present in a traditional medical consultation: non-verbal communication, face-to-face physical examination or the feeling of privacy or individualized medical attention.

A study published by the Journal of Medical Internet Research (Donaghy et al., 2019) revealed the concerns of patients when performing virtual consultations. They listed the absence of physical contact in the consultation and the limitation of nonverbal communication -such as gestures and facial expressions-. All this made it impossible to generate a more personal connection with the doctor and, therefore, the experience of the online consultation was valued negatively.

Some patients do prefer to perform physical consultations because they feel safer and more comfortable in known settings. Going to a medical center provides patients with a sense of security which reinforces confidence in the given diagnosis and treatment.

In conclusion, we can affirm that the lack of face-to-face interaction is a barrier that patients face when making use of telemedicine. Personal connections and certain tangible aspects in the consultation itself are highly valued by these patients.

Limitations in diagnosis and treatment: Remote clinical evaluation sometimes mean that the medical appointment is not as exhaustive or accurate as a face-to-face medical consultation. These limitations affect patients' adoption of these technologies and also physicians' restricted ability to accurately diagnose diseases or provide appropriate treatment. Some of these limitations may be:

-Limited physical examination: The absence of direct contact with the patient can result in a complex physical examination. A remote examination may be insufficient depending on the referred condition or pathology.

-Diagnostic tests: Some diagnoses require of tests like the x-rays, ultrasounds, etc. The lack of these tests in telemedicine can reduce the ability to diagnose diseases.

Limited medical intervention: There are situations where medical treatment requires of physical procedures. This is where telemedicine can be a barrier for both the patient and the physician.

In conclusion, the limitation in diagnosis and treatment is a barrier that imposes and reduces the use of telemedicine for patient with a necessity for physical examination. Despite these limitations, telemedicine is very valuable for many chronic diseases and monitoring situations, follow-ups, etc.

Resistance to changes: This is a barrier that is quite common and noticeable in both patients and health professionals. The reluctance to adopt new technologies and methods of health care is increased when the level of digital literacy of users is low. There are different dimensions preventing changes towards an online consultation:

-Familiarity and comfort within the traditional consultation: The habit of a traditional consultation model means safety for some patients; this safety feeling is stronger than that of change. Switching to telemedicine may require of some kind of mindset process. According to Adler-Milstein et al. (2016) familiarity with an existing model can influence resistance to adopting telemedicine.

- Quality: There is a fear among patients about telemedicine not offering the same quality of service as a face-to-face consultation. This may be due to a barrier already mentioned above, that of a lack of physical contact and communication.
- Work processes: Health professionals are sometimes reluctant to making changes in their daily consultation routine and in work processes.
- Negative perceptions: Resistance to change can also be influenced by previous negative experiences. When patients and practitioners have had previous negative experiences, they tend to turn to the alternative face-to-face consultation and, prefer to continue their usual consultation routine.

5. HEALTH MARKETING AND ITS IMPLICATION IN HEALTH LITERACY

Digital transformation in the health sector is a challenge both economically and socially. The results of the research highlight the many different barriers undermining the use of telemedicine. Bearing in mind the barriers studied, there is still work to be done to achieve a greater acceptance and literacy of digital health uses. This is why we invited 4 health marketing professionals to a focus group, for them to draw proposals and break those digital health barriers felt by patients so as to improve health literacy within society.

Some of these action proposals of marketing professionals to be implemented to improve health literacy are as follows:

1. **Improvement of awareness:** It is necessary to carry out some work to improve the education and awareness of both health professionals and patients for them to understand the benefits of telemedicine and its effectiveness. The government of every country is to encourage the use of these digital tools and help patients acquire the corresponding knowledge. To do so, they propose to include the creation of explanatory and informative materials on telemedicine and its benefits -like keeping track of personal diseases, - etc. Conducting workshops or educational seminars detailing some uses and applications -like preparing more interactive events to help users interact in real time and address their concerns or questions-. The use of social media or awareness campaigns launched to encourage patients' exploration of their uses. Real experiences always generate more links. Sharing patients' stories with a positive experience is fundamental -like the explanation of how the use of telemedicine has changed their lives-. These can humanize technology and help patients feel strong enough to improve their digital health literacy and experiences.

Awareness and improved education towards a more digitized health system. Transmitting accurate and reliable information of large medical institutions or of the government itself helps promoting the acceptance of telemedicine and improves literacy levels of both patients and health professionals.

2. Generation of trust: According to the barriers studied, we have observed how, for some patients, trust and privacy in the practice are very precious variables. This is why we propose the improvement of trust through marketing: with the generation of messages and materials to address patients' concerns. These could also highlight the security measures and regulations involved for online consultations to meet the same requirements as physical ones.
3. Real experiences: Through marketing, health centers can also launch real messages with patients' stories, success stories and testimonies. In this way, patients will feel more identified and less reluctant to make use of these digital tools.
4. Improvement of users 'experiences: The market trend is changing towards a more technological society, so we can help the whole society acquire an acceptable level of literacy to improve in the use of such tools. We propose to carry out actions with health providers for them to listen and then meet the needs of the population to further facilitate their use of these tools. Providing a more intuitive and simple use for example, supported by some patient care system in case of doubts.
5. Because of the previous action, the use of chatbots is proposed. Messaging applications are more than consolidated on the market. This is why they consider the use of chatbots as a digital marketing strategy in the health sector. In this way, user service is automated when requesting an appointment

or consulting health information for example. Chatbots help simplify the query process, but they must be configured beforehand.

6. Finally, it is important to achieve inclusive digital health by means of actions. Some populations cannot make use of health technologies, whichever of the previous actions are taken. A particular attention to these populations with situations of greater social, economic, geographical, or cultural vulnerability, is fundamental. ICTs have a great potential to reduce inequalities in health, but actions must be developed to: enhance the access to information or prevention tools, to access healthcare and provide a closer digital inclusion. Actions such as: (1) The provision of some help –with health advisors for example- for the most vulnerable patients to understand and practice the use of online medical appointments. (2) The collaboration with local organizations, like associations or community centers, to provide them with an access to resources and training programs, to further improve their digital health literacy. (3) The access to mobile devices in communities with low literacy levels, for them to use digital health apps and resources, providing less use concerns.

These actions are aimed at increasing and improving digital health literacy equitably in all areas. While working to reinforce these measures to ensure literacy is not a problem anymore, it is important to favor research on the real impact of digital literacy levels in patient health.

The perspective from the point of view of marketing professionals opens up an area that can be worked on to enhance satisfaction and, above all, the adoption of these technologies by society. Marketing professionals emphasize that there is still much work to be done, firstly, to thoroughly understand the needs that will arouse the desire of these consumers and, secondly, to meet their expectations: ease of use and user experience.

Telemedicine presents a revolutionary potential to overcome in the future the barriers it faces. By removing or reducing these barriers while improving digital health literacy, we aim at a society that is enabled to benefit from the digital health advantages provided.

REFERENCES

Adler-Milstein, J., Kvedar, J., & Bates, D. W. (2016). Telehealth Among US Hospitals: Several Factors, Including State Reimbursement and Licensure Policies, Influence Adoption. *Health Affairs*, *35*(12), 2330–2337. doi:10.1377/hlthaff.2016.0445 PMID:24493762

Ahern, D. K., Kreslake, J. M., Phalen, J. M., & Bock, B. (2006). What is eHealth (6): Perspectives on the evolution of eHealth research. *Journal of Medical Internet Research*, *8*(1), e4. doi:10.2196/jmir.8.1.e4 PMID:16585029

Allen, A., & Allen, D. (1995). Telemedicine programs: 2nd annual review reveals doubling of programs in a year. *Telemedicine Today*, *3*(2), 10–14.

Arkorful, V. E., Shuliang, Z., Muhideen, S., Basiru, I., & Hammond, A. (2020, September 09). Adoption: The Mediating Role of Electronic Health. *International Journal of Public Administration*, *43*(12), 1013–1028. Advance online publication. doi:10.1080/01900692.2019.1664569

Arkorful, Zhao, Muhideen, Basiru, & Hammond. (2019). *An Empirical Investigation of Health Practitioners Technology*. Academic Press.

Asamblea Mundial de la Salud. WHA58.28 Cibersalud. Novena sesión plenaria, 25 de mayo de 2005 - Comisión A, séptimo informe.

Ata, R., & Yildirim, K. (2019). Exploring Turkish pre-service teachers' perceptions and views of digital literacy. *Education Sciences*, *9*(1), 1–16. doi:10.3390/educsci9010040

Baker, D. W., Wolf, M., Feinglass, J., Thompson, J., Gazmararian, J., & Huang, J. (2007). Health literacy and mortality among elderly persons. *Archives of Internal Medicine*, *167*(14), 1503–1509. doi:10.1001/archinte.167.14.1503 PMID:17646604

Barrios, K. V., Orozco-Nuñez, D. M., Pérez-Navas, E., & Conde-Cardona, G. C. (2021). Nuevas recomendaciones de la versión PRISMA 2020 para revisiones sistemáticas y metaanálisis. *Acta Neurologica Colombiana*, *37*(2), 105–106. doi:10.22379/24224022373

Bashshur, R. L. (1995). Telemedicine effects: Cost, quality, and access. *Journal of Medical Systems*, *19*(2), 81–91. doi:10.1007/BF02257059 PMID:7602255

Belliger, A., & Krieger, D. J. (2018). *The Digital Transformation of Healthcare*. Progress in IS.

Bokolo, A. J. (2019). Use of Telemedicine and Virtual Care for Remote Treatment in Response to COVID-19 Pandemic. *Journal of Medical Internet Research*, *22*(12), e19415. doi:10.2196/19415

Bronfman, S., & Pelegrín, O. (2018). *The digital revolution in management education*. Retrieved from https://globalfocusmagazine.com/the-digital-revolution-in-management-education/

Burnett, C., Davies, J., Merchant, G., & Rowsell, J. (2014). *New Literacies around the Globe: Policy and Pedagogy*. Routledge. doi:10.4324/9781315867311

Chang, B. L., Bakken, S., Brown, S. S., Houston, T. K., Kreps, G. L., Kukafka, R., & Stavri, P. Z. (2004). Bridging the digital divide: Reaching vulnerable populations. *Journal of the American Medical Informatics Association : JAMIA*, *11*(6), 448–457. doi:10.1197/jamia.M1535 PMID:15299002

Chen, E. M., Andoh, J. E., & Nwanyanwu, K. (2022). Socioeconomic and demographic disparities in the use of telemedicine for ophthalmic care during the COVID-19 pandemic. *Ophthalmology*, *129*(1), 15–25. doi:10.1016/j.ophtha.2021.07.003 PMID:34245753

Cline, R. J. W., & Haynes, K. M. (2001). Consumer health information seeking on the internet: The state of the art. *Health Education Research*, *16*(6), 671–692. doi:10.1093/her/16.6.671 PMID:11780707

DeWalt, D. A., Dilling, M. H., Rosenthal, M. S., & Pignone, M. P. (2007). Low parental literacy is associated with worse asthma care measures in children. *Ambulatory Pediatrics*, *7*(1), 25–31. doi:10.1016/j.ambp.2006.10.001 PMID:17261479

Donaghy, E., Atherton, H., Hammersley, V., McNeilly, H., Bikker, A., Robbins, L., Campbell, J. L., & McKinstry, B. (2019). Acceptability, benefits, and challenges of video consulting: A qualitative study in primary care. *The British Journal of General Practice*, *69*(686), e586–e594. doi:10.3399/bjgp19X704141 PMID:31160368

Eberly, L. A., Kallan, M. J., Julien, H. M., Haynes, N., Khatana, S. A., Nathan, A. S., Snider, C., Chokshi, N. P., Eneanya, N. D., Takvorian, S. U., Anastos-Wallen, R., Chaiyachati, K., Ambrose, M., O'Quinn, R., Seigerman, M., Goldberg, L. R., Leri, D., Choi, K., Gitelman, Y., ... Adusumalli, S. (2020, December 01). Patient characteristics associated with telemedicine access for primary and specialty ambulatory care during the COVID-19 pandemic.[. *JAMA Network Open*, *3*(12), e2031640. doi:10.1001/jamanetworkopen.2020.31640 PMID:33372974

Fu, J. (2013). ICT in Education: A Critical Literature Review and Its Implications. *International Journal of Education and Development Using Information and Communication Technology*, 112–125.

Gopal, G., Suter-Crazzolara, C., Toldo, L., & Eberhardt, W. (2019). Beyond Adoption: A New Framework for Theorizing and Evaluating Nonadoption, Abandonment, and Challenges to the Scale-Up, Spread, and Sustainability of Health and Care Technologies. *J Med Internet Res*. doi:10.2196/jmir.8775

Greenhalgh, T. (2020). Whose digital health? More-inclusive approaches to understanding and action on digital health. *BMJ (Clinical Research Ed.)*, *368*, m390. doi:10.1136/bmj.m390

Kreps, G. L. (2006). Communication and racial inequities in health care. *The American Behavioral Scientist*, *49*(6), 760–774. doi:10.1177/0002764205283800

Kumar, R., Sharma, K., Assaf, M., Sharma, B., & Naidu, S. (2019). Development of an Assistive Tongue Drive System for Disabled Individuals. In A. Nayak & A. Sharma (Eds.), Lecture Notes in Computer Science: Vol. 11672. *PRICAI 2019: Trends in artificial intelligence. PRICAI 2019*. Springer. doi:10.1007/978-3-030-29894-4_41

Lattimore, C. M., Kane, W. J., Fleming, M. A., Martin, A. N., Mehaffey, J. H., Smolkin, M. E., Ratcliffe, S. J., Zaydfudim, V. M., Showalter, S. L., & Hedrick, T. L. (2021, October 08). Disparities in telemedicine utilization among surgical patients during COVID-19.[. *PLoS One*, *16*(10), e0258452. doi:10.1371/journal.pone.0258452 PMID:34624059

Lee, T. H. (2014). *The strategy that will fix health care*. Academic Press.

Logan, A. G., McIsaac, W. J., Tisler, A., Irvine, M. J., Saunders, A., Dunai, A., Rizo, C. A., Feig, D. S., Hamill, M., Trudel, M., & Cafazzo, J. A. (2007). Mobile phone-based remote patient monitoring system for management of hypertension in diabetic patients. *American Journal of Hypertension*, *20*(9), 942–948. doi:10.1016/j.amjhyper.2007.03.020 PMID:17765133

Lorence, D. P., Park, H., & Fox, S. (2006). Racial disparities in health information access: Resilience of the digital divide. *Journal of Medical Systems*, *30*(4), 241–249. doi:10.100710916-005-9003-y PMID:16978003

Marilyn, J. (1996). Telemedicine: A Guide to Assessing Telecommunications in Health Care. Knowledge Management in Digital Change, 311-326. doi:10.1007/978-3-319-73546-7_19

Martin, A., & Grudziecki, J. (2006). DigEuLit: Concepts and Tools for Digital Literacy Development. *Innovation*.

Matarín Jiménez, T.M. (2015). *Social networks in prevention and health promotion. A review of the current*. Academic Press.

Montserrat Canal, J. M., Suárez-Girón, M., Egea, C., Embid, C., Matute-Villacís, M., de Manuel Martínez, L., Orteu, Á., González-Cappa, J., Tato Cerdeiras, M., & Mediano, O. (2021). Spanish Society of Pulmonology and Thoracic Surgery positioning on the use of telemedine in sleep-disordered breathing and mechanical ventilation. Arch Bronconeumol (Engl Ed), 57(4), 281-290. doi:10.1016/j.arbr.2021.02.001

Nand, R., & Sharma, B. (2019). Meta-heuristic approaches to tackle skill based group allocation of students in project-based learning courses. In *IEEE Congress on Evolutionary Computation (CEC)* (pp. 1782–1789). 10.1109/CEC.2019.8789987

Neuhauser, L., & Kreps, G. L. (2003). Rethinking communication in the e-health era. *Journal of Health Psychology*, *8*(1), 7–22. doi:10.1177/1359105303008001426 PMID:22113897

Paramio Pérez, G., Almagro, B. J., Hernando Gómez, Á., & Aguaded Gómez, J. I. (2015). Validación de la escala eHealth Literacy (eHEALS) en población universitaria española. *Revista Española de Salud Pública*, *89*(3), 329–338. doi:10.4321/S1135-57272015000300010 PMID:26388346

Reddy, P., Sharma, B., & Chaudhary, K. (2020). Digital literacy: A review of literature. *International Journal of Technoethics*, *11*(2), 65–94. doi:10.4018/IJT.20200701.oa1

Rippen, H. E., & Yasnoff, W. A. (2004). Building the national health information infrastructure. *Journal of American Health Information Management Association*, *75*(5), 21–24. PMID:15141583

Sageena, G., Sharma, M., & Kapur, A. (2021). Evolution of Smart Healthcare: Telemedicine During COVID-19 Pandemic. *J. Inst. Eng. India Ser. B*, *102*(6), 1319–1324. doi:10.100740031-021-00568-8

Salcedo Aparicio, D.M., Ibarra Peña, K.A., Ceballos Muñoz, V.I., & Pazmiño Peñafiel, E.S. (2022). Digital meanings: multimodal communications and multiliteracy. *RECIMUNDO*, 147-154. .(3).junio.2022.147-154 doi:10.26820/recimundo/6

Sarkar, S. (2012). The Role of Information and Communication Technology (ICT) in Higher Education for the 21st Century. *The Science Probe*, 30-41.

Schillinger, D. (2002). Association of health literacy with diabetes outcomes. *Journal of the American Medical Association*, *288*(4), 475–478. doi:10.1001/jama.288.4.475 PMID:12132978

Serhrouchni, S., & Malmartel, A. (2021). Diagnostic agreement between telemedicine on social networks and teledermatology centers. *Annals of Family Medicine*, *19*(1), 24–29. doi:10.1370/afm.2608 PMID:33431387

Simond, S. K. (1974). Health education as a social policy. *Health Education Monographs*, *2*(1_suppl), 1–25. doi:10.1177/10901981740020S102

Smith, A. C., Thomas, E., Snoswell, C. L., Haydon, H., Mehrotra, A., Clemensen, J., & Caffery, L. J. (2020). Telehealth for global emergencies: Implications for coronavirus disease 2019 (COVID-19). *Journal of Telemedicine and Telecare*, *26*(5), 309–313. doi:10.1177/1357633X20916567 PMID:32196391

Strehle, E. M., & Shabde, N. (2006). One hundred years of telemedicine: Does this new technology have a place in paediatrics? *Archives of Disease in Childhood*, *91*(12), 956–959. doi:10.1136/adc.2006.099622 PMID:17119071

Tenforde, M. W., Kim, S. S., Lindsell, C. J., Billig Rose, E., Shapiro, N. I., Files, D. C., Gibbs, K. W., Erickson, H. L., Steingrub, J. S., Smithline, H. A., Gong, M. N., Aboodi, M. S., Exline, M. C., Henning, D. J., Wilson, J. G., Khan, A., Qadir, N., Brown, S. M., Peltan, I. D., ... Feldstein, L. R.IVY Network Investigators. (2020, July 31). CDC COVID-19 Response Team; IVY Network Investigators. Symptom Duration and Risk Factors for Delayed Return to Usual Health Among Outpatients with COVID-19 in a Multistate Health Care Systems Network - United States, March-June 2020. *MMWR. Morbidity and Mortality Weekly Report*, *69*(30), 993–998. doi:10.15585/mmwr.mm6930e1 PMID:32730238

Urrútia, G., & Bonfill, X. (2010). Declaración PRISMA: Una propuesta para mejorar la publicación de revisiones sistemáticas y metaanálisis. *Medicina Clínica*, *135*(11), 507–511. doi:10.1016/j.medcli.2010.01.015 PMID:20206945

Whaley, C. M., Pera, M. F., Cantor, J., Chang, J., Velasco, J., Hagg, H. K., Sood, N., & Bravata, D. M. (2020, November 2). Changes in health services use among commercially insured US populations during the COVID-19 pandemic.[. *JAMA Network Open*, *3*(11), e2024984. doi:10.1001/jamanetworkopen.2020.24984 PMID:33151319

Yepes-Nuñez, J. J., Urrutia, G., Romero-Garcia, M., & Alonso-Fernandez, S. (2021). The PRISMA 2020 statement: An updated guideline for reporting systematic reviews. *Revista Española de Cardiología (English Ed.)*, *74*(9), 790–799. PMID:34446261

Yin, H. S., Dreyer, B. P., Foltin, G., van Schaick, L., & Mendelsohn, A. L. (2007). Association of low caregiver health literacy with reported use of nonstandardized dosing instruments and lack of knowledge of weight-based dosing. *Ambulatory Pediatrics*, *7*(4), 292–298. doi:10.1016/j.ambp.2007.04.004 PMID:17660100

Zamora, H. & Clingerman, E.M. (2011). *Health literacy among older adults: A systematic literature review*. Academic Press.

Zamora, H., & Clingerman, E. M. (2011, October). Health Literacy Among Older Adults: A Systematic Literature Review. *Journal of Gerontological Nursing*, *37*(10), 41–51. doi:10.3928/00989134-20110503-02 PMID:21634314

Chapter 9
A Review of the Colombian Healthcare System:
Challenges and Opportunities

Gustavo Adolfo Girón-Restrepo
Universitat Jaume I, Spain & Antonio José Camacho University, Colombia

Sandra Tena-Monferrer
https://orcid.org/0000-0002-3153-8271
Universitat Jaume I, Spain

Juan Carlos Fandos-Roig
Universitat Jaume I, Spain

ABSTRACT

This chapter, of a descriptive nature, aims to highlight the challenges that the Colombian healthcare system is facing. The widespread discontent and protests of society over the last few years have led to the proposal that the current government of Colombia presented to the Congress of the Republic for its reform. Bill 339 of 2023 seeks to improve access conditions for the most vulnerable households while also reducing the administrative barriers causing delays in payments to hospitals and specialist appointments. However, it should be stated that the healthcare system is a truly broad and complex ecosystem, so it is not an easy task to assess the outcomes of the potential reforms. Besides, Colombia brings together highly relevant heterogeneous factors, almost like no other country in Latin America, a complex geography, interculturality, unemployment, and social inequality, among many others. Consequently, this work presents and brings together the social, political, economic, and academic perceptions of this new scenario that arises in the potential change.

DOI: 10.4018/979-8-3693-0679-6.ch009

1. INTRODUCTION TO THE COLOMBIAN CONTEXT

It is said that Colombia has always had two ideological tendencies, the "Santanderista" and the "Bolivarista" and this is due to a historical dispute between the liberator Simón Bolívar and the well-known lawman Francisco De Paula Santander. Bolívar made Santander understand that Colombia had many laws and few political subjects to enforce them. As the centuries passed, Colombia continued in this trend of going deeply into the regulations. This has led to great achievements such as having one of the most advanced constitutionalism in Latin America.

More than 200 years have passed, and the division of thought continues. According to the historian Julio Roberto Galindo (Galindo, 2019), it is the Bolivarian tendency that embodies the thought that alludes to personal freedoms and thought and the Santanderista that marks the legacy of order and legality. Paradoxically, both trends share a privileged place in the National shield with the expression "Freedom and order" (Galindo, 2019).

In 1830 Bolívar resigned his mandate (in 1828 he had been the victim of an attempted coup d'état at the hands of Santander's followers) and Colombia was divided. On December 17, 1830, Bolívar died and in 1832 Santander was called from his exile to be the president of New Granada.

Citing the historian Galindo (Galindo, 2019), all this directly influences the evolution as a nation, since before the national front, two parties always governed, either the liberal or the conservative. Each one with its own tendencies, and although today other political parties have already gained ground, Colombia continues to be framed in the two ways of conceiving the State. However, the art of good governance in Colombia will be achieved when someone finds a way to successfully combine these two trends (Galindo, 2019).

Many decades passed before health gained a place on the national political agenda in Colombia. The political power decided to include health as part of the government system with the constitution of 1886 (Colombia, 1886). This constitution had very different characteristics from the current one and governed the country's destinies for 105 years. As the highest legal framework of the nation, and in particular, centralist in nature, it served as the foundation for the organization of public health as a function of the state. Under its protection, Law 30 of 1886 was enacted, creating the Central Hygiene Board, defining for the first time a state structure in charge of the health problems of the Colombian population. Among the main functions of the central Hygiene Board were: 1) control of epidemic diseases, 2) environmental sanitation, and 3) everything related to the control of ports within the guidelines of the International Sanitary Conventions and the international market pressures. However, this first attempt is too limited due to the lack of resources, infrastructure, political will, and the reality of a divided country.

The government and its leaders identified the need to organize and generate solid health policies, which is why laws began to be enacted that would allow a restructuring of the model. Law 33 of 1913 stands out, which created the Higher Health Council, making it dependent on the Ministry of Government and with direct advice from the National Academy of Medicine. The same Law establishes three more levels in the organization of health: the Departmental Hygiene Boards, the Health Boards, and the Health Commissions. Next, law 32 of 1918 that converts the previous Board into the National Hygiene Directorate, dependent on the Ministry of Public Instruction. In 1925 the Ministry changed its name to Public Instruction and Health, its main function was focused on educational problems and was focused on "Hygiene and education, and as such it needs to penetrate deeply into the brain of the communities so that they can understand it." assimilate", clearly there were already some notions of the importance of the environment and conditions to promote healthy environments (Health Promotion).

Health functioned in this way until 1945, managing only health aspects, a health system with very poor scope. Curative-preventive-specialized care was financed by patients or religious institutions of a charitable nature, for this reason the model was colloquially called "the charity model."

In 1945, the national provident fund was created, in charge of serving public sector employees. And, at the same time, the Social Security Institute was created by Law 90 of 1946, which served employees in the private sector. It cannot be denied that a giant leap was made in terms of population insurance. However, they continued to have very little coverage in the most disadvantaged strata; this model lasted until 1975.

By decree 056 of 1975, the National Health System was created under the supply subsidy scheme. The resources were transferred directly to hospitals, health centers and health posts (Public Network). It had a basic organization for its direction at the national, sectional, and local levels, as defined by said decree in "Article 37: As of March 15, 1975, to receive aid or contributions that come directly or indirectly from the nation. or the budget of the Sectional Health Services, any hospital institution or health organization attached or linked to the National Health System must comply with the standards established in this Decree and in the other provisions on the National Health System.

In 1977, by decree 1650, the Colombian Social Insurance Institute was transformed into the Social Insurance Institute. The workers became officials with the right to collective bargaining. This period was characterized by the geographical expansion of social security coverage of the private sector in Colombia, and this is how we ended up having the three health systems that coexisted before Law 100 of 1993. These three systems according to Tafur & Prada (2019), were the German Bismarck model of insurance for low-income workers, financed based on wages (former Social Insurance Institute). Beveridge's English model, financed by taxes, aimed at the uninsured population (state-financed Public Network, National Health System) and the private system based on voluntary insurance (private clinics).

In 1990, Law 10 was issued, within the framework of very notable internal and global changes. In the 90s, the Washington Consensus was created, a list that included economic policies for Latin America prepared by different international financial organizations. This became the model applied by several Latin American countries, including Colombia.

The 20th century was coming to an end and a new world order was reflected where capitalism reigned, and neoliberalism was the new economic model. This largely led in some Latin countries to the privatization of state industries, downsizing in the public sector, and deregulation of business; promoted by the International Monetary Fund and the World Bank. All this with the objective of reducing the power, the monopoly of the state and stimulating private initiative. This completely changed the way the markets and the Colombian economy were managed. Health was not immune to this, which is why after three years of application of the law of January 10, 1990, which reorganized the National Health System. Exactly on December 23, 1993, the General System of Comprehensive Social Security Law 100 was born, which contains 4 books, in order they are 1) General Pension System, 2) General System of Social Security in Health, 3) Professional Risks and 4) Complementary Social Services.

This law sought to expand health coverage through two regimes, one contributory (population with the ability to pay) and another subsidized (poor insured population), with a scheme to expand the provision of health services that covers spouses and children underage. age or adults up to 25 years old students dependent on parents, but even allowing the inclusion of parents and third-degree blood relatives, this model continues to be the Colombian health model today (Vélez, 2016).

Contrary to what many believe, Neoliberalism or new liberalism is not a concept or a term or a new model, it appeared years after the end of the First World War and in summary its primary function is to limit the power of the state in economic and social matters. legal. Those who defend this theory constantly promote free trade and the deregulation of markets, instilling the idea that private administration is much more efficient than public administration. This is colloquially called "Privatization", in this way state intervention in spending and investment is reduced, affecting (in some cases) public health, public education and all sectors that the state must guarantee to civil society.

Law 100 that creates the Colombian Social Security Health System framed in its second chapter, is an essentially neoliberal system since it allows the creation of Private Companies that serve as administrators among patients (or users of the health system) and their Health Providing Institutions (IPS). These Private Companies, called Health Promotion Entities (EPS) or Benefit Plan Administration Companies (EAPB) are the ones who manage public resources, contract with the Service Providers, pay for the adequate provision of health services to the Providing Institutions. (IPS) and manage the risk of getting sick, currently health insurance covers 99.6% of the Colombian population (Vélez, 2016).

Analyzing the main reforms that have taken place in recent years in the Colombian healthcare system, we find three main modifications: law 1122 of 2007, law 1438 of 2011 and law 1751 of 2015. Through the first modification of 2007, changes were made to the general social health security system, with the priority being to improve the provision of services to users. With this objective, reforms were carried out in the aspects of management, universalization, and financing. Strengthening the balance between the actors of the system. This law is commonly known as the "financing law", since it increased the health tax in Colombia by 0.5% for the contributory regime, going from 12% to 12.5%.

Later, in 2011, an important change occurred with the inclusion of provisions to establish the unification of the Benefit Plan for all residents of the country. The universality of insurance and the guarantee of portability or provision of benefits anywhere in the country, within a framework of financial sustainability. Finally, with Law 1751 of February 16, 2015, health became a fundamental right. Health, understood as health promotion, disease prevention, diagnosis, treatment, recovery, rehabilitation, and palliative care. All of this became guaranteed, under the responsibility of the State, to all people, without distinction of any kind. For the first time, a law made it clear that, in matters of health, people have duties to themselves and to the health system. Promoting the need for each person to take care of themselves by adopting, for example, healthy habits.

2. CHALLENGES OF THE COLOMBIAN HEALTHCARE SYSTEM

According to Agudelo et al. (2011), the progress of the General Social Security Health System is optimistic, but it has not managed to achieve universality and has stagnated in access to services and equity. We do not agree with the statement regarding universality, since having such a high percentage of coverage puts Colombia among the healthcare systems with the best coverage globally. However, accessibility to health services and equity represent two of the biggest weaknesses of the healthcare system.

It is evident that substantial improvements have been made to the health system in Colombia and that Law 100 allowed all citizens, regardless of their social status, to have access to the health system. However, it is also important to understand that there are very complex structural problems that make people, especially those who live in deep Colombia, who have been excluded for some social reason or who do not have the economic means, see how a crusade to be able to have accessibility to health services.

The commodification of health is the starting point. This concept highlights the scenario in which the administrators of the EPS system (Health Promotion Entity) do not transfer the resources corresponding to the IPS (Health Providing Institutions) for the procedures carried out. Consequently, IPS does not pay workers and therefore some services stop working, with patients being directly affected. This fact is a clear contradiction of the Constitution because the economic factor cannot be an excuse, especially when in Colombia health is a fundamental right reiterated by the Constitutional Court and reaffirmed with law 1751 of 2015 (Colombia, 2015). Health cannot be conditioned by economic factors and the state must guarantee it.

Under this premise, throughout this section the main barriers that users expose when accessing health system services will be listed.

2.1 Lack of Solvency

According to (Restrepo-Zea et al., 2014), the lack of solvency among some users, despite being insured, is why many times, to access services or medicines, additional payments or indirect costs must be made, especially in medicines or so-called high-cost diseases. Consequently, this lack of ability to pay delays care because covering the costs of carrying out diagnostic tests, travel or treatment becomes impossible. In this scenario there is only one way out, to assert your right through legal means, most times by filing protection actions.

2.2 Geographical Barriers

Geographic barriers depend on multiple factors, they can be urban or rural and are directly affected by the fragmentation of the network that the EPS Health Promotion Entity has (Restrepo-Zea et al., 2014). This situation forces users to make trips, in some cases excessive, both within the city and in rural areas. And in extreme cases, between municipalities. Without considering such important factors as great distances, the transportation difficulties presented by cities, towns, municipalities, the patient's health conditions and the lack of economic resources. Here a gigantic structural problem of the system becomes vitally important and that is that the best human and technological resources are found in the large capitals, this makes the problem of access to health in the country's villages and towns extremely difficult and much more difficult. when the illness suffered by the patient is terminal or wrongly called high cost.

Latin America is one of the most inequitable regions in the world, where Colombia holds second place only surpassed by Brazil. The member countries of the Organization for Economic Cooperation and Development -OECD- gave Colombia a Gini coefficient (coefficient that measures the inequality of countries) of 0.53 in 2019 before the pandemic began. Post-pandemic impact has further increased inequality, pushing the Gini coefficient up to 0.54 in 2020 and dragging around 3.6 million more people into poverty.

It is important to understand that these inequalities have a lot to do with the existence of 11 million Colombians who live in rural areas according to the National Department of Statistics -DANE- (DANE, 2022a). This becomes a major problem when it is observed that the Health system's delivery chain is developed fundamentally in urban centers concentrated in the 5 large cities of the country (Bogotá, Medellín, Cali, Barranquilla and Cartagena). However, in small municipalities, in departments such as Amazonas, Vaupés or the Caribbean, there is not the same infrastructure. Not to mention that in large economically developed urban centers, it can be mixed with the business of complementary plans and prepaid medicines.

The most socioeconomically vulnerable populations have less accessibility to health services and were the ones who had the highest deaths from coronavirus, as shown by the Economic Commission for Latin America and the Caribbean -ECLAC- in its study Mortality from COVID-19 and inequalities by level socioeconomic and by territory (Cruz & Henrique, 2021). In Colombia, the -DANE- figures regarding monetary poverty are 39.3% (DANE, 2022b), an eloquent figure, without mentioning that 22.6% of Colombians could only have two meals a day (Portafolio, 2022).

In a biodiverse country, with enough fertile lands to achieve food sovereignty, more than 10 million people are tolerating what should not be tolerated. These inequities are reproduced by the health system, the best services are available in large cities., the same as the Intensive Care Units -ICU- and highly complex services.

2.3 Labor Barriers

In Colombia, the underground economy is an harm that is increasing; in March 2023, the proportion of underground employment was 58.2%, according to data from the National Department of Statistics (DANE, 2023). The lack of legal employment in one form or another has become a barrier to accessing services for several citizens. Although the subsidized regime meets this need, the other side of the coin is that person who has a stable job, is diagnosed with a serious illness and after a while ends up quitting their job to avoid difficulties with their employers and colleagues due to the number issues.

2.4 Administrative Barriers

These arise from the insurer, the provider, the contract they have and the service plan. These include the insufficient hiring of personnel, suppliers, providers, the procedures to access the service and the cancellation of contracts with providing institutions without immediately meeting the need. In the latter case, it is the patients who are severely affected, as they do not receive treatments due to lack of contract with an IPS, a clinical laboratory, a diagnostic aid center or a medication supplier (Restrepo-Zea et al., 2014). The system should prohibit the transfer of administrative problems between system actors to patients or users.

Another element that must be studied is the job insecurity of the health sector; many health workers do not know what social benefits are. 71.3% of health workers are outsourced under "precarious" forms of contracting according to information provided by the Ministry of Health and the National Attorney's Office collected by the media outlet el tiempo in 2021 (El Tiempo, 2021). Outsourced contracts, indirect links, by union, by event and even verbal agreements are what abounds in the sector. The largest staff in the health sector is nursing. Fundamentally, they are women, with low incomes, hired to provide services ranging from $1,500,000 to $3,000,000 depending on whether it is a professional or technical level, this according to the talent.com portal (it should be noted that social benefits are not received for the provision of services).

2.5 Benefit Plan Administration Companies (EAPB) or Health Promotion Entities (EPS)

In Colombia, the issue of EPS has been very difficult and highly controversial. These private companies are the ones who manage public resources, contract with service providers, pay for the adequate provision of health services to Health Providing Institutions (IPS) and manage the risk of getting sick. However, there are multiple complaints of denial-of-service provision, authorization of third and fourth level procedures, and delivery of high-cost medications. For this reason, an approach that has been carried out recurrently is the definitive establishment of the direct line. Let the state be the one to directly transfer the health money to the different IPS of the country, as the resources and health money (which are public resources that come from taxes and contributions) are required in the pockets of the workers. They are the human capital that supports health. And in the IPS, which are the centers that will generate user attention, however, much of this income ends up in the accounts of the administrators (EPS-EAPB). The amounts of money accumulated by the Benefit Plan Administration Companies -EAPB-, previously called Health Promotion Companies -EPS- were quite large during the Covid-19 pandemic. The EPS obtained an indisputable profitability. For example, the well-known "New EPS" generated income in 2020 of 9.9 billion pesos with an increase of 25.7% compared to 2019, Sura generated income of 5.9 billion with an increase of 26.2% compared to 2019, Sanitas generated income of 4 billion and Total Health generated income of 3.9 billion (Portfolio, 2021). While some hospitals and clinics lost economic resources with the closure of some services and outpatient care, for this reason the question arises regarding the need for these Health System Administrators.

Multiple proposals have been put forward to try to solve this problem, among them, 1) leave only the EPS that are working well and have fewer complaints from users, liquidate the others, 2) leave a single EPS that manages all public resources, 3) that it is the territorial entities (state organizations of the municipal or departmental order) who manage public money, taking away the management of the money from the EPS, 4) their definitive disappearance has even been proposed.

It is worth understanding that in a world where economic globalization is expanding and becoming more tangible every day, and where the prevailing economic system is capitalist, a balance between the humanistic and the monetary factor is inevitably needed to function better. It is not possible to provide high quality health if the workers in the sector do not have a high humanization component, are well remunerated financially, have contracts that provide them with job stability but at the same time the System is economically balanced and the public health money It is reaching where it needs to reach, to the workers in the sector and to the Institutions that provide Health services. Thus, users will most likely be able to receive the care they seek within their diagnostic particularities. However, today we have a health system with a fiscal gap of 10 billion and there are no real solutions in this regard (La República, 2019).

As a personal approach, the solution cannot be to hand over the total management of health resources to the Colombian state; our political history has led us in the last 5 decades to reveal decadent scandals regarding corruption, clientelism, bureaucracy and power ambitions. generated by officials and public servants elected by popular vote, appointed in administrative careers, or chosen to hold positions of free appointment and removal, for this reason, this proposal generates great concern for us.

Clearly there are some problems of form and substance that still need to be reviewed and corrected. The administration and management of health organizations has been demanding various challenges to guarantee the fundamental right to health and adaptation in the Colombian regulatory context. Situations such as the closure of several EPS or EAPB (benefit plan management companies) and the transfer of said users to other EPS or EAPB, due, among many other causes, to the financing or loss of economic resources, generate a quite complex panorama. for system administration. However, it is paradoxical that in the latest survey published by the Colombian Ministry of Health and Social Protection, 64% of the people surveyed rate the service provided by the EPS in Colombia as good (Colombian Association of Integral Medicine Companies, 2022). For this reason, it is important to carry out a detailed study on the situations that currently raise alerts in the Colombian health sector.

On the other hand, the achievements that the Colombian Health system has had throughout these 30 years of operation cannot be denied. We can highlight that the country has one of the lowest out-of-pocket health expenses in Latin America, it is the only one below 4% according to (ConsultorSalud, 2019). This information is very relevant, since household finances are not affected by possible health problems that any of its members may have. Likewise (ConsultorSalud, 2019) reports that per capita spending on health is the lowest in the entire area, since it is only US$358; while in the rest of the countries in the region it exceeds US$1,000, such as Chile (US$1,244), Brazil (US$1,114), Argentina (US$1,071); and according to the study, even in Mexico (US$505) and Venezuela (US$384) more is spent on health than in Colombia (ConsultorSalud, 2019).

Another achievement to highlight is access to health, which is understood in the country as coverage or insurance, according to the Ministry of Health and Social Protection, by June 2022 coverage was almost universal, 99.6% of the The Colombian population has EPS insurance, which leads us to almost universal insurance, with a distribution of 24,399,839 people in the Contributory Regime and 24,745,934 in the Subsidized Regime (Minsalud, 2022). This is an achievement because before Law 100, social security coverage was only 23%, while 13% attended private clinics, 40% in the official sector, and 25% of the total population was unprotected (Vélez, 2016). However, it is important to clarify that before Law 100, any Colombian could attend public hospitals regardless of their ability to pay and without being restricted from using x or y healthcare center or hospital (Vélez, 2016).

According to (OPS, 2022), Colombia has improved in almost all public health indicators. For example, between 2000 and 2020, infant mortality decreased from 25.8 to 16.8 per 1,000 live births, which implies a decrease of 34.9%. The percentage of low-birth-weight births (less than 2500 g) increased from 7.6% to 9.5% between 2002 and 2019, while adherence to exclusive breastfeeding in the infant population up to 6 months represented 25.8% in 2000 and 46.8% in 2005. (OPS, 2022)

Regarding the immunization strategy, in 2019 measles vaccination coverage was 95%, which represents an increase of seven percentage points compared to coverage in 2000 (OPS, 2022).

The maternal mortality ratio for 2017 was estimated at 83 per 100,000 live births, which represents a reduction of 11.7% compared to the value estimated for 2000. In relation to fertility, it is estimated that, in 2017, Women had an average of 1.8 children throughout their reproductive lives. In the specific case of adolescent fertility, a reduction of 36.1% is observed, if the rate of 98.8 live births per 1,000 women aged 15 to 19 in 2000 is compared with the figure of 63.1 in 2021. Regarding prenatal care, between 2000 and 2019 there is an increase in the percentage of pregnant people who attended four or more prenatal care consultations during pregnancy, since this went from 72.6% to 83 .9%. On the other hand, 98.5% of births were attended by trained personnel in 2019 (OPS, 2022).

In 2019, according to (PAHO, 2022), the adjusted rate of potentially avoidable premature mortality in Colombia was 183.7 deaths per 100,000 inhabitants, which is equivalent to a decrease of 46.1% compared to the rate of 340. 9 registered in 2000. In this sense, the country presented a rate in 2019 that was 19% lower than that reported for the Region of the Americas. Of potentially avoidable premature deaths, the rate due to preventable causes in 2019 was 113.2 per 100,000 inhabitants, a figure 17.4% lower than the regional rate, while the rate related to treatable causes rose to 70.5 per 100,000 inhabitants. 100,000 inhabitants, compared to a regional average of 89.6 (OPS, 2022).

Regarding the general mortality rate adjusted by age, according to (OPS, 2022), in 2019 it was 4.4 per 1,000 inhabitants, which implies a decrease of 31.2% compared to 2000 (6.4 deaths per 1000 inhabitants) (PAHO, 2022).

For this reason, public health indicators confirm efforts that are reflected in a decrease in infant mortality, low birth weight, breastfeeding, immunization, maternal mortality, adolescent fertility, and potentially avoidable premature deaths, among others, clearly not You can ignore an effort that shows tangible results, although the system has flaws (mentioned above), ignoring its progress would not be responsible.

Added to this whole panorama is the global crisis that occurred with the SARS-Cov-2 pandemic, stimulating an intense debate between academia, social sectors, political actors, and professionals linked to the health sector. The health problem has been worsening due to the fiscal gap that has been growing year after year for several decades and amounts to more than 10 billion pesos (La República, 2019) and with the social outbreak of April 2022, health It became part of the National political agenda due to the file of reform 010 that was being processed in the Congress of the Republic, but when the president changed in 2022, the new administration presented a bill to carry out a structural reform to the Health System. Colombian, for this reason the big question arises: What are the challenges and trends facing the Colombian Health system?

3. IMPROVEMENT AREAS IN THE COLOMBIAN HEALTHCARE SYSTEM

Clearly, the system must improve, or must be reformed, preserving and enhancing the achievements that have been achieved in these 30 years, but some fundamental structural factors persist that must be solved. Firstly, the current strong economic deficit, no government has addressed this problem in a profound way, momentary solutions have been given, but until now the fiscal gap persists, and the liquidation of EPS is a constant. Secondly, the barriers to accessibility to health services are continuous, especially in populations that are far from large cities, which we call deep Colombia. And, thirdly, information systems. Technology must be seen as a means, not as an end; databases must have adequate information, seeking an information system that is integrable and interoperable. It must be seen as an issue of digital transformation; an adequate technological system must be worked on through Internet access and coverage. It is about bringing the internet to citizens, not just to the home, so that organizations can use support networks with complete data, providing information on how the population group is doing in terms of health. Throughout the following subsections, four important components in the possible reform of the health system are presented.

3.1 Public Health

The reform should contemplate the element of public health in more depth, delve into and articulate with the ten-year public health plan, understanding the importance of these components in a robust health system that is in line with international guidelines.

Any reform must have health as a fundamental right as a precept, health authorities should evaluate health indicators, develop public policies to strengthen health systems and have social determinants as a fundamental principle, work on them and attack them, this inevitably leads us to strengthening of intersectoral articulation.

There are various formulas to work on this aspect. From the provision of the service (individual actions), actions with the health authority (collective interventions) (public health policies), and in the superstructure (at the national level), thus more impact and results are generated. The individual approach gives results in quality if real access is achieved, not just potential access in large urban centers, but it is necessary to clearly articulate it with the collective intervention plan that already exists. We have been working on this for a long time, but it must be improved because the real articulation with the different actors is not potentially being seen in the community, more so in the communities that are far from the large urban centers.

Articulating and connecting all this is the central focus, health systems must be based on primary care. Primary care is not a minor issue, it must be seen as a main issue, for this purpose, even the academy becomes a main actor to instill this change in thinking. Universal access and coverage is proposed, something that Colombia is well advanced in. Resilient health systems, understanding the importance of strengthening the capacity of the first levels of complexity.

The structures of the system must be rethought to find the point of synergy between functions, resources, and forms, understanding that the essential function is the formulation of public policies, but the fragmentation between individual and collective provision continues to be a complex problem.

3.2 Primary Healthcare Strategy: APS

By analyzing the strategy, we seek to understand that APS is an approach to health that includes the entire society and that aims to guarantee the greatest health based on the needs of the people, as close as possible. to the people.

The reform says that the APS will be developed by the state through the public and state IPS -ISES- for this reason responsibility is being taken away from the territorial entity. There is a dissociation between public health and institutions providing health services; it is important to understand that territorial entities must be strengthened and not take away their functions, considering the differential approach.

The provision of services is differential, we need to clearly identify the rural population from the urban population. It is necessary to collect manual and technical information, the manual collection of information cannot be left aside, it is important to register people to have current and relevant information.

The PHC is carried out in the places of greatest risk (assemblies, jobs, schools, sports centers), where the individuals are, this is different with people in rural areas, a differential approach.

Community participation is of vital importance even for the delivery of medicines in rural areas and their different conglomerates.

3.3 Comprehensive and Integrated Networks

Networks do not work in the best way and are claimed as a necessity. All levels complain about integration and feedback. Comprehensive RIIS networks, understood as the set of organizations that provide coordinated and efficient health services with family and community orientation, should present clinical results by health status to the population they serve.

First situation, integrated networks and comprehensive networks are two different things, the differences come from the WHO, law 1438 and 1441 of 2016.

Great concentration of networks in urban areas and less concentration in rural areas, with a large presence of the private sector in urban areas, but very little presence in rural areas.

They are necessary for the organization of networks:

- Technical elements: the determining criteria of the networks that have to do with assistance, governance, risk management, knowledge management.
- Assistance: Risk management, knowledge management
- Organization and management: trust through agreements between all those involved.
- Assignment of incentives: For network members who meet global goals.
- In the proposal for Comprehensive Resolving Care Centers -Capris-: leave the formation of extramural teams and transportation options well established.
- Technical and operational regulation of telemedicine as a great help within the sector.
- Information technologies: single public health information system.

Resolving capacity of the sectors, relocating personnel, continuous training strategies, according to the model and the needs of the population.

3.4 Information Systems

Unique comprehensive online health information system, two fundamental questions: why is it needed? And do you have the conditions and infrastructure for a great information system? Technology should be seen as a means, not an end. Databases must have adequate information, seeking an information system that is integrable and interoperable. Working as a digital transformation issue, an adequate technological system must be worked on through Internet access and coverage. It is about bringing the internet to citizens, not just to the home, so that organizations can use support networks with complete data, providing information on how the population group is doing in terms of health.

Second, the governance of the data by analyzing it, managing it and allowing its quick and accessible consultation, always thinking about the data model that must be generated. In terms of health to have the articulation, after this you can see the information system with two conditions: integrable and interoperable, in which the system is going to be developed, what are the technological environments, guidelines must be given from the technological part, digital government, digital transformation, smart cities, are the necessary policies to have adequate technological development.

Privacy cannot be left aside, especially if we talk about patients in the health system, a digital transformation must be carried out, not an information system.

Data sources must be exact, complete, and coherent, the quality of the data is very important for their respective analysis.

Technology is a means, but the primary asset is built through accurate and clear data, the source, quality, and security must be harmonized, digital security has only recently been guaranteed through public policy in Colombia. The data model is important to have a clear and functional information system.

The concept of public health has always been a broad and structured concept. However, those who are not technicians or experts in this field are unable to demonstrate the limits of Public Health and the need for it within a health model that meets the expectations of a multicultural and pluriform society.

For Héctor Abad Gómez (Abad, 2012), public health, understood as it has traditionally been done, a discipline that prevents and treats collective diseases (biological or traumatic fundamentally), expands towards a much more social, more comprehensive vision or discipline., we call this polyatry (from polis = city-state and iatry = study, treatment, cure). What makes public health a totally new profession, not only multidisciplinary but transdisciplinary, seeking to harmonize the other disciplines or professions that have emerged until now in the course of the history of human culture: medicine, public health, epidemiology, anthropology, sociology, social psychology, economics, politics (Abad, 2012). For this reason, the public health worker tends to be a political actor that seeks the vindication of the most disadvantaged subjects in society.

We cannot see social security and public health solely as health promotion, health maintenance, care and rehabilitation, because there are multiple circumstances that directly influence the appearance of the disease. These range from decent housing, adequate food (food sovereignty), quality education and stable employment to, even, the political situation of the country, for this reason it is very important to understand that the coordination between the actors will allow clearer positive effects in society.

4. CONCLUSION

Clearly, there are many points that must be evaluated to understand the complex scenario of a healthcare systema like the Colombian one. Colombia brings together highly relevant heterogeneous factors, almost like no other country in Latin America. A complex geography, infrastructure that must be renewed or updated in several remote regions. But not only health infrastructure, secondary and tertiary roads represent a major mobility problem for the inhabitants of the areas that are popularly identified as "deep Colombia." Also, interculturality, the specific particularities of some populations, unemployment, and the consequent social inequalities are some of the most important challenges to be faced.

For these reasons, a government that is committed to improving the healthcare system must be in total synergy with a change that entails a deep understanding of the theoretical model of the social determinants of health. But at the same time, it should guarantee the economic resources to achieve this systematic and gradual change of all these components that affect the health-disease process of the residents. If we do not have the economic resource guaranteed, the purpose of change will be registered as a profound social discourse that did not materialize in the reality of the Colombian who lives in a difficult environment for whom the minimum for a dignified life is not guaranteed.

The current general social security healthcare system has had important achievements that should not be omitted. We cannot retrocede to the old subsidy scheme nor to the health supply without any control. At the same time, we should not take away functions from territorial organizations and a mechanism should be sought so that current administrators improve the provision of services and administrative barriers are reduced. The current system has very important achievements, ignoring them does not contribute to reflection. The union of institutional and personal strengths with the opportunities that the outside offers us is key to creating a strategic roadmap. Colombia must have well identified the strengths of the current healthcare system, but also understand the opportunities that could arise from a reform of the system. All that remains is to relate the internal and external strengths, so the country can grow and provide a better quality of life to citizens. This is why we consider it very important to support and enhance the achievements so that the healthcare reform that Colombia requires can be built.

REFERENCES

Abad, H. (2012). *Fundamentos éticos de la salud pública*. https://www.udea.edu.co/wps/wcm/connect/udea/fea72810-e0f6-44f4-ba18-9d932411d04b/fundamentos_eticos_sp_hag.pdf?MOD=AJPERES

AgudeloC. A.CardonaJ.OrtegaJ.RobledoR. (2011). Sistema de salud en Colombia: 20 años de logros y problemas. *Ciênc. Saúde Coletiva, 16*(6). https://doi.org/https://doi.org/10.1590/S1413-81232011000600020

Asociación Colombiana de empresas de medicina integral. (2022). *Encuesta del Ministerio de Salud confirma satisfacción de usuarios con sus EPS*. https://acemi.org.co/encuesta-del-ministerio-de-salud-confirma-satisfaccion-de-usuarios-con-sus-eps/

Colombia, R. (1886). *Constitución política de 1886*.

Colombia. (2015). *Ley estatutaria 1751*.

ConsultorSalud. (2019). *Gastos de bolsillo en Latinoamérica*. https://consultorsalud.com/gastos-de-bolsillo-en-latinoamerica/

Cruz, H., & Henrique, J. (2021). Mortalidad por COVID-19 y las desigualdades por nivel socioeconómico y por territorio. *CEPAL*. https://www.cepal.org/es/enfoques/mortalidad-covid-19-desigualdades-nivel-socioeconomico-territorio

DANE. (2022a). *Situación de las mujeres rurales desde las estadísticas oficiales Serie notas estadísticas octubre 18 de 2022*.

DANE. (2022b, April 26). *Pobreza monetaria y pobreza monetaria extrema*. DANE. https://www.dane.gov.co/index.php/estadisticas-por-tema/pobreza-y-condiciones-de-vida/pobreza-monetaria

DANE. (2023, March). *Empleo informal y seguridad social*. https://www.dane.gov.co/index.php/estadisticas-por-tema/mercado-laboral/empleo-informal-y-seguridad-social#:~:text=Informaci%C3%B3n%20agosto%20%2D%20octubre%202022&text=Finalmente%2C%20para%20el%20total%20de,anterior%20(47%2C1%25)

El tiempo. (2021, January 9). *El 71% del personal de salud tiene un contrato tercerizado*. El Tiempo. https://www.eltiempo.com/justicia/servicios/procuraduria-advierte-tercerizacion-laboral-de-medicos-y-personal-de-salud-en-hospitales-559693

Galindo, J. R. (2019, August 7). *Bolívar y Santander: dos tendencias opuestas que han marcado nuestra historia*. Blog Universidad Libre. https://blog.unilibre.edu.co/news/bolivar-y-santander-dos-tendencias-opuestas-que-han-marcado-nuestra-historia/

La República. (2019). *El déficit de la salud se financiará con deuda pública: Juan Pablo Uribe*. https://www.larepublica.co/economia/el-deficit-de-la-salud-se-financiara-con-deuda-publica-juan-pablo-uribe-2827267

Minsalud. (2022). Colombia llegó al aseguramiento universal en salud al alcanzar el 99,6%. *Minsalud*. https://www.minsalud.gov.co/Paginas/Colombia-llego-al-aseguramiento-universal-en-salud-al-alcanzar-el-99.6.aspx#:~:text=Seguidamente%2C%20la%20viceministra%20de%20Protecci%C3%B3n,839%20personas%20en%20el%20R%C3%A9gimen

OPS. (2022). *Salud en las Américas, perfil de Colombia.* Organización Panamericana de La Salud. https://hia.paho.org/es/paises-2022/perfil-colombia#:~:text=Para%20el%202021%20se%20estimaron,de%20los%20habitantes%20del%20pa%C3%ADs

Portafolio. (2021, June 13). *Las 10 EPS más grandes del país, según sus ingresos operacionales.* Portafolio. https://www.portafolio.co/negocios/empresas/las-10-eps-mas-grandes-del-pais-segun-sus-ingresos-en-2020-552928

Portafolio. (2022, July 27). *Panorama de seguridad alimentaria en el país mejoró en junio de 2022.* Portafolio. https://www.portafolio.co/economia/finanzas/alimentos-cuantas-comidas-al-dia-consumen-los-colombianos-segun-el-dane-568760

Restrepo-Zea, J. H., Silva-Maya, C., Andrade-Rivas, F., & Vh-Dover, R. (2014). Acceso a servicios de salud: Análisis de barreras y estrategias en el caso de Medellín, Colombia. *Revista Gerencia y Políticas de Salud, 13*(27), 236–259. doi:10.11144/Javeriana.rgyps13-27.assa

Tafur, L. A., & Prada, S. (2019). El Sistema General de Seguridad Social en Salud de Colombia. *PROESA.* https://docplayer.es/142078983-Proesa-el-sistema-general-de-seguridad-social-en-salud-de-colombia-luis-alberto-tafur-calderon-md-esp-sergio-i-prada-mpa-phd.html

Vélez, M. (2016). *La salud en Colombia, pasado, presente y futuro de un Sistema en crisis.* Academic Press.

Chapter 10
Cross-Sector Partnerships and Relationship Marketing in Healthcare:
The Example of Fairy Tale Therapy in Children's Hospitals in Poland

Agnieszka Żak
https://orcid.org/0000-0003-1602-1757
Cracow University of Economics, Poland

Kakhaber Djakeli
University of Georgia, Georgia

Edyta Bielińska-Dusza
Cracow University of Economics, Poland

ABSTRACT

The aim of this chapter is to assess the potential of fairy tale therapy as a comprehensive relationship marketing tool in the context of cross-sectoral partnerships. The chapter enriches the existing literature on the increasing importance of cross-sectoral collaboration in addressing important social problems, with an emphasis on the use of fairy tale therapy. It also contributes to the debate on the role of fairy tale therapy in building relationships in the health sector. The chapter characterises the issues of relationship marketing, cross-sector partnerships, and one method of bibliotherapy such as fairy tale therapy. Among the factors influencing intersectoral partnerships, those that foster them and those that hinder collaboration will be identified and analysed. The publication uses the case study method as a research method. The chapter will present and analyse a cross-sector partnership between hospitals, businesses, and an NGO that created a fairy-tale therapy programme in children's wards of selected hospitals in Poland.

DOI: 10.4018/979-8-3693-0679-6.ch010

The assumption that a company's true capital is its good relationships with its environment is the basis of collaboration based on relationship marketing (Morgan & Hunt, 1994). Today, in healthcare marketing, relationships take on a new and special significance. They are the foundation for trust, loyalty and success in the long term (Yildirim, Amarat & Akbolat, 2022). Relationships put the patient at the centre and enable the comprehensive satisfaction of their needs, which is crucial in the context of health and medical care (Molina-Mula & Gallo-Estrada, 2020). Relationships in healthcare today are becoming more interactive, personalised, trust-based (Sutherland et al. 2022), and require adaptation to a changing environment (Menatti, Bich & Saborido, 2022). Social and digital marketing offers significant opportunities for organizations through lower costs, better brand awareness and increased sales (Dwivedi et al., 2021). Adapting marketing strategies to the demands of the digital world can help build lasting and rewarding relationships with patients (Chauhan, 2015). Strong relationships with healthcare providers enable better coordination of care and continuity of treatment at different stages. With digital data and analytics tools, communications and offerings can be tailored to individual patient needs and preferences. Personalisation, in turn, allows stronger relationships to be built as patients feel understood and valued. Thus, digital technology provides new tools and communication channels (Pascucci, Savelli & Gistri, 2023), but it is the relationship that remains the key element in building lasting and valuable connections with patients (Molina-Mula & Gallo-Estrada, 2020).

Relationship building is probably the most demanding and time-consuming challenge in the process of developing partnerships (Lasker et al. 2001). It remains crucial, however, because the essence of successful collaboration is the quality of the personal and professional relationships between the people involved (Kerka, 1997). The best collaboration requires extensive connections between many people at many levels and is possible when organizations develop structures, processes and skills to overcome organizational and interpersonal differences.

Relationship marketing in healthcare focuses on meeting patient needs, wants and desires by listening, responding, providing and adapting (Dwivedi et al., 2021). Adopting a relationship marketing approach in healthcare institutions and assessing the importance of its dimensions will benefit the effectiveness of marketing strategies (Ersoy & Tehci, 2023). Fairy tale therapy implemented in children's hospitals can be considered as an example of modern healthcare marketing. Fairy tale therapy can play an important role during therapy and recovery, especially among children who are in hospitals for long periods of time and away from home. Cross-sector partnerships and relationship marketing can also play an important role in the promotion and implementation of innovative therapeutic approaches. Children's hospitals have the opportunity to establish partnerships with community organizations, foundations or other entities interested in supporting children in their recovery. These types of partnerships can provide access to funding, expertise, volunteers or other resources needed to deliver story therapy. They can also help to raise the profile and visibility of the fairy tale therapy program through joint campaigns and promotional activities. However, it is worth noting that the implementation of projects in cross-sector partnerships can be strengthened or weakened by a number of factors (Zhu et al., 2019), as described in relation to the case study.

In the available literature, there is a lack of perception of fairy tale therapy delivered through cross-sector partnerships as a multi-faceted healthcare relationship marketing instrument. This innovative approach to healthcare can differentiate a hospital and attract the attention of patients and their families, while building the image of the hospital as a place where innovative methods are used for the benefit of patients. This chapter aims to fill this gap.

The chapter is structured as follows. The first section presents a general overview of the literature related to relationship marketing, cross-sector partnerships and fairy tale therapy as a method to support the healing process. Then, in order to justify our study, it is explained why fairy tale therapy can be seen as an example of modern healthcare marketing. This section is followed by a description of the research design, starting with a presentation of the research method and then the means of data analysis. The description of the research project includes the characteristics of the partners involved in the collaboration of the fairy tale therapy program implemented since 2017, including the results and impact of the partnership from the beneficiaries' perspective. The second part of the chapter identifies and analyses the factors affecting cross-sector partnerships, both facilitating and hindering collaboration. Finally, the implications and limitations of the research conducted are discussed.

LITERATURE REVIEW

Relationship Marketing

To understand contemporary marketing, it is very important to study business exchange relationships from a relational and sustainable perspective (Möller & Halinen 2000). Many authors recognise that the new paradigm of marketing is relationship marketing (see Sheth & Parvatiyar, 1995; Möller & Halinen 2000; Veloutsou, Saren & Tzokas, 2002; Grönroos, 2000), which is considered to be at the forefront of marketing practices for services (Astuti & Nagase, 2014), due to the close interactions with customers (Sin et al., 2006).

Relationship marketing (RM) is a concept of market action whose effectiveness depends on establishing bonds with market participants. It is a dialogue-based process aimed at building mutually beneficial long-term relationships between a company and its customers and other stakeholder groups (Astuti & Nagase, 2014), in such a way as to achieve the objectives of the partners involved (Grönroos, 1994). RM definitions primarily emphasise the importance of building as well as consolidating and strengthening mutually positive and mutually beneficial partnerships. The development of long-term relationships is made possible by creating an atmosphere of mutual trust, which is built primarily through communication processes and sustained cooperation between partners (Grönroos, 2000; Morgan & Hunt, 1994). Essentially, therefore, relationship marketing is based on relationships, networks and interactions, focused on 'win-win' relationships with individual customers and where value is created together (Gummesson, 2002). The type of relationship depends on the object of the relationship and the actors who form it. In the literature, the concept of RM has been described by six components: trust, bonding, communication, shared value, empathy, and reciprocity (see Ersoy & Tehci, 2023; Sin et al., 2002).

The originator of the relationship marketing concept is considered to be Berry (1995), who defined relationship marketing as creating, maintaining and enriching a relationship with a customer. A company can build consumer trust in three ways: through the communication process, through the guarantee of its services and by ensuring the highest possible standards of its actions (Berry, 1995). The main features of relationship marketing include an emphasis on the quality of customer service and a focus on customer retention, a long-term scale of action, constant communication and monitoring of the situation with the customer, creating new value for the customer or helping to create partnerships both internally and externally – with suppliers, intermediaries, to create the value expected by the customer (Gordon, 1998).

The premise of the RM concept is to build relationships based on loyalty (Gilaninia et al., 2011). Underlying this perspective is the recognition that customer retention is as important as customer acquisition (Berry 2002); consequently, particularly in service industries, this has led to the original 4-P marketing mix approach being extended to include people, processes and physical evidence (Booms and Bitner 1981). Yildirim and team (2022) argue that a number of factors can be identified that are effective in ensuring patient loyalty. These include, for example, healthcare institutions taking into account patient complaints, service quality and patient satisfaction, corporate image, hospital reputation, trust and doctors' reputation (Yildirim et al, 2022).

Relationship marketing has a significant potential in the context of public healthcare, based on its advocacy of building relationships between providers and customers and between providers and their suppliers. It is important to transform public health care from a primarily provider- and product-based service to a truly relationship-oriented service (Wright & Taylor, 2005). Building relationships with patients is critical to the success of many healthcare organizations (Wagner et al., 1994). As a determinant of relationship quality, trust is fundamental to patient satisfaction (Han & Hyun, 2015). In turn, effective communication is crucial for empathy in care and understanding of the patient in relation to healthcare quality (Ersoy & Tehci, 2023). Relationship marketing practices should contribute to patients leaving the healthcare facility satisfied. It is believed that feeling special and valuable, in addition to social benefits and trust, will positively influence patient loyalty (Yildirim, Amarat & Akbolat, 2022). Ensuring patient satisfaction can encourage patients to continue to use the same institution. For these reasons, for shaping, enhancing and maintaining patient loyalty, understanding relationship marketing – which aims to earn trust, ensure loyalty and communicate with customers in a timely, reliable and proactive manner – occupies an important place in the service sector (Taleghani et al., 2011).

Cross-Culture Partnerships

Relationship marketing is well suited to establishing and maintaining successful, long-term relational exchanges (Barroso-Méndez et al., 2014). This, in turn, translates into the success of cross-sector partnerships, which are a key tool in building and maintaining long-term, valuable relationships between organizations operating in different sectors (Bryson, Crosby & Stone, 2006). Companies are increasingly collaborating across the boundaries of their sectors, and these collaborations are taking place in a variety of configurations. This results in a situation where it is particularly important to properly match partners and take care of the entire process of cooperation implementation, which should result in a long and effective partnership (Bielinska - Dusza, 2021).

Cross-sector partnerships (CSPs) are relatively intensive, voluntary and long-term interactions between organizations from two or more sectors (business, government and/or civil society) to address social or environmental problems (Clark & Crane, 2018; Bryson & Crosby, 2015), such as healthcare, economic development or environmental sustainability (Waddock, 1991). These relationships can vary widely in scope and length, as well as in the number of partners (Austin & Seitanidi, 2012; Selsky & Parker, 2005). Cross-sector alliances can often have three or more partners, due to the need for diversity of goals, business strategies and expertise (Arya & Salk, 2006).

A key feature of cross-sectoral partnerships is the diverse nature of the partners and the focus mainly on social rather than business issues. Partners' objectives and approaches to solving a social problem often vary due to being influenced by distinctly different stakeholder groups (Selsky & Parker, 2005).

The differences relate to the nature and scope of the problem they are expected to contribute to and the means by which they do so.

The main benefits for partners can be considered in multiple contexts (see Lakin & Scheubel 2010; Parmigiani & Rivera-Santos, 2011). Companies may be motivated to improve their image or legitimacy or attract better employees, not-for-profit organizations may seek to influence social change while improving their own status, and government agencies may respond to increasing demands for efficiency and accountability. These varying motivations often make this form of partnership difficult to create and manage. Power imbalances can also make this form of relationship challenging (Parmigiani & Rivera-Santos, 2011). Despite this, cross-sector partnerships may become the preferred form of collaboration in the 21st century (Vestergaard et al., 2021). Their prevalence and practice is even expected to increase exponentially (Porter & Kramer, 2011).

In addition to the benefits achieved individually by the partners involved, it is worth highlighting the benefits achieved by two specific groups of beneficiaries. These are the benefits for employees and project partners (e.g. society). This aspect is highlighted by Lakin and Scheubel (2010), according to whom employee involvement is an integral part of corporate social engagement strategies. The personal involvement of employees in the communities where they work and live makes being active in community life a reality. When informal networks receive formal support from management, participation reaches a significant intensity. Employee engagement can be seen as a '*triple* win'– for employees, communities and the company. Communities receive valuable support, as well as access to a range of skills and resources from the private sector. Employees gain personal satisfaction from contributing to the community, experience themselves and others in different roles, and gain new skills and experience. Such activities also motivate employees in their daily work and enhance the image and reputation of the company (Lakin and Scheubel, 2010).

There is a need in the literature for partnerships to promote health and wellbeing (Towe et al. 2016). As Noh and co-authors (2022) believe, today's changing healthcare environment requires hospitals to address population health issues and commit to working with their communities. Population health at the community level depends on a wide range of determinants, such as clinical, genetic, behavioural, social and environmental factors (Noh et al., 2022). To address the broad spectrum of determinants beyond clinical factors and achieve the goal of improving population health, hospitals should collaborate with various community sectors and stakeholders, rather than taking sole responsibility for population health (Mac McCullough et al., 2019).

Bringing different sectors and organizations together in healthcare has many benefits (Buse & Walt, 2000). For example, it influences the creation of lasting and valuable relationships with patients, their families and the community. Collaboration between different sectors, such as hospitals, charities, businesses or public institutions, also enables access to different resources, knowledge and experiences (Cankar & Petkovsek, 2013). This is extremely important in developing and promoting innovative approaches to care for, for example, sick children. These partnerships can help to obtain funding, human resources and community support, which is crucial for the success of such projects.

Participation in cross-sector partnerships can therefore be an important element of hospitals' offerings because, by working with other organizations, it enables them to expand their services and deliver comprehensive care to patients. This care can include not only the medical aspect, but also social support, education and other services related to health and well-being (Towe et al., 2016). This builds patient loyalty and influences their perception of the hospital as a provider of valuable services. The hospital can promote the partners in its marketing communications, and the partners can recommend the hospital to their customers and community members. In this way, both parties can support each other and build a positive image. Cross-sector partnerships also allow the hospital to reach new target groups (Vestergaard et al., 2021). By collaborating with other organizations, a hospital can reach new customers, patients and communities that may be interested in its services. This in turn opens up new market opportunities and potential sources of growth. Cross-sector partnerships can also help to strengthen community engagement around the hospital (Maiolini et al., 2022). Joint projects, community events or charitable initiatives organised in collaboration with partners attract the attention and involvement of the local community. This builds social connectedness and a positive image of the hospital as an institution committed to the well-being of the local community (Cronin et al., 2022).

Fairy Tale Therapy

Although health-related sectors (such as health care and public health) play a key role in health promotion, they cannot solve many societal issues affecting health alone. The opportunity to align the resources and contributions of different sectors to address these issues is offered by cross-sector collaboration (Zhu et al., 2019). Intersectoral partnerships implemented under the concept of relationship marketing in health care can play an important role in the promotion and implementation of innovative therapeutic approaches, such as fairy tale therapy in children's hospitals.

Numerous empirical studies have shown that children manifest anxieties and fears related to illness and hospitalisation, which are very difficult experiences for children and their families (Haristiani, Wahyuningsih & Susaldi, 2022; Lamani et al., 2021). There are many methods to reduce anxiety among hospitalised children (Ouzts, 1991). For example, Margherita, Martino, Recano and Camera (2014) list a large number of tools available to support children's and/or family's difficult experiences described in the literature: clown therapy, music therapy, pet therapy, book therapy, art therapy and virtual mentoring, play and online group support.

The above points to the possibility of applying, among other things, bibliotherapy to this type of therapy. Defining the term bibliotherapy (book therapy) is challenging (McMillen & Pehrsson, 2004). The term, proposed by Samuel Crothers in 1916, is a combination of the Greek words for therapy and books (Crothers, 1916 after McMillen & Pehrsson, 2004). Already the ancient Greeks were aware of the therapeutic power of books by placing the phrase 'Healing place of the soul' above the door of the ancient library at Thebes. But older than literacy is the sharing of stories. Before written language, bards and story-tellers wove the beauty of language into individual and collective experience, giving voice to pain and activating the healing process (Berns, 2004). The foundations for the scientific treatment of bibliotherapy were laid by Bruno Bettelheim (1976), who, based on numerous clinical studies, argued that literature was able to play an important role in child development. In general, bibliotherapy is a process of dynamic interaction between the reader's personality and literature under the guidance of a trained helper (Lucas & Soares, 2013). Bibliotherapy, therefore, is the therapeutic use of literature (Cohen, 1993) to reduce anxiety among hospitalised children (Naina & Pooja, 2023). It can also be considered as an adjunct to other therapies (see e.g. McMillen & Pehrsson, 2004; Pardeck & Pardeck, 1998; Riordan & Wilson, 1989).

While bibliotherapy usually uses classical and lyrical works of high artistic merit, fairy tales, fables and stories that have a happy ending, are distinguished by a clear axiology (good triumphs over evil), are instructive and show how the characters deal with their own fears are of value in fairy tale therapy. Fairy tale therapy is a specific type of bibliotherapy that consists of a system of instruments and procedures aimed at promoting development and improving health (Kuciapinski, 2014). It includes narrative methods and reading passages based on fantasy and involves a narrator and people, animals, objects and even plants that come to life. Telling imaginary stories, which can include not only fairy tales but also fables, myths, legends and other folklore stories, which are very well suited to address the topic, is very valuable from a pedagogical and psychological point of view. For the fairy tale has a specific function in the natural life of the individual (Bettelheim 1976) and offers new dimensions to the child's imagination. Emotional aspects can enter his consciousness and are processed by his imagination, so that these elements gradually become tolerated (Margherita et al., 2014). The fairy tale thus provides a road map that helps children find their way and meanings (Tsitsani et al. 2011). The suggestive story serves as a springboard for discussion and dialogue (Berns, 2004). According to Betteelheim (1976), fairy tale therapy influences the child psyche through identification with a positive protagonist, shapes the child's personality, inspires the child to overcome difficulties encountered and familiarises the children with previously unknown concepts, feelings and phenomena. The method helps to solve personal dilemmas and is also a kind of support in the process of achieving security. It can also be a way to meet children's needs (Kuciapinski, 2014).

Story time therapy is an educational tool that builds bonding and shared understanding, addresses emotional needs, supports the child's psychological development and strengthens his or her sense of self-worth, and helps with problem solving. This three-step process to support a child's emotional development includes reading, structured conversation and educational play. Conscious storytelling and educational play shape the children's personality and imagination. At the same time, the little one learns to communicate his or her own emotions and take on new challenges. Since children tend to model the characters they identify with, story therapy becomes useful in identifying the thoughts and feelings of the characters so that children can identify, explore and express their own thoughts, behaviour and feelings (Gladding & Gladding, 1991; Prater et al., 2006). This method also helps to increase empathic understanding of others as it promotes interpersonal skills and emotional maturity. It also enhances self-expression and self-esteem. Additionally, by raising awareness that others have similar problems or situations, and by providing children with factual information about the problems they are experiencing, it promotes a sense of belonging and reduces conflict. Emotions such as stress, anxiety and loneliness can be reduced. Bibliotherapy also improves problem-solving and coping skills (Mitchell-Kamalie, 2002).

Fairy tale therapy can be particularly valuable in helping children who are unable to cope with the emotional distress associated with real-life situations. This is because it helps tame emotions (especially anxiety), relaxes, calms, develops communication skills and supports children to concentrate. The rationale for using books as a coping mechanism for emotional and behavioural problems in children, or as a teaching tool, is based on the assumption that people identify with similar characters (Lucas & Soares, 2013). Children often have difficulty identifying and communicating their feelings. In contrast, children's engagement in reading allows them to empathise with the characters portrayed in the book, thus gaining insight into a variety of life issues they may face or experience, such as illness, separation, death, poverty, disability, alienation and others (Lucas & Soares, 2013). This identification and insight leads to emotional release, new goal-directed behaviours and new ways of interacting with others (Gladding & Gladding, 1991). Research suggests that bibliotherapy reduces anxiety (Prater et al., 2006), influences both behaviour and attitudes of students (Cook et al., 2006), and imparts social and developmental skills (Prater et al., 2006). Research shows that the regular practice of bibliotherapy during hospitalisation can produce the desired reduction in anxiety among children (Lamani et al., 2021; Ouzts, 1991; Yati et al., 2017). Adamo et al. (2008) studied fairy tale therapy workshops in children's oncology wards. In all cases, the researchers noted that the use of fairy tale therapy reduced anxiety and fear in participants and increased reported and observed coping skills and self-efficacy.

As Borecka (2001) writes, by using bibliotherapy it is possible to influence certain spheres of a person's life (mental, intellectual, social, emotional) and to some extent to interfere with their behaviour. Bibliotherapy is an effective therapeutic method used among people of all ages, cultures and backgrounds (Pehrsson & McMillen, 2005). Importantly, it must be conducted by a trained person (such as a psychologist, a teacher or a librarian). Bibliotherapy can therefore support the healing process in hospital wards, sanatoriums, social care facilities or schools, among others (Borecka, 2001).

Bibliotherapy as a tool can be used in many ways, independently or together with other intervention methods. It can be used in occupational therapy as an adjunctive form, i.e. as a tool in the hands of a professional therapist. This is the original meaning of the term, which is strongly determined by the second term with medical overtones (therapy). At the same time, fairy tale therapy has gone beyond the framework of psychotherapy and acquired a parallel meaning - a special contact with the child, a method of solving his or her problems, assisting in his or her development. It is then used not by psychologist-therapists, but also by parents, carers or teachers.

Although fairy tale therapy has many advantages, its effectiveness may be limited by various factors (e.g. availability of books, lack of motivation to read or children's withdrawal). Some of these limitations can be overcome through regular implementation and use of group discussions and other activities (Gladding & Gladding, 1991). Other limitations can be identified if the facilitator has limited knowledge of human development and developmental issues and insufficient knowledge of relevant literature. Therefore, facilitators need to be adequately trained.

Fairy tale therapy brings with it a number of additional values. The most important of these are the promotion of reading and social education. In their work, Selin and Graube (2017), on the other hand, strongly emphasise another aspect of fairy tale therapy conducted in children's hospitals. They see it as a community building tool. Developing as a reader is part of a child's becoming an individual – when you can find out what you like, love, when you can discuss it with another person. Being moved by literature is about experience. The moment a child is introduced to a story, they gain inner strength and understand how literature and life works. Focusing, recognising and grasping details, imagining faces and following the events in a book helps to understand society and the interactions between people. A children's hospital may be a small and often forgotten place, but it is essential to building a strong and healthy society. Engaging with the book promotes healthy thinking and attitudes that allow children to take their own practical experiences with them when they leave hospital. Focusing on patients' and parents' reactions to bibliotherapy activities shows what reading projects can do for children and for society (Selin & Graube, 2017).

Fairy Tale Therapy as an Example of Modern Healthcare Marketing

The planning and implementation of marketing activities for hospitals is a very important part of their operation and development. It is worth emphasising at this point that the most important goal of any healthcare facility should be to act in the service of the patient (Greene et al., 2012). Fairy tale therapy in children's hospitals can be considered as an example of modern healthcare marketing. Among other things, it represents an innovative approach to healthcare that differentiates the hospital, attracts the attention of patients and their families as well as the media and builds the image of the hospital as a place where innovative methods are used for the benefit of patients.

Some of the most important objectives of healthcare marketing activities include: creating and maintaining a positive corporate image, communicating with potential patients, attracting new patients, gaining the trust of current patients who become 'ambassadors' of the healthcare facility in their community or offering and communicating about new services and treatments, the purchase of innovative equipment or new medical staff members (see e.g. Berkowitz, 2021; Balogun & Ogunnaike, 2017; Jenkinson et al, 2002; Otani et al., 2010; Waters et al., 2016; Wu, 2011). Fairy tale therapy can help to create a positive image of the hospital as an institution that cares not only for the physical health but also for the emotional wellbeing of patients. By promoting this form of therapy and its benefits, the hospital can influence public awareness of children's mental health and the need for therapeutic support. This type of therapy engages children emotionally and creates positive experiences. This, in turn, can help build personalised emotional connections with patients and their families, which are important in relationship marketing. Fairy tale therapy can also be considered as a unique service offering of the hospital, setting it apart from other medical facilities. Allowing it to build the trust of patients and their families and influencing their loyalty to the hospital. Strengthening its reputation, creating a positive image and enabling it to achieve a competitive advantage on the healthcare market. In addition, positive feedback and recommendations from patients and their families can be a valuable communication and promotional tool for the hospital (Berger et al., 2020; Castro et al., 2016). At the same time, informing the wider community about the use of a unique form of therapy can attract the attention of the media, patients and their families, as well as potential donors and business partners.

MATERIALS AND METHODS

Qualitative research is used to study a variety of phenomena related to individuals, groups and organizations (Ding & Ferràs Hernández, 2023) and is an important methodological basis for many scientific disciplines. Therefore, during the course of the research, it was decided to use the case study as the main research method, involving the detailed study of a single case, usually in the context of a real phenomenon or problem (Heale & Twycross, 2018). Case study is a research methodology, typically seen in social and life sciences (Heale & Twycross, 2018). Researchers describe how case studies explore complex phenomena in a natural setting to increase understanding (Hamel et al., 1993; Yin, 2009). This method examines a real, contemporary, limited system (case) or multiple limited systems (cases) over time, through detailed, in-depth data collection involving multiple sources of information, and reports a case description and case themes (Creswell & Creswell, 2017; Thomas, 2021). It can also be used to explore complex and multidimensional issues, understand context, examine processes and analyse interactions between different factors, in this case between different partners (Heale & Twycross, 2018). Compared to other research methods, the case study offers the richest range of techniques and tools for data acquisition and analysis. Data sources can include observations, interviews, company documents, newspaper articles, surveys, and databases maintained by various institutions.

In the course of the research, it was decided to augment the case study method with a free interview technique, supported by email interviewing (James, 2007; Opdenakker, 2006), as well as participant observation. In addition, secondary data were also used for the analysis: documents (reports), information on websites and publications (see Brzustewicz et al., 2022). It is also worth quoting Sofaer (1999), who believes that qualitative methods have been and can be used in health services and health policy research. Qualitative research methods are valuable in providing descriptions of complex phenomena;

tracing unique events or illuminating the experiences and interpretations of events by actors with different roles (Sofaer, 1999).

The analysis of the literature on the subject, together with the secondary materials collected, allowed the formulation of four main research questions to which the study responds. These are as follows:

Q.1. How is the process of fairy tale therapy implemented within the framework of a tripartite cross-sector partnership between hospitals, companies and an NGO whose volunteers conduct fairy tale therapy in children's wards of selected hospitals in Poland?
Q.2. What factors are conducive to the implementation of a fairy-tale therapy program in the cross-sector partnership under study?
Q.3. What factors hinder the cooperation of partners involved in the implementation of fairy tale therapy in children's hospital wards?
Q.4. Can the fairy tale therapy method implemented in a cross-sector partnership be considered as a multi-faceted relationship marketing instrument?

In order to find an answer to the research questions posed in this way, interviews were conducted with representatives of both the Foundation (CEO, a volunteer personally involved in the project), the company (Sustainability and Internal Communication Expert, a volunteer personally involved in the project) and the hospital (Promotion and Marketing Department). All interviews were conducted in July 2023. Secondary data were also analysed: documents (social reports published by the Company and data on fairy tale therapy collected between 2017 and 2022 by the Foundation), information on websites and publications (see Brzustewicz et al., 2022), which were also relevant to this project. It should be emphasised that this multidimensional approach allows for a holistic and integrated understanding of the problem under study.

RESULTS

It was pointed out above that the primary research method is the case study. The choice of method was dictated by the fact of a limited population and the fact that this method allows for a detailed and in-depth understanding of a specific phenomenon in its real-life context. In this case, the focus is on presenting a project for the use of hospital-based fairy tale therapy implemented in a cross-sector partnership (see Tab.1) as a multi-faceted relationship marketing instrument. The aim of this chapter is to assess the potential of fairy tale therapy as a comprehensive relationship marketing tool in the context of cross-sector partnerships. This partnership has been implemented since 2017 between an NGO (a foundation), a loan company and a children's hospital from one of Poland's large cities1 . The main aim of the cross-sector collaboration is to improve the wellbeing of sick children in hospital wards, including helping them cope with their emotions through the use of story therapy. This is in line with both the NGO's mission, the company's social goals and the hospital's strategic objectives.

Table 1. Partnership overview

Partnership
– partners: NGO – business – hospitals – duration: 2017 – ongoing – main aim: Advancing well-being of ill children in hospital wards, including helping them to cope with their emotions through story therapy, – fairy tale therapy conducted according to the model: reading – discussing – practising, – nationwide coverage (13 Polish cities); approximately 60 hours per week, – more than 200 volunteers and 26 coordinators after comprehensive training in fairy tale therapy, – beneficiaries: patients in children's hospital wards, pupils in children's homes and in aid and care institutions, – in 2021, the cooperation program covered 100,000 beneficiaries.
Business partner
– in Poland since 1997, – a subsidiary of an international financial group listed on the London Stock Exchange, – more than 1,600 employees, – brands present in Poland, the Czech Republic, Hungary, Romania, Finland, Estonia, Lithuania, Latvia, Spain and Australia and Mexico, – providing cash loans to individual customers, – motive for cooperation: development of the corporate volunteering program (CV).
NGO partner
– established in 2013, – fairytales-tellers, over 50 hours of fairytale therapy per week, 77 cooperating cities and 54 benches on city streets, – purpose: to promote engaged reading, teach relationship building through books and provide community education Train volunteers in the use of fairy tale therapy and coordinate a fairy tale therapy project in hospitals, – 1.8 mil collected books, over 1000 opened libraries, nearly 500 trained, – motive for cooperation: development of the idea of fairy-tale therapy in hospitals, financial and organizational support.
Hospital partner
– has been operating since 1876, – one of the oldest paediatric hospitals in Poland, – 10 wards, 22 specialist clinics, more than 500 employees, – 198 beds, 77,000 consultations, 8,000 patients per year, – the hospital's mission: to promote health and treat all children in need in the spirit of the slogan: "We fight for a child's life, health and smile", – motive for cooperation: to meet the needs and expectations of patients by enriching the treatment offer with non-standard forms of therapy; to extend cooperation in the field of health promotion and protection.

Source: own preparation

Partners

NGO Partner (The Foundation)

The Foundation was founded in 2013. The Foundation's mission is to support children and young people in hospitals and to promote reading. It uses the book to build quality relationships – from relationships with oneself, to relationships in one's immediate environment, to relationships between entire communities and institutions. The Foundation involves hundreds of people acting together to inspire and support. Its activities bring together various communities, from actors, singers and journalists to politicians and government employees, as well as patients, students and parents.

The Foundation – in cooperation with companies and institutions – runs social support programs through which it pursues two Sustainable Development Goals: good quality education (Goal 4) and good health and quality of life (Goal 3).

Thanks to the social movement, it has more than 450 hospitals under its wing. The Foundation helps its beneficiaries by setting up libraries and therapy rooms, as well as by implementing a bibliotherapy program. Social Campaigns carried out by the Foundation include: The Great Book Collection, Benches (in the shape of open books) - Imagination Trail. Since its inception, it has been guided by the slogan – *Give away your Book – Create a Library – Inspire Others*. The Foundation's activities are supported by people well-known from the world of media, culture, art and literature. Thanks to continuously cultivated relationships, unconventional (extraordinary) promotional activities can be carried out together.

Through its activities, the Foundation can be proud of the following achievements: 1.8 mil collected books, over 1000 opened libraries, nearly 500 (465) trained fairytales-tellers, over 50 hours of fairytale therapy per week, 77 cooperating cities and 54 benches on city streets.

The slogan *Give Away Your Books* is being implemented through the Great Book Collection. It is a nationwide campaign, that begins with a press conference attended by the Foundation's Ambassadors, representatives of ministries and the media. For one month, a public collection of books is being held in Poland's largest cities, which, after sorting, will go to libraries in hospitals and care and aid institutions.

Along with thousands of collection points, books are being collected by, among others, the Presidential Palace, the Office of the Children's Rights Ombudsman, The Parliament, the Ministry of National Education, the presidents of patronage cities, theatres, museums, municipal stadiums, kindergartens, schools and the inhabitants of Poland. The Great Book Collection is supported by a nationwide media campaign (including on Polish Television, Polish Radio and numerous local media). Promotion in the media is accompanied by an extensive digital and outdoor campaign. As part of the Great Book Collection, the Foundation organizes numerous reading events in public spaces, such as conferences, readings in urban and hospital spaces, as well as promotional stands at the Book Fair.

The essence of PR and communication activities is not just to inform, but to strive for change. Effective communication is not an end in itself, but only a path to the goal of changing behaviour or attitudes. From a marketing point of view, it is worth emphasising that the Great Book Collection is a social campaign that every year brings not only media effects, but above all social effects.

Activities under the slogan *Create a library* are a response to the expectations of Polish hospitals. The Foundation conducted a survey of the needs of public hospitals under the patronage of the Ministry of Health. Based on the results, a group of beneficiaries was selected and an appropriate set of activities was created for each group. New Libraries for Small Patients and Libraries for Adults are being opened. The Foundation has hundreds of hospitals under its permanent care - patients can use the library without hindrance and even take home a favourite book. The libraries are established thanks to business and institutional partners who allocate part of their budgets to community activities. The libraries are opened together with the Foundation's ambassadors in the presence of the media, representatives of public institutions, business partners and the beneficiaries themselves. The events are accompanied by fairy tale therapy workshops, fairytale therapy workshops and interactive theatre plays.

What *inspires* people living in Polish cities are the benches. These are urban furniture in the shape of open books that decorate public spaces. The benches provide residents with inspiring artworks and free access to audio books. Each bench has a unique design and an artistic ambassador. Well-known artists, journalists, singers, actors and illustrators were invited to create inspiring bench designs. The benches are placed in specially dedicated locations in urban spaces to promote reading, as well as other cultures and arts.

A non-governmental organization pursues its objectives, inter alia, through cooperation with state and local government institutions, health care institutions, other non-governmental organizations and individuals. Such cooperation may take the form of organizational support, partial or total financing of an undertaking or assistance in obtaining the necessary funds from other sources. Examples of such activities include the creation of libraries, employee volunteer fairy-tale therapy, preparation of educational publications (e.g. therapeutic fairy tales for very young oncology patients) and making them available free of charge (in the form of eBooks and audiobooks). The Foundation also organizes in-house training in fairy tales and bibliotherapy for company employees and then coordinates a program in which volunteers hold regular meetings with children or seniors in institutions. The program can also be conducted online or by telephone.

The events of recent years (the pandemic, war in Ukraine) have also put the Foundation's activities on a different track. In response to the social isolation (pandemic lockdown) during the prevailing outbreak of the COVID-19 virus, the Foundation's activities were enriched by an *online* fairy tale therapy program, taking place via the Internet. These were book encounters conducted live via LIVE reports on Instagram by 20 ambassadors – people well-known in the media world. During the pandemic, the Foundation also ran the "Books - for health!" campaign, which supported hospital patients and wards of care and support institutions with literature. The campaign was intended to draw attention to the problems resulting from long-term isolation – disrupted interpersonal relationships, a sense of destabilization, heightened anxiety or long-term loneliness. These activities complemented traditional treatment methods and supported the mental sphere, which is of great importance in the healing process.

In 2022, waves of refugees, especially children, were in need of support due to the war in Ukraine. Polish and Ukrainian publishers, educators, NGOs and others responded immediately by making content available for free on their websites. As the Foundation's mission is to promote reading, social education and relationship building, links to the most interesting materials were published on the website: e-books with fairy tales, audiobooks, coloring books and educational materials.

The Business Partner

One of the Foundation's partners in social activities is a leader on the Polish lending market, a company that is part of an international financial group based in the UK. The group operates in Central and Eastern Europe, Mexico and Australia. It has been operating in Poland for more than 25 years and its services have been used by more than 4 million Poles to date. The company has been repeatedly awarded the titles of Ethical Company, Top Employer award. "Top Brand" and "Winner European Customer Centricity Award 2020, and in 2022 it received the "Fair To Women" award.

The company actively supports campaigns that improve the lives of local communities and smaller groups in need of help. It is an organisation committed to partnerships and cooperation with other business and social entities. It has implemented more than 500 social projects, passing on to the social environment the commitment of company volunteers as well as significant project funding. Since 2006, it has been implementing an employee volunteering program, caring for local communities, running financial education programs and planting trees. Many initiatives are long-term programs with the same beneficiary. The diverse projects allow a large number of employees to be selected and involved, thereby making a positive impact on the environment in which the company operates. For example, in 2021, 275 employees and client advisors carried out 29 projects, contributing 1,350 hours of volunteering. Assistance went to more than 770,000 beneficiaries. Employees are given time off on a selected day of the year to carry out volunteering activities.

In 2020-2021, during the COVID-19 pandemic, the company supported local hospitals with financial and in-kind assistance. In 2022, in turn, the company rented a house for Ukrainian women with young children who had to flee their country because of the war, and company volunteers renovated and equipped it within three weeks. To this day, Ukrainian women with children find shelter and psychological support in the 'Mother's Home'.

The company has been working with the Foundation since 2017 and has carried out many valuable, long-term activities for the benefit of many thousands of recipients, e.g. in 2021 the cooperation program with the Foundation helped 100,000 beneficiaries. Books were collected for the Foundation at the company's facilities. Together, dozens of hospital libraries were opened. The foundations of a volunteer fairy tale therapy structure were established in a dozen locations. Office space was made available for staff training in fairy-tale therapy. Trained company volunteers visit young patients in hospitals and conduct fairy tale therapy activities for them – in addition to reading, they discuss readings, conduct exercises, play games and spend time with the patients. Many of the company's employees, including members of the board of directors, are involved in supporting young patients during difficult times in hospital. Every year before Christmas, they visit children staying in the wards of the pediatric hospital, give them presents and read books. In pandemic, a telephone bibliotherapy session was held jointly with the Foundation for senior citizens from a *nursing home*.

As emphasized during the interview, the benefits are probably different for each volunteer, but the strengthening of interpersonal and communication skills and openness were repeated in the interviews. For the *interviewee*, who also visited the young patients, the most important thing was the feeling that the visit helped, and took their minds off their everyday hospital life. Encounters on hospital wards made her once again aware of the hierarchy of life values and what is most important in life. The benefits for employees carry over into benefits for the company. The volunteer experience has strengthened the commitment of the team. The courage to take on new challenges. A good example is the aforementioned Mother's Home. It is a place of refuge for pregnant women and women with young children who had to flee from war-torn Ukraine. The idea for its creation was born three days after Russia's attack on Ukraine. It took less than a month to find the facility and refurbish it with the efforts of company volunteers. Had it not been for previous experience with, among other things, fairy-tale therapy, it would probably have been more difficult for the employees to achieve such a spectacular effect.

The Hospital Partner

The Regional Specialized Children's Hospital is one of the oldest pediatric hospitals in Poland, having been in operation since 1876. It currently consists of 10 wards, 22 specialist clinics and has 198 beds. Every day, more than 500 employees care for the smallest patients, in the spirit of the motto: "We fight for the life, health and smile of the child". Every year, the hospital provides 77,000 consultations, and hospitalizes 8,000 patients.

The hospital's mission is to promote health and treat all children in need living in Kraków and the Małopolska voivodship, as well as neighboring voivodships, with particular emphasis on psychiatry, rheumatology, neurology, allergology, gastrology, endocrinology and pulmonology. It fulfils this mission through specialized diagnostics and therapy within the framework of inpatient treatment and specialist outpatient clinics, constantly improving the quality of services, improving the skills of the staff, adapting to the needs and expectations of patients, improving the conditions of patients' hospitalization and the work of the staff. Among the hospital's strategic objectives is the expansion of cooperation in the field of health promotion and protection. The treatment offer is enriched by non-standard forms of therapy in which patients using the services of the hospital and the ward participate, including: dogotherapy, fairy tale therapy or horticultural therapy (garden therapy).

One of the hospital's departments is the Clinical Psychiatry Ward for Children. It is a child psychiatry centre that provides continuous, comprehensive, all-round care in many forms, including: inpatient, day treatment, outpatient, individual, group, family or therapeutic community therapy. A strong emphasis is placed on the psychiatry of the young child. If necessary, short inpatient stays of the child with the mother are possible. The unit is very experienced in the diagnosis and treatment of holistic developmental (including autism), behavioural and nutritional disorders. It strives to make the patient's treatment a process and to have a permanent team of therapists working with the patient wherever possible. Speech therapy care is also provided as an ongoing element to support patient development.

According to Dalton and co-authors (2020), public health emergencies such as pandemic take a toll on both physical and mental health. Children are particularly vulnerable to such situations, due to their limited understanding of events. They may not be able to communicate their feelings in the same way as adults. Children, due to their inability to escape physical and psychological harm, have limited coping strategies. Conversely, school closures and separation from friends in younger and older children can cause stress and anxiety. Psychological suffering can also be exacerbated by media coverage of crisis events and unverified information circulating on social media (Dalton et al., 2020). The authors of 'The State of the World's Children 2021' report call on national governments and public and private sector partners to commit to improving the mental health of all children and protecting those in need. Among the demands are investments in prevention efforts, programs for parents and caregivers or tackling the taboo on mental illness (Keeley, 2021). Imran and colleagues (2020) also postulate that prioritising mental health, including child and adolescent mental health, should be an essential component of any universal, community-led response to the COVID-19 pandemic (Imran et al., 2020). Concern for the mental health of young children and the sense of responsibility of the volunteers involved meant that one of the first hospital wards to which the fairy tale therapy program returned after the pandemic was the Psychiatry Ward for Children in Regional Specialised Children's Hospital.

Overview of the Partnership: Fairy Tale Therapy Program in Children's Hospitals

The fairy tale therapy program, implemented in Polish hospitals, is a CSR program created for a business entity by a non-governmental organisation (the Foundation). The program was planned in such a way as to use not only the financial potential, but also the personal, organizational and content-related potential of the business partner. The implementation of the project was preceded by an analysis and consideration of the needs of beneficiaries and volunteers. Importantly, at its core was the compatibility of the partners' organizational goals, which influenced the course of the partnership. This is a rare model of cooperation between a large financial institution and an NGO, in which both entities are partners, supporting each other with their resources and achieving tangible social results – far from greenwashing and sham activities.

Fairy-tale education means reading books, discussing and playing together with children. Volunteers visit hospitals and children's homes, carrying out story-education meetings with the foundation's youngest beneficiaries. Their aim is to show the children's guardians (parents, educators, teachers) a concrete tool through which it is possible to build a deep relationship with the child, to identify and name emotions together with him or her, and to support him or her in difficult experiences. In this case, developmental bibliotherapy is implemented, which can be used by teachers and other helpers to facilitate normal development and self-actualisation in an essentially healthy population, as opposed to clinical bibliotherapy, which is used by trained professionals dealing with serious emotional or behavioural problems (McMillen & Pehrsson, 2004).

After opening a hundred libraries, the Foundation looked for a scientifically researched tool to use books as psychological support. This is how a program of first fairy tale therapy and then bibliotherapy was developed, both involving the use of the therapeutic function of literature. This is of particular relevance in hospital centres as well as in aid and care institutions.

Initially, the Foundation made contact with the establishments itself. The person responsible for contacting the beneficiaries agreed on the details and a cooperation agreement was signed. Suggestions from local coordinators were also used. There was never any trouble with the establishments, they were very willing to cooperate, seeing many benefits, already described in the context of fairy tale therapy. Contracts were always renewed, demonstrating a desire to continue the program.

The program has over 200 volunteers and 26 coordinators. Each volunteer, prior to the start of the fairytale therapy meetings, undergoes a comprehensive training in fairytale therapy. During the workshop, volunteers gain knowledge and skills on fairy tale therapy and identifying their own emotions. Volunteers are supervised by local coordinators who accompany them on their first visits to the centres.

In the period 2017 - 2020 (before the COVID-19 pandemic), fairy tale therapy took place periodically, up to 28 times a week, for nearly 60 hours, in institutions located in 13 Polish cities. It was conducted in many different paediatric wards – cardiology, oncology, haematology, orthopaedics, psychiatry or internal medicine. Weekly meetings are listed on the schedule (see tab. 2).

Table 2. Weekly fairy tale therapy meetings

Day of the Week	Location (on a Given Day)	Number of Cities (on a Given Day)	Number of Hours (on a Given Day)
Mondays	hospitals, children's homes	2	5
Tuesdays	hospitals, care institution	8	21,5
	hospitals, children's home	8	16,5
Thursdays	hospitals, children's home, care institution	8	15,5

Source: own preparation based on materials from The Foundation

Among the most important benefits resulting from the mutual cooperation of the actors involved were the increased success of all parties' undertakings thanks to the use of synergies, mutual inspiration or gaining insights from a different perspective and the exchange of experiences and skills between the partners, as well as the value for the local community and increased public trust in all actors. During the implementation of the project, between 2017 and 2022, several hundred thousand children were the beneficiaries. It is worth noting that, according to *interviewees from the* Foundation, Parents also benefit from the project. They often listen or ask what the fairy tale therapy method is all about and this is also a very important aspect of the fairy tale activities. From the company's perspective, the participation of selected employees in the project as volunteers has raised the social awareness of other employees and increased interest in volunteering within the company. Company volunteers emphasised that the project had an impact on all aspects of their lives, both inside and outside the organisation. It improved relationships between employees and made them rely on each other more, in a way that they were ready to help each other in their private lives as well. Participation in the project increased employees' awareness of the social problems around them and, as a result, their willingness to help others increased. At an organizational level, positive relationships between employees increased their satisfaction and fostered greater commitment to their work. In turn, increased employee engagement encouraged the company to increase support for the implementation of future editions of the project (Brzustewicz et al., 2022).

The fairy tale therapy program, in a modified form, also took place during the pandemic when all hospitals were closed. Two programs were launched in 2020. The first involved evening fairy tale therapy meetings led by ambassadors (40 meetings, 26 ambassadors involved). The second program, on the other hand, was online story time with volunteers (31 story times) who met with children in hospital wards before the pandemic. In 2021, on the other hand, a special tele-library therapy program for senior citizens was launched, an online fairy tale therapy program was introduced and 113 fairy tale therapy educators were trained (also online). After the lockdown was lifted, fairy tale therapy was reactivated in two cities. The Foundation has recently received grants to develop this program in children's hospital wards, which gives hope for thriving activities in the years to come.

Factors Facilitating Cross-Sectoral Collaboration During the Implementation of a Fairy Tale Therapy Program in Hospitals

Zhu and co-authors (2019) list among the factors affecting cross-sector partnerships both those that foster them and those that hinder collaboration. Based on this typology, seven facilitating factors and four inhibiting factors can be identified, based on information gleaned from interviews and conversations, analyses of reports and the authors' own observations (one of the co-authors participates as a volunteer in a fairy tale therapy program).

Thus, among the facilitating factors for mobilising cross-sector collaborations are:

1. **Shared values** – at an organizational level, for all partners, meeting the needs of beneficiaries was paramount from the outset. The alignment of the organisation's strategic goals, the sharing of complementary resources and the high level of commitment of top management enabled the partnership to work together. The action of the partners on the basis of shared values led to positive changes in the social awareness of employees and strengthened the commitment of the company and the Foundation to CSR goals, which, as Brzustewicz and her team (2022) note, indicates the emergence of social impact.
2. **Durability of cooperation** – cooperation was facilitated by effective communication between partners and an atmosphere of mutual trust. In the case in question, the comprehensiveness and longevity of the activities initiated together are also characteristic. These elements allowed for the development of a long-term trilateral relationship. Reflecting on the experience of partnership, as well as on individual values and emotions, is an important source of learning that helps to understand and appreciate the differences encountered (Battisti, 2009). The Foundation highly values the partnership with the company and claims that the collaborative model created together can be a model of action for cross-sector partnerships. The partnership with the Foundation is also rated very highly by the Company. Its cooperation arouses a great deal of positive emotion among

employees, advisors, customers and also cooperating companies. Thanks to the cooperation with the Foundation, the company is sure that the needed help goes to the right places. During visits to the hospital ward by the volunteers conducting fairy tale therapy, the little patients often ask about the next visit and expect it to continue, suggesting that fairy tale therapy is a meaningful element for children during their hospital stay.

3. **Commitment of employees and volunteers** – a successful collaboration would not be possible without the commitment of employees. The company's volunteers are part of the Foundation's team and work together to achieve the mission. In addition to the donated funds, they are realistically involved in the Foundation's activities – they donate books, receive training in story therapy, attend library openings and regularly visit young patients in paediatric wards. Participation in the project has been a source of great emotional commitment and satisfaction for the volunteers, which ultimately motivates them to continue their involvement in the project. As a result, the value offered to the beneficiaries is unique and provides an opportunity to create wider social change. Satisfaction with the introduction of this form of activation into the employee volunteering offer is rated very highly by the company. The company conducts satisfaction surveys on the activities offered after successive editions of its volunteering programs, including fairy tale therapy conducted in paediatric wards. The conclusions of the regular surveys are very satisfying. Volunteers appreciate that volunteering has given them the chance to do something good and to strengthen their skills. They also appreciate that the company is involved in such activities both financially and organisationally. From the company's perspective, the participation of selected employees in the project as volunteers has increased the social awareness of other employees and increased interest in volunteering within the company. Involvement in the fairy tale therapy process was shown not only by the volunteers and beneficiaries (little patients), but also by their families and medical staff. This is important, as the health service needs service-oriented and customer-focused staff who develop informed relationships with clients. The RM approach is extremely important, especially because of the critical role of the human factor in health service delivery (Ersoy & Tehci, 2023).
4. **Hospitals openness** – the analysed hospital joined the project in 2017. The introduction of this form of activation into the department's offer, as well as the cooperation with partners, are rated very highly by the hospital. There are a number of benefits that the hospital sees from this form of contact with patients (both for the hospital, staff and patients). The hospital is building its positive image in the province. As bibliotherapy is not intended as a treatment but as a complement to it (Caldin, 2009), it provides an opportunity to broaden and diversify children's activities and allows them to be observed in new situations. The activities help children to calm down, exercise concentration and imagination, and invite them to reflect and talk about important topics. Hospital staff, recognising the range of benefits, have been very open and supportive of the implementation of this program.
5. **Health-promoting context** – a collaboration between different sectors allows access to different resources, knowledge and experiences. This is extremely important in developing and promoting innovative approaches to working with, for example, sick children. In the case study, shared values, activism and cooperation are promoted. The need for mental and emotional support for children and young people, especially after the pandemic, is indisputable and recognised by many communities. Here, cross-sector partnerships focus on improving the wellbeing of children on hospital wards and their emotional support. Partners help to secure funding, human resources and community support, which is crucial to the success of such projects.

6. **Cross-sector leadership and governance** – it is important to emphasise that on the part of each partner, board members and middle managers are very much involved in the project. Through this activity, they inspire their employees and others to take action. The culture of volunteering is very much entrenched in the company, as an employee volunteering program has been in place since 2006. Not only rank-and-file employees but also directors and board members get involved in projects. When the company started working with an NGO in 2017, employees, in addition to setting up shared libraries or collecting books, also joined in the fairy tale therapy program. This approach allowed the company to actively use the potential of its volunteers and involve them in another new type of assistance – competence volunteering. Company volunteers trained by the Foundation's experts in fairy tale therapy use the knowledge they gain at meetings in hospitals. Senior management is also involved in the action of reading to children who are in paediatric wards. The company's CEO and members of the management team visit children in the paediatric hospital on the occasion of Santa Claus.
7. **Supporting activities** – social campaigns, such as the creation of libraries, the Great Book Collection, Benches (in the shape of open books) or inviting people known from the world of media, culture, art and literature to take part in promotional activities – these initiatives facilitate partner recognition and partnership building, which translates into easier acquisition of sponsorship and funding.

On the other hand, the following factors stand out among the challenges inhibiting cross-sectoral cooperation when implementing a fairy tale therapy program in hospitals

1. **The mental load on volunteers** – the fairy tale therapy is challenging. It is working with the emotions of both children and volunteers. Therefore, it is a good idea to prepare well for the activities. Before each visit, the volunteer should answer the question whether he or she is ready for the meeting today, whether he or she has the energy and strength to share it with others. After the meeting, he or she should leave himself or herself space and time to reflect, to talk to a more experienced person. Peer support is extremely important, especially when volunteers visit 'difficult' hospital wards, e.g. paediatric cardiology, oncology, haematology or psychiatry.
2. **Moral and organizational constraints** – in the opinion of the *interviewee* from the Company, fairy tale therapy classes are a special kind of volunteering. In story therapy, the most important thing is to follow the child and his/her needs. The number of pages read or the precise adherence to the lesson plan is not important. Sometimes, just being willing to do the activities is enough. Sometimes the fairy tale therapy is not carried out due to the children's bad mood. It is therefore important to be open to the little patient, but also to his or her loved ones, who sometimes accompany him or her to the hospital. It is also important to be able to withdraw if the patient is tired or unwell. In some cases, especially for children with trauma or difficult experiences, the use of some elements of story therapy may need to be used with caution to avoid triggering unwanted emotional reactions.

In contrast, the limitations identified by the hospital associated with the provision of fairy tale therapy are the difficulties in delivering the program in larger groups of patients. As Pardeck & Pardeck (1993) suggest: "the ideal group size is between six and eight participants. The group should be homogeneous. The members of the group should be of a similar age or be more or less at the same developmental level, so that the book chosen is suitable for all members of the group". Due to the variety of patients staying in the same ward at any given time and place, it is sometimes very difficult to fulfil these conditions. Another issue is also that sometimes children may seem uninterested or distracted (Lucas & Soares, 2013). However, it is worth bearing in mind that some children can absorb information even when their backs are turned to the storyteller. This suggests individual differences in learning styles, but also indicates that the beneficial effects of bibliotherapy may only become apparent after some time (Berns, 2004).

There are also limited opportunities to use fairy tale therapy in a wider context as a valuable external communication and promotional tool for the hospital. It is very important to respect the intimacy and dignity of young patients and to protect their image and sensitive data. In some situations, for example in a psychiatry or haematology department, it is forbidden or undesirable to capture images of children participating in fairy tale therapy on any audiovisual media.

3. **Financial and staffing constraints** – constraints of this kind can inhibit the creation, operation and maintenance of cross-sectoral cooperation. Limited external sources of funding (such as grants) and reliance largely on funds raised from sponsors and partners, limit opportunities to engage in new initiatives or expand existing ones. In addition, difficulties in recruiting volunteers for some programs can also be a threat, undermining their sustainability. The effectiveness of bibliotherapy may also be limited by the availability of books or materials or resources. Others are related to insufficient knowledge of the person conducting the fairy tale therapy. This may relate, for example, to developmental problems of children and adolescents as well as the selection of appropriate literature. Hence, the demand for proper preparation and training of all volunteers is extremely important.
4. **Geographical dispersion** - the structure of cross-sector partnerships is influenced by geographical location, with which certain cultural factors or material resources are associated (Awad, 2023). In addition, the dispersion of beneficiaries creates logistical challenges and influences the choice of facility in a given city. In addition to the needs of the hospital, the ability of volunteers to commute, coming from different parts of the city and even suburban areas, is also taken into account. Among other things, the public transport network and connections to other parts of the city are important. Access is also facilitated by existing cycle paths and the number of parking spaces in the hospital car park. It is also worth emphasising that our study refers to the presentation of the application of fairy tale therapy in one hospital in Poland, while the fairy tale therapy program is implemented in 13 Polish cities. This has the effect of limiting, among other things, the possibility of frequent interpersonal contacts between partners, coordinators and volunteers.

DISCUSSION AND CONCLUSION

This study extends the existing literature on the growing use of intersectoral collaboration in addressing important social problems through the use of story-telling. An existing three-way cross-sector partnership between hospitals, businesses and an NGO is taking action to improve the mental health of hospitalised children. The fairy tale therapy program conducted in selected children's hospitals can at the same time be seen as a marketing instrument to support relationship building in health care.

When analysing the partnership, one can see the interconnectedness of interests between the partners. The results show that each partner brings complementary resources that are relevant to achieving the partnership's mission. The relatively close cooperation between partners leads to interaction value from the point of view of all organizations involved. Cross-sector partnership refers to a collaboration in which all participants were fully and equally involved. This is in line with the work of Morgan & Hunt (1994), who argue that the development of long-term relationships is possible by creating an atmosphere of mutual trust built primarily through processes of communication and sustained collaboration between partners. The previously cited factors of trust, bonding, communication, shared value, empathy, and reciprocity (Sin et al., 2002) influence the relationship between partners. The research conducted also allowed for the identification and analysis of factors that foster and constrain cross-sectoral cooperation. Their analysis in the context of the implementation of the current or similar programs will enable positive factors to be strengthened and negative factors to be counteracted.

Fairy tale therapy can be integrated into children's hospital provision in a way that is not only effective, but also strategic. By involving partners from different sectors, it can create strong synergies that benefit both the children and the organizations involved in the therapy. Children's hospitals can establish partnerships with community organizations, foundations or other stakeholders interested in supporting children in their recovery. They can also provide access to funding, expertise, volunteers or other resources needed to deliver story therapy. These partnerships can also help to raise the profile and visibility of the fairy tale therapy program through joint campaigns and promotional activities. Fairy tale therapy can also be a tool for working with the local community. Collaborating with community organizations, schools or foundations that promote children's health and well-being can strengthen relationships with local stakeholders and build the hospital's reputation as a place where patients are treated holistically. However, it is important to note that despite the marketing aspects, fairy tale therapy in children's hospitals is primarily aimed at providing therapeutic support and improving the wellbeing of young patients. Marketing here is a tool to promote and reach the right people, but it should not override the primary goal, which is the health and well-being of patients.

Our analysis has several limitations. To generalise the results, more similar community projects offered in other locations should be analysed. Although they may be similar, their complexity and unique characteristics may affect the formation and implementation of cross-sector partnerships and the outcomes of the byway program. The local context can significantly influence the types of collaborations and the factors contributing to their success. Our findings may not reflect the diversity of experiences in other areas. Secondly, our data on cross-sectoral activities was reported by key informants, no larger scale research was conducted. Thirdly: children were not included in the interviews, even though they are the largest and most important group of beneficiaries. Based on the ethical principle of respect for persons, parental consent and child consent function together to protect the child and promote self-determination (Roth-Cline & Nelson, 2013). Parents or legal guardians must give their consent (written or verbal) to the implementation of research involving the child, and in many cases must be present during the research. This rule should absolutely apply to any type of research involving children (whether medical or marketing). It is not in every case possible for a parent to accompany a child during a hospital stay, and hence, for this group of beneficiaries, participant observation has been limited. Due to the turnover of patients in hospital wards, it is also difficult to assess unequivocally its effectiveness in relation to a specific child.

In an era of disruptive technology, revolutionary change, pervasive digitisation and artificial intelligence, healthcare systems around the world are transforming and changing. The goal of these changes is to make healthcare more affordable, accessible, acceptable, collaborative and positive. The advancement of digital technology and its impact on every area of life is happening continuously on a global scale. However, it will not replace real, deep relationships and artificial intelligence will not teach how to deal with emotions.

REFERENCES

Adamo, S. M., Serpieri, S. A., De Falco, R., Di Cicco, T., Foggia, R., Giacometti, P., & Siani, G. (2008). Tom Thumb in hospital: The fairy tale workshop in a paediatric oncology and haematology ward. *Psychodynamic Practice*, *14*(3), 263–280. doi:10.1080/14753630802141865

Arya, B., & Salk, J. E. (2006). Cross-sector alliance learning and effectiveness of voluntary codes of corporate social responsibility. *Business Ethics Quarterly*, *16*(2), 211–234. doi:10.5840/beq200616223

Astuti, H. J., & Nagase, K. (2014). Patient loyalty to healthcare organizations: Relationship marketing and satisfaction. *International Journal of Management and Marketing Research*, *7*(2), 39–56.

Austin, J. E., & Seitanidi, M. M. (2012b). Collaborative value creation: A review of partnering between nonprofits and businesses. Part 2: Partnership processes and outcomes. *Nonprofit and Voluntary Sector Quarterly*, *41*(6), 929–968. doi:10.1177/0899764012454685

Awad, M. H. (2023). Place and the structuring of cross-sector partnerships: The moral and material conflicts over healthcare and homelessness. *Journal of Business Ethics*, *184*(4), 933–955. doi:10.100710551-023-05360-w PMID:37168486

Balogun, B., & Ogunnaike, O. (2017). Healthcare Organisations in a global marketplace: A systematic Review of the literature on healthcare marketing. *SSRN*, *1*(5). Advance online publication. doi:10.2139srn.3047747

Barroso-Méndez, M. J., Galera-Casquet, C., & Valero-Amaro, V. (2014). Partnerships between businesses and NGOs in the field of corporate social responsibility: A model of success from the perspective of relationship marketing. *Journal of Relationship Marketing*, *13*(1), 1–27. doi:10.1080/15332667.2014.882626

Berger, S., Saut, A. M., & Berssaneti, F. T. (2020). Using patient feedback to drive quality improvement in hospitals: A qualitative study. *BMJ Open*, *10*(10), e037641. doi:10.1136/bmjopen-2020-037641 PMID:33099495

Berkowitz, E. N. (2021). *Essentials of health care marketing*. Jones & Bartlett Learning.

Berns, C. F. (2004). Bibliotherapy: Using books to help bereaved children. *Omega*, *48*(4), 321–336. doi:10.2190/361D-JHD8-RNJT-RYJV

Berry, L. L. (1995). Relationship marketing of services—Growing interest, emerging perspectives. *Journal of the Academy of Marketing Science*, *23*(4), 236–245. doi:10.1177/009207039502300402

Berry, L. L. (2002). Relationship marketing of services perspectives from 1983 and 2000. *Journal of Relationship Marketing*, *1*(1), 59–77. doi:10.1300/J366v01n01_05

Bettelheim, B. (1976). *The Uses of Enchantment: The Meaning of Fairy Tales*. Vintage. doi:10.1037/e309842005-008

Bielińska-Dusza. E. (2021). Znaczenie współpracy międzyorganizacyjnej w przedsiębiorstwach z branży kreatywnej. In Trendy w badaniu przedsiębiorczości. Uniwersytet Ekonomiczny w Katowicach.

Booms, B. H., & Bitner, M. J. (1981). Marketing Strategies and Organization Structures for Service Firms. In *Marketing of Services*. American Marketing Association.

Borecka, I. (2001). *Biblioterapia: teoria i praktyka; poradnik*. Wydawn. SBP.

Bryson, J. M., Crosby, B. C., & Stone, M. M. (2006). The design and implementation of Cross-Sector collaborations: Propositions from the literature. *Public Administration Review*, *66*(s1), 44–55. doi:10.1111/j.1540-6210.2006.00665.x

Bryson, J. M., Crosby, B. C., & Stone, M. M. (2015). Designing and implementing cross-sector collaborations: Needed and challenging. *Public Administration Review*, *75*(5), 647–663. doi:10.1111/puar.12432

Brzustewicz, P., Escher, I., Hatami, A., Hermes, J., Keränen, A., & Ulkuniemi, P. (2022). Emergence of social impact in company–NGO relationships in corporate volunteering. *Journal of Business Research*, *140*, 62–75. doi:10.1016/j.jbusres.2021.11.089

Buse, K., & Walt, G. (2000). Global public-private partnerships: Part I - a new development in health? *Bulletin of the World Health Organization*, *78*, 549–561. PMID:10885184

Cankar, S. S., & Petkovsek, V. (2013). Private and public sector innovation and the importance of cross-sector collaboration. *Journal of Applied Business Research*, *29*(6), 1597–1606. doi:10.19030/jabr.v29i6.8197

Castro, E. M., Van Regenmortel, T., Vanhaecht, K., Sermeus, W., & Van Hecke, A. (2016). Patient empowerment, patient participation and patient-centeredness in hospital care: A concept analysis based on a literature review. *Patient Education and Counseling*, *99*(12), 1923–1939. doi:10.1016/j.pec.2016.07.026 PMID:27450481

Chauhan, M. K. (2015). How relationship marketing can add value to your practice. *Medical Economics*, *92*(24), 61. PMID:26875312

Clarke, A., & Crane, A. (2018). Cross-Sector Partnerships for Systemic Change: Systematized Literature Review and Agenda for Further Research. *The Journal of Business*, *150*(2), 303–313. doi:10.100710551-018-3922-2 PMID:30996499

Cohen, L. J. (1993). Discover the healing power of books. *AJN The American Journal of Nursing*, *93*(10), 70–74. PMID:8213951

Cook, K. E., Earles-Vollrath, T., & Ganz, J. B. (2006). Bibliotherapy. *Intervention in School and Clinic*, *42*(2), 91–100. doi:10.1177/10534512060420020801

Creswell, J. W., & Creswell, J. D. (2017). *Research design: Qualitative, quantitative, and mixed methods approaches*. Sage publications.

Cronin, C. E., Singh, S. R., Turner, J. S., & Evashwick, C. J. (2022). Hospitals' contributions to their communities: Should they be regulated? *Frontiers in Public Health*, *10*, 1064210. doi:10.3389/fpubh.2022.1064210 PMID:36504974

Crothers, S. M. (1917). *A literary clinic*. Houghton Mifflin.

Dalton, L., Rapa, E., & Stein, A. (2020). Protecting the psychological health of children through effective communication about COVID-19. *The Lancet. Child & Adolescent Health, 4*(5), 346–347. doi:10.1016/S2352-4642(20)30097-3 PMID:32243784

Ding, B., & Hernández, X. F. (2023). Case study as a methodological foundation for Technology Road-mapping (TRM): Literature review and future research agenda. *Journal of Engineering and Technology Management, 67*, 101731. doi:10.1016/j.jengtecman.2023.101731

Dwivedi, Y. K., Ismagilova, E., Hughes, D. L., Carlson, J., Filieri, R., Jacobson, J., Jain, V., Karjaluoto, H., Kefi, H., Krishen, A. S., Kumar, V., Rahman, M. M., Raman, R., Rauschnabel, P. A., Rowley, J., Salo, J., Tran, G. A., & Wang, Y. (2021). Setting the future of digital and social media marketing research: Perspectives and research propositions. *International Journal of Information Management, 59*, 102168. doi:10.1016/j.ijinfomgt.2020.102168

Ersoy, Y., & Tehci, A. (2023). Relationship marketing orientation in healthcare organizations with the AHP method. Internal and external customer perspective. *Operations Research and Decisions, 33.*

Gilaninia, S., Almani, A. M., Pournaserani, A., & Mousavian, S. J. (2011). Relationship marketing: A new approach to marketing in the third millennium. *Australian Journal of Basic and Applied Sciences, 5*(5), 787–799.

Gordon, I. H. (1998). *Relationship Marketing*. John Wiley & Sons.

Greene, S. M., Tuzzio, L., & Cherkin, D. (2012). A framework for making patient-centered care front and center. *The Permanente Journal, 16*(3), 49–53. doi:10.7812/TPP/12-025 PMID:23012599

Grönroos, C. (1994). Quo vadis, marketing? Toward a relationship marketing paradigm. *Journal of Marketing Management, 10*(5), 347–360. doi:10.1080/0267257X.1994.9964283

Grönroos, C. (2000). Creating a relationship dialogue: Communication, interaction and value. *The Marketing Review, 1*(1), 5–14. doi:10.1362/1469347002523428

Gummesson, E. (1994). Broadening and specifying relationship marketing. *Asia-Australia Marketing Journal, 2*(1), 31–43. doi:10.1016/S1320-1646(94)70276-8

Hamel, J., Dufour, S., & Fortin, D. (1993). *Case study methods* (Vol. 32). Sage Publications. doi:10.4135/9781412983587

Han, H., & Hyun, S. S. (2015). Customer retention in the medical tourism industry: Impact of quality, satisfaction, trust, and price reasonableness. *Tourism Management, 46*, 20–29. doi:10.1016/j.tourman.2014.06.003

Haristiani, R., Wahyuningsih, W., & Susaldi, S. (2022). Effect of Storytelling Therapy can Reduces Anxiety for Children with Leukemia at DR Wahidin Sudiro Husodo Hospital in Makassar. *Jurnal Ilmiah Ilmu Keperawatan Indonesia, 12*(02), 88–92. doi:10.33221/jiiki.v12i02.1877

Heale, R., & Twycross, A. (2018). What is a case study? *Evidence-Based Nursing, 21*(1), 7–8. doi:10.1136/eb-2017-102845 PMID:29146764

Imran, N., Zeshan, M., & Pervaiz, Z. (2020). Mental health considerations for children & adolescents in COVID-19 Pandemic. *Pakistan Journal of Medical Sciences, 36*(COVID19-S4), S67.

James, N. (2007). The use of email interviewing as a qualitative method of inquiry in educational research. *British Educational Research Journal, 33*(6), 963–976. doi:10.1080/01411920701657074

Jenkinson, C., Coulter, A., Bruster, S., Richards, N., & Chandola, T. (2002). Patients' experiences and satisfaction with health care: Results of a questionnaire study of specific aspects of care. *Quality & Safety in Health Care, 11*(4), 335–339. doi:10.1136/qhc.11.4.335 PMID:12468693

Keeley, B. (2021). *On My Mind--Promoting, Protecting and Caring for Children's Mental Health.* UNICEF.

Kerka, S. (1997). *Developing Collaborative Partnerships*. Practice Application Brief. ERIC Clearinghouse on Adult, Career, and Vocational Education.

Kindig, D. A., & Isham, G. (2014). Population health improvement: A community health business model that engages partners in all sectors. *Frontiers of Health Services Management, 30*(4), 3–20. doi:10.1097/01974520-201404000-00002 PMID:25671991

Kuciapiński, M. J. (2014). The therapeutic and educational properties of fairytale therapy in the early stages of children's development. *Pedagogika Rodziny, 4*(2), 77–93. doi:10.2478/fampe-2014-0019

Lakin, N., & Scheubel, V. (2010). *Corporate Community Involvement : The Definitive Guide to Maximizing Your Business' Societal Engagement.* Routledge.

Lamani, T. R., Sajjan, S. B., & Natekar, D. S. (2021). Effectiveness of bibliotherapy in reducing the level of anxiety among hospitalized children in selected hospital at Bagalkot. *International Journal of Research in Engineering. Science and Management, 4*(3), 153–156.

Lasker, R. D., Weiss, E. S., & Miller, R. (2001). Partnership synergy: A practical framework for studying and strengthening the collaborative advantage. *The Milbank Quarterly, 79*(2), 179–205. doi:10.1111/1468-0009.00203 PMID:11439464

Lucas, C. V., & Soares, L. (2013). Bibliotherapy: A tool to promote children's psychological well-being. *Journal of Poetry Therapy, 26*(3), 137–147. doi:10.1080/08893675.2013.823310

Mac McCullough, J., Singh, S. R., & Leider, J. P. (2019). The importance of governmental and nongovernmental investments in public health and social services for improving community health outcomes. *Journal of Public Health Management and Practice, 25*(4), 348–356. doi:10.1097/PHH.0000000000000856 PMID:31136508

Maiolini, R., Versari, P., Rullani, F., & Seitanidi, M. M. (2022). The role of community participation in cross-sector social partnerships. *Nonprofit and Voluntary Sector Quarterly*, •••, 08997640221130696.

Margherita, G., Martino, M. L., Recano, F., & Camera, F. (2014). Invented fairy tales in groups with onco-haematological children. *Child: Care, Health and Development, 40*(3), 426–434. doi:10.1111/cch.12076 PMID:23672257

McMillen, P. S., & Pehrsson, D. E. (2004). Bibliotherapy for hospital patients. *Journal of Hospital Librarianship, 4*(1), 73–81. doi:10.1300/J186v04n01_07

Menatti, L., Bich, L., & Saborido, C. (2022). Health and environment from adaptation to adaptivity: A situated relational account. *History and Philosophy of the Life Sciences*, *44*(3), 1–28. doi:10.100740656-022-00515-w PMID:35980478

Molina-Mula, J., & Gallo-Estrada, J. (2020). Impact of nurse-patient relationship on quality of care and patient autonomy in decision-making. *International Journal of Environmental Research and Public Health*, *17*(3), 835. doi:10.3390/ijerph17030835 PMID:32013108

Möller, K., & Halinen, A. (2000). Relationship marketing theory: Its roots and direction. *Journal of Marketing Management*, *16*(1-3), 29–54. doi:10.1362/026725700785100460

Morgan, R. M., & Hunt, S. D. (1994). The commitment-trust theory of relationship marketing. *Journal of Marketing*, *58*(3), 20–38. doi:10.1177/002224299405800302

Naina, M., & Pooja, G. (2023). Effectiveness of Bibliothreapy in Reducing the Level of Anxiety among Hospitalised Children. *International Journal of Science and Research (Raipur, India)*, *9*(10), 15. doi:10.21275/SR23303103505

Noh, E., Begun, J. W., White, K. M., & Potthoff, S. J. (2022). US hospital engagement in cross-sector partnerships for population health improvement in socioeconomically distressed counties. *Public Health*, *205*, 55–57. doi:10.1016/j.puhe.2022.01.020 PMID:35235880

Opdenakker, R. J. G. (2006). Advantages and disadvantages of four interview techniques in qualitative research. In *Forum Qualitative Sozialforschung= Forum: Qualitative Social Research*, *7*(4), art-11.

Otani, K., Waterman, B., Faulkner, K. M., Boslaugh, S., & Dunagan, C. W. (2010). How patient reactions to hospital care attributes affect the evaluation of overall quality of care, willingness to recommend, and willingness to return. *Journal of Healthcare Management*, *55*(1), 25–38. doi:10.1097/00115514-201001000-00006 PMID:20210071

Ouzts, D. T. (1991). The emergence of bibliotherapy as a discipline. *Reading Horizons*, *31*(3), 199–206.

Pardeck, J. T., & Pardeck, J. A. (1998). *Children in foster care and adoption: A guide to bibliotherapy*. Greenwood Press.

Parmigiani, A., & Rivera-Santos, M. (2011). Clearing a path through the forest: A meta-review of interorganizational relationships. *Journal of Management*, *37*(4), 1108–1136. doi:10.1177/0149206311407507

Parmigiani, A., & Rivera-Santos, M. (2011). Clearing a path through the forest: A meta-review of interorganizational relationships. *Journal of Management*, *37*(4), 1108–1136. doi:10.1177/0149206311407507

Pascucci, F., Savelli, E., & Gistri, G. (2023). How digital technologies reshape marketing: Evidence from a qualitative investigation. *Italian Journal of Marketing*, *2023*(1), 27–58. doi:10.100743039-023-00063-6

Porter, M. E., & Kramer, M. R. (2011). Tworzenie wartości dla biznesu i społeczeństwa. *Harvard Business Review Polska, 99.*

Prater, M. A., Johnstun, M. L., Dyches, T. T., & Johnstun, M. R. (2006). Using children's books as bibliotherapy for at-risk students: A guide for teachers. *Preventing School Failure*, *50*(4), 5–10. doi:10.3200/PSFL.50.4.5-10

Riordan, R. J., & Wilson, L. S. (1989). Bibliotherapy: Does it work? *Journal of Counseling and Development, 67*(9), 506–508. doi:10.1002/j.1556-6676.1989.tb02131.x

Roth-Cline, M., & Nelson, R. M. (2013). Parental permission and child assent in research on children. *The Yale Journal of Biology and Medicine, 86*(3), 291. PMID:24058304

Selin, E., & Graube, K. (2017). *Reading aloud to children in hospital. Bibliotherapy as a community builder.* Paper presented at IFLA WLIC 2017 – Wrocław, Poland – Libraries. Solidarity. Society. in Session 138 - Literacy and Reading, Libraries for Children and Young Adults, Public Libraries and School Libraries. https://library.ifla.org/id/eprint/1784

Selsky, J. W., & Parker, B. (2005). Cross-sector partnerships to address social issues: Challenges to theory and practice. *Journal of Management, 31*(6), 849–873. doi:10.1177/0149206305279601

Sheth, J. N., & Parvatiyar, A. (1995). The evolution of relationship marketing. *International Business Review, 4*(4), 397–418. doi:10.1016/0969-5931(95)00018-6

Sin, L. Y., Alan, C. B., Yau, O. H., Lee, J. S., & Chow, R. (2002). The effect of relationship marketing orientation on business performance in a service-oriented economy. *Journal of Services Marketing, 16*(7), 656–676. doi:10.1108/08876040210447360

Sin, L. Y., Tse, A. C., Chan, H., Heung, V. C., & Yim, F. H. (2006). The effects of relationship marketing orientation on business performance in the hotel industry. *Journal of Hospitality & Tourism Research (Washington, D.C.), 30*(4), 407–426. doi:10.1177/1096348006287863

Sofaer, S. (1999). Qualitative methods: What are they and why use them? *Health Services Research, 34*(5 Pt 2), 1101. PMID:10591275

Sutherland, B. L., Pecanac, K., LaBorde, T. M., Bartels, C. M., & Brennan, M. B. (2022). Good working relationships: How healthcare system proximity influences trust between healthcare workers. *Journal of Interprofessional Care, 36*(3), 331–339. doi:10.1080/13561820.2021.1920897 PMID:34126853

Taleghani, M., Gilaninia, S., & Mousavian, S. J. (2011). The role of relationship marketing in customer orientation process in the banking industry with focus on loyalty (Case study: Banking industry of Iran). *International Journal of Business and Social Science, 2*(19).

Thomas, G. (2021). How to do your case study. *How to do your case study*, 1-320.

Towe, V. L., Leviton, L., Chandra, A., Sloan, J. C., Tait, M., & Orleans, T. (2016). Cross-sector collaborations and partnerships: Essential ingredients to help shape health and well-being. *Health Affairs, 35*(11), 1964–1969. doi:10.1377/hlthaff.2016.0604 PMID:27834234

Tsitsani, P., Psyllidou, S., Batzios, S. P., Livas, S., Ouranos, M., & Cassimos, D. (2012). Fairy tales: A compass for children's healthy development–a qualitative study in a Greek island. *Child: Care, Health and Development, 38*(2), 266–272. doi:10.1111/j.1365-2214.2011.01216.x PMID:21375565

Tzokas, N., & Saren, M. (2004). Competitive advantage, knowledge and relationship marketing: Where, what and how? *Journal of Business and Industrial Marketing, 19*(2), 124–135. doi:10.1108/08858620410524007

Veloutsou, C., Saren, M., & Tzokas, N. (2002). Relationship marketing: What if…? *European Journal of Marketing*, *36*(4), 433–449. doi:10.1108/03090560210417255

Vestergaard, A., Langevang, T., Morsing, M., & Murphy, L. (2021). Partnerships for development. Assessing the impact potential of cross-sector partnerships. *World Development*, *143*, 105447. doi:10.1016/j.worlddev.2021.105447

Waddock, S. A. (1991). A typology of social partnership organizations. *Administration & Society*, *22*(4), 480–515. doi:10.1177/009539979102200405

Wagner, H. C., Fleming, D., Mangold, W. G., & LaForge, R. W. (1994). Relationship marketing in health care. *Marketing Health Services*, *14*(4), 42. PMID:10154636

Waters, S., Edmondston, S. J., Yates, P. J., & Gucciardi, D. F. (2016). Identification of factors influencing patient satisfaction with orthopaedic outpatient clinic consultation: A qualitative study. *Manual Therapy*, *25*, 48–55. doi:10.1016/j.math.2016.05.334 PMID:27422597

Wright, G. H., & Taylor, A. (2005). Strategic partnerships and relationship marketing in healthcare. *Public Management Review*, *7*(2), 203–224. doi:10.1080/14719030500091251

Wu, C. C. (2011). The impact of hospital brand image on service quality, patient satisfaction and loyalty. *African Journal of Business Management*, *5*(12), 4873.

Yati, M., Wahyuni, S., & Islaeli, I. (2017). The effect of storytelling in a play therapy on anxiety level in pre-school children during hospitalization in the general hospital of Buton. *Public Health of Indonesia*, *3*(3), 96–101. doi:10.36685/phi.v3i3.134

Yildirim, Y., Amarat, M., & Akbolat, M. (2022). Effect of relationship marketing on hospital loyalty: The mediating role of patient satisfaction. *International Journal of Pharmaceutical and Healthcare Marketing*, *16*(3), 337–353. doi:10.1108/IJPHM-01-2021-0010

Yin, R. K. (2009). *Case Study Research. Design and Methods* (4th ed.). SAGE Publications.

Zhu, X., Weigel, P., Baloh, J., Nataliansyah, M., Gunn, N., & Mueller, K. (2019). Mobilising cross-sector collaborations to improve population health in US rural communities: A qualitative study. *BMJ Open*, *9*(11), e030983. doi:10.1136/bmjopen-2019-030983 PMID:31699729

KEY TERMS AND DEFINITIONS

Bibliotherapy: A therapeutic approach using books and other forms of literature used to support a patient's mental health.

Case Study: One of the qualitative research methods, the main aim of which is to illustrate a certain case as well as possible. It provides an in-depth analysis of a specific phenomenon. It includes a detailed analysis of the case, goals, objectives, motives, and actions.

Cross-Sector Collaboration: A process where organizations from different sectors come together to focus their expertise and resources on a complex issue important to the community they want to support.

Fairy Tale Therapy: An important method of support and therapeutic influence for children, which can help them to deal effectively with emotions or difficult situations (e.g., illness, pain, frustration).

Partnerships: A voluntary, cooperative relationship between participants (partners) from different sectors, established to achieve a common objective or undertake a specific task and share the risks, responsibilities, resources, competences, and benefits.

Relationship Marketing: Is a relationship management strategy that emphasises customer, patient, etc. satisfaction and loyalty.

Relationships: Interrelationships with other actors (individuals, groups, organizations) in the interpersonal space.

ENDNOTE

1 All information about partners, their activities, collaborations, etc. used in this section is taken from websites, CSR reports, internal documents and also from interviews with staff and volunteers.

Chapter 11
The Application of Design Thinking in Healthcare Marketing:
A Systematic Review

Ioseb Gabelaia
https://orcid.org/0000-0002-6323-6913
Graceland University, USA

ABSTRACT

For this chapter, the systematic review was selected to allow a deep dive and exploration of application design thinking in marketing for healthcare organizations. Moreover, there needs to be more literature that highlights using design thinking in healthcare as a major tool to create awareness and promotion of developed models that enhance the patient experience. This systematic review explores the use and impact of design thinking in healthcare marketing. By synthesizing existing literature, the current study provides comprehension of the theoretical bases, methodologies, and effects of employing design thinking principles in healthcare marketing strategies. Particularly today, technological advancements oblige organizations to be technologically savvy and provide the best future solutions to the customers, in our case, to the patients.

INTRODUCTION

In the digital era, design thinking has grasped substantial interest in various industries, including healthcare, due to its capacity to generate innovative, patient-centered solutions. As a problem-solving approach, design thinking features processes from empathizing, ideation, prototyping, and repetition to address complex challenges. For instance, it encourages a change from a provider-centric to a patient-centric model by vigorously involving patients and healthcare professionals in the design process. By incorporating diverse perceptions and the idea of co-creation, design thinking fosters a subconscious understanding of patients' preferences and experiences, serving as a basis for designing tailored solutions for the industry.

DOI: 10.4018/979-8-3693-0679-6.ch011

The content in this book chapter is organized comprehensively, allowing the reader to follow the material step by step: (1) first, the systematic review process is highlighted, followed by literature analysis. (2) Second, the author presents systematic review findings, the cornerstone of building a three-way approach. (3) Third, the author showcases the three-way approach using design thinking in healthcare marketing.

1. A SYSTEMATIC LITERATURE REVIEW

1.1. A Systematic Literature Review Process

The author used a systematic literature review to explore the impact of design thinking on healthcare marketing. This approach allowed the author to retrieve various research studies and highlight gaps in existing knowledge.

A systematic literature review includes techniques to identify, evaluate, and synthesize all accessible evidence on a particular topic (Gough et al., 2017). Besides, unlike traditional, a systematic review uses a structured procedure to reduce bias and ensure objectivity. A systematic literature review defines a specific research topic, and a protocol highlighting the criteria for including or excluding is drafted (Gough et al., 2017). Lastly, the quality of materials is assessed, and relevant data is extracted. The extracted data is analyzed and synthesized to draw tactical conclusions (Gough et al., 2017). By synthesizing the findings from multiple studies, systematic literature reviews provide a reliable and trustworthy overview of the existing research on a particular topic.

For this book chapter, the systematic literature review presents a deep dive into applying design thinking in healthcare marketing for healthcare organizations. As the research topic is new for modern healthcare marketing in the digital era, there is a need to have literature highlighting the use of design thinking in healthcare marketing as a significant tool to create awareness and promote developed models that enhance the patient experience.

Today, organizations are extensively focused on providing maximum satisfaction and experience to their clients. Marketing specialists in healthcare are tasked to learn and comprehend the wants of patients through various media communication channels. Exploring the needs of target consumers allows healthcare marketers to develop strategic decisions and eventually make a profit for the organizations.

This systematic review explores the use and impact of design thinking in healthcare marketing. By synthesizing existing literature, the current study provides comprehension of the theoretical bases, methodologies, and effects of employing design thinking principles in healthcare marketing strategies. The primary job is to create an overarching image that represents healthcare organizations. Especially today, where technological advancements oblige organizations to be technologically savvy and provide the best future solutions tailored to the patient's needs/wants.

Marketing is a valuable instrument for businesses; however, with design thinking philosophy and tools, it enhances brand awareness, drives growth, acquires and retains customers, and promotes engagement. For this book chapter, it was essential to explore resources that address design thinking in healthcare marketing and showcase its impact on creating sustainable solutions.

A systematic literature review consists of four major stages: identification, screening, eligibility, and inclusion (Gough et al., 2017). To ensure the goodness and trustworthiness of the data collection and analysis, the author identified key themes, developed evaluation methods, and established objectives.

Besides, the systematic review used exclusion and inclusion criteria while selecting the literature for this book chapter. Overall, there were four inclusion and exclusion criteria shown in Table 1.

Stage 1- Identification. Various electronic databases were explored for this systematic literature review to detect relevant studies. Overall, 1054 scientific journals and reports were investigated. Figure 1 shows that 432 were from Scopus, 321 from WoS, and 301 from Google Scholar. One of the significant criteria was ranked journals. Identifying current work concerning healthcare marketing and discovering the knowledge gap was essential.

Moreover, ranked journals must have been published within the last seven years between 2015-2023. The search used keywords such as design thinking, healthcare marketing, digital era, and marketing strategies. This enabled the author to generate a wide range of data collection and established criteria for exclusion, allowing the author to filter various journals for eligibility.

Table 1. Inclusion and exclusion criteria for a systematic literature review

Inclusion Criteria	Exclusion Criteria
-Ranked Journals	- Articles mentioned Design thinking but did not investigate deeply
-Published 2015-2023	- Articles mentioned Healthcare Marketing but did not explore deeply
-Search Keywords: Design Thinking, Healthcare marketing, Digital Era, Marketing Strategies	-Articles that were within the Design thinking context but did not explore topics particular to marketing
-Goodness and Trustworthiness	- Articles mentioning general marketing, but not associated with healthcare

Stage 2- Screening. Stage two in a systematic literature review is a screening process. First, 1054 articles must be checked for duplicates, as they could be found in all available databases. To avoid duplicates, the author cross-checked all available literature. Titles, publishing years, publishers, and more were assessed. Accordingly, 268 duplicate articles from three databases were eliminated from the proportion. The author used a second round of filtering to exclude articles that were not accessible, and data would not been extracted. After this process, only 475 articles were selected for the research. To conclude the screening process, the third round of filtering was conducted. This time, article titles were screened, and 111 articles were eliminated.

Stage 3- Eligibility. Stage three examines articles for eligibility, where a more rigorous process is applied due to goodness and trustworthiness. In order to validate and build marketing strategies with design thinking, the sources from where data is extracted must be effective. The first step was to screen articles based on abstracts. Four exclusion criteria guided the author. However, it must be noted that if the abstract met at least two exclusion criteria, they were eliminated from the selection.

Consequently, 184 articles were eliminated from the proportion, which left 180 articles for eligibility. The second round was to explore full texts. This process was time-consuming, and after almost three weeks of reading and evaluating materials, 133 articles were eliminated. All exclusion criteria were applied in this process, such as articles that mentioned Design thinking but did not investigate deeply, articles that mentioned Healthcare Marketing but did not explore deeply, articles that were within the Design thinking context but did not explore topics particular to marketing and articles mentioning general marketing but not associated with healthcare. This approach removed additional characteristics that could interfere with the study's success or increase the risk of an adverse consequence.

Figure 1. A systematic literature review process

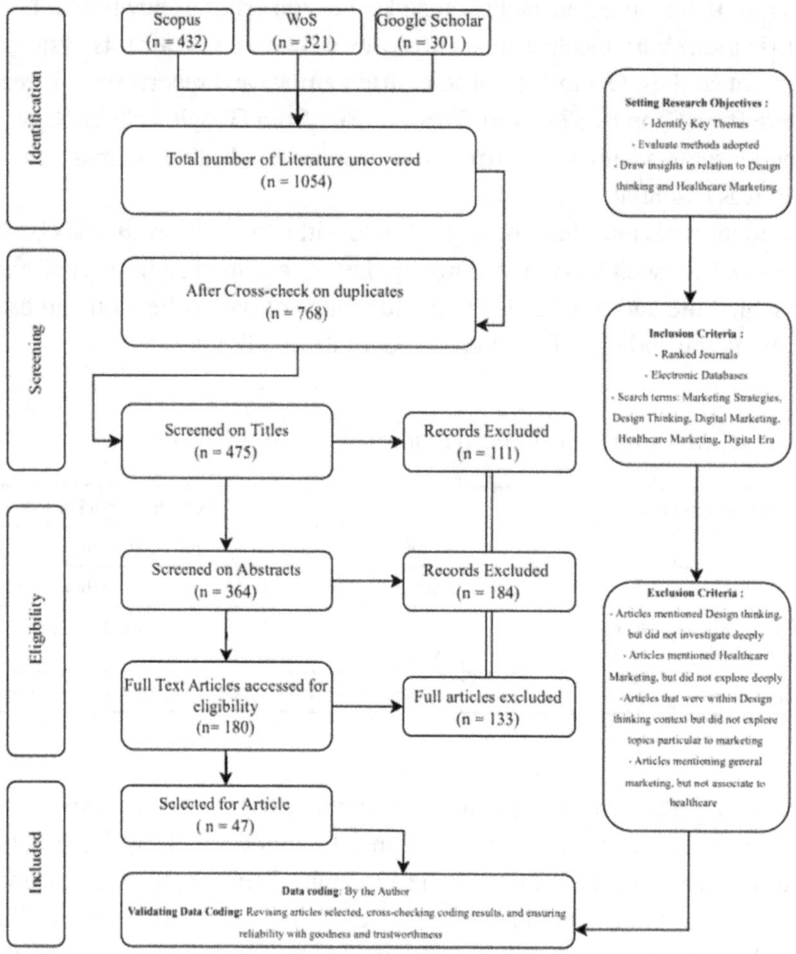

Stage 4- Inclusion. The fourth stage is the inclusion stage. The author, with specific inclusion and exclusion criteria, defined characteristics of design thinking in healthcare marketing and included forty-seven reports and articles that met the eligibility criteria. After selection, to validate the data, additional cross-checking of selected articles was performed to ensure goodness and trustworthiness.

1.2. A Systematic Review: Overview

1.2.1. Healthcare Marketing

Healthcare marketing has undertaken a transformative journey driven by technological advancements, changing patient expectations, and the need for efficient and personalized healthcare services (Gilligan & Lowe, 2018). This evolution can be explored scientifically by investigating the obscure interaction of various factors shaping the healthcare marketing environment (Berkowitz, 2022). The dynamic evolution affected the healthcare systems, generating significant changes and imposing healthcare marketing as an indispensable element of health brands (Purcarea, 2019).

The COVID-19 Pandemic has influenced many sectors worldwide (Renu, 2021). The healthcare system is undergoing a fundamental transformation fueled by regulatory shifts that reward value over volume and unprecedented technological capabilities advances (Agarwal et al., 2018). Moreover, new technologies have revolutionized nearly every aspect of human existence, including how firms market products and services to consumers (Grewal et al., 2019).

Traditionally, marketing has not focused on healthcare (Han & Hwang, 2015). Nevertheless, healthcare has a long tradition of leveraging and integrating data from multiple sources and using analytics to inform product offerings, recommendations, and personalized patient experiences to drive patient value (Grewal et al., 2019). In this sense, the shifting healthcare landscape, fueled by technological advances and regulatory shifts, requires a marketing approach as it transforms from a sector that has provided patient care using episodic and reactive measures to one that relies on continuous and proactive assessments, from reimbursement-based to evidence-based medicine, from rewarding volume to rewarding value and from being provider-centered to being patient-centered (Ludvigsson et al., 2019; Grewal et al., 2019).

One significant aspect of healthcare marketing is employing big data and analytics (Liu et al., 2017). Healthcare providers and marketers now have access to vast patient data, permitting for sophisticated analysis of demographics, preferences, and health patterns (Berkowitz, 2022). This data can be influenced through advanced statistical techniques to create targeted marketing strategies, warranting that healthcare services are accurately tailored to meet individual needs (Carrera & Bridges, 2015).

Additionally, the rise of digital platforms and social media has revolutionized patient engagement (Ng & Russell-Bennett, 2015; Berkowitz, 2022). Scientific studies have shown that active use of social media can improve patient education, accelerate communication between healthcare providers and patients, and even impact healthcare decision-making processes (Gereffi, 2020). This shift towards digital channels has widened the reach of healthcare marketing efforts and paved the way for innovative approaches such as telemedicine and wearable health devices, enabling continuous patient monitoring and proactive healthcare interventions (Mends-Brew & Asiamah, 2018; Gereffi, 2020).

Ethics and transparency are integral to healthcare marketing from a scientific standpoint (Mends-Brew & Asiamah, 2018; Berkowitz, 2022). Studies highlight the importance of building trust between healthcare providers and patients (Purcarea, 2019; Asiamah et al., 2018).

1.2.2. Marketing Strategies in the Digital Era

The digital era has transformed the marketing environment, restructuring how businesses interact with consumers (Diez-Martin et al., 2019; Purwanto, 2022). Through accurate scientific study, numerous significant strategies have emerged, driving profitable marketing campaigns in the digital age (van Esch & J, 2021).

Data-driven decision-making lies at the basis of modern marketing strategies (Royle & Laing, 2015; Imelda et al., 2019). Through advanced analytics, businesses can process vast amounts of data, acquiring deep insights into consumer behavior and preferences (Peter & Vecchia, 2020; Caliskan et al., 2020). Data-driven marketing increases customer targeting and facilitates businesses to predict trends, optimize pricing strategies, and personalize customer experiences, steering to higher engagement and transformation rates (Olson et al., 2021).

Social media platforms have become formidable tools for digital marketing, a phenomenon considerably studied in the scientific community (Katsikeas et al., 2020; Kim et al., 2021; Imelda et al., 2019). Research shows that social media marketing success is strengthened when tailored to specific platforms and target demographics (Darma & Noviana, 2020). Businesses can construct content that resounds with their audience by analyzing user communications and preferences, encouraging community engagement and brand loyalty (Purnomo, 2023).

Search Engine Optimization (SEO) and content marketing are pivotal in improving online visibility (Herhausen et al., 2020). Studies have shown that strategic keyword optimization and high-quality, relevant content substantially advance website rankings on search engines (Saura, 2021; Adiyono et al., 2021). Businesses influencing these scientific insights can guarantee that their content is sympathetic to users and associates with search engine algorithms, encouraging organic traffic and brand credibility (Busca & Bertrandias, 2020).

Additionally, the digital era has witnessed the advance of influencer marketing, a strategy analytically proven to drive consumer trust and purchasing decisions (Kim et al., 2021; Kotler, 2020). Consumers recognize influencers as trustworthy sources, indicating heightened brand authenticity and recognition (Veleva & Tsvetanova, 2020; Pandey et al., 2020). By spotting influencers whose values align with their own, businesses can establish genuine partnerships that resound with the influencer's audience, increasing their reach and market influence (Junusi, 2020; Madanaguli et al., 2021).

1.2.3. Design Thinking

Design thinking, a human-centered problem-solving methodology, has become a scientific approach to innovation (Lewrick et al., 2020; Dell'era et al., 2020). Grounded in empirical research, this method raises creativity and addresses complex problems by highlighting empathy, collaboration, and iterative prototyping (Braun & Clarke, 2022). Besides, design thinking's effectiveness is improving innovation processes (Lewrick et al., 2020; Deitte & Omary, 2019). Designers gain reflective insights into user needs by understanding end-users through in-depth qualitative research (Kimbell, 2015). These insights form the foundation of ideation and problem framing, ensuring solutions are rooted in real user experiences (Kim & Park; Hennessey & Mueller, 2020).

Moreover, design thinking supports multidisciplinary collaboration, integrating diverse perspectives from psychology, engineering, and business (Anupam, 2021). Besides, it shows that diverse teams generate a more comprehensive range of ideas, leading to more innovative solutions (Pande & Bharathi, 2020; Bhandari, 2022). Furthermore, prototyping and iteration, critical principles of design thinking, are verified by a cognitive approach (Abookire et al., 2020). Reiterative testing and improvement leverage cognitive learning processes, supporting designers to adapt and advance solutions based on user feedback (Henriksen et al., 2017), (Kim & Park, 2021).

2. A SYSTEMATIC REVIEW: FINDINGS

The systematic review findings show that design thinking promotes a human-centered approach to healthcare marketing, emphasizing empathy, collaboration, and reiterative problem-solving. By integrating diverse views, design thinking pushes multidisciplinary teams to understand and recognize patient needs, foster innovative solutions, and increase patient experience. This is illustrated in Figure 2.

The examined studies showcased the usage of design thinking principles in various aspects of healthcare marketing, including brand development, communication strategies, service design, and patient engagement. The findings showed its increased role in the industry, challenged by technological advancements. Based on a systematic literature review, branding is fundamental in the healthcare sector, considerably affecting patients' and stakeholders' reputations, trust, and reliability toward healthcare organizations. A robust brand image heightens a healthcare organization's credibility, advances patient assertion, and encourages trust-based relationships. This trust is critical in healthcare decision-making processes, influencing patients' choice of healthcare providers and services. Therefore, design thinking application in marketing permits practitioners to tailor campaigns to the right audience. Moreover, a well-established brand can differentiate, conveying its unique value proposition and quality of care to generate a competitive advantage. Besides, applying design thinking permits marketing professionals to evaluate cost vs value-based decision-making and effectively allocate marketing resources.

Effective branding with design thinking can accelerate consistent communication, further health marketing campaigns, and gather public support. Besides, a vigorous brand in healthcare rouses pride among employees, aligning them with the organization's mission and values, which are fundamental for effectiveness. Eventually, in an era where patient experience is central, strategic branding contributes to the financial success of healthcare organizations.

By utilizing design thinking in healthcare marketing, organizations can potentially witness positive outcomes such as enhancing patient engagement and satisfaction by including them in decision-making, refining their experiences, and offering personalized care, Figure 2. Secondly, it fosters the development of innovative healthcare solutions, such as patient-centered technologies and user-friendly medical devices. Lastly, design thinking urges interdisciplinary cooperation, promoting partnerships between healthcare professionals, engineers, and other stakeholders to tackle complex healthcare challenges.

Figure 2. The impact of design thinking in healthcare marketing

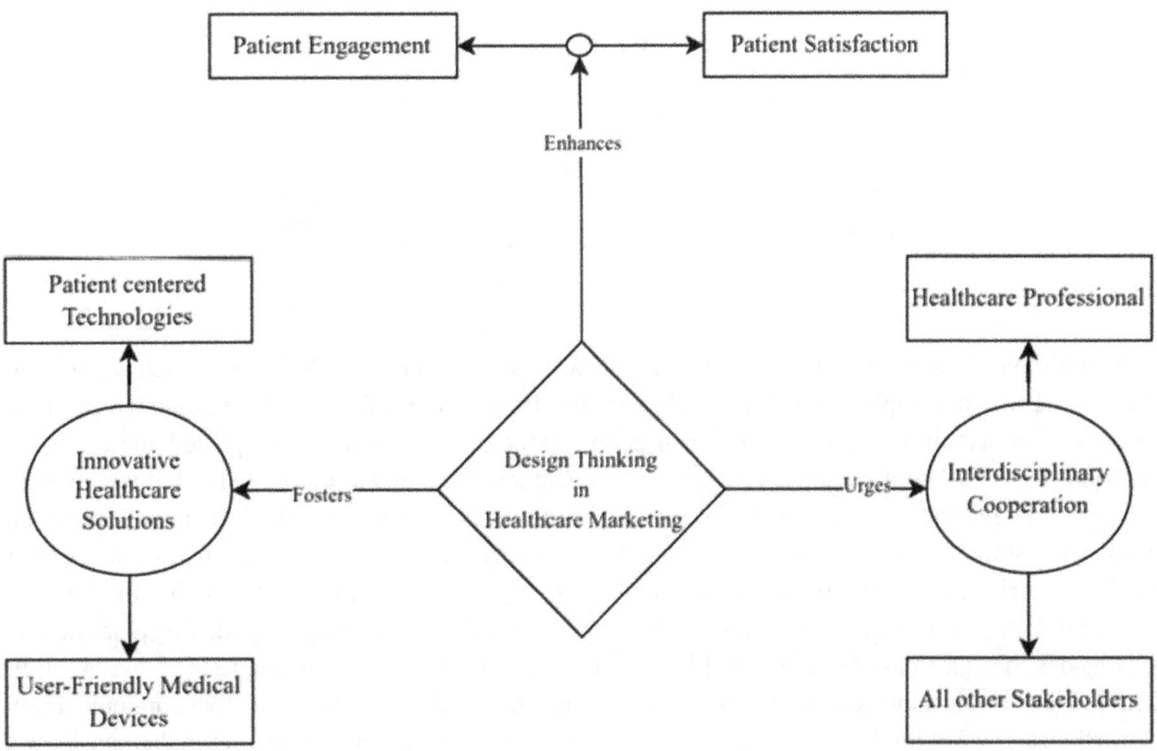

The nature of design thinking permits continuous improvement and modification of solutions to healthcare marketing (Lewrick et al., 2020). Hence, rapid prototyping and testing assist healthcare providers in identifying and tackling potential defects early in the design process, resulting in more effective and efficient intermediations. Likewise, design thinking accelerates a culture of innovation within healthcare businesses, supporting experimentation and risk-taking and emphasizing user-centered consequences.

On the other hand, despite the many benefits, employing and implementing design thinking in healthcare is challenging. Resistance to change, resource constraints, and the need for interdisciplinary collaboration can present difficulties, Figure 3. Organizations that adopt design thinking in marketing can exhibit improved patient results, boosted efficiency, and superior healthcare experiences.

Resistance to change is a standard barrier healthcare organizations face when implementing new initiatives or strategies, and marketing is not an exclusion. Decision-makers may resist change because of a fear of the unknown, loss of control, or other concerns. However, design thinking, a problem-solving approach that highlights empathy and creativity, can be operational in adopting resistance to change while developing marketing campaigns. By utilizing design thinking principles, marketing specialists in healthcare can better understand the needs, concerns, and proportions of the audiences affected by the change. Marketing specialists can acquire deep insights through sympathetic research techniques such as interviews, observations, and surveys. These insights allow them to tailor their change initiatives in marketing to address the concerns and needs of the audiences involved.

Figure 3. Design Thinking in healthcare marketing: Two spaces

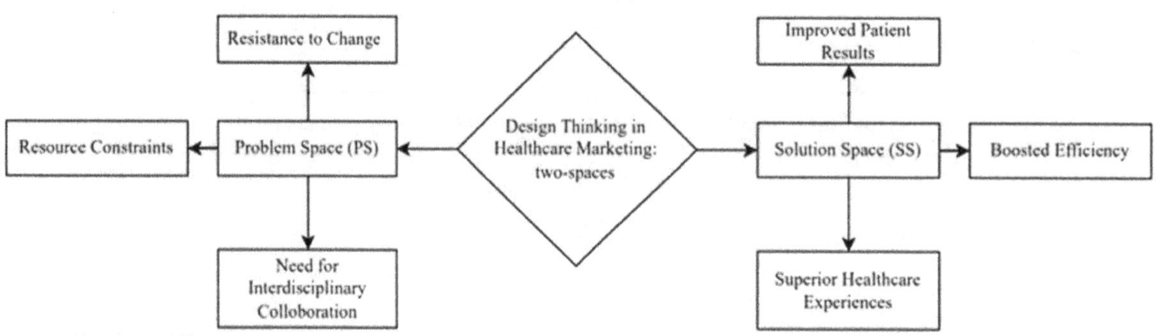

In addition, design thinking encourages a collaborative and interdisciplinary approach (Lewrick et al., 2020). Involving employees and stakeholders in the design process for marketing campaigns nurtures a sense of ownership and inspiration. When people feel that their views are respected and are active contributors to the developing marketing tactics and strategies, they are more likely to embrace them. Likewise, the reiterative nature of design thinking permits healthcare marketing specialists to test and polish their strategies in response to feedback. Rapid prototyping facilitates the identification of potential issues early and making mandatory adjustments to any campaign. It provides 10-15% flexibility to change and adapt to the market environment. This approach builds confidence for marketing practitioners.

Besides, design thinking accelerated the identification of unmet patient requests (Lewrick et al., 2020). Likewise, it improved tailored marketing campaigns, leading to more effective communication. Nevertheless, design thinking cultivated a culture of innovation within healthcare organizations. Design thinking promotes interdisciplinary collaboration and co-creation with various stakeholders from various disciplines. This collaborative approach stimulated a shared understanding of marketing goals. Consequently, it facilitated positioning marketing strategies with broader organizational goals and objectives.

It is critical to note that the reviewed studies identified the practical advantages of design thinking in healthcare marketing. Implementing and executing design thinking principles enhanced patient engagement, brand perception, and equity and increased patient satisfaction and customer loyalty, figure 3.

Design thinking, when used in the context of brand equity in healthcare, can be an influential instrument for building and improving the value of a brand. The following design thinking principles were discovered from the literature review that can positively influence brand equity.

- Innovative Product and Service Design: Through ideation and prototyping, design thinking promotes innovative solutions. Healthcare businesses can develop compelling products and services in the healthcare market by continuously refining ideas based on patient feedback. Innovative offerings enhance brand equity as they establish a unique awareness in the minds of consumers.
- Understanding Customer Needs. Design thinking arises with a deep understanding of the Customer's viewpoint. A healthcare marketing specialist can identify patient needs and desires. Interpreting these characteristics enables healthcare organizations to create and deliver experiences that meet customer expectations, thus increasing customer satisfaction and loyalty.
- Brand Communication and Storytelling. Marketing specialists apply design thinking principles in brand communication and storytelling. Healthcare organizations can strengthen their brand identity by producing narratives that resonate with the target audience and evoke emotional responses. Besides, authentic brand stories help build trust and credibility, essential elements of brand equity. Customers tend to use user and brand-generated content, increasing brand engagement.

Still, the systematic literature review also detected some challenges and limitations. Implementing and utilizing design thinking in healthcare marketing requires organizational commitment, resources, and a compassionate culture. Some studies recounted resistance to change, hierarchical structures, and a lack of interdisciplinary cooperation as obstacles to successful application, Figure 3. Also, the long-term sustainability and scalability of design thinking proposals within healthcare organizations endured areas of further consideration. Lastly, the review highlighted that design thinking elements are for short-term use rather than long-term.

Marketers in the healthcare sector face fascinating challenges in achieving target goals (Berkowitz, 2022). This systematic review of findings emphasizes the potential of design thinking to revolutionize and transform healthcare marketing by positioning patients at the center of marketing strategies. Incorporating design thinking principles aids healthcare organizations in recognizing patients' perspectives better. Moreover, it enables marketers in healthcare to create appealing experiences and prepare marketing campaigns that echo their target audience.

3. APPLICATION OF DESIGN THINKING IN HEALTHCARE MARKETING

Healthcare marketing suggests the techniques healthcare marketing specialists use to attract patients, build relationships, and boost their products and services. In today's competitive healthcare landscape, successful marketing is fundamental for hospitals, clinics, pharmaceutical companies, and individual practitioners to influence their target audience and, more importantly, to differentiate themselves from competitors. Hence, this book chapter aims to highlight the impact of design thinking in healthcare marketing.

A systematic literature review provided an opportunity to define, analyze, and provide a framework for how to apply design thinking in healthcare marketing (Lewrick et al., 2020). Consequently, the author developed a three-way approach, applying design thinking in healthcare marketing. All these steps are shown below in a step-by-step guide.

Step one in the three-way approach is using the double-diamond model (Lewrick et al., 2020). The Double Diamond model is a design thinking framework developed by the British Design Council. It illustrates the design process, highlighting the significance of divergent and convergent thinking in problem-solving. This approach is vital in healthcare, as the healthcare market is complex and requires a strategic, patient-centered approach. Therefore, the authors accept the probability of using a double-diamond model to filter the environment and identify the problem. Finally, the model contains four apparent stages- discover, define, develop, and deliver, in two diamond shapes (Lewrick et al., 2020), illustrated in Figure 4.

- Discover. The first diamond begins with the Discover stage, where healthcare marketing specialists engage themselves in the problem space. This phase encompasses extensive research and brainstorming sessions. The goal is to derive a deep understanding of the problem and detect opportunities for innovation.
- Define. In the second diamond, the Define stage involves blending the information gathered during the discovery phase. Healthcare marketing specialists analyze the research findings, identify patterns, and define the problem statement. This stage is decisive for marketing specialists to frame and ensure a targeted approach in the successive stages.
- Develop. In the third stage, Develop, stress, and emphasis are on divergent thinking. Healthcare marketing specialists explore various ideas and solutions to the defined problem. Brainstorming, ideation sessions, and prototyping are everyday activities and must be encouraged.
- Deliver: The final stage, Deliver, includes convergent thinking. Healthcare marketing specialists evaluate and filter the generated solutions, judging feasibility, viability, and desirability. Marketing specialists develop a prototype marketing plan for various campaigns and tests. This process ensures that solutions are user-friendly and functional.

The Double Diamond model is necessary in a three-way approach as it sets a tone for understanding and recognizing the audience's needs. It stimulates and navigates healthcare marketing specialists in the complexities of the design process in healthcare marketing, nurturing creativity and innovation while safeguarding a patient-centered and problem-focused result.

Step two in the Three-way Approach is TOWS with DMAIC Roadmap for root-cause analysis, illustrated in Figure 5. This step is a complex approach, as healthcare marketing specialists must have a deep knowledge of their organization. For this reason, step one must be completed first. We assess healthcare organizations' marketing in this stage based on the TOWS and DMAIC approaches. Healthcare marketing specialists must address the cause, not the symptom. Step two ensures that information used to develop marketing campaigns is validated and focused on the value driver development.

Figure 4. Step one in the three-way approach: Double diamond model

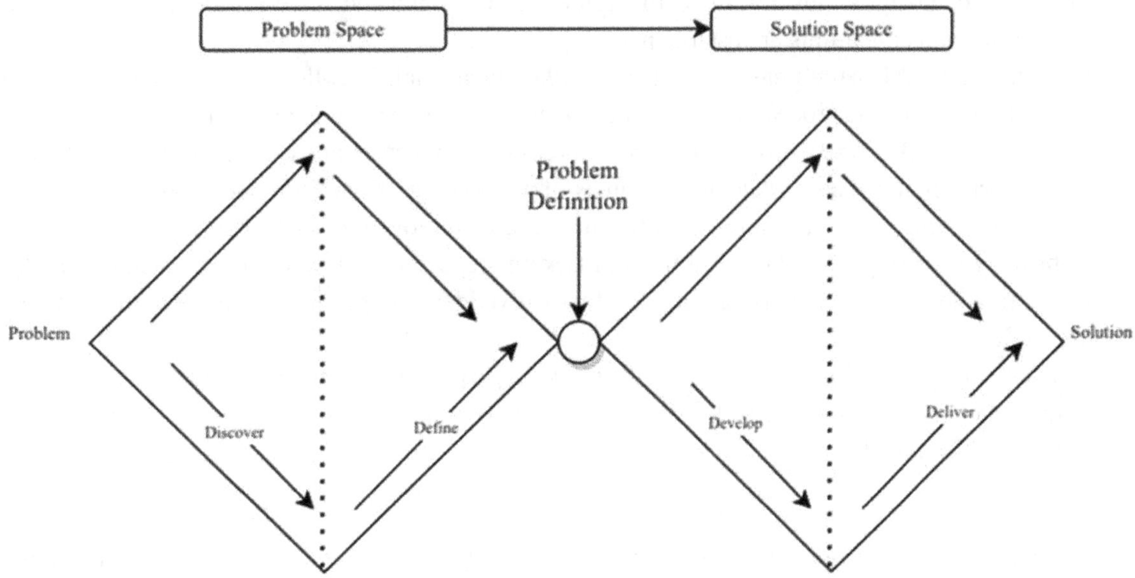

The TOWS analysis (Threats, Opportunities, Weaknesses, Strengths) is the first piece of this model, shown in Figure 5. It requires RCA (root-cause analysis). Moreover, the TOWS is a strategic planning tool that aids organizations in accessing internal and external environments. In conjunction with a SWOT analysis, it facilitates the formulating of action plans, especially for marketing specialists. The TOWS approach matches internal factors with external factors to create specialized strategies, such as

- Strengths (S) – Opportunities (O) Strategies (SO) - Identify how internal strengths can be used to exploit external opportunities. Besides, it influences the healthcare organization's strengths to benefit from available opportunities.
- Strengths (S) – Threats (T) Strategies (ST) - Determine how internal strengths can be used to moderate external threats. Besides, it focuses on using internal strengths to stabilize potential threats.
- Weaknesses (W) – Opportunities (O) Strategies (WO) - Identify strategies to seize internal weaknesses by taking advantage of external opportunities. Besides, it aims to minimize weaknesses by leveraging available opportunities.
- Weaknesses (W) – Threats (T) Strategies (WT) - Develop strategies to master internal weaknesses and avoid external threats. Besides, it focuses on reducing both internal weaknesses and external threats.

The second phase is the DMAIC roadmap. DMAIC is an acronym and has five data-driven phases of a process improvement (enhance quality and reduce defects) approach through Six Sigma methodologies. Each letter signifies a phase: Define, Measure, Analyze, Improve, and Control.

- Define. In the Define phase, healthcare marketing specialists define the goals and objectives of the marketing campaigns. Besides, the campaign to be developed and solved is identified. Moreover, boundaries and constraints are established.
- Measure. In the Measure phase, healthcare marketing specialists collect relevant data to measure the current state of the process. Data is collected analytically to recognize the process performance.
- Analyze. In the Analyze phase, healthcare marketing specialists analyze the collected data to identify patterns, root causes of defects, and areas of process variation. Moreover, statistical analysis, process mapping, and cause-and-effect techniques are employed for analysis.
- Improve. In the Improve phase, healthcare marketing specialists develop and implement marketing campaigns to address target audiences. Innovative ideas are generated, and potential solutions are evaluated.
- Control. In the Control phase, healthcare marketing specialists implement control measures to sustain the improvements. Besides, key performance indicators are monitored. Lastly, ongoing monitoring and feedback mechanisms are established.

Figure 5. Step two in the three-way approach: TOWS with DMAIC roadmap for root-cause analysis

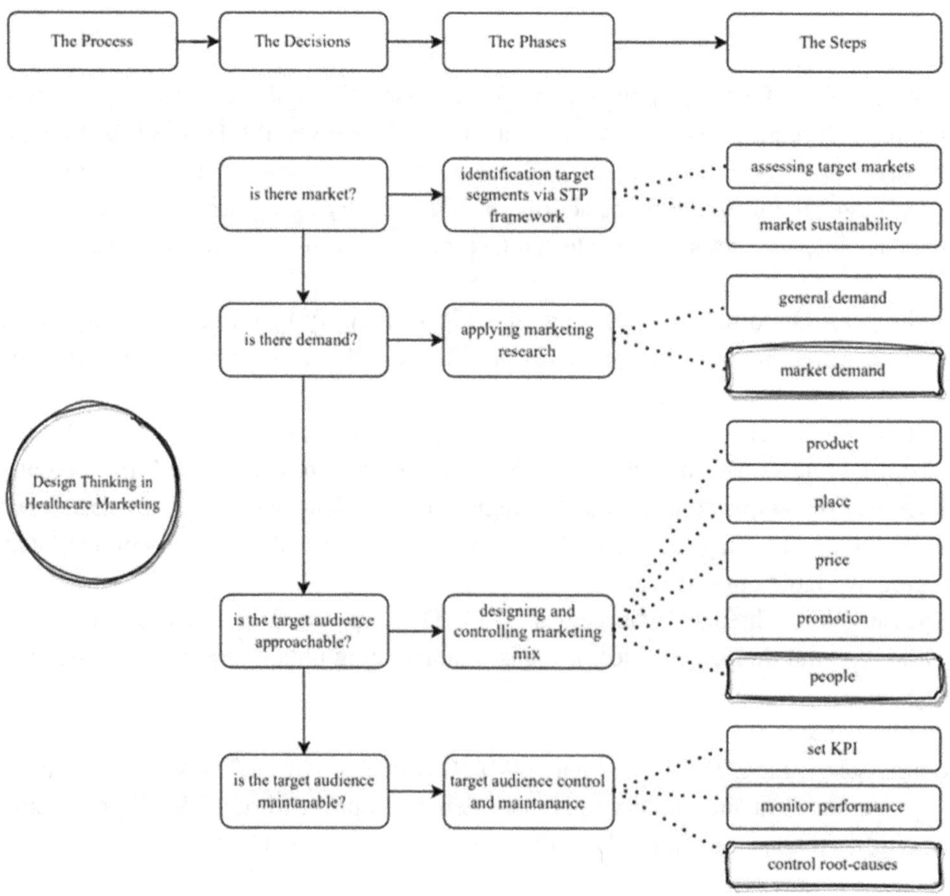

Step three in the Three-way approach is a detailed map applying Design Thinking in Healthcare Marketing, illustrated in Figure 6. First, recognize that it has four key elements: processes, decisions, phases, and steps. Each step is fundamental for healthcare marketing specialists, as the first two steps in a three-way approach prepare them to design specific marketing campaigns tailored to the target audiences.

The process in this book chapter, and for the model, is design thinking in healthcare marketing. It is followed by the decision stage, where healthcare marketing specialists address whether there is a market for the marketing campaigns if there is a demand to develop marketing campaigns, if the target audience is approachable, and lastly, if the target audience is maintainable. This step ensures that the dollar amount is allocated and spent according to the healthcare organization's budgets and controls. Moreover, it allows to track dollar amounts to the customer and back.

The next is the phases stage. Each previous inquiry is broken down in more depth. To address the market, healthcare marketing specialists are tasked to use STP frameworks to identify market segments better and position them in customers' minds. It also leads to managing market sustainability. Market research is required to evaluate spending and expenditure when addressing the demand. It is critical to know the difference between general and market demand.

To address audience approachability, healthcare marketing specialists must design and control the marketing mix. The fifth P (People) must be part of the proportion in health care. Furthermore, healthcare marketing specialists must establish audience control and maintenance benchmarks such as KPIs and more for the target audience maintenance.

Figure 6. Step three in the three-way approach: Applying design thinking in healthcare marketing

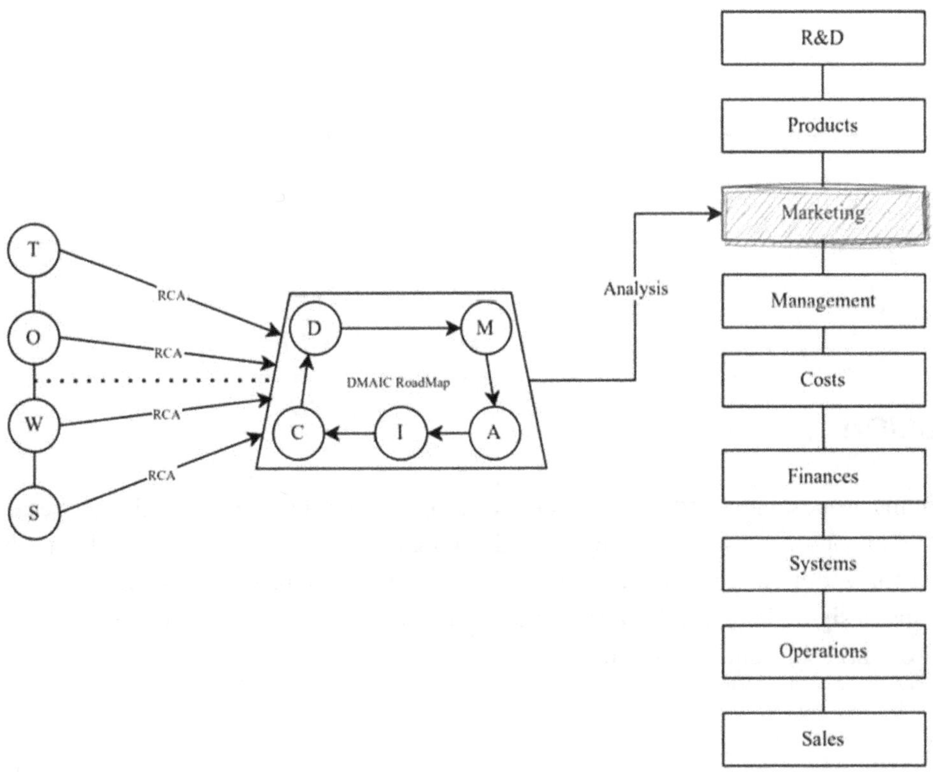

In brief, the three-way approach is a tactical approach highlighting how design thinking can be part of healthcare marketing. Healthcare marketing is a very particular sector. Moreover, due to a lack of resources and requirements for CSR, marketing specialists must be practical in developing effective marketing campaigns with less expenditure.

Effective healthcare marketing campaigns attract new patients and foster patient loyalty and trust. Using design thinking, healthcare organizations can demonstrate a positive reputation by employing ethical, patient-centric strategies and expanding their patient base, as shown in Figure 7. Figure 7 dictates that successful implementation brings efficiency, innovation, quality, and responsiveness to the customers. Moreover, healthcare organizations are more value-driven rather than cost-driven.

Figure 7. The benefit of applying design thinking in healthcare marketing

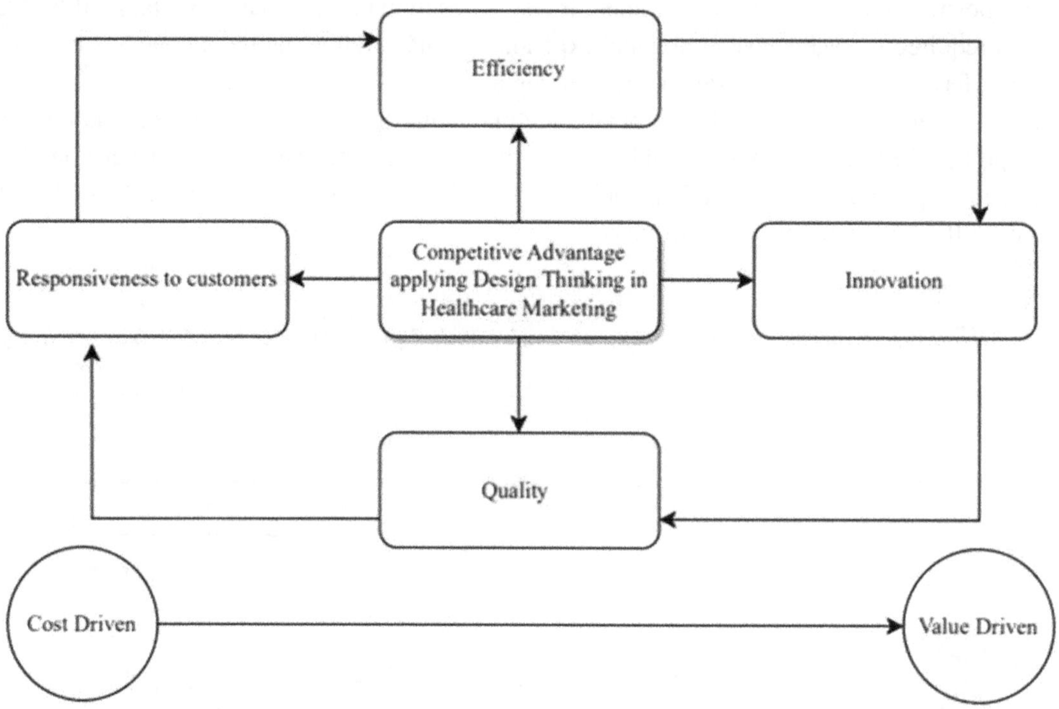

CONCLUSION

Design thinking proposes a valued framework for tackling complex healthcare challenges besides creating patient-centered solutions. By combining empathy, collaboration, and testing into the design process, healthcare organizations can better understand patient needs and improve and foster a culture of innovation. Adopting design thinking in healthcare marketing can transform the healthcare sector, eventually improving patient results and experiences.

Design thinking in healthcare marketing highlights the magnitude of the end-to-end customer experience. Brands steadily deliver positive and notable experiences at every touchpoint, and building strong emotional connections with customers is fundamental for healthcare organizations. Besides, these emotional connections enhance brand loyalty and sponsor positive brand associations.

Moreover, design thinking promotes continuous improvement. Healthcare organizations that progress based on changing customer needs and market trends remain relevant. This flexibility guarantees that the brand remains valuable to its audience, sustaining and increasing brand equity.

Using the TOWS with DMAIC, healthcare marketing specialists can develop a more comprehensive set of marketing campaigns that address individual audience needs, outlining internal and external factors. This approach encourages a proactive outlook and provides a structured strategic planning and decision-making framework, allowing healthcare organizations to align their resources and capabilities effectively.

Lastly, design thinking in healthcare marketing empowers marketing specialists to create patient-centric, innovative, and emotionally meaningful brand experiences. By concentrating on understanding customer needs, delivering unique and consistent experiences, and adjusting to change, design thinking in healthcare marketing impacts drastically building and sustaining brand equity. Besides, successful implementation brings efficiency, innovation, quality, and responsiveness to the customers. Hence, healthcare organizations are more value-driven rather than cost-driven.

FUTURE RESEARCH

The author recommends future research. Future research should tackle the challenges and barriers to implementing design thinking in healthcare marketing. It should examine its long-term influence on organizational performance, patient outcomes, and healthcare delivery.

REFERENCES

Abookire, S., Plover, C., Frasso, R., & Ku, B. (2020). *Health Design Thinking: An Innovative Approach in Public Health to Defining Problems and Finding Solutions*. Public Health Education and Promotion. doi:10.3389/fpubh.2020.00459

Adiyono, G., Rahmat, T. Y., & Anindita, R. (2021). Digital Marketing Strategies To Increase Online Business Sales Through Social Media. *Journal Of Humanities, Social Science, Public Administration and Management*, *1*(2), 31–37. doi:10.51715/husocpument.v1i2.58

Agarwal, R., Dugas, M., Gao, G., & Kannan, P. K. (2018). Emerging technologies and analytics for a new era of value-centered marketing in healthcare. *Journal of the Academy of Marketing Science*, *48*(1), 9–23. doi:10.100711747-019-00692-4

Anupam, T. (2021). Using Rapid Design Thinking to Overcome COVID-19 Challenges in Medical Education. *Academic Medicine*, *96*(1), 56–61. doi:10.1097/ACM.0000000000003718 PMID:32889947

Asiamah, N., Opuni, F. F., & Mensah, H. K. (2018). The nexus between internal marketing in hospitals and organizational commitment: Incorporating the mediation roles of key job characteristics. *International Journal of Healthcare Management*, *13*(sup1), 385–399. doi:10.1080/20479700.2018.1551951

Berkowitz, E. N. (2022). *Essentials of Healthcare Marketing*. Jones & Bartlett Learning.

Bhandari, A. (2022). Design Thinking: From Bibliometric Analysis to Content Analysis, Current Research Trends, and Future Research Directions. *Journal of the Knowledge Economy*. Advance online publication. doi:10.100713132-022-00920-3

Braun, V., & Clarke, V. (2022). Conceptual and design thinking for thematic analysis. *Qualitative Psychology*, *9*(1), 3–26. doi:10.1037/qup0000196

Busca, L., & Bertrandias, L. (2020). A Framework for Digital Marketing Research: Investigating the Four Cultural Eras of Digital Marketing. *Journal of Interactive Marketing*, *49*(1), 1–19. doi:10.1016/j.intmar.2019.08.002

Caliskan, A., Deniz, Y., Özen, Ö., & Ozturkoglu, Y. (2020). Digital transformation of traditional marketing business model in new industry era. *Journal of Enterprise Information Management*, *34*(4), 1252–1273. doi:10.1108/JEIM-02-2020-0084

Carrera, P. M., & Bridges, J. F. (2015). Globalization and healthcare: Understanding health and medical tourism. *Expert Review of Pharmacoeconomics & Outcomes Research*, *6*(4), 447–454. doi:10.1586/14737167.6.4.447 PMID:20528514

Darma, G., & Noviana, P. (2020). Exploring Digital Marketing Strategies during the New Normal Era in Enhancing the Use of Digital Payment. *Journal Mantik*, *4*(3).

Deitte, L., & Omary, R. (2019). The Power of Design Thinking in Medical Education. *Academic Radiology*, *26*(10), 1417–1420. doi:10.1016/j.acra.2019.02.012 PMID:30867087

Dell'era, C., Magistretti, S., Cautela, C., Verganti, R., & Zurlo, F. (2020, June). MAgistretti, S. C., Cautela, C., Verganti, R., & Zurlo, F. (2020). Four kinds of design thinking: From ideating to making, engaging, and criticizing. *Creativity and Innovation Management*, *29*(2), 324–344. Advance online publication. doi:10.1111/caim.12353

Diez-Martin, F., Blanco-Gonzalez, A., & Prado-Roman, C. (2019). Research Challenges in Digital Marketing: Sustainability. *Sustainability (Basel)*, *11*(10), 2839. Advance online publication. doi:10.3390u11102839

Gereffi, G. (2020). What does the COVID-19 pandemic teach us about global value chains? The case of medical supplies. *Journal of International Business Policy*, *3*(3), 287–301. doi:10.105742214-020-00062-w

Gilligan, C., & Lowe, R. (2018). *Marketing and Healthcare Organizations*. Academic Press.

Gough, D., Oliver, S., & Thomas, J. (2017). Introducing Systematic Reviews. In D. Gough, S. Oliver, & J. Thomas (Eds.), *An Introduction to Systematic Reviews* (3rd ed.). Sage Publications Ltd.

Grewal, D., Hulland, J., Kopalle, P. K., & Karahanna, E. (2019). The future of technology and marketing: A multidisciplinary perspective. *Journal of the Academy of Marketing Science*, *48*(1), 1–8. doi:10.100711747-019-00711-4

Han, H., & Hwang, J. (2015). Growing competition in the healthcare tourism market and customer retention in medical clinics: New and experienced travellers. *Current Issues in Tourism*, *21*(6), 680–702. doi:10.1080/13683500.2015.1104292

Hennessey, E., & Mueller, J. (2020). Teaching and Learning Design Thinking (DT). *Canadian Journal of Education*, 498–521.

Henriksen, D., Richardson, C., & Mehta, R. (2017). Design thinking: A creative approach to educational problems of practice. *Thinking Skills and Creativity*, *26*, 140–153. doi:10.1016/j.tsc.2017.10.001

Herhausen, D., Miočević, D., Morgan, R. E., & Kleijnen, M. H. (2020). The digital marketing capabilities gap. *Industrial Marketing Management*, *90*, 276–290. doi:10.1016/j.indmarman.2020.07.022

Imelda, D. C., Fenni, F., & Deveia, R. (2019). Digital marketing strategy in promoting product. *Management and Entrepreneurship: Trends of Development*, *4*(10), 58–66. Advance online publication. doi:10.26661/2522-1566/2019-4/10-05

Junusi, R. (2020). Digital Marketing During the Pandemic Period; A Study of Islamic Perspective. *Junusi*, *2*(1), 15. Advance online publication. doi:10.21580/jdmhi.2020.2.1.5717

Katsikeas, C., Leonidou, L., & Zeriti, A. (2020). Revisiting international marketing strategy in a digital era: Opportunities, challenges, and research directions. *International Marketing Review*, *37*(2), 405–424. doi:10.1108/IMR-02-2019-0080

Kim, J., Jang, S., & Lee, K. H. (2021). Evolution of digital marketing communication: Bibliometric analysis and network visualization from key articles. *Journal of Business Research*, *130*, 552–563. doi:10.1016/j.jbusres.2019.09.043

Kim, Y. S., & Park, J. A. (2021). Design Thinking in the Framework of Visual Thinking and Characterization of Service Design Ideation Methods Using Visual Reasoning Model. *The Design Journal*, 931-953. doi:10.1080/14606925.2021.1977497

Kimbell, L. (2015). Rethinking Design Thinking: Part I. *Design and Culture*, *3*(3), 285–306. doi:10.2752/175470811X13071166525216

Kotler, M. (2020). Marketing Environment in the Digital Transformation. *Marketing Strategy in the Digital Age*, 3-45.

Lewrick, M., Link, P., & Leifer, L. (2020). *The Design Thinking Toolbox*. Wiley. doi:10.15358/9783800657520

Liu, J. X., Goryakin, Y., Maeda, A., Bruckner, T., & Scheffler, R. (2017). Global Health Workforce Labor Market Projections for 2030. *Human Resources for Health*, *15*(11), 11. Advance online publication. doi:10.118612960-017-0187-2 PMID:28159017

Ludvigsson, J. F., Svedberg, P., Olén, O., Bruze, G., & Neovius, M. (2019). The longitudinal integrated database for health insurance and labour market studies (LISA) and its use in medical research. *European Journal of Epidemiology*, *34*(4), 423–437. doi:10.100710654-019-00511-8 PMID:30929112

Madanaguli, A. T., Dhir, A., Talwar, S., Singh, G., & Escobar, O. (2021). Business to business (B2B) alliances in the healthcare industry: A review of research trends and pertinent issues. *Journal of Business and Industrial Marketing*, *37*(8), 1688–1705. doi:10.1108/JBIM-01-2021-0060

Mends-Brew, E., & Asiamah, N. (2018). Improving health workers' organisational commitment: Drawing lessons from the interaction between internal marketing and key job characteristics. *International Journal of Healthcare Management, 13*(sup1), 318–328. doi:10.1080/20479700.2018.1548152

Ng, S., & Russell-Bennett, R. (2015). The Role of Affect in Consumer Evaluation of Health Care Services. *Health Marketing Quarterly, 32*(1), 31–47. doi:10.1080/07359683.2015.1000708 PMID:25751317

Olson, E. M., Olson, K. M., Czaplewski, A. J., & Key, T. M. (2021). Business strategy and the management of digital marketing. *Business Horizons, 64*(2), 285–293. doi:10.1016/j.bushor.2020.12.004

Pande, M., & Bharathi, V. (2020). Theoretical foundations of design thinking – A constructivism learning approach to design thinking. *Thinking Skills and Creativity, 36*, 100637. Advance online publication. doi:10.1016/j.tsc.2020.100637

Pandey, N., Nayal, P., & Rathore, A. S. (2020). Digital marketing for B2B organizations: Structured literature review and future research directions. *Journal of Business and Industrial Marketing, 35*(7), 1191–1204. doi:10.1108/JBIM-06-2019-0283

Peter, M. K., & Vecchia, M. D. (2020). The Digital Marketing Toolkit: A Literature Review for the Identification of Digital Marketing Channels and Platforms. *New Trends in Business Information Systems and Technology*, 251-265. doi:10.1007/978-3-030-48332-6_17

Purcarea, V. L. (2019). The impact of marketing strategies in healthcare systems. *Journal of Medicine, 93-96*(2), 93–96. Advance online publication. doi:10.25122/jml-2019-1003 PMID:31406509

Purnomo, Y. J. (2023). Digital Marketing Strategy to Increase Sales Conversion on E-commerce Platforms. *Journal of Contemporary Administration and Management, 1*(2), 54–62. Advance online publication. doi:10.61100/adman.v1i2.23

Purwanto, A. (2022). How The Role of Digital Marketing and Brand Image on Food Product Purchase Decisions? An Empirical Study on Indonesian SMEs in the Digital Era. *Journal of Industrial Engineering & Management Research.*

Renu, N. (2021). Innovative Healthcare Marketing Strategies during COVID-19. *Journal of Marketing Management, 9*(2), 45–49. doi:10.15640/jmm.v9n2a7

Royle, J., & Laing, A. (2015). The digital marketing skills gap: Developing a Digital Marketer Model for the communication industries. *International Journal of Information Management, 34*(2), 65–73. doi:10.1016/j.ijinfomgt.2013.11.008

Saura, J. R. (2021). Using Data Sciences in Digital Marketing: Framework, methods, and performance metrics. *Journal of Innovation & Knowledge, 6*(2), 92–102. doi:10.1016/j.jik.2020.08.001

van Esch, P., & Stewart Black, J. (2021). Artificial Intelligence (AI): Revolutionizing Digital Marketing. *Australasian Marketing Journal, 29*(3), 199–203. Advance online publication. doi:10.1177/18393349211037684

Veleva, S., & Tsvetanova, A. (2020). *Characteristics of the digital marketing advantages and disadvantages*. IOP Con. doi:10.1088/1757-899X/940/1/012065

Chapter 12
The Role of AI in Elevating Hospital Service Quality:
Framework, Development, and Applications

Mustufa Haider Abidi
https://orcid.org/0000-0001-5609-5705
Advanced Manufacturing Institute, King Saud University, Saudi Arabia

Syed Hammad Mian
https://orcid.org/0000-0002-9780-0842
Advanced Manufacturing Institute, King Saud University, Saudi Arabia

Ateekh Ur Rehman
https://orcid.org/0000-0003-2265-5828
Department of Industrial Engineering, College of Engineering, King Saud University, Saudi Arabia

Hisham Alkhalefah
Advanced Manufacturing Institute, King Saud University, Saudi Arabia

Yusuf Siraj Usmani
https://orcid.org/0000-0001-5812-6413
Department of Industrial Engineering, College of Engineering, King Saud University, Saudi Arabia

ABSTRACT

Artificial intelligence (AI) is now becoming an integral part of human life. It is finding applications in almost all domains, such as healthcare, marketing, business development, manufacturing, transportation, etc. This chapter explores the applications of AI in enhancing hospital service quality and presents a framework for its development. The chapter begins by providing an overview of hospital service quality and highlighting the role of AI in healthcare. It emphasizes the importance of enhancing hospital service quality and introduces the need for an AI-driven framework. The foundations of AI in healthcare are then discussed, including its evolution and different types of AI technologies. The challenges in implementing AI in healthcare are also addressed. The chapter also includes applications that illustrate the successful application of AI. The framework development section focuses on understanding the current hospital service landscape and defining key metrics for hospital service quality.

DOI: 10.4018/979-8-3693-0679-6.ch012

1. FOUNDATIONS OF ARTIFICIAL INTELLIGENCE IN HEALTHCARE

This section explains the basics of artificial intelligence in healthcare field. It explains the growth of AI in healthcare domain, as well as its different types, and highlights key challenges.

1.1 Evolution of AI in Healthcare

AI has significantly transformed the healthcare industry, revolutionizing the way healthcare services are delivered. The evolution of AI in healthcare has been driven by advancements in computing power, availability of vast amounts of healthcare data, and breakthroughs in machine learning algorithms (Yu, Beam, & Kohane, 2018). In the early stages, AI was primarily used for rule-based expert systems, where predefined rules were programmed to mimic human expertise in diagnosing diseases and recommending treatments (Davenport & Kalakota, 2019). However, with the advent of machine learning, AI systems became capable of learning from data and improving their performance over time. This led to the development of predictive models and decision support systems that could analyze large datasets to identify patterns, predict outcomes, and assist healthcare professionals in making informed decisions (Rong, Mendez, Bou Assi, Zhao, & Sawan, 2020). Figure below shows the application of AI in healthcare:

Figure 1. Applications of AI in healthcare
Source: Adapted from Pandya et al. (2021)

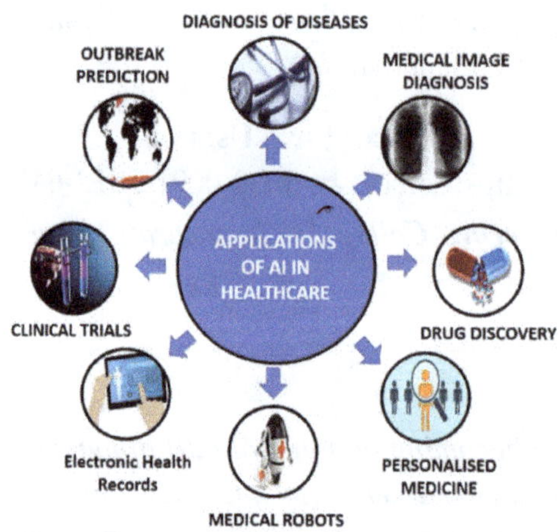

Over the years, AI in healthcare has witnessed remarkable progress. From image recognition algorithms that can detect anomalies in medical images with high accuracy, to natural language processing models that can extract valuable information from unstructured clinical notes, AI has expanded its reach across various healthcare domains (Jiang et al., 2017). It has demonstrated its potential in areas such as radiology, pathology, genomics, drug discovery, and personalized medicine.

1.2 Types of AI in Healthcare

Different types of AI utilized in healthcare are as follows:

a. Machine Learning: Machine learning is a branch of AI that enables computers to learn and make predictions or decisions without being explicitly programmed. In healthcare, machine learning algorithms are trained on large datasets to recognize patterns and generate insights (Verma & Verma, 2022). Supervised learning algorithms, such as support vector machines and neural networks, are commonly used for tasks like disease classification, predicting patient outcomes, and identifying optimal treatment plans (Amann et al., 2020). Unsupervised learning algorithms, such as clustering and dimensionality reduction techniques, help uncover hidden patterns in healthcare data, aiding in patient segmentation and population health management.
b. Natural Language Processing (NLP): NLP is a subfield of AI that focuses on enabling computers to understand and process human language. In healthcare, NLP techniques are applied to analyze electronic health records, clinical notes, research papers, and patient-generated data. NLP models can extract valuable information from unstructured text, such as identifying medical conditions, extracting medication information, and detecting adverse events. NLP-powered chatbots and virtual assistants also enhance patient engagement and provide personalized healthcare information (Solanki, Rajawat, Gadekar, & Patil, 2023).
c. Robotics and Automation: Robotics and automation technologies are transforming surgical procedures, diagnostics, and patient care. Robotic surgical systems enable precise and minimally invasive procedures, reducing patient trauma and improving surgical outcomes (Rick, 2017). Autonomous robots can assist in repetitive tasks, such as medication dispensing and logistics, enhancing efficiency and reducing human error. Automation of administrative tasks, such as billing and coding, streamlines operations, freeing up healthcare professionals' time for patient care.
d. Expert Systems: Expert systems are AI-based computer programs that mimic human decision-making in specific domains. They employ knowledge bases and inference engines to provide expert-level advice and recommendations. In healthcare, expert systems assist in diagnosis, treatment planning, and decision support (Li, Asch, & Shah, 2020). They integrate medical guidelines, clinical protocols, and patient data to generate personalized recommendations for healthcare professionals.
e. Computer Vision: Computer vision refers to the field of AI that focuses on enabling computers to understand and interpret visual information. In healthcare, computer vision algorithms analyze medical images, such as X-rays, CT scans, and MRIs, to identify abnormalities, assist in diagnosis, and aid in surgical planning (Rahane, Dalvi, Magar, Kalane, & Jondhale, 2018). Deep learning-based architectures, such as convolutional neural networks, have shown exceptional performance in image classification, segmentation, and object detection tasks.
f. Digital marketing: Digital marketing has become an integral component of the healthcare industry, offering healthcare organizations unprecedented opportunities to connect with patients, improve brand visibility, and drive patient engagement (Grbic, Stimac Grbic, Stimac, & Sostar, 2019). By employing a strategic and tailored approach to digital marketing, healthcare providers can enhance their online presence, deliver personalized care experiences, and ultimately, contribute to better patient outcomes. Embracing the power of digital marketing is no longer a choice but a necessity for healthcare organizations seeking to thrive in the digital era (Mondal et al., 2022). It includes, content marketing, social media marketing, marketing through email, patient's feedback and testimonials record online, etc.

1.3 Key Challenges in Implementing AI in Healthcare

Despite the immense potential of AI in healthcare, several challenges must be addressed for successful implementation:

a. Data privacy and security concerns: Healthcare data is sensitive and subject to stringent privacy regulations. Safeguarding patient information and ensuring compliance with data protection laws is crucial when developing and deploying AI systems (Schönberger, 2019).
b. Regulatory and ethical considerations: AI algorithms and systems need to adhere to ethical guidelines, ensuring fairness, transparency, and accountability. Regulatory frameworks should be established to assess the safety and efficacy of AI technologies before their widespread adoption (Schönberger, 2019).
c. Interoperability challenges: Healthcare data is often stored in different formats and systems, making data integration and interoperability complex. Establishing data standards and interoperability protocols is crucial for effective AI implementation.
d. Staff training and acceptance of AI technologies: Healthcare professionals need to be trained to effectively utilize AI technologies and understand their limitations. Promoting a culture of acceptance and trust in AI systems among healthcare staff is essential for successful integration.

Addressing these challenges requires collaboration between AI experts, healthcare professionals, policymakers, and regulatory bodies. By overcoming these hurdles, AI can contribute significantly to improving healthcare service quality and patient outcomes.

2. SOME APPLICATIONS OF AI IN HEALTHCARE

This section presents some of work reported in the literature for the application of AI in different domains of healthcare.

2.1 AI-Driven Patient Triage and Prioritization

The application of AI algorithms for efficient patient triage and prioritization, aiming to optimize resource allocation and minimize patient waiting times is presented (Wee et al., 2022). By leveraging machine learning techniques, hospitals can develop predictive models that analyze various patient data points, such as symptoms, medical history, vital signs, and risk factors, to determine the severity and urgency of each case.

These AI algorithms can accurately categorize patients based on the severity of their condition, allowing healthcare professionals to prioritize those requiring immediate attention. By implementing an AI-driven patient triage system, hospitals have reported significant reductions in patient waiting times and improved resource utilization. Patients with critical conditions are identified and treated promptly, leading to better clinical outcomes.

2.2 AI-Enabled Radiology Diagnosis

This is one of the most explored applications of AI in healthcare (Hosny, Parmar, Quackenbush, Schwartz, & Aerts, 2018). The field of radiology plays an essential role in the diagnosis of several medical conditions. AI algorithms have demonstrated significant potential in the analysis of medical images, including X-rays, CT (computer tomography) scans, and MRIs (Magnetic resonance imaging), with the aim of aiding radiologists in achieving precise and quick diagnoses. Deep learning techniques, namely convolutional neural networks (CNNs), have exhibited remarkable efficacy in tasks such as image classification, segmentation, and anomaly detection (Yamashita, Nishio, Do, & Togashi, 2018).

Through the use of CNN models trained on extensive datasets containing annotated medical images, AI systems can acquire the capability to discern nuanced anomalies and furnish radiologists with supplementary perspectives. AI algorithms have the potential to decrease the time required for interpretation, improve the accuracy of diagnoses, and aid radiologists in identifying initial indications of diseases like cancer. The use of AI into the field of radiology diagnostics holds promise for enhancing patient care, streamlining treatment planning processes, and maximizing workflow efficiency.

2.3 Robotics and Automation in Surgery

Robotic surgical systems are an example of AI-driven technology that has revolutionized surgical procedures (Rivero-Moreno et al., 2023). These systems offer enhanced precision, dexterity, and visualization, allowing surgeons to perform minimally invasive surgeries with greater accuracy. By leveraging robotic arms and advanced imaging technologies, surgeons can navigate complex anatomical structures and perform intricate procedures with minimal invasiveness (Kamel, 2023).

Robotic surgery has demonstrated numerous benefits, including reduced blood loss, shorter hospital stays, faster recovery times, and improved surgical outcomes. The AI-powered robotic systems can aid surgeons in precise movements, filtering out tremors, and providing real-time feedback. As a result, patients experience less trauma, decreased post-operative complications, and improved quality of life.

2.4 Personalized Care Pathways for Chronic Disease Management

Chronic diseases require ongoing management and personalized treatment plans. AI technologies can analyze patient data, including medical records, genetics, lifestyle factors, and treatment responses, to develop personalized care pathways (Ng, Kartoun, Stavropoulos, Zambrano, & Tang, 2021). By integrating machine learning algorithms, healthcare providers can predict disease progression, identify high-risk patients, and recommend tailored interventions.

Personalized care pathways offer numerous benefits, such as improved treatment effectiveness, reduced hospitalizations, and better patient engagement. For example, in the management of diabetes, AI algorithms can analyze patients' glucose levels, dietary patterns, and activity data to optimize insulin dosages and provide personalized recommendations for lifestyle modifications (Tarumi et al., 2021). These tailored interventions empower patients to actively participate in their care and achieve better health outcomes.

2.5 Virtual Assistants and Bots for Patient Education and Support

AI-powered virtual assistants and chatbots have gained popularity in providing patient education and support (Aggarwal, Tam, Wu, Li, & Qiao, 2023). These conversational agents can interact with patients, answer their questions, provide health information, and offer emotional support. By leveraging natural language processing algorithms, virtual assistants can understand patients' queries and respond in a conversational manner.

Virtual assistants enhance patient engagement, promote self-management, and improve healthcare literacy (Roca, Hernández, Sancho, García, & Alesanco, 2020). For instance, patients can use chatbots to learn about their medical conditions, access medication information, schedule appointments, and receive reminders for follow-up care. These virtual agents are available 24/7, offering personalized support and reducing the burden on healthcare staff. Moreover, they contribute to increased patient satisfaction and empowerment.

These applications exemplify the effective utilization of AI within the healthcare sector, illustrating its profound influence on the overall quality of hospital services. Healthcare facilities have observed advancements in patient triage, radiological diagnosis, surgical precision, chronic illness management, and patient engagement through the utilization of AI algorithms and technology. These achievements underscore the potential of AI in transforming the provision of healthcare, enhancing patient results, and elevating the overall caliber of hospital services. The progressive development of AI is anticipated to have a progressively significant role in influencing the trajectory of healthcare in the future.

3. FRAMEWORK DEVELOPMENT FOR ENHANCING HOSPITAL SERVICE QUALITY

This section explains about the development of a framework that will alleviate the hospital service quality by utilizing the AI tools. Figure 2 shows the major building blocks of the framework.

Figure 2. Major building blocks of the proposed framework

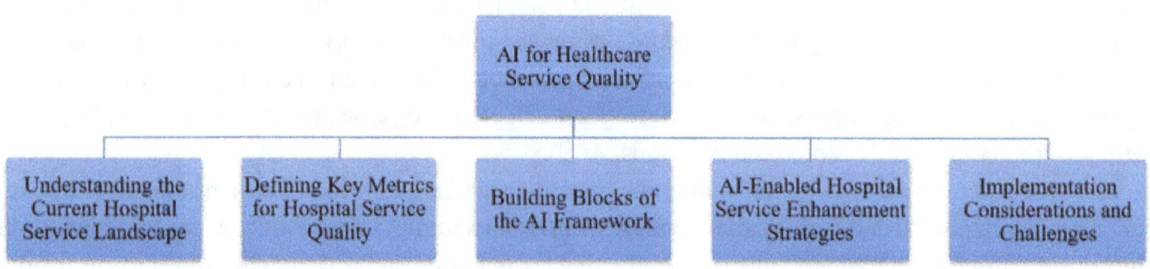

3.1 Understanding the Current Hospital Service Landscape

To enhance hospital service quality, it is essential to have a comprehensive understanding of the current landscape, including challenges, opportunities, patient expectations, staffing considerations, and existing technologies and systems. By conducting a thorough assessment, healthcare institutions can identify areas for improvement and develop targeted strategies. Figure 3 below shows the different areas to be covered under understanding the current landscape.

Figure 3. Areas to be covered under understanding the current landscape

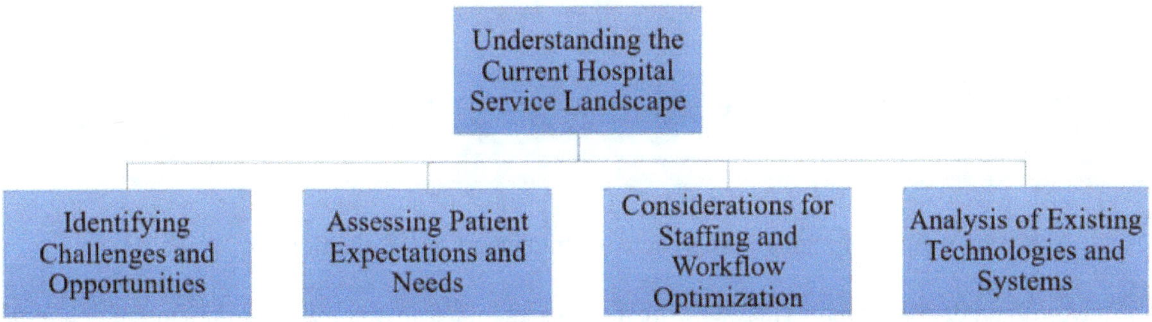

a. Identifying Challenges and Opportunities: This involves analyzing the key challenges faced by hospitals in delivering high-quality services. These challenges could include long waiting times, inefficient care coordination, limited access to healthcare services, inadequate communication between care providers, and high healthcare costs. Simultaneously, opportunities such as advancements in technology, process improvements, and patient-centric care models should be identified.
b. Assessing Patient Expectations and Needs: Understanding patient expectations is crucial for providing high-quality healthcare services. Conducting surveys, focus groups, and analyzing patient feedback can help identify areas where hospitals can improve, such as reducing wait times, enhancing communication, and ensuring personalized and empathetic care.
c. Considerations for Staffing and Workflow Optimization: Hospital service quality is greatly influenced by staffing and workflow efficiency. Assessing current staffing levels, skill sets, and workload distribution can help identify areas where improvements can be made. Streamlining workflows, optimizing shift scheduling, and leveraging AI-enabled tools for resource allocation and task automation can enhance efficiency and productivity.
d. Analysis of Existing Technologies and Systems: Evaluating the effectiveness of existing technologies and systems is crucial for determining areas where AI can be integrated to enhance service quality. This includes electronic health record systems, communication platforms, patient portals, and other healthcare information systems. Identifying gaps or areas where technology can be optimized will inform the development of the AI framework.

3.2 Defining Key Metrics for Hospital Service Quality

Defining key metrics is vital for assessing and measuring the impact of AI-enabled interventions on hospital service quality. Figure 4 shows the key metrics to be considered for hospital service quality.

Figure 4. Key metrics to be considered for hospital service quality

The following metrics provide a comprehensive framework for evaluation:

a. Access and Waiting Times: This metric focuses on reducing wait times for appointments, procedures, and tests. It measures the time from appointment scheduling to actual service delivery, aiming to optimize resource allocation and minimize patient waiting.
b. Care Coordination and Continuity: Effective care coordination ensures seamless transitions between different healthcare providers and settings. Metrics such as care transitions, care plan adherence, and patient handoffs can help evaluate the effectiveness of AI-based interventions in improving care coordination and continuity.
c. Patient Safety and Satisfaction: Patient safety and satisfaction are essential components of high-quality healthcare services. Metrics such as adverse events, medication errors, patient-reported outcomes, and satisfaction surveys can provide insights into the impact of AI on patient safety and overall satisfaction levels.
d. Cost-effectiveness and Efficiency: Measuring the cost-effectiveness and efficiency of AI-enabled interventions is crucial for assessing their impact on healthcare operations. Metrics such as resource utilization, cost per patient, and productivity gains can help evaluate the financial benefits of AI implementation.
e. Communication and Information Exchange: Effective communication and information exchange among healthcare providers, patients, and caregivers are vital for quality care delivery. Metrics such as communication timeliness, information accuracy, and patient engagement levels can gauge the effectiveness of AI-based tools in improving communication and information exchange.

3.3 Building Blocks of the AI Framework

Developing an effective AI framework involves integrating various building blocks to optimize hospital service quality. Figure 5 depicts the building blocks for the AI framework.

Figure 5. Building blocks for the AI framework

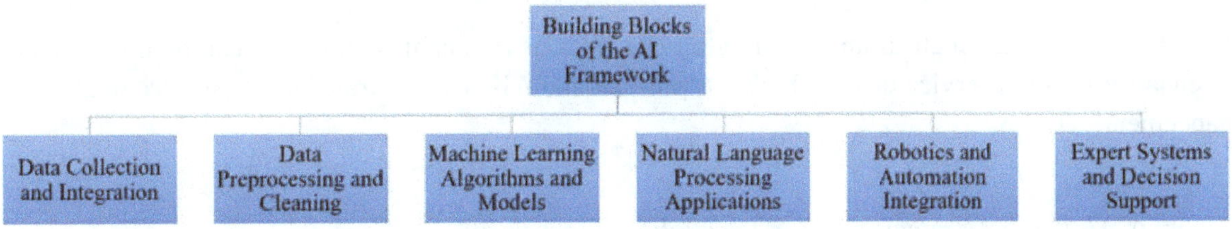

These building blocks include:

a. Data Collection and Integration: Efficient data collection mechanisms should be established to capture relevant patient data, clinical information, and operational data. This may involve leveraging electronic health records, wearable devices, Internet of Things (IoT) sensors, and other data sources. Integrating these disparate data sources is crucial for creating a holistic view of patients and healthcare processes.

b. Data Preprocessing and Cleaning: Raw healthcare data often contains noise, missing values, and inconsistencies. Data preprocessing techniques, such as data cleaning, normalization, and feature engineering, are necessary to ensure data quality and reliability. Preprocessed data forms the foundation for accurate AI model development and analysis.

c. Machine Learning Algorithms and Models: Selecting appropriate machine learning algorithms and models is crucial for leveraging AI capabilities. Supervised learning algorithms, such as decision trees, random forests, and deep neural networks, can be employed for tasks like disease prediction, risk stratification, and treatment outcome analysis. Unsupervised learning algorithms, such as clustering and anomaly detection, can uncover hidden patterns and trends in healthcare data.

d. Natural Language Processing Applications: Natural Language Processing (NLP) techniques can extract meaningful information from unstructured clinical notes, research articles, and patient feedback. NLP algorithms can be applied for tasks like sentiment analysis, clinical coding, entity recognition, and clinical decision support. NLP applications can significantly enhance information retrieval, knowledge extraction, and clinical documentation processes.

e. Robotics and Automation Integration: AI-powered robotics and automation technologies can streamline various healthcare processes, improving efficiency and reducing errors. Robotic process automation can automate administrative tasks, such as data entry and billing, freeing up healthcare professionals' time for direct patient care. Robotic surgical systems can enhance surgical precision, reducing complications and recovery times.

f. Expert Systems and Decision Support: Expert systems, built upon medical knowledge bases and inference engines, can provide decision support to healthcare professionals. These systems can assist in diagnosis, treatment planning, drug interactions, and clinical guidelines adherence. By incorporating expert systems into the AI framework, healthcare professionals can benefit from expert-level insights and recommendations.

3.4 AI-Enabled Hospital Service Enhancement Strategies

Based on the defined metrics and building blocks, various AI-enabled strategies can be implemented to enhance hospital service quality. Figure 6 presents the AI-enabled strategies for service quality enhancement.

Figure 6. AI-enabled strategies for service quality enhancement

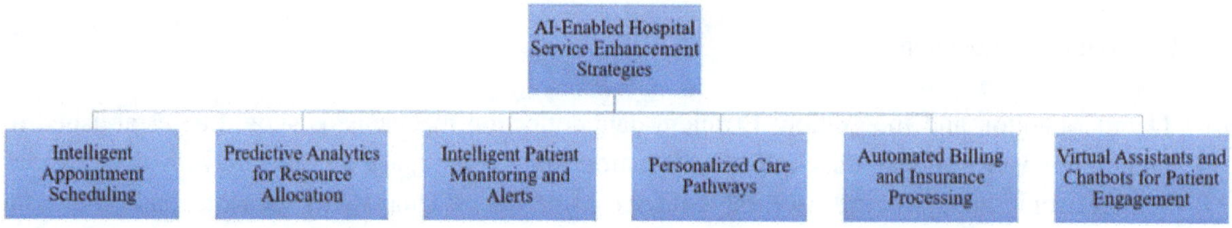

These strategies are as follows:

a. Intelligent Appointment Scheduling: AI algorithms can optimize appointment scheduling by considering factors such as patient preferences, clinician availability, and anticipated service times. Intelligent scheduling can reduce patient wait times, minimize no-shows, and improve overall resource utilization.
b. Predictive Analytics for Resource Allocation: By analyzing historical data and real-time information, predictive analytics models can accurately forecast patient demand, resource needs, and patient flow patterns. This enables proactive resource allocation, reducing bottlenecks, optimizing staffing levels, and ensuring efficient service delivery.
c. Intelligent Patient Monitoring and Alerts: AI-powered monitoring systems can continuously analyze patient data, such as vital signs, lab results, and patient-reported data, to identify potential risks and provide early warnings. Automated alerts and notifications can prompt healthcare professionals to intervene promptly, improving patient safety and reducing adverse events.
d. Personalized Care Pathways: By leveraging patient data, clinical guidelines, and machine learning algorithms, personalized care pathways can be developed. These pathways consider individual patient characteristics, medical history, and preferences to create tailored treatment plans. Personalized care pathways enhance treatment effectiveness, patient engagement, and healthcare outcomes.
e. Automated Billing and Insurance Processing: AI algorithms can streamline billing and insurance processes by automating coding, claim submission, and reimbursement calculations. This reduces administrative burdens, minimizes billing errors, and expedites financial transactions, improving overall operational efficiency.
f. Virtual Assistants and Chatbots for Patient Engagement: AI-powered virtual assistants and chatbots can provide personalized patient education, answer frequently asked questions, and offer support and guidance. These virtual agents can engage patients, assist with appointment scheduling, medication reminders, and provide health information, empowering patients to actively participate in their care.

3.5 Implementation Considerations and Challenges

Implementing AI in healthcare requires careful consideration of several factors and addressing associated challenges. Major factors and challenges for AI implementation in healthcare is presented in Figure 7.

Figure 7. Major factors and challenges for AI implementation in healthcare

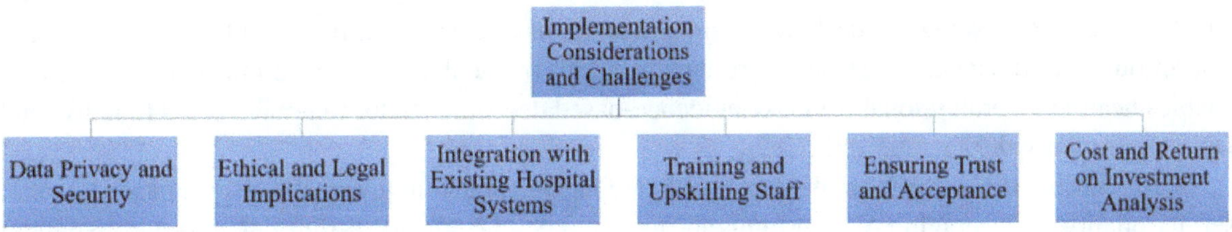

Some of major factors and challenges are described here:

a. Data Privacy and Security: Healthcare data contains sensitive patient information, necessitating robust security measures and adherence to privacy regulations. AI systems should comply with data protection laws, ensuring patient privacy and data confidentiality.
b. Ethical and Legal Implications: AI algorithms should adhere to ethical guidelines and transparency principles. Clear accountability and responsibility frameworks need to be established to ensure the fair and responsible use of AI in healthcare.
c. Integration with Existing Hospital Systems: Integrating AI technologies with existing hospital systems, such as electronic health records and other healthcare information systems, can be complex. Ensuring interoperability, data exchange standards, and seamless integration are crucial for successful implementation.
d. Training and Upskilling Staff: Healthcare professionals need to be trained to effectively use AI-enabled tools and understand their limitations. Providing training programs, workshops, and continuous education on AI technologies will facilitate successful adoption.
e. Ensuring Trust and Acceptance: Gaining trust and acceptance from healthcare professionals, patients, and stakeholders is vital for the successful implementation of AI systems. Transparent communication, addressing concerns, and demonstrating the value and benefits of AI technologies are crucial in building trust.
f. Cost and Return on Investment Analysis: Conducting a comprehensive cost and return on investment analysis is necessary to evaluate the economic feasibility and benefits of AI implementation. This analysis should consider factors such as infrastructure costs, training expenses, efficiency gains, and improved patient outcomes.

Healthcare institutions can successfully use AI to improve hospital service quality, patient experiences, and healthcare outcomes by taking these implementation factors and challenges into account.

4. DISCUSSION AND CONCLUSION

The integration of AI in healthcare service quality enhancement has significant implications for healthcare delivery. The utilization of AI technologies offers numerous benefits, including improved diagnostic accuracy, enhanced patient safety, streamlined workflows, cost savings, and increased patient engagement. The application of AI in hospital service quality can lead to improved patient outcomes, increased operational efficiency, and higher patient satisfaction rates.

One of the key advantages of AI is its ability to process and analyze vast amounts of data quickly and accurately. By leveraging machine learning algorithms and deep learning architectures, healthcare institutions can extract valuable insights from patient data, medical records, and clinical guidelines. This enables healthcare professionals to make evidence-based decisions, tailor treatment plans to individual patients, and provide personalized care.

In conclusion, the integration of AI in healthcare has the potential to significantly enhance hospital service quality. By leveraging AI algorithms and technologies, healthcare institutions can improve patient triage, diagnostic accuracy, surgical precision, chronic disease management, and patient engagement. However, successful implementation requires addressing challenges related to data privacy, ethical considerations, integration, staff training, and trust-building. With careful planning, collaboration, and continuous evaluation, AI can be a transformative force in enhancing hospital service quality, ultimately leading to improved patient outcomes and experiences. This chapter explored the foundations of AI in healthcare, the development of a framework for enhancing hospital service quality, and presented applications showcasing successful AI implementations.

The framework developed in this chapter provides a roadmap for healthcare institutions to enhance hospital service quality through AI-driven strategies. By understanding the current hospital service landscape, defining key metrics for quality assessment, and leveraging the building blocks of the AI framework, hospitals can develop targeted interventions. Intelligent appointment scheduling, predictive analytics, intelligent patient monitoring, personalized care pathways, automated billing, and virtual assistants are some of the strategies that can be implemented to enhance hospital service quality.

ACKNOWLEDGMENT

The authors extend their appreciation to the Deputyship for Research & Innovation, "Ministry of Education" in Saudi Arabia for funding this research work through the project number (IFK-SUDR_H105).

REFERENCES

Aggarwal, A., Tam, C. C., Wu, D., Li, X., & Qiao, S. (2023). Artificial Intelligence–Based Chatbots for Promoting Health Behavioral Changes: Systematic Review. *Journal of Medical Internet Research*, *25*, e40789. doi:10.2196/40789 PMID:36826990

Amann, J., Blasimme, A., Vayena, E., Frey, D., & Madai, V. I. (2020). Explainability for artificial intelligence in healthcare: A multidisciplinary perspective. *BMC Medical Informatics and Decision Making*, *20*(1), 310. doi:10.118612911-020-01332-6 PMID:33256715

Davenport, T., & Kalakota, R. (2019). The potential for artificial intelligence in healthcare. *Future Healthcare Journal, 6*(2), 94–98. doi:10.7861/futurehosp.6-2-94 PMID:31363513

Grbic, M., Stimac Grbic, D., Stimac, L., & Sostar, Z. (2019). Digital marketing in healthcare. *European Journal of Public Health, 29*(Supplement_4), ckz186.077. Advance online publication. doi:10.1093/eurpub/ckz186.077

Hosny, A., Parmar, C., Quackenbush, J., Schwartz, L. H., & Aerts, H. J. W. L. (2018). Artificial intelligence in radiology. *Nature Reviews. Cancer, 18*(8), 500–510. doi:10.103841568-018-0016-5 PMID:29777175

Jiang, F., Jiang, Y., Zhi, H., Dong, Y., Li, H., Ma, S., Wang, Y., Dong, Q., Shen, H., & Wang, Y. (2017). Artificial intelligence in healthcare: Past, present and future. *Stroke and Vascular Neurology, 2*(4), 230–243. doi:10.1136vn-2017-000101 PMID:29507784

Kamel, I. S. (2023). The role of robotics and automation in surgery: Critical review of current and emerging technologies. *Futurity Medicine, 2*(1), 23–35. doi:10.57125/FEM.2023.03.30.03

Li, R. C., Asch, S. M., & Shah, N. H. (2020). Developing a delivery science for artificial intelligence in healthcare. *npj. Digital Medicine, 3*(1), 107. doi:10.103841746-020-00318-y PMID:32885053

Mondal, T., Mugaloremutt Jayadeva, S., Pani, R., Subramanian, M., P, A., & Sumana, B. (2022). E marketing strategy in health care using IoT and Machine Learning. *Materials Today: Proceedings, 56*, 2087–2091. doi:10.1016/j.matpr.2021.11.417

Ng, K., Kartoun, U., Stavropoulos, H., Zambrano, J. A., & Tang, P. C. (2021). Personalized treatment options for chronic diseases using precision cohort analytics. *Scientific Reports, 11*(1), 1139. doi:10.103841598-021-80967-5 PMID:33441956

Pandya, S., Thakur, A., Saxena, S., Jassal, N., Patel, C., Modi, K., Shah, P., Joshi, R., Gonge, S., Kadam, K., & Kadam, P. (2021). A Study of the Recent Trends of Immunology: Key Challenges, Domains, Applications, Datasets, and Future Directions. *Sensors (Basel), 21*(23), 7786. Advance online publication. doi:10.339021237786 PMID:34883787

Rahane, W., Dalvi, H., Magar, Y., Kalane, A., & Jondhale, S. (2018). *Lung Cancer Detection Using Image Processing and Machine Learning HealthCare.* Paper presented at the 2018 International Conference on Current Trends towards Converging Technologies (ICCTCT), Comibatore, India. 10.1109/ICCTCT.2018.8551008

Riek, L. D. (2017). Healthcare robotics. *Communications of the ACM, 60*(11), 68–78. doi:10.1145/3127874

Rivero-Moreno, Y., Echevarria, S., Vidal-Valderrama, C., Pianetti, L., Cordova-Guilarte, J., Navarro-Gonzalez, J., ... Acero-Alvarracín, K. (2023). Robotic Surgery: A Comprehensive Review of the Literature and Current Trends. *Cureus, 15*(7), e42370. doi:10.7759/cureus.42370 PMID:37621804

Roca, S., Hernández, M., Sancho, J., García, J., & Alesanco, Á. (2020). *Virtual Assistant Prototype for Managing Medication Using Messaging Platforms.* Paper presented at the XV Mediterranean Conference on Medical and Biological Engineering and Computing – MEDICON 2019, Cham, Switzerland.

Rong, G., Mendez, A., Bou Assi, E., Zhao, B., & Sawan, M. (2020). Artificial Intelligence in Healthcare: Review and Prediction Case Studies. *Engineering (Beijing), 6*(3), 291–301. doi:10.1016/j.eng.2019.08.015

Schönberger, D. (2019). Artificial intelligence in healthcare: A critical analysis of the legal and ethical implications. *International Journal of Law and Information Technology*, *27*(2), 171–203. doi:10.1093/ijlit/eaz004

Solanki, R. K., Rajawat, A. S., Gadekar, A. R., & Patil, M. E. (2023). Building a Conversational Chatbot Using Machine Learning: Towards a More Intelligent Healthcare Application. In M. B. Garcia, M. V. Lopez Cabrera, & R. P. P. de Almeida (Eds.), *Handbook of Research on Instructional Technologies in Health Education and Allied Disciplines* (pp. 285–309). IGI Global. doi:10.4018/978-1-6684-7164-7.ch013

Tarumi, S., Takeuchi, W., Chalkidis, G., Rodriguez-Loya, S., Kuwata, J., Flynn, M., . . . Kawamoto, K. (2021). Leveraging Artificial Intelligence to Improve Chronic Disease Care: Methods and Application to Pharmacotherapy Decision Support for Type-2 Diabetes Mellitus. *Methods Inf Med, 60*(S 01), e32-e43. doi:10.1055/s-0041-1728757

Verma, V. K., & Verma, S. (2022). Machine learning applications in healthcare sector: An overview. *Materials Today: Proceedings*, *57*, 2144–2147. doi:10.1016/j.matpr.2021.12.101

Wee, C. K., Zhou, X., Sun, R., Gururajan, R., Tao, X., Li, Y., & Wee, N. (2022). Triaging Medical Referrals Based on Clinical Prioritisation Criteria Using Machine Learning Techniques. *International Journal of Environmental Research and Public Health*, *19*(12), 7384. doi:10.3390/ijerph19127384 PMID:35742633

Yamashita, R., Nishio, M., Do, R. K. G., & Togashi, K. (2018). Convolutional neural networks: An overview and application in radiology. *Insights Into Imaging*, *9*(4), 611–629. doi:10.100713244-018-0639-9 PMID:29934920

Yu, K.-H., Beam, A. L., & Kohane, I. S. (2018). Artificial intelligence in healthcare. *Nature Biomedical Engineering*, *2*(10), 719–731. doi:10.103841551-018-0305-z PMID:31015651

Chapter 13
Policy for Digitalization of the Georgian Healthcare System

Revaz Gvelesiani
Ivane Javakhishvili Tbilisi State University, Georgia

Irina Gogorishvili
Ivane Javakhishvili Tbilisi State University, Georgia

ABSTRACT

The work aims to characterize and analyze the economic policy of healthcare development in Georgia and, in particular, the policy of digitalization of healthcare. The healthcare system in Georgia has been characterized as a mixture of Bismarck and Beveridge models, with the government's universal healthcare program recently expanding, the goal of which is to increase the affordability of health services for the population. The work describes the goals, tools, institutions, and problems of Georgia's development policy and digitalization of healthcare. In conclusion, the authors consider those areas that should be maximally strengthened in the policy for digitalizing healthcare in Georgia to achieve the goals successfully.

INTRODUCTION

The territory of Georgia is 69,700 square kilometers. According to the 2014 census, the population is 3.7 million. After the collapse of the Soviet Union, namely in 1991, Georgian statehood was restored. It should also be noted that the unfavorable economic situation, the low solvency of newly created (based on privatization) private enterprises, and the lack of a unified database of payers have always been severe obstacles to developing healthcare and social insurance. Informal out-of-pocket payments have become widespread due to limited government funding for the health care system. The private insurance companies created during this period were less interested in the healthcare market.

With the help of the United States and EU countries, Georgia overcame the most difficult challenges and problems that generally arose in all countries during such a period. Gross domestic product per capita increased from US$3,233 to US$6,571 between 2010 and 2023 (World Ometers, n.d.).

DOI: 10.4018/979-8-3693-0679-6.ch013

Economic growth has had a significant impact on improving the population's health status, which has a positive impact on the process of achieving health-related sustainable development goals. As of 2020, the average life expectancy from birth for men is 68.8 years, and for women it is 77.8 years. In Georgia, women live on average nine years longer than men. (World Life Expectancy, n.d.).

GEORGIAN HEALTHCARE SYSTEM

Until 1995, the Soviet healthcare model existed in Georgia, which then virtually completely excluded (due to the lack of financial resources at the disposal of the state) the implementation of the interests of poor citizens.

According to Article 37 of the 1995 Constitution of Georgia (adopted on August 24, 1995), the state declared for the first time that the burden of responsibility for health care was distributed among various state entities, and health care services were no longer accessible. What was new to the country's citizens was that the state's responsibility was no longer comprehensive, but that obligations were determined by state health care programs and industry management (regulatory) mechanisms. The public still had the right to access medical services provided by government healthcare programs. In reality, due to the highly meager healthcare funding from the state, the population had nothing (Verulava, 2022).

The financing of the health care system was initially carried out according to the social insurance model (Bismarck model). With the introduction of the social insurance system, the funding party (the insurance company or the Ministry of Health) and the providers were separated. The financed party had the right to choose a medical institution at its discretion, which increased competition between them and, therefore, positively impacted the quality of service.

Reforms in the healthcare sector began in 2004, but actual steps were taken in Resolution N11 of the Georgian government of 2007, which adopted the "Master Plan for the Development of Hospitals." This meant the creation of 100 multidisciplinary hospitals (with 7,800 beds) in the country, but there were no financial resources in the regions, and the plan remained unrealized.

Since 2007, the transition to a tax model (Beveridge model) has begun because, for developing countries, the tax system has an advantage over the social insurance model. Particularly in those developing countries where the informal sector is more developed, the Beveridge model has the potential to spread more rapidly. However, the tax system burdens the state budget. In addition, there is uneven funding as it may result in subsidization of the self-employed, but not necessarily the poor. Thus, for Georgia, as a country with a small, open, and developing market, a system of financing health care through general taxes (the Beveridge model) was then appropriate.

Until 2013, the low level of economic development (with a meager state budget) hampered the implementation of set goals in the healthcare sector, and a significant part of them turned out to be unattainable.

Since 2013, in parallel with the Beveridge model, a state program of universal healthcare was launched, which aims to increase the financial accessibility of medical services for the population. All citizens of Georgia are provided with essential medical services under public and private insurance programs. For example, in 2017, compared to 2012, the volume of government allocations for the health sector doubled and increased from 365 million GEL to 800 million GEL. (Ministry of Health, n.d.a) We share the views of health policy researchers who believe that income growth increases the costs of health care and the costs of managing this process. (Hagenaars et al., 2017)) At the same time, it should be noted that the introduction of telemedicine and artificial intelligence technologies should reduce management costs and increase the efficiency of the healthcare system. However, this also has tools and institutions for the implementation of economic health policy in Georgia.

The main goal of the state health policy is to improve the health status of the population of Georgia through universal access to health services, eliminating inequalities and equitable sharing of financial burdens.

The goals subordinated to the primary goal of health protection are:

1. Improving health sector management;
2. Increasing the fairness and efficiency of the health care financing system;
3. Development of human resources in the healthcare sector;
4. Ensuring access to high-quality, effective, and safe medicines and medical products;
5. Strengthening the health management information system;
6. Improving the quality of medical services;
7. Strengthening the health system to improve preparedness and response to threats.

The central government institutions implementing health policy in Georgia are:

- Ministry of Internally Displaced Persons from the Occupied Territories, Labour, Health and Social Affairs of Georgia; (Ministry of Health, n.d.b)
- LLC National Center for Disease Control and Public Health named after L. Sakvarelidze;
- NHA – National Health Agency (NHA);
- LSI – Medical and Pharmaceutical Regulatory Agency
- SSI – Information Technology Agency;
- LSI – Center for Emergency Response and Assistance Coordination.

Important tools for implementing health policy on the territory of the state and in the legal space are:

- Law of Georgia "On Health Protection" 1997;
- Law of Georgia "On Health Insurance" of 1997, which was declared invalid as of July 1, 2007;
- Law of Georgia on the rights of patients. Accepted 05/05/2000;
- Law of Georgia "On Medical Activities," adopted on June 8, 2001; And
- The Law of Georgia on HIV/AIDS was adopted on November 17, 2009.

It should also be noted that these tools are constantly being improved.

"Georgia Solidarity Fund" (founded in June 2014) aims to support children diagnosed with cancer and young people under the age of 22, which includes financing diagnostics and treatment in Georgia and abroad. In 2013, the Georgian government, in a socially oriented budget, has unprecedentedly increased (almost doubled) the health sector's budget. However, several expensive medical services remain that available government resources cannot fully cover. Based on international experience, the organization mobilizes financial resources based on voluntary donations from citizens and the public and private sectors. The funds raised are used for the treatment of the beneficiaries of the fund. Treatment is financed in Georgia (in the amount of the share remaining outside the state program) and abroad.

At this stage, the fund collects financial resources from the following sources: stable voluntary micro-donations from the salaries of civil servants; similar voluntary donations from citizens working in the private sector; one-time donations; Integration of a charitable component into a product by companies; charity events and auctions; Patronage (the company fully covers the treatment costs of one beneficiary). 100% of the funds mobilized in the fund are used to finance the treatment of beneficiaries. For maximum transparency of activities, the Solidarity Fund is managed by the Supervisory Board and the Standing Commission, which, along with the public sector, includes representatives of the non-governmental and private sectors, as well as the UN permanent coordinator in Georgia. The state covers the administrative costs of the fund.

The state concept of the Georgian healthcare system – "Universal healthcare and quality management to protect patients' rights" – was adopted on December 29, 2014. The mentioned state concept covered the period 2014-2020.

The state concept of the healthcare system identified ten main priorities:

1. Health in all policies - a common state multi-sectoral approach - several multi-sectoral strategies have been approved, and their implementation has begun with the participation of various ministries: Georgian State Tobacco Control Strategy (2013); National Strategy for the Prevention and Control of HIV/AIDS for 2016–2018 (2016); National et al. 2016–2020 (2016); Georgian et al. for Promoting Maternal and Newborn Health for 2017–2030 (2017); National strategy for the prevention and control of non-communicable diseases in Georgia for 2017-2020 (from 2023 the state will fully finance liver transplantation for GEL 120,000) (Ministry of Health, 2023)

National Strategy for Eliminating Hepatitis C in Georgia for 2016–2020 (2016). It should be noted here that organ transplant recipients could not exercise the right to determine disability status, for which appropriate changes were introduced in January of this year, and liver, heart, or kidney transplantation is the basis for determining significant disability status.

2. Development of health sector management. Developing a strategy and action plan for the development of the Georgian healthcare system has begun and will be completed soon. One of the most critical tasks is the harmonization of rules in the field of pharmaceuticals, safe blood, human organs and tissues, tobacco, and alcohol with the current legislation of the European Union.
3. Improving the health care financing system - work was divided into the introduction of strategic procurement mechanisms, payment based on results, and various cost containment methods (selective contracting, DRG).
4. Development of the quality of medical services - a document on the classification of medical institutions has been prepared, permitting conditions for inpatient institutions to be clarified. By the year's end, a strategy for developing hospital and primary health care was developed.
5. Development of human resources in the healthcare sector - since 2014, funding has begun for the postgraduate education of medical applicants for their employment in mountainous and border regions. Since 2016, with the support of the US Threat Reduction Agency (DTRA), the implementation of the British Medical Journal (BMJ) online platform has begun in Georgia. Since 2017, participation in the continuing medical education system has become mandatory for persons working in the perinatal service.
6. Development of health care management information systems. In 2014, an electronic register of patients in hospitals was introduced. Since 2015, an electronic register of diseases registered in institutions providing outpatient services and a new system for recording malignant neoplasms

(population cancer register) have been implemented. Since 2016, a mobile and tablet application of the National Preventive Vaccination Calendar and an "electronic module for monitoring the health of pregnant women and newborns" (birth register) have been introduced. Table 1. presents the objectives, tools, and challenges of strengthening the health management information system.

7. Strengthening the health of mothers and children - the perinatal regionalization project started in 2015 and ended in 2017, which involves determining the levels of institutions providing perinatal services, their roles, and responsibilities. In 2016, specific treatment for pregnant women with sexually transmitted diseases (syphilis) was started. Since 2018, the state has funded eight prenatal visits.

Improving the prevention and treatment of priority infectious diseases - the Hepatitis C Elimination Program was launched in 2015. Since 2017, the Samegrelo-Upper Svaneti region began integrating the detection of HIV, tuberculosis, and hepatitis C into the PJD component. A transition plan for funding programs to combat AIDS and tuberculosis was developed. In order to prevent drug-resistant forms of tuberculosis, the dispensary service for patients has been strengthened.

9. Improving the prevention and control of priority non-communicable diseases - the regulatory framework for controlling tobacco use has been introduced since May 2018. A drug program for the treatment of chronic diseases was launched, and a population-based cancer registry was launched. Since 2015, the development of community-based mental health services began.
10. Development of the public health system. Since 2014, Georgia has actively supported the implementation of the global health security initiative, which is based on the aspects of preventing, detecting, and responding to risks caused by infectious diseases. Of the 11 action packages under the initiative, Georgia places particular emphasis on the "real-time epidemic surveillance" action package and supports the "zoonotic diseases" and "national laboratory system" action packages (Ministry of Health, n.d.c).

Even partial implementation of these priorities has significantly improved the healthcare situation in Georgia. The mortality rate is decreasing throughout the world, and so is Georgia. The reason for this is, first of all, the development of the healthcare sector. New technologies and treatments being introduced into healthcare are increasing the ability to detect and control diseases at an early stage. As a result, despite population growth, the aging process continues, and the proportion of the elderly population increases, ultimately reducing the mortality rate. (Verulava & Jorbenadze, 2021)

The Georgian National Health Strategy for 2022-2030 was approved by the Government of Georgia Resolution N230 in 2022. This document is the main instrument of health policy. It includes Georgia's obligations in the European Association, which imply cooperation in protecting public health, improving security, and protecting human rights. The document is also a key component of sustainable development and economic growth.

Regular monitoring and evidence-based evaluation will be carried out annually, with a report prepared within 60 calendar days after the end of the reporting year and a progress report every six months. The assessment of the National Health Strategy will be carried out in two stages. The interim assessment of the strategy will take place in the first half of 2026, when the necessary data on the indicators presented in the strategy's logical framework are fully available, and the final assessment will take place at the last stage of policy implementation, but no later than the first half of 2031 (Legislative Herald of Georgia, n.d.).

Table 1. Strengthening health management information systems

Tasks	triggers	Problems	Negative Consequences	Strengthening Digital Health Management
Goal 5.1 Strengthening digital governance	Capacities for e-health policy implementation and IT service management need to be strengthened.	Lack of electronic analytical tools for assessing the effectiveness of government health programs	mismanagement of Health data and digital health	Strengthening digital health governance
Goal 5.2 Strengthening e-health structure and services and improving the quality and electronic data interchange system	Availability of a single repository of health data	Limited use of e-health solutions	The need to improve the structure and services of the electronic health system (e-health)	Strengthening the structure and services of e-health, improving the electronic system and the quality of data exchange
Goal 5.3 Promoting the implementation of telemedicine services of digital health technologies	Lack of necessary infrastructure and capabilities to use digital health technologies (including the use of telemedicine regarding mHealth solutions)	Low access to digital health		Promoting the introduction of digital technologies and telemedicine services

Source: Brief overview of the Georgian healthcare system https://www.moh.gov.ge/uploads/files/2018/Failebi/06.08.2018 .pdf

Among the strategy's priorities, the fifth goal is strengthening health management information systems (Ministry of Health, n.d.d)

Health information systems (HMIS) play an increasingly important role in the healthcare system; they are designed to manage health-related data and are used by various stakeholders, including healthcare providers, patients, and government decision-makers.

Further strengthening the health management information system in Georgia (Goal 5) includes the implementation of the following three sub-goals: improving the national structure of e-health, digital health, and governance; strengthening the architecture and services of the electronic health care system by improving the electronic system itself and the quality of data exchange; and strengthening digital health technologies and telemedicine services.

The indicator for achieving the fifth goal is the health information system productivity index. Its base indicator for 2020 is 24, and in 2030, we should reach 30.

Subgoal 5.1 – Strengthening digital health governance. The indicator reflects the proportion of service providers in the electronic health reporting system (eHealth). The 2020 baseline is 93%, and the 2030 target is 100%. The main problems of the policy for the development of healthcare management information systems are:

1. Georgia does not yet have a national e-health strategy and a corresponding action plan;
2. There is no effective implementation of the electronic health system policy based on the need to strengthen the management capacity of IT services;
3. more analytical tools must be used to assess the effectiveness of government health programs.

Subordinate goal 5.2. Strengthening the architecture and services of e-health, improving the electronic system, and the quality of data exchange. Outcome indicator for achieving the goal: the proportion of medical institutions that have "Brief information about the patient," electronic medical records, electronic prescriptions, and in connection with a single electronic platform. The baseline for 2020 is 82%, with 100% to be achieved in 2030.

The objectives of this secondary goal are the need to improve the architecture and maintenance of the electronic health system, the availability of a single repository of health data (including medical records and national registries), and low use of electronic health solutions (e-health solutions), such as electronic prescriptions.

Subordinate goal 5.3. Promoting the implementation of digital health technologies and telemedicine services. Outcome indicator: Proportion of primary centers in rural areas using digital e-health technologies in their daily activities. The base rate for 2020 was 6.5%, the availability of 50 primary healthcare centers, and the target rate for 2030 was 100%. A significant challenge in achieving success is the limited use of mobile and digital technologies in healthcare.

Telemedicine has played an essential role in combating the spread of the coronavirus pandemic. It promoted physical distancing and remote treatment of illnesses at the primary healthcare level. Telemedicine platforms have proven ideal for combating infectious disease outbreaks. However, with their help, medical personnel, when communicating remotely with a patient, only in some instances determine in which case the patient's condition can be remotely managed and when he needs to visit a medical facility.

REDMED is the first innovative telemedicine platform in Georgia, with which you can choose the desired doctor based on his rating and ratings of other patients. The company unites 300 doctors and 20 medical areas. Provides telephone and video consultation with a doctor or a visit to the apartment and the purchase of necessary pharmaceutical products through courier delivery at the PSP pharmacy. The doctor issues the card during a home visit to the patient after issuing a prescription. Within 24 hours from the date of the visit, to check the information, the patient can use the application to ask questions to the doctor and receive timely feedback (REDMED, n.d.).

It is equally important to support the creation of creative products related to digitalization in the Georgian higher education system. DigitalMed is the first Georgian system based on artificial intelligence for the medical field, which speaks to you in Georgian and has the ability to process and analyze the information received and, as a result, make a primary diagnosis, recommend the patient to visit the clinic and the appropriate doctor. The product, created with the help of specially developed unique algorithms, is exceptional and replaces diagnostic procedures and doctor consultations with new approaches. (DigitalMed project, n.d.) It was built on the medical portal journal. ge, which offers the use of the product to all site visitors.

Fifty outpatient clinics in Georgian villages are already equipped with digital equipment, and the introduction of digital technologies in rural areas is expanding (based on a UN project and financial assistance from the European Union).

Mobile health services and health applications have great potential in the development of health-related information and services. Mobile medical services for vaccination, intelligent monitoring, and other services are already operational. To support existing activities, economic policies and legislation related to health care are already being developed, as well as the development of appropriately qualified personnel, technical support, and coordination. Significant efforts are needed to reduce inequalities in access to e-health services in rural areas, urban settlements, and various demographic and social groups (refugees, ethnic minorities, socially vulnerable people, and the LGBTQ group).

With technical support from the World Bank, an e-health strategy is being developed to create an appropriate, secure digital environment. At the same time, work is underway to make fiscal decisions to limit existing infrastructure and financing challenges.

Georgia has actively begun work to improve the capacity of medical personnel, digital technologies, and e-health. These activities should be implemented by developing and implementing eHealth-focused training programs. It is obvious that the use of media plays a vital role in increasing the efficiency of processes associated with the digitalization of the healthcare system. The provision of services by medical personnel, healthcare organizations, and medical associations must have comprehensive characteristics. In this regard, policymakers must always consider the behavioral culture of economic interest groups and the population.

Following the development of telemedicine and artificial intelligence in Georgia, the following problems and risks have been identified:

1. In most mountainous regions and villages of Georgia, there is a problem with access to high-speed Internet;
2. Georgian legislation does not regulate telemedicine services and mainly considers telemedicine a teleconsultation between two doctors. During the pandemic, the provision of telemedicine care directly between the doctor and the patient has increased, so in some instances, some rules have often had to be relaxed;
3. It is essential to develop guidelines for telehealth services (for example, minimum standard of patient screening), develop quality management indicators, and reflect them in healthcare programs. To date, this work is progressing, but very slowly;
4. A decision was made to introduce a number of telemedicine services, including preventive and door-to-door telemonitoring, cost-effective services, and products adapted abroad from the point of view of their integration into insurance packages. Although the decision has been made, it has not yet been implemented;
5. In the digital health development policy, it is necessary to take into account the problem of digital inequality - the healthcare of those individuals who, at this stage, cannot be covered by telemedicine services due to infrastructural or technological limitations;
6. Against the backdrop of the spread of electronic histories and electronic insurance, millions of personal data (results of examinations, analyses, and consultations) are posted on the portal of the Ministry of Health and the servers of various providers in the virtual space. This is a potential target for cyberhackers who can cause financial, reputational, or political damage. At this stage of development of the economic digitalization policy in Georgia, there is no special legislation that government agencies could use to regulate software services containing artificial intelligence. However, in some other areas, the Constitution of Georgia and other legislative acts establish several requirements for regulatory services that government agencies apply to the use of artificial intelligence. To eliminate the problems and risks associated with the development of telemedicine and artificial intelligence in healthcare, the following measures must be taken:
    - Access to broadband (high-speed) Internet needs to be expanded to facilitate accelerated development of e-health. Coordination of high-speed (broadband) Internet and affordable tariff policy for the population in remote, mountainous, and border areas must be implemented. It is also essential to promote the availability of technological equipment necessary for the implementation of telemedicine in primary healthcare centers and hospitals in these regions;

- Existing electronic programs, electronic records, insurance platforms, and communication systems in Georgia should implement the following:
  a) assessing the level of confidentiality and security of patient data and making appropriate changes based on the creation of unified mechanisms for protecting information systems;
  b) consideration of modern approaches to cybersecurity and reflection of this problem in the strategic plan for national cybersecurity;
  c) ensuring high standards of data protection, privacy, and cybersecurity in the healthcare sector in Georgia;
  d) preparation and implementation of a strategic plan for the development of e-health, mHealth, and telemedicine and related regulatory changes (note: during the pandemic, it is desirable to maintain a less restrictive regulatory regime in order to achieve maximum effect from services, the main thing is to ensure the security of data and networks.);
- It is strengthening cooperation with the European Union in e-health, mobile health, and telemedicine. This needs to be done by assessing the improvement and effectiveness of e-health applications and systems in combating the pandemic. Also, the main directions that have already been established in the documents of the European Commission can be considered components of the regulation and route plan of the designated territory for Georgia. In particular, the electronic platform www.geocase.ge should become (international interoperability of healthcare systems, harmonization of electronic history standards, quality standards, reliability, and data security, use of big data in public health, epidemiological surveillance and contact tracing applications, mobile implementation of telemedicine strategies and telemonitoring, effective and safe use of personal electronic medical records, networks and resources of remote psychiatric care, artificial intelligence, etc.) as the basis for the most accelerated development of patient-centric integrated e-health through digital innovation.
- Expansion of joint projects of modern applications and innovative technologies that contribute to health security in the future long-term scientific framework of the European Union - Horizon Europe - a program based on considering network cooperation in long-term plans. The global pandemic health crisis has provided an unexpected opportunity to unlock the power of health systems, both by testing good practices and identifying vulnerabilities and problems. Georgia needs to make the most of this chance;
- Georgia is a country with a small open economy and a developing market, where up to 0.5 million citizens of Georgia and foreign countries live as refugees. Among them are many cyber criminals who have already tried to commit crimes on Georgian territory. We hope that the Georgian government (as appropriate) will develop capabilities to combat and prevent cybercrime in the healthcare system at an accelerated pace with the help of artificial intelligence technologies.

CONCLUSION

Over the past ten years, due to reforms to the health system, overall health expenditure and government budget allocations have increased significantly. However, the risk of impoverishment due to healthcare costs remains high for citizens.

In order to increase the economic efficiency of the healthcare system, modern quality control and compensation systems for medical institutions have been introduced, including the "Payment for Results" model. The development of the primary healthcare system and the expansion of its functions are paramount for the financial sustainability of the healthcare system and the control of rising costs.

In preventive services, it is desirable to invest more financial resources to strengthen primary, secondary, and tertiary prevention of diseases with the highest burden of morbidity and mortality. This will protect populations with chronic diseases from very high healthcare costs.

Simultaneously with the development of a market economy in Georgia, mass privatization of medical institutions was carried out, which lagged behind the development of their regulatory framework. The legal mechanisms for the digitalization of the healthcare system also need to catch up to the requirements for regulating the results of projects and reforms we face in relations with the European Union and other international organizations. Problems arise for patients in obtaining safe and high-quality medical services and for doctors regarding their rights to protection, which exist in the context of systematic analysis and management of medical errors.

The problem is the implementation of generally accepted methods for ensuring the quality of medical care. Regarding infrastructure and human resources, existing quality and safety mechanisms (permits, licenses, and certification systems) need to be improved, expanded, and continuously improved monitoring mechanisms.

Assessing the quality of care and implementing evidence-based practices at the level of medical institutions could be better. Problems associated with qualified personnel (resources) and their uneven geographical distribution represent severe obstacles to implementing quality health services. There are enough qualified doctors in Georgia, but very few highly qualified specialists are among them. Today, a highly qualified specialist accepts an offer from abroad and leaves Georgia. Digitalization of the Georgian healthcare system will slow down this process, as doctors will be allowed to work on outsourcing based on the introduction of telemedicine.

It is crucial to constantly develop evidence-based systems to support clinical practice and adapt them to modern requirements. It should include the continuous development and improvement of mechanisms for standardization, financing, and monitoring of both education and medical services.

Particular attention should be paid (through economic policy instruments such as taxes, national qualification standards, etc.) to the smooth operation of statistical and surveillance systems. There should be a uniform commitment, monitoring, and evaluation policy for public and private institutions in public health programs, excluding any benefits. Where we are dealing with people's health, lobbying is not allowed.

REFERENCES

DigitalMed project. (2018). Artificial Intelligence Can Make A Preliminary Diagnosis. https://btu.edu.ge/ proeqti-digitalmed -tsinastsari-diagnozis-dasmas-khelovnuri-inteleqti-shedzlebs/

Hagenaars, L.L., Klazinga, N.S., Mueller, M., Morgan, D. & Jeurissen, P. P. T. (2017). How and why do countries differ in their healthcare governance and financing-related administrative expenditure? An analysis of OECD countries by healthcare system.

Legislative Herald of Georgia. (n.d.) Agreement between Georgia, on the one hand, and the European Union and the European Atomic Energy Union and their member states, on the other hand. International Treaty and Agreement of Georgia. 11. 09. 2014. https://matsne

Ministry of Health. (2023). The state will fully finance liver transplantation for GEL 120,000. *Surgery, 07*, 19. https://www.moh.gov.ge/en/news/

Ministry of Health. (n.d.b) Ministry of Internally Displaced Persons from the Occupied Territories, Labour, Health and Social Affairs of Georgia. https://www.moh.gov.ge/en/460/

Ministry of Health. (n.d.a) Universal Health Program. Ministry of Internally Displaced Persons from the Occupied Territories, Labour, Health and Social Affairs of Georgia. https://www.moh.gov.ge/ka/529

Ministry of Health. (n.d.c) A brief overview of the Georgian healthcare system. https://www.moh.gov.ge/uploads/files /2018/Failebi/ 06.08.2018.pdf

Ministry of Health. (n.d.d) Georgian National Health Strategy for 2022-2030. 63-70. https://www.moh.gov.ge/uploads/publicinformation/2022/05/04/3749f20341220a6dc1ab60c0d4f3b895.pdf

REDMED. (n.d.) Online Clinic For Georgian Immigrants Is Now Available. https://georgians.gr/redmed-for-georgians/

World Life Expectancy. (n.d.) World Health Rankings Live Longer, Live Better. https://www.worldlife-expectancy.com/country-health-profile/georgia

World Ometers. (n.d.) https://www.worldometers.info/gdp/gdp per capita.

Verulava, T. (2022). Factors influencing medical students' choice of family medicine. *Family Medicine & Primary Care Review, 113017.*

Verulava, T., & Jorbenadze, A. (2021). Context and issues of social health insurance introduction in Georgia. *Arch Balk Med Union.*, *56*(3), 349–357. doi:10.31688/ABMU.2021.56.3.09

Chapter 14
Strategic and Positive Business Communication for Healthcare

Lela Abdushelishvili
International Black Sea University, Georgia

ABSTRACT

The healthcare field is full of various challenges, such as implementing new technologies, not enough skilled workforce, stress, and anxiety. Patients' ability to communicate effectively may also be affected by their condition, medication, pain, and/or anxiety. Therefore, what is needed for the healthcare professionals is good strategic communication skills and maintaining positivity and simplicity to ensure patient safety, wellbeing, and the overall efficiency of busy healthcare organizations. Besides, serious problems may arise from poor quality communication. If professional communication skills vary in quality, then a patient's understanding of their health status may lack context, completeness, and accuracy – often causing confusion and potential harm. Communication failures in hospitals and medical practices are responsible for malpractice claims, resulting in deaths and high costs.

1. INTRODUCTION

Healthcare industry went through serious changes over the past two decades: COVID-19 pandemic, overloaded hospitals, last-minute changing circumstances and a lot of anxiety. For the first time in history, a health crisis has shut down the entire global economy. This made healthcare institutions and professionals move toward value-based care, improve overall wellness of population and decrease illnesses and complications. Besides, there were reported cases of information overload, unclearly structured messages and statements which confused people and let them feel stressed and frustrated. So, it became extremely essential to clearly, positively and strategically communicate and pass messages with the view of leading to win-win solutions and outcomes as well as develop positive attitudes and be able to handle critical situations effectively in both face-to-face and online/digital communication.

COVID-19 pandemic significantly contributed to the change of the healthcare environment: procedures were quickly altered, hospitals found themselves confronted with the shortage of staff, there was high demand on quick information analysis and making timely and critical decisions. During 2020, the

DOI: 10.4018/979-8-3693-0679-6.ch014

pandemic has become a major health concern in the whole world. In fact, the number of those who died of this infection amounts to two million.

Additional challenge came up as a result of big technological innovations: strong digital platforms became extremely necessary, a lot of data accumulated and its privacy issues arose, deep fake content creation was reported, too much focus on automation was made. Besides, patients demanded doctors to meet their expectations and even serve as heroes, experts, creators of positive patient experience and just close friends of theirs in order to ensure positivity and calm atmosphere. The added challenge was clinical communication practices changed by this infection. In other words, the regular face-to-face communication changed into remote and distance practices. This led to certain barriers to communication as almost all consultations became video based and the use of virtual assistants emerged.

Notably, COVID-19 created such challenges that the field of healthcare has never experienced before and some big changes for the better emerged. One of them is developing resilience and innovation. In other words, use of telehealth emerged. If before video healthcare visits were not regarded useful, now they proved to be otherwise. Besides, the amount of requests for such virtual visits required technology update and simplification of the process to meet the needs. Therefore, online consultations were used intensively and, in fact, they proved to be successful which helped healthcare establishments to move towards a good balance of face-to-face and distance appointments and, thus, provide even more effective consultations.

Because of the increased need, people began working in joint cooperation and attempted to defeat the crisis which led to breaking down hierarchy and promoted more intense sense of cooperation and collaboration.

One negative outcome of the pandemic was the issue with mental health. In other words, people were afraid of becoming ill and they had practically no interaction which increased anxiety and boredom. As a result, negative emotions accumulated inside them and the need for sharing their stories arose. As John Bonamo, MD, Chief Medical and Quality Officer at RWJ Barnabas Health (https://www.rwjbh.org/blog/2022/january/how-covid-19-is-reshaping-healthcare/) stated, “Everybody has a story and it is important for us to take the time to listen and, if necessary, become an advocate or a resource for the patient”. Indeed, listening to the patient and his/her story, demonstrating to him/her that they are cared for and listened to makes significant impact on his/her mental health and, thus, sets him/her for positivity.

COVID-19 advised medical field representatives to be flexible. What this meant was that old regulations and rules no more were applied and the so-called functional flexibility came in which meant giving different roles to different employees. This also is linked to job rotation which encompasses workers taking various tasks related to their shift working schemes or special requirements and demands of the medical institution.

Thus, taking into consideration all the above-stated, anxiety rose, many last-minute changing circumstances arose, psychological state of individuals got critical and, therefore, effective strategic communication skills and maintaining positivity and simplicity proved to be extremely significant to ensure patient wellbeing, calm and quiet interaction between colleagues and provide timely and quality service.

Undoubtedly, communication lies at the heart of effective healthcare. In a fast-paced and complex industry, the art of communication is extremely significant for healthcare leaders to ensure engagement, make their teams more empowered and activate a culture of transparency.

It is due to poor communication that the potential for medical errors is increased and a negative working environment is created. This leads to a lower quality of patient care which has a negative effect on clinical outcomes. When health care professionals are not communicating effectively, patient safety is at risk for several reasons: lack of critical information, misinterpretation of information, unclear orders over the telephone, and overlooked changes in status. Lack of communication creates situations where medical errors can occur. Therefore, special strategies and techniques used will make sure the situation is more or less coordinated and taken care of.

2. STRATEGIC AND POSITIVE BUSINESS COMMUNICATION FOR HEALTHCARE PROFESSIONALS

Effective communication can have a positive impact on the relationships between the patient and the provider dynamic. It lets patients know better what the condition of their own health is and, thus, be able to plan and implement health and wellness strategies. It can also help patients develop a comprehensive understanding of current care strategies involving their health, including acute health situations.

Communication can also help develop a sense of trust between the patient and provider, which might make it easier for patients to adhere to a provider's recommendations. These elements can lead to several key potential long-term benefits, such as reduced patient visits, reduced costs and improved patient outcomes.

The increased presence of technology makes effective communication even more important in health care. It can help mitigate the potential impact of health misinformation that could otherwise lead patients to make poor or improper decisions about their health. It can also help improve communication among other health care professionals who may need to coordinate care across multiple facilities. This can also lead to improved opportunities for delivering care.

Because technology constantly evolves, it is crucial to periodically reinvigorate communication for health care providers to meet patient expectations. This will help to avoid further misunderstandings and crisis.

Besides, patient portals developed by healthcare facilities will allow patients to get access to health care information. Educational health information can be placed on the patient's portal that is relevant to the patient's specific health needs. Clinical summaries can be made accessible. These summaries can be a review of the patient's last appointment or a summary of recent test results with explanations. The summaries can also include recommendations, such as the need for follow-up appointments.

Using simple language helps to overcome the challenges. Language is the most powerful tool of communication. Communication of ideas, thoughts, opinions and emotional expressions, social interaction, using the power of sound help to maintain effective communication in healthcare and ensure positivity.

When a healthcare worker communicates effectively, s/he makes sure every patient is approached individually, respectfully and with the view of understanding his/her concerns or worries as well as thoughts and opinions. In this process such skills as active listening, paying attention, gathering main points come to the front.

For nurses, good communication in healthcare means approaching every patient interaction with the intention to understand the patient's concerns, experiences, and opinions. This includes using verbal and nonverbal communication skills, along with active techniques. As a result, interaction is maintained, engagement is made, active listening is present, complaints are heard, engagement is provided, feedback is encouraged and the culture of collaboration and empowerment is enhanced.

Communication with patients and their family members enhances patient experience and even leads to better outcomes. In this process it is essential to emphasize the importance of active listening and use of simple language to make sure that the information given is understood easily.

In the era of digital, technological progress and advancement a lot of tools are at the disposal of healthcare professionals to provide better and professional communication since effective communication is the main backbone or successful operation in the healthcare field. Therefore, it is essential to engage and communicate effectively with patients and their families, promote transparency, enhance patient engagement and lead them to better outcomes. This helps to create a collaborative and patient-centered environment thus leading to effective communication towards positive development and change.

Improving communication in healthcare will not only help to ensure the best level of care is provided to patients and clinical outcomes are improved, effective and efficient communication helps to drive down the cost of healthcare provision.

One of the most effective communication strategies to improve patient safety is to structure conversations to ensure information is accurately transferred between two people and a useful approach is SBAR, an acronym for Situation, Background, Assessment, Recommendation. Michael Leonard, MD, Physician Leader for Patient Safety, along with colleagues Doug Bonacum and Suzanne Graham at Kaiser Permanente of Colorado (Evergreen, Colorado, USA) developed this technique. The SBAR technique has been implemented widely at health systems such as Kaiser Permanente. Please provide your information to download the SBAR Tool.

This approach is particularly useful for nurse-nurse communications during shift handovers and for nurse-physician conversations.

Conversations should start with Situation – who is calling, to which patient the call refers, and the reason for the call. Concise Background information is then provided about the patient and his/her condition. Information is then provided about the Assessment of the patient. The caller then provides their Recommendation or asks for recommendations on the best course of action to take. The person who initiates the call then asks the receiver to repeat the information to make sure it has been understood.

Adding structure to the conversation ensures relevant information is rapidly, accurately, and efficiently transferred. It is also useful getting people to think about what they are about to communicate beforehand to ensure all the necessary information is passed on.

3. THE STICC AND BATHE PROTOCOLS IN COMMUNICATION STRATEGIES FOR HEALTHCARE

The STICC protocol has been adopted in several industries for providing structure to briefings and ensuring critical information has been understood.

- Situation – Explain the situation and the problem
- Task – Explain the recommended course of action
- Intent – Explain why that action should be taken
- Concern – Explain any issues that may arise and what to look out for
- Calibrate – Invite the person to say if they do not understand. Ask if there is any reason why an action cannot be taken and for the receiver to express any concerns.

Effective communication with patients is essential for passing on essential information and making sure that information is understood. Good communication also improves the patient experience, which improves patient satisfaction. There are several communication strategies in healthcare that can be adopted to improve communication with patients.

The BATHE Protocol-is a useful for establishing a rapport with a patient and to put them at their ease. The purpose of this communication strategy is not to solve any problems the patient has. Instead the aim is to give the patient reassurances and to listen to their concerns. This approach has proved to be effective in outpatient settings at improving the patient experience and patient satisfaction scores.

- Background – What is going on in your life?
- Affect – How does that affect you?
- Troubles – What troubles are you experiencing?
- Handling – How are you handling them?
- Empathetic Statement – E.g. That must be very difficult for you.

The AWARE Approach to Patient Interaction - is a useful protocol for improving the patient experience. Healthcare professionals should Announce their presence, Welcome the patient and smile, Ask if there is anything the patient needs, Review the interaction and explain why it was important and when the patient will need to be seen again, then Exit with kindness.

Patient teach back is a useful communication strategy in healthcare that nurses and physicians can adopt to make sure important information has been effectively communicated and understood by the patient. Patients may say they have understood what they have been told even when they are not totally clear about what has been said. This approach helps to make sure that important information has been properly understood. This communication strategy can help to prevent readmissions. After communicating information to a patient, ask the patient to repeat back what they have been told in their own words.

4. THE IMPORTANCE OF PATIENT SATISFACTION IN HEALTHCARE

The importance of patient satisfaction in healthcare cannot be overstated. When patients have a high level of satisfaction with the care they receive from a healthcare provider, patient outcomes are likely to be better. Patients are also more likely to remain with the same healthcare provider. If a patient has a bad experience, he/she could change providers and share the bad experience on social media, the internet, or word of mouth. That could easily make it harder for healthcare providers to attract patients.

Patient satisfaction is a good measure of quality of care, which is why a percentage of reimbursement for Medicare is linked to patient satisfaction scores from Hospital Consumer Assessment of Healthcare Providers and Systems (HCAHPS) surveys.

4.1. Take Advantage of New Communication Tools for Patient Satisfaction

These communication strategies in healthcare will help to ensure information is transferred effectively and efficiently; however, communication strategies in healthcare will only go so far. Healthcare organizations also need to provide modern communication systems to facilitate better communication. Today, smartphones and other portable electronic devices allow people to communicate quickly, effectively, and confidentially in the outside world. These technologies can also be used to improve communication in healthcare, although many hospitals are still reliant on one-way communication tools such as pagers and faxes. A great deal of time is wasted in healthcare playing phone tag, chasing up physicians and nurses to make sure information has been received.

HIPAA-compliant text messaging platforms allow all members of a care team to communicate with each other efficiently and effectively. These platforms allow healthcare professionals to keep all members of the care team in the loop and ensure information is communicated with the right people at the right time. These platforms can support text, audio, and video calls and can be used for quick consults, to contact any member of the care team, to transfer information accurately at shift changes and other patient handoffs, and allow healthcare providers to easily provide telehealth services to remote patients.

Healthcare providers that have replaced pagers and faxes with these advanced healthcare communications solutions have been able to improve efficiency and productivity, increase staff morale, reduce medical errors, improve patient satisfaction scores, and cut costs.

One of the most effective communication strategies to improve patient safety is to structure conversations to ensure information is accurately transferred between two people. One of the most useful approaches is SBAR, an acronym for Situation, Background, Assessment, Recommendation.

The key purpose of strategies is to add structure to communications. Consequently, each of these strategies can be adapted to suit specific circumstances provided the strategy remains consistent to ensure that handovers, briefings, and consultations follow the same patterns to prevent omissions or misunderstandings.

Because of the different nature of the scenarios, there is no one-size-fits-all communication strategy in healthcare that is suitable for all scenarios and trying to tailor one strategy to address organization-wide communication issues could create more problems than it solves.

While some strategies do not provide the opportunity for questions or objections, their purpose is to communication a course of action, justify it, and ensure the course of action has been understood. Other strategies are more interactive inasmuch as allow for questions and/or objections. Teams should decide which strategy (or version of the strategy) is appropriate for specific scenarios.

With some communication tools, teams can upload templates to ensure each element of the communication is covered and nothing is omitted or overlooked. This can be a very useful feature during handovers when stressful situations could result in forgetfulness or shortcuts being taken that might mitigate the effectiveness of the communication strategy.

5. CONCLUSION

The 21st century in the time of active hybrid communications. The physical and digital channels of communication between the doctor and patient already competing with each other (Gigauri & Djakeli, 2021). Many patients to rationalize the use of the time already turn in the side of virtual e-visits to physicians. The generational marketing shows us how it is important to know more insides about the patients. For example, the patients of generation Z, have high willingness of online booking of the visit to the doctor and digital engagement from the side of health organization. But members of X generation, still continue to lead in physical, verbal communication with gatekeeper medicine, their doctors, family physicians, representatives of secondary healthcare. Even if healthcare will be innovatively developed to the new era of virtual surgeries, and this type of surgery operations will be in guidelines of well developed, high industrial countries (Djakeli, 2012). Still baby boomer and generation x members will continue to wish all medicine into form of physical communication. That's why we see that communication has many problems and barriers. Various types of communication barriers in healthcare are physical and environmental, physical or biological, language, personal, emotional, socio-psychological, cultural. They significantly affect the process and outcome and hinder efficiency. From this perspective, strategic and positive communication plays a significant role to overcome those barriers and challenges and ensure positive and flawless environment to provide wellbeing and room for further development.

Thus, the scientific research about the healthcare communication must be focused on effective ways of overcoming psychological, behavioral and economic barriers to provide clinics and individuals with tangible and useful evidence based knowledge on how to become more trustful, mutually understandable, efficient and effective to achieve the positive long term communication with patient.

REFERENCES

Arruda, W. (2017). What LinkedIn will look like in the future - and the actions you need to take now. *Forbes*. Available at https://www.forbes.com/ sites/ williamarruda/ 2017/ 06/ 30/ what-linkedin-will-look-like-in-the-future-and-the-actions-you-need-to-take-now/ #3fd3b0bd5c6f

Baker, T. (2019). *Nine barriers to effective workplace communication*. IIDM. Available at https://www.iidmglobal.com/ expert_talk/ expert-talk-categories/ managing-people/ staff_communication/ id3264-nine-barriers-to-effective-workplace-communication.html

Bednarz, K. (2016). *11 tips for effective communication through Skype*. LinkedIn. Available at https://www.linkedin.com/ pulse/effective-communication-through-skype-katherin-bednarz

Benjamin, T. (n.d.). *How to effectively communicate remotely*. Chron. Available at https://smallbusiness.chron.com/ effectively-communicate-remotely-33662.html

Clampitt, P. G., & Girard, D. (1993). Communication satisfaction: A useful construct? *New Jersey Journal of Communication, 1*(2), 84–102. Available at http://imetacomm.com/ wp-content/ themes/ Structure%20Premium%20White/ organic_structure_white/ downloads/ Metacomm_UsefulConstruct.pdf

Djakeli, K. (2012). Matrix of Brand Awareness and a Positive Image as a Success Factor in Political PR. *Journal in Humanities*, 31-35.

Dorsey, K. (2017). The 10 pros and cons about working from home that you need to know right now. Available at https://www.insider.co.uk/ news/10-pros-cons-working-home-10455197

Fisher, C. (2017). Ready for the robots: survey says job candidates are mostly okay with AI Apps in the application process. *Allegis*. Available at https://blog.allegisglobalsolutions.com/ ready-for-the-robots-survey-says-job-candidates-are-mostly-okay-with-ai-apps-in-the-application-process

Gigauri, I., & Djakeli, K. (2021). National Health Reforms in Georgia during 1994-2021 and their Success. *HOLISTICA–Journal of Business and Public Administration, 12*(2), 102–108. doi:10.2478/hjbpa-2021-0017

Grainger, C. (n.d.). *How to write a compelling LinkedIn profile summary that gets noticed.* TopCV blogpost. Available at https://www.topcv.co.uk/ career-advice/ linkedin-profile-summary

Ibrahim, M. M., El-Khedr, S. M., & Nosek, L. J. (2013). Effective communication and job satisfaction among staff nurses working in paediatric intensive care units. *Life Science Journal, 10*(1), 2661–2669. Available at https://www.researchgate.net/ publication/ 261359002_Effective_Communication_and_Job_Satisfaction_among_Staff_Nurses_Working_in_Pediatric_Intensive_Care_Units

NFON. (2018). *4 reasons why generation Z brings a human communication style to the workplace.* Available at https://www.nfon.com/ en/ news/ press/ blog/ blog-detail/ 4-reasons-why-generation-z-brings-a-human-communication-style-to-the-workplace

Pierce, D. (2018). *Step into your new virtual office.* Wired blogpost. Available at https://www.wired.com/ story/ augmented-reality-in-the-workplace/

Rycraft, S. (2018). *7 benefits of using LinkedIn.* LinkedIn blogpost. Available at https://www.linkedin.com/ pulse/ 7-benefits-using-linkedin-sarah-rycraft

Sawa, D. (2019). Extreme loneliness or the perfect balance? How to work from home and stay healthy. *The Guardian Health & Wellbeing*. Available at https://www.theguardian.com/ lifeandstyle/ 2019/ mar/ 25/ extreme-loneliness-or-the-perfect-balance-how-to-work-from-home-and-stay-healthy

UK VIP. (n.d.). *The four basic styles of communication.* University of Kentucky Violence Intervention and Prevention Centre. Available at https://www.uky.edu/ hr/ sites/ www.uky.edu.hr/ files/ wellness/ images/ Conf14_FourCommStyles.pdf

Woods, D. (2010). *Poor communication between managers and employees wastes time and impacts productivity.* HR. Available at http://www.hrmagazine.co.uk/ article-details/ poor-communication-between-managers-and-employees-wastes-time-and-impacts-productivity

Compilation of References

Abad, H. (2012). *Fundamentos éticos de la salud pública.* https://www.udea.edu.co/wps/wcm/connect/udea/fea72810-e0f6-44f4-ba18-9d932411d04b/fundamentos_eticos_sp_hag.pdf?MOD=AJPERES

Abdullah, M., Madain, A., & Jararweh, Y. (2022, November). ChatGPT: Fundamentals, applications and social impacts. *2022 Ninth International Conference on Social Networks Analysis, Management and Security (SNAMS)*, 1-8. 10.1109/SNAMS58071.2022.10062688

Abid, A., Roy, S. K., Lees-Marshment, J., Dey, B. L., Muhammad, S. S., & Kumar, S. (2023). Political social media marketing: A systematic literature review and agenda for future research. *Electronic Commerce Research*, 1–36. doi:10.100710660-022-09636-7

Abookire, S., Plover, C., Frasso, R., & Ku, B. (2020). *Health Design Thinking: An Innovative Approach in Public Health to Defining Problems and Finding Solutions.* Public Health Education and Promotion. doi:10.3389/fpubh.2020.00459

Aceto, G., Persico, V., & Pescapé, A. (2020). Industry 4.0 and Health: Internet of Things, Big Data, and Cloud Computing for Healthcare 4.0. *Journal of Industrial Information Integration, 18.* doi:10.1016/j.jii.2020.100129

Acheson, R. M. (1978). The definition and identification of need for health care. *Journal of Epidemiology and Community Health, 32*(1), 10–15. doi:10.1136/jech.32.1.10 PMID:262581

Adamo, S. M., Serpieri, S. A., De Falco, R., Di Cicco, T., Foggia, R., Giacometti, P., & Siani, G. (2008). Tom Thumb in hospital: The fairy tale workshop in a paediatric oncology and haematology ward. *Psychodynamic Practice, 14*(3), 263–280. doi:10.1080/14753630802141865

Adams, C. P., & Brantner, V. V. (2006). Estimating the cost of new drug development: Is it really $802 million? *Health Affairs, 25*(2), 420–428. doi:10.1377/hlthaff.25.2.420 PMID:16522582

Adiyono, G., Rahmat, T. Y., & Anindita, R. (2021). Digital Marketing Strategies To Increase Online Business Sales Through Social Media. *Journal Of Humanities, Social Science, Public Administration and Management, 1*(2), 31–37. doi:10.51715/husocpument.v1i2.58

Adler-Milstein, J., Kvedar, J., & Bates, D. W. (2016). Telehealth Among US Hospitals: Several Factors, Including State Reimbursement and Licensure Policies, Influence Adoption. *Health Affairs, 35*(12), 2330–2337. doi:10.1377/hlthaff.2016.0445 PMID:24493762

Agarwal, R., Dugas, M., Gao, G., & Kannan, P. K. (2018). Emerging technologies and analytics for a new era of value-centered marketing in healthcare. *Journal of the Academy of Marketing Science, 48*(1), 9–23. doi:10.100711747-019-00692-4

Agatemor, C., Ibsen, K. N., Tanner, E. E., & Mitragotri, S. (2018). Ionic liquids for addressing unmet needs in healthcare. *Bioengineering & Translational Medicine, 3*(1), 7–25. doi:10.1002/btm2.10083 PMID:29376130

Aggarwal, A., Tam, C. C., Wu, D., Li, X., & Qiao, S. (2023). Artificial Intelligence–Based Chatbots for Promoting Health Behavioral Changes: Systematic Review. *Journal of Medical Internet Research*, *25*, e40789. doi:10.2196/40789 PMID:36826990

Aghdam, Z. N., Rahmani, A. M., & Hosseinzadeh, M. (2021). The role of the Internet of Things in healthcare: Future trends and challenges. *Computer Methods and Programs in Biomedicine*, *199*, 105903. doi:10.1016/j.cmpb.2020.105903 PMID:33348073

AgudeloC. A.CardonaJ.OrtegaJ.RobledoR. (2011). Sistema de salud en Colombia: 20 años de logros y problemas. *Ciênc. Saúde Coletiva, 16*(6). https://doi.org/https://doi.org/10.1590/S1413-81232011000600020

Ahern, D. K., Kreslake, J. M., Phalen, J. M., & Bock, B. (2006). What is eHealth (6): Perspectives on the evolution of eHealth research. *Journal of Medical Internet Research*, *8*(1), e4. doi:10.2196/jmir.8.1.e4 PMID:16585029

Ahmed, S., Alqasmi, I., Ashrafi, D. M., Choudhury, M. M., Rahman, M. K., & Mohiuddin, M. (2023). Determining the intention to use app-based medicine service in an emerging economy. *International Journal of Healthcare Management*, 1–15. doi:10.1080/20479700.2023.2198186

Ahuja, A. S., Polascik, B. W., Doddapaneni, D., Byrnes, E. S., & Sridhar, J. (2023). The digital metaverse: Applications in artificial intelligence, medical education, and integrative health. *Integrative Medicine Research*, *12*(1), 100917. doi:10.1016/j.imr.2022.100917 PMID:36691642

Alkaissi, H., & McFarlane, S. I. (2023). Artificial hallucinations in ChatGPT: Implications in scientific writing. *Cureus*, *15*(2). Advance online publication. doi:10.7759/cureus.35179 PMID:36811129

Allen, A., & Allen, D. (1995). Telemedicine programs: 2nd annual review reveals doubling of programs in a year. *Telemedicine Today*, *3*(2), 10–14.

Alonzo, D., & Popescu, M. (2021). Utilizing social media platforms to promote mental health awareness and help seeking in underserved communities during the COVID-19 pandemic. *Journal of Education and Health Promotion*, *10*. Advance online publication. 1 doi:0.4103/jehp.jehp_21_21 PMID:34222531

Alshakhs, F., & Alanzi, T. (2018). The evolving role of social media in health-care delivery measuring the perception of health-care professionals in Eastern Saudi Arabia. *Journal of Multidisciplinary Healthcare*, *11*, 473–479. doi:10.2147/JMDH.S171538 PMID:30275699

Amann, J., Blasimme, A., Vayena, E., Frey, D., & Madai, V. I. (2020). Explainability for artificial intelligence in healthcare: A multidisciplinary perspective. *BMC Medical Informatics and Decision Making*, *20*(1), 310. doi:10.1186/s12911-020-01332-6 PMID:33256715

Anderson, S. T., Nasr, L., & Rayburn, S. W. (2018). Transformative service research and service design: Synergistic effects in healthcare. *Service Industries Journal*, *38*(1-2), 99–113. doi:10.1080/02642069.2017.1404579

Annual Report 2022-23. (n.d.). Department of Pharmaceuticals, Ministry of Chemicals & fertilizers, Government of India. Available at: https://pharmaceuticals.gov.in/sites/default/files/Annual%20Report%202022-23%20Final-3_0.pdf

Anupam, T. (2021). Using Rapid Design Thinking to Overcome COVID-19 Challenges in Medical Education. *Academic Medicine*, *96*(1), 56–61. doi:10.1097/ACM.0000000000003718 PMID:32889947

Aras, R. (2011). Social marketing in healthcare. *The Australasian Medical Journal*, *4*(8), 418–424. doi:10.4066/AMJ.2011.626 PMID:23393528

Archer MSA. (2008). investopedia.com

Arenal, A., Armuna, C., Feijoo, C., Ramos, S., Xu, Z., & Moreno, A. (2020). Innovation ecosystems theory revisited: The case of artificial intelligence in China. *Telecommunications Policy*, *44*(6), 101960. doi:10.1016/j.telpol.2020.101960

Arkorful, Zhao, Muhideen, Basiru, & Hammond. (2019). *An Empirical Investigation of Health Practitioners Technology*. Academic Press.

Arkorful, V. E., Shuliang, Z., Muhideen, S., Basiru, I., & Hammond, A. (2020, September 09). Adoption: The Mediating Role of Electronic Health. *International Journal of Public Administration*, *43*(12), 1013–1028. Advance online publication. doi:10.1080/01900692.2019.1664569

Arruda, W. (2017). What LinkedIn will look like in the future - and the actions you need to take now. *Forbes*. Available at https://www.forbes.com/ sites/ williamarruda/ 2017/ 06/ 30/ what-linkedin-will-look-like-in-the-future-and-the-actions-you-need-to-take-now/ #3fd3b0bd5c6f

Arya, B., & Salk, J. E. (2006). Cross-sector alliance learning and effectiveness of voluntary codes of corporate social responsibility. *Business Ethics Quarterly*, *16*(2), 211–234. doi:10.5840/beq200616223

Asamblea Mundial de la Salud. WHA58.28 Cibersalud. Novena sesión plenaria, 25 de mayo de 2005 - Comisión A, séptimo informe.

Asiamah, N., Opuni, F. F., & Mensah, H. K. (2018). The nexus between internal marketing in hospitals and organizational commitment: Incorporating the mediation roles of key job characteristics. *International Journal of Healthcare Management*, *13*(sup1), 385–399. doi:10.1080/20479700.2018.1551951

Asociación Colombiana de empresas de medicina integral. (2022). *Encuesta del Ministerio de Salud confirma satisfacción de usuarios con sus EPS*. https://acemi.org.co/encuesta-del-ministerio-de-salud-confirma-satisfaccion-de-usuarios-con-sus-eps/

Association of Accessible Medicines. (2017). *Generic Drug Access and Savings in the U.S.* Available at https://accessiblemeds.org/sites/default/files/2017-07/2017-AAM-Access-Savings-Report-2017-web2.pdf

Assumptions for the Draft Act on Financing Medical Care in Poland Based on the legislative initiative of the Senator of the Second Term of the Republic of Poland, Zygmunt Hortmanowicz of 17 December 1991.

Asti, W. P., Handayani, P. W., & Azzahro, F. (2021). Influence of trust, perceived value, and attitude on customers' repurchase intention for e-grocery. *Journal of Food Products Marketing*, *27*(3), 157–171. doi:10.1080/10454446.2021.1922325

Astuti, H. J., & Nagase, K. (2014). Patient loyalty to healthcare organizations: Relationship marketing and satisfaction. *International Journal of Management and Marketing Research*, *7*(2), 39–56.

Ata, R., & Yildirim, K. (2019). Exploring Turkish pre-service teachers' perceptions and views of digital literacy. *Education Sciences*, *9*(1), 1–16. doi:10.3390/educsci9010040

Austin, J. E., & Seitanidi, M. M. (2012b). Collaborative value creation: A review of partnering between nonprofits and businesses. Part 2: Partnership processes and outcomes. *Nonprofit and Voluntary Sector Quarterly*, *41*(6), 929–968. doi:10.1177/0899764012454685

Averill, R. F., Muldoon, J. H., Vertrees, J. C., Goldfield, N. I., Mullin, R. L., Fineran, E. C., Mona Z. Zhang, B.S., SteinbeckB., & Grant, T. (1998). *The evolution of casemix measurement using diagnosis related groups (DRGs)*. Wallingford: 3M Health Information Systems.

Awad, M. H. (2023). Place and the structuring of cross-sector partnerships: The moral and material conflicts over healthcare and homelessness. *Journal of Business Ethics*, *184*(4), 933–955. doi:10.100710551-023-05360-w PMID:37168486

Azam, M., Khan, A. Q., & Ozturk, I. (2019). The effects of energy on investment, human health, environment and economic growth: Empirical evidence from China. *Environmental Science and Pollution Research International*, *26*(11), 10816–10825. doi:10.100711356-019-04497-4 PMID:30778925

Baabdullah, A. M., Alalwan, A. A., Rana, N. P., Kizgin, H., & Patil, P. (2019). Consumer use of mobile banking (M-Banking) in Saudi Arabia: Towards an integrated model. *International Journal of Information Management*, *44*, 38–52. doi:10.1016/j.ijinfomgt.2018.09.002

Baker, T. (2019). *Nine barriers to effective workplace communication.* IIDM. Available at https://www.iidmglobal.com/ expert_talk/ expert-talk-categories/ managing-people/ staff_communication/ id3264-nine-barriers-to-effective-workplace-communication.html

Baker, D. W., Wolf, M., Feinglass, J., Thompson, J., Gazmararian, J., & Huang, J. (2007). Health literacy and mortality among elderly persons. *Archives of Internal Medicine*, *167*(14), 1503–1509. doi:10.1001/archinte.167.14.1503 PMID:17646604

Bala, M., & Verma, D. (2018). A critical review of digital marketing. *International Journal of Management, IT & Engineering*, *8*(10), 321–339.

Balogun, B., & Ogunnaike, O. (2017). Healthcare Organisations in a global marketplace: A systematic Review of the literature on healthcare marketing. *SSRN*, *1*(5). Advance online publication. doi:10.2139srn.3047747

Barei, F., & Ross, M. (2015). The refinement of the super generic concept: Semantic challenge for product re-innovation? *Generics and Biosimilars Initiative (GaBI) Journal*, *4*(1), 25–32.

Barrios, K. V., Orozco-Nuñez, D. M., Pérez-Navas, E., & Conde-Cardona, G. C. (2021). Nuevas recomendaciones de la versión PRISMA 2020 para revisiones sistemáticas y metaanálisis. *Acta Neurologica Colombiana*, *37*(2), 105–106. doi:10.22379/24224022373

Barroso-Méndez, M. J., Galera-Casquet, C., & Valero-Amaro, V. (2014). Partnerships between businesses and NGOs in the field of corporate social responsibility: A model of success from the perspective of relationship marketing. *Journal of Relationship Marketing*, *13*(1), 1–27. doi:10.1080/15332667.2014.882626

Bartosiak, N. (2021). *Human Resources Management during a Pandemic in Selected Corporations in the Pharmaceutical Industry. Dissertation.* Academy of War Art.

Bashshur, R. L. (1995). Telemedicine effects: Cost, quality, and access. *Journal of Medical Systems*, *19*(2), 81–91. doi:10.1007/BF02257059 PMID:7602255

Basińska-Zych, A., & Springer, A. (2021). Organizational and individual outcomes of health promotion strategies—A review of empirical research. *International Journal of Environmental Research and Public Health*, *18*(2), 383. doi:10.3390/ijerph18020383 PMID:33419033

Bednarz, K. (2016). *11 tips for effective communication through Skype.* LinkedIn. Available at https://www.linkedin.com/ pulse/effective-communication-through-skype-katherin-bednarz

Belliger, A., & Krieger, D. J. (2018). *The Digital Transformation of Healthcare.* Progress in IS.

Belz, F.-M., & Peattie, K. (2012). *Sustainability Marketing.* Wiley & Sons.

Ben Ayed, M., & El Aoud, N. (2017). The patient empowerment: A promising concept in healthcare marketing. *International Journal of Healthcare Management*, *10*(1), 42–48. doi:10.1080/20479700.2016.1268326

Benjamin, T. (n.d.). *How to effectively communicate remotely*. Chron. Available at https://smallbusiness.chron.com/effectively-communicate-remotely-33662.html

Berger, S., Saut, A. M., & Berssaneti, F. T. (2020). Using patient feedback to drive quality improvement in hospitals: A qualitative study. *BMJ Open*, *10*(10), e037641. doi:10.1136/bmjopen-2020-037641 PMID:33099495

Berkowitz, E. N. (2022). *Essentials of Healthcare Marketing*. Jones & Bartlett Learning.

Berkowitz, E. N. (2021). *Essentials of Health Care Marketing* (5th ed.). Jones & Bartlett Learning.

Berkowitz, E. N. (2021). *Essentials of health care marketing*. Jones & Bartlett Learning.

Berkowitz, E. N., & Flexner, W. (1980). The market for health services: Is there a non-traditional consumer? *Journal of Health Care Marketing*, *1*(1). PMID:10251474

Bernhardt, J. M. (2006). Improving health through health marketing. *Preventing Chronic Disease*, *3*(3). PMID:16776874

Berns, C. F. (2004). Bibliotherapy: Using books to help bereaved children. *Omega*, *48*(4), 321–336. doi:10.2190/361D-JHD8-RNJT-RYJV

Berry, L. L. (1995). Relationship marketing of services—Growing interest, emerging perspectives. *Journal of the Academy of Marketing Science*, *23*(4), 236–245. doi:10.1177/009207039502300402

Berry, L. L. (2002). Relationship marketing of services perspectives from 1983 and 2000. *Journal of Relationship Marketing*, *1*(1), 59–77. doi:10.1300/J366v01n01_05

Bettelheim, B. (1976). *The Uses of Enchantment: The Meaning of Fairy Tales*. Vintage. doi:10.1037/e309842005-008

Bhandari, A. (2022). Design Thinking: From Bibliometric Analysis to Content Analysis, Current Research Trends, and Future Research Directions. *Journal of the Knowledge Economy*. Advance online publication. doi:10.100713132-022-00920-3

Bhattacharya, S., Maddikunta, P. K. R., Pham, Q. V., Gadekallu, T. R., Chowdhary, C. L., Alazab, M., & Piran, M. J. (2021). Deep learning and medical image processing for coronavirus (COVID-19) pandemic: A survey. *Sustainable Cities and Society*, *65*, 102589. doi:10.1016/j.scs.2020.102589 PMID:33169099

Bielińska-Dusza. E. (2021). Znaczenie współpracy międzyorganizacyjnej w przedsiębiorstwach z branży kreatywnej. In Trendy w badaniu przedsiębiorczości. Uniwersytet Ekonomiczny w Katowicach.

Bocken, N. (2021). Sustainable Business Models. In W. Leal Filho, A. M. Azul, L. Brandli, A. Lange Salvia, & T. Wall (Eds.), *Decent Work and Economic Growth. Encyclopedia of the UN Sustainable Development Goals*. Springer. doi:10.1007/978-3-319-95867-5_48

Bokolo, A. J. (2019). Use of Telemedicine and Virtual Care for Remote Treatment in Response to COVID-19 Pandemic. *Journal of Medical Internet Research*, *22*(12), e19415. doi:10.2196/19415

Booms, B. H., & Bitner, M. J. (1981). Marketing Strategies and Organization Structures for Service Firms. In *Marketing of Services*. American Marketing Association.

Borecka, I. (2001). *Biblioterapia: teoria i praktyka; poradnik*. Wydawn. SBP.

Braun, V., & Clarke, V. (2022). Conceptual and design thinking for thematic analysis. *Qualitative Psychology*, *9*(1), 3–26. doi:10.1037/qup0000196

Bredl, K., & Bösche, W. (Eds.). (2013). *Serious games and virtual worlds in education, professional development, and healthcare*. IGI Global. doi:10.4018/978-1-4666-3673-6

Bridges, J. F., Janssen, E. M., Ferris, A., & Dy, S. M. (2018). Project Transform: Engaging patient advocates to share their perspectives on improving research, treatment and policy. *Current Medical Research and Opinion, 34*(10), 1755–1762. doi:10.1080/03007995.2018.1440199 PMID:29429378

Bronfman, S., & Pelegrín, O. (2018). *The digital revolution in management education.* Retrieved from https://globalfocusmagazine.com/the-digital-revolution-in-management-education/

Bryman, A., & Bell, E. (2011). *Business Research Methods* (3rd ed.). Oxford University Press.

Bryson, J. M., Crosby, B. C., & Stone, M. M. (2006). The design and implementation of Cross-Sector collaborations: Propositions from the literature. *Public Administration Review, 66*(s1), 44–55. doi:10.1111/j.1540-6210.2006.00665.x

Bryson, J. M., Crosby, B. C., & Stone, M. M. (2015). Designing and implementing cross-sector collaborations: Needed and challenging. *Public Administration Review, 75*(5), 647–663. doi:10.1111/puar.12432

Brzustewicz, P., Escher, I., Hatami, A., Hermes, J., Keränen, A., & Ulkuniemi, P. (2022). Emergence of social impact in company–NGO relationships in corporate volunteering. *Journal of Business Research, 140*, 62–75. doi:10.1016/j.jbusres.2021.11.089

Buchanan, L., Kelly, B., Yeatman, H., & Kariippanon, K. (2018). The effects of digital marketing of unhealthy commodities on young people: A systematic review. *Nutrients, 10*(2), 148. doi:10.3390/nu10020148 PMID:29382140

Burnett, C., Davies, J., Merchant, G., & Rowsell, J. (2014). *New Literacies around the Globe: Policy and Pedagogy.* Routledge. doi:10.4324/9781315867311

Busca, L., & Bertrandias, L. (2020). A Framework for Digital Marketing Research: Investigating the Four Cultural Eras of Digital Marketing. *Journal of Interactive Marketing, 49*(1), 1–19. doi:10.1016/j.intmar.2019.08.002

Buse, K., & Walt, G. (2000). Global public-private partnerships: Part I - a new development in health? *Bulletin of the World Health Organization, 78*, 549–561. PMID:10885184

Çağlıyor, S., Tosun, P., & Uray, N. (2022). Communicating value in healthcare marketing from a social media perspective. In *New Perspectives in Operations Research and Management Science: Essays in Honor of Fusun Ulengin* (pp. 143–170). Springer International Publishing. doi:10.1007/978-3-030-91851-4_6

Caliskan, A., Deniz, Y., Özen, Ö., & Ozturkoglu, Y. (2020). Digital transformation of traditional marketing business model in new industry era. *Journal of Enterprise Information Management, 34*(4), 1252–1273. doi:10.1108/JEIM-02-2020-0084

Cameron, A., Mantel-Teeuwisse, A. K., Leufkens, H. G., & Laing, R. O. (2012). Switching from originator brand medicines to generic equivalents in selected developing countries: How much could be saved? *Value in Health, 15*(5), 664–673. doi:10.1016/j.jval.2012.04.004 PMID:22867775

Cankar, S. S., & Petkovsek, V. (2013). Private and public sector innovation and the importance of cross-sector collaboration. *Journal of Applied Business Research, 29*(6), 1597–1606. doi:10.19030/jabr.v29i6.8197

Carlsson-Szlezak, P., Reeves, M., & Swartz, P. (2020). What coronavirus could mean for the global economy. *Harvard Business Review*, 3.

Carrera, P. M., & Bridges, J. F. (2015). Globalization and healthcare: Understanding health and medical tourism. *Expert Review of Pharmacoeconomics & Outcomes Research, 6*(4), 447–454. doi:10.1586/14737167.6.4.447 PMID:20528514

Carrera, P. M., & Dalton, A. R. (2014). Do-it-yourself healthcare: The current landscape, prospects and consequences. *Maturitas, 77*(1), 37–40. doi:10.1016/j.maturitas.2013.10.022 PMID:24287177

Castro, E. M., Van Regenmortel, T., Vanhaecht, K., Sermeus, W., & Van Hecke, A. (2016). Patient empowerment, patient participation and patient-centeredness in hospital care: A concept analysis based on a literature review. *Patient Education and Counseling*, *99*(12), 1923–1939. doi:10.1016/j.pec.2016.07.026 PMID:27450481

Chakraborty, C. (Ed.). (2022). *Digital Health Transformation with Blockchain and Artificial Intelligence*. CRC Press. doi:10.1201/9781003247128

Chandra, P. (2019). Surviving Generics – Top Pharma Brand Marketing Strategies. *Linkedin*. Available at https://www.linkedin.com/pulse/surviving-generics-top-pharma-brand-marketing-phanish-chandra

Chang, B. L., Bakken, S., Brown, S. S., Houston, T. K., Kreps, G. L., Kukafka, R., & Stavri, P. Z. (2004). Bridging the digital divide: Reaching vulnerable populations. *Journal of the American Medical Informatics Association : JAMIA*, *11*(6), 448–457. doi:10.1197/jamia.M1535 PMID:15299002

Chattu, V. K. (2021). A review of artificial intelligence, big data, and blockchain technology applications in medicine and global health. *Big Data and Cognitive Computing*, *5*(3), 41. doi:10.3390/bdcc5030041

Chaudhuri, S. (2016). Reverse payment deals in patent disputes and its impact on competition. *ET Healthworld*. Available at https://health.economictimes.indiatimes.com/news/pharma/reverse-payment-deals-in-patent-disputes-and-its-impact-on-competition/52024742

Chauhan, M. K. (2015). How relationship marketing can add value to your practice. *Medical Economics*, *92*(24), 61. PMID:26875312

Chaves Prasetya, T. A. E., & Wardani, R. W. K. (2023). Systematic review of social media addiction among health workers during the pandemic Covid-19. *Heliyon*, *9*(6), e16784. doi:10.1016/j.heliyon.2023.e16784 PMID:37274718

Chen, E. M., Andoh, J. E., & Nwanyanwu, K. (2022). Socioeconomic and demographic disparities in the use of telemedicine for ophthalmic care during the COVID-19 pandemic. *Ophthalmology*, *129*(1), 15–25. doi:10.1016/j.ophtha.2021.07.003 PMID:34245753

Chen, Y. Y., Li, C. M., Liang, J. C., & Tsai, C. C. (2018). Health Information Obtained From the Internet and Changes in Medical Decision Making: Questionnaire Development and Cross-Sectional Survey. *Journal of Medical Internet Research*, *20*(2), e47. doi:10.2196/jmir.9370 PMID:29434017

Chiu, C. M., Hsu, M. H., Lai, H., & Chang, C. M. (2012). Re-examining the influence of trust on online repeat purchase intention: The moderating role of habit and its antecedents. *Decision Support Systems*, *53*(4), 835–845. doi:10.1016/j.dss.2012.05.021

Christina, M. B. (2021). Drugs Shortages Amid the COVID-19 Pandemic. *U. S. Pharmacist*, *46*(2), 25–28.

Cianciara, D. (Ed.). (2010). *Public Health - a Review of Issues*. Medical Center for Postgraduate Education – School of Public Health.

Ciron Pharma. (2021). *Marketing Strategies of Pharmaceutical Products of India*. Available at https://www.cironpharma.com/blog/pharmaceutical-products-in-india-marketing-strategies/

Clampitt, P. G., & Girard, D. (1993). Communication satisfaction: A useful construct? *New Jersey Journal of Communication, 1*(2), 84–102. Available at http://imetacomm.com/ wp-content/ themes/ Structure%20Premium%20White/ organic_structure_white/ downloads/ Metacomm_UsefulConstruct.pdf

Clar, C., Dyakova, M., Curtis, K., Dawson, C., Donnelly, P., Knifton, L., & Clarke, A. (2014). Just telling and selling: current limitations in the use of digital media in public health: a scoping review. *Public Health*, *128*(12), 1066–1075. doi:10.1016/j.puhe.2014.09.009 PMID:25443388

Clarke, A., & Crane, A. (2018). Cross-Sector Partnerships for Systemic Change: Systematized Literature Review and Agenda for Further Research. *The Journal of Business, 150*(2), 303–313. doi:10.100710551-018-3922-2 PMID:30996499

Cline, R. J. W., & Haynes, K. M. (2001). Consumer health information seeking on the internet: The state of the art. *Health Education Research, 16*(6), 671–692. doi:10.1093/her/16.6.671 PMID:11780707

Cohen, L. J. (1993). Discover the healing power of books. *AJN The American Journal of Nursing, 93*(10), 70–74. PMID:8213951

Colombia, R. (1886). *Constitución política de 1886.*

Colombia. (2015). *Ley estatutaria 1751.*

ConsultorSalud. (2019). *Gastos de bolsillo en Latinoamérica.* https://consultorsalud.com/gastos-de-bolsillo-en-latino-america/

Cook, K. E., Earles-Vollrath, T., & Ganz, J. B. (2006). Bibliotherapy. *Intervention in School and Clinic, 42*(2), 91–100. doi:10.1177/10534512060420020801

Cooper, P. D. (Ed.). (1994). *Health care marketing: A foundation for managed quality.* Jones & Bartlett Learning.

Corbin, C. L., Kelley, S. W., & Schwartz, R. W. (2001). Concepts in service marketing for healthcare professionals. *American Journal of Surgery, 181*(1), 1–7. doi:10.1016/S0002-9610(00)00535-3 PMID:11248166

Cortez, N. (2008). Patients without borders: The emerging global market for patients and the evolution of modern health care. *Industrial Law Journal, 83*, 71.

Coventry, L., & Branley, D. (2018). Cybersecurity in healthcare: A narrative review of trends, threats and ways forward. *Maturitas, 113*, 48–52. doi:10.1016/j.maturitas.2018.04.008 PMID:29903648

Creswell, J. W., & Creswell, J. D. (2017). *Research design: Qualitative, quantitative, and mixed methods approaches.* Sage publications.

Crié, D., & Chebat, J. C. (2013). Health marketing: Toward an integrative perspective. *Journal of Business Research, 66*(1), 123–126. doi:10.1016/j.jbusres.2012.09.002

Cronin, C. E., Singh, S. R., Turner, J. S., & Evashwick, C. J. (2022). Hospitals' contributions to their communities: Should they be regulated? *Frontiers in Public Health, 10*, 1064210. doi:10.3389/fpubh.2022.1064210 PMID:36504974

Crothers, S. M. (1917). *A literary clinic.* Houghton Mifflin.

Cruz, H., & Henrique, J. (2021). Mortalidad por COVID-19 y las desigualdades por nivel socioeconómico y por territorio. *CEPAL.* https://www.cepal.org/es/enfoques/mortalidad-covid-19-desigualdades-nivel-socioeconomico-territorio

Cutting Edge Information. (2004). *Combating Generics: Pharmaceutical Brand Defense.* Available at http://www.PharmaGenerics.com

Da Silva Etges, A. P. B., Ruschel, K. B., Polanczyk, C. A., & Urman, R. D. (2020). Advances in value-based healthcare by the application of time-driven activity-based costing for inpatient management: A systematic review. *Value in Health, 23*(6), 812–823. doi:10.1016/j.jval.2020.02.004 PMID:32540239

Da Silva, E. C., & Mazzon, J. A. (2016). Developing social marketing plan for health promotion. *International Journal of Public Administration, 39*(8), 577–586. doi:10.1080/01900692.2015.1023447

Dahlstrom, R., & Crosno, J. L. (2022). Sustainable Marketing. Chicago Business Press.

Dalton, L., Rapa, E., & Stein, A. (2020). Protecting the psychological health of children through effective communication about COVID-19. *The Lancet. Child & Adolescent Health*, *4*(5), 346–347. doi:10.1016/S2352-4642(20)30097-3 PMID:32243784

DANE. (2022a). *Situación de las mujeres rurales desde las estadísticas oficiales Serie notas estadísticas octubre 18 de 2022.*

DANE. (2022b, April 26). *Pobreza monetaria y pobreza monetaria extrema.* DANE. https://www.dane.gov.co/index.php/estadisticas-por-tema/pobreza-y-condiciones-de-vida/pobreza-monetaria

DANE. (2023, March). *Empleo informal y seguridad social.* https://www.dane.gov.co/index.php/estadisticas-por-tema/mercado-laboral/empleo-informal-y-seguridad-social#:~:text=Informaci%C3%B3n%20agosto%20%2D%20octubre%202022&text=Finalmente%2C%20para%20el%20total%20de,anterior%20(47%2C1%25)

Darma, G., & Noviana, P. (2020). Exploring Digital Marketing Strategies during the New Normal Era in Enhancing the Use of Digital Payment. *Journal Mantik*, *4*(3).

Darwiesh, A., El-Baz, A. H., Abualkishik, A. Z., & Elhoseny, M. (2023). Artificial Intelligence Model for Risk Management in Healthcare Institutions: Towards Sustainable Development. *Sustainability, 15*(1), 420.

Davenport, T., & Kalakota, R. (2019). The potential for artificial intelligence in healthcare. *Future Healthcare Journal*, *6*(2), 94–98. doi:10.7861/futurehosp.6-2-94 PMID:31363513

Davidson, A., & Simonetto, M. (2005). Pricing strategy and execution: An overlooked way to increase revenues and profits. *Strategy and Leadership*, *33*(6), 25–33. doi:10.1108/10878570510631639

Dawes, T. J., de Marvao, A., Shi, W., Fletcher, T., Watson, G. M., Wharton, J., Rhodes, C. J., Howard, L. S. G. E., Gibbs, J. S. R., Rueckert, D., Cook, S. A., Wilkins, M. R., & O'Regan, D. P. (2017). Machine learning of three-dimensional right ventricular motion enables outcome prediction in pulmonary hypertension: A cardiac MR imaging study. *Radiology*, *283*(2), 381–390. doi:10.1148/radiol.2016161315 PMID:28092203

De Veirman, M., Hudders, L., & Nelson, M. R. (2019). What is influencer marketing and how does it target children? A review and direction for future research. *Frontiers in Psychology*, *10*, 2685. doi:10.3389/fpsyg.2019.02685 PMID:31849783

Deitte, L., & Omary, R. (2019). The Power of Design Thinking in Medical Education. *Academic Radiology*, *26*(10), 1417–1420. doi:10.1016/j.acra.2019.02.012 PMID:30867087

Dell'era, C., Magistretti, S., Cautela, C., Verganti, R., & Zurlo, F. (2020, June). MAgistretti, S. C., Cautela, C., Verganti, R., & Zurlo, F. (2020). Four kinds of design thinking: From ideating to making, engaging, and criticizing. *Creativity and Innovation Management*, *29*(2), 324–344. Advance online publication. doi:10.1111/caim.12353

Desai, V., & Vidyapeeth, B. (2019). Digital marketing: A review. *International Journal of Trend in Scientific Research and Development*, *5*(5), 196–200. doi:10.31142/ijtsrd23100

Detsky, A. S. (2011). What patients really want from health care. *Journal of the American Medical Association*, *306*(22), 2500–2501. doi:10.1001/jama.2011.1819 PMID:22166610

DeWalt, D. A., Dilling, M. H., Rosenthal, M. S., & Pignone, M. P. (2007). Low parental literacy is associated with worse asthma care measures in children. *Ambulatory Pediatrics*, *7*(1), 25–31. doi:10.1016/j.ambp.2006.10.001 PMID:17261479

Diez-Martin, F., Blanco-Gonzalez, A., & Prado-Roman, C. (2019). Research Challenges in Digital Marketing: Sustainability. *Sustainability (Basel)*, *11*(10), 2839. Advance online publication. doi:10.3390u11102839

DigitalMed project. (2018). Artificial Intelligence Can Make A Preliminary Diagnosis. https://btu.edu.ge/ proeqti-digitalmed -tsinastsari-diagnozis-dasmas-khelovnuri-inteleqti-shedzlebs/

DiMasi, J. A., Hansen, R. W., & Grabowski, H. G. (2003). The price of innovation: New estimates of drug development costs. *Journal of Health Economics*, *22*(2), 151–185. doi:10.1016/S0167-6296(02)00126-1 PMID:12606142

Ding, B., & Hernández, X. F. (2023). Case study as a methodological foundation for Technology Roadmapping (TRM): Literature review and future research agenda. *Journal of Engineering and Technology Management*, *67*, 101731. doi:10.1016/j.jengtecman.2023.101731

Djakeli, K. (2012). Matrix of Brand Awareness and a Positive Image as a Success Factor in Political PR. *Journal in Humanities*, 31-35.

Djakeli, K. (2018). From disruptive marketing to the new model of prestigious branding. Quality - Access to Success, 19(166), 71-76.

Djakeli. (2013). Analyzing Success and Failure of Two Health Reforms in Independent Georgia. *Journal of Business, 2*(2), 5-14. https://jb.ibsu.edu.ge/jms/index.php/jb/article/view/56

Djakeli, K. (2023). Sustainable Healthcare Reforming Model Based on Marketing: Case of Georgia. In I. Gigauri, M. Palazzo, & M. Ferri (Eds.), *Handbook of Research on Achieving Sustainable Development Goals With Sustainable Marketing* (pp. 271–287). IGI Global. doi:10.4018/978-1-6684-8681-8.ch014

Dodokh, A., & Al-Maaitah, M. A. (2019). Impact of social media usage on organizational performance in the Jordanian dead sea cosmetic sector. *European Journal of Business and Management*, *11*(2), 75–91.

Donabedian, A. (1974). *Aspects of Medical Care Administration*. Harvard University Press.

Donaghy, E., Atherton, H., Hammersley, V., McNeilly, H., Bikker, A., Robbins, L., Campbell, J. L., & McKinstry, B. (2019). Acceptability, benefits, and challenges of video consulting: A qualitative study in primary care. *The British Journal of General Practice*, *69*(686), e586–e594. doi:10.3399/bjgp19X704141 PMID:31160368

Donovan, R. J. (2011). The role for marketing in public health change programs. *Australian Review of Public Affairs, 10*(1), 23-40.

Dorsey, K. (2017). The 10 pros and cons about working from home that you need to know right now. Available at https://www.insider.co.uk/ news/10-pros-cons-working-home-10455197

Duflos, G., & Lichtenberg, F. R. (2012). Does competition stimulate drug utilization? The impact of changes in market structure on US drug prices, marketing and utilization. *International Review of Law and Economics*, *32*(1), 95–109. doi:10.1016/j.irle.2011.08.003

Dwivedi, Y. K., Ismagilova, E., Hughes, D. L., Carlson, J., Filieri, R., Jacobson, J., Jain, V., Karjaluoto, H., Kefi, H., Krishen, A. S., Kumar, V., Rahman, M. M., Raman, R., Rauschnabel, P. A., Rowley, J., Salo, J., Tran, G. A., & Wang, Y. (2021). Setting the future of digital and social media marketing research: Perspectives and research propositions. *International Journal of Information Management*, *59*, 102168. doi:10.1016/j.ijinfomgt.2020.102168

Dyer, O. (2004). NHS takes makers of generic drugs to court for price fixing. *BMJ (Clinical Research Ed.)*, *329*(7456), 12. doi:10.1136/bmj.329.7456.12-a PMID:15231602

Eberly, L. A., Kallan, M. J., Julien, H. M., Haynes, N., Khatana, S. A., Nathan, A. S., Snider, C., Chokshi, N. P., Eneanya, N. D., Takvorian, S. U., Anastos-Wallen, R., Chaiyachati, K., Ambrose, M., O'Quinn, R., Seigerman, M., Goldberg, L. R., Leri, D., Choi, K., Gitelman, Y., ... Adusumalli, S. (2020, December 01). Patient characteristics associated with telemedicine access for primary and specialty ambulatory care during the COVID-19 pandemic.[. *JAMA Network Open*, *3*(12), e2031640. doi:10.1001/jamanetworkopen.2020.31640 PMID:33372974

Eichner, M. J., McClellan, M. B., & Wise, D. A. (1998). *Insurance or Self-Insurance? Variation, Persistence, and Individual Health Accounts*. University of Chicago Press.

El tiempo. (2021, January 9). *El 71% del personal de salud tiene un contrato tercerizado*. El Tiempo. https://www.eltiempo.com/justicia/servicios/procuraduria-advierte-tercerizacion-laboral-de-medicos-y-personal-de-salud-en-hospitales-559693

Elkington, J. (1998). *Cannibals with Forks: The Triple-Bottom Line For 21st Century Business*. New Society Publishers.

Elton, J., & O'Riordan, A. (2016). *Healthcare disrupted: Next generation business models and strategies*. John Wiley & Sons.

Enumah, Z. O. (2022). Therapeutic citizens or therapeutic refugees? An examination of triage, refugeehood, and referral health care in Tanzania. *Social Science & Medicine*, *298*, 114837. doi:10.1016/j.socscimed.2022.114837 PMID:35247780

Ersoy, Y., & Tehci, A. (2023). Relationship marketing orientation in healthcare organizations with the AHP method. Internal and external customer perspective. *Operations Research and Decisions, 33*.

Fahmi, K., Sihotang, M., Hadinegoro, R. H., Sulastri, E., Cahyono, Y., & Megah, S. I. (2022). Health Care SMEs Products Marketing Strategy: How the Role of Digital Marketing Technology through Social Media? *UJoST-Universal Journal of Science and Technology*, *1*(1), 16–22.

Farah, M. F. (2017). Application of the theory of planned behavior to customer switching intentions in the context of bank consolidations. *International Journal of Bank Marketing*, *35*(1), 147–172. doi:10.1108/IJBM-01-2016-0003

Farris, P. W., Hanssens, D. M., Lenskold, J. D., & Reibstein, D. J. (2015). Marketing return on investment: Seeking clarity for concept and measurement. *Applied Marketing Analytics*, *1*(3), 267–282.

Feldstein, M., & Gruber, J. (1994). *A Major Risk Approach to Health Insurance Reform.* NBER Working Paper no. 4852. National Bureau of Economic Research.

Feldstein, M. (1971). A New Approach to National Health Insurance. *The Public Interest*, *23*, 93–105.

Fisher, C. (2017). Ready for the robots: survey says job candidates are mostly okay with AI Apps in the application process. *Allegis*. Available at https://blog.allegisglobalsolutions.com/ ready-for-the-robots-survey-says-job-candidates-are-mostly-okay-with-ai-apps-in-the-application-process

Ford, R. C., & Fottler, M. D. (2000). Creating customer-focused health care organizations. *Health Care Management Review*, *25*(4), 18–33. doi:10.1097/00004010-200010000-00003 PMID:11072629

Fox, E. (2017). How Pharma Companies Game the System to Keep Drugs Expensive. *Harvard Business Review*. Available at https://hbr.org/2017/04/how-pharma-companies-game-the-system-to-keep-drugs-expensive

France, K. R., & Grover, R. (1992). What is the health care product? *Marketing Health Services*, *12*(2), 31. PMID:10119211

Freire, Y., Sánchez, M. G., Suárez, A., Joves, G., Nowak, M., & Díaz-Flores García, V. (2023). Influence of the use of social media on patients changing dental practice: A web-based questionnaire study. *BMC Oral Health*, *23*(1), 365. doi:10.118612903-023-03078-9 PMID:37277765

Friedman, M. (1982). *Capitalism and freedom (1962). Whether government control over the provision of education through public schools is also efficient is a quite different matter.* Academic Press.

Fu, J. (2013). ICT in Education: A Critical Literature Review and Its Implications. *International Journal of Education and Development Using Information and Communication Technology*, 112–125.

Galani, V. (2017). Choice of better medicine in India: Branded vs generic medicine. *Pharmacy & Pharmacology International Journal*, *5*(3), 124–125. doi:10.15406/ppij.2017.05.00125

Galindo, J. R. (2019, August 7). *Bolívar y Santander: dos tendencias opuestas que han marcado nuestra historia*. Blog Universidad Libre. https://blog.unilibre.edu.co/news/bolivar-y-santander-dos-tendencias-opuestas-que-han-marcado-nuestra-historia/

Gereffi, G. (2020). What does the COVID-19 pandemic teach us about global value chains? The case of medical supplies. *Journal of International Business Policy*, *3*(3), 287–301. doi:10.105742214-020-00062-w

Gerke, S., Stern, A. D., & Minssen, T. (2020). Germany's digital health reforms in the COVID-19 era: Lessons and opportunities for other countries. *NPJ Digital Medicine*, *3*(1), 94. doi:10.103841746-020-0306-7 PMID:32685700

Ghalavand, H., Panahi, S., & Sedghi, S. (2020). Opportunities and challenges of social media for health knowledge management: A narrative review. *Journal of Education and Health Promotion*, *9*, 1–5. PMID:32766329

Ghanbarzadeh, R., Ghapanchi, A. H., Blumenstein, M., & Talaei-Khoei, A. (2014). A decade of research on the use of three-dimensional virtual worlds in health care: A systematic literature review. *Journal of Medical Internet Research*, *16*(2), e47. doi:10.2196/jmir.3097 PMID:24550130

Gigauri, I., & Djakeli, K. (2021b). Remote working challenges for Georgian social enterprises in the context of the current pandemic. *HOLISTICA – Journal of Business and Public Administration, 12*(3), 39-53. doi:10.2478/hjbpa-2021-0021

Gigauri, I., & Djakeli, K. (2021c). National Health Reforms in Georgia during 1994-2021 and their Success. *HOLISTICA – Journal of Business and Public Administration, 12*(2), 102-108. doi:10.2478/hjbpa-2021-0017

Gigauri, I., Apostu, S. A., & Popescu, C. (2023). Digital Transformation: Threats and Opportunities for Social Entrepreneurship. In Two Faces of Digital Transformation: Technological Opportunities versus Social Threats (pp. 1-17). Emerald Publishing Limited.

Gigauri, I., Janjua, L. R., Panait, M., & Guillen, F. P. (2023). Exploring the Nexus Between Financial Inclusion, Poverty, Digitalization and Sustainable Development Goal. *LUMEN Proceedings, 19*, 63-81. 10.18662/lumproc/gekos2022/06

Gigauri, I., & Djakeli, K. (2021a). Expecting Transformation of Marketing During the Post-Pandemic New Normal: Qualitative Research of Marketing Managers in Georgia. *International Journal of Sustainable Economies Management*, *10*(2), 1–18. doi:10.4018/IJSEM.2021040101

Gigauri, I., Palazzo, M., & Ferri, M. A. (Eds.). (2023). *Handbook of Research on Achieving Sustainable Development Goals With Sustainable Marketing*. IGI Global. doi:10.4018/978-1-6684-8681-8

Gil Guzman, J. M., Hernandez-Fernandez, A., & Canales-Ronda, P. (2021). Bringing social marketing closer to the disability field. *Journal of Social Marketing*, *11*(4), 321–341. doi:10.1108/JSOCM-06-2020-0105

Gilaninia, S., Almani, A. M., Pournaserani, A., & Mousavian, S. J. (2011). Relationship marketing: A new approach to marketing in the third millennium. *Australian Journal of Basic and Applied Sciences*, *5*(5), 787–799.

Gilbert, T., Ural, A., & Lopez, M. (2012). Five Branded Generic Strategies to Master for Global Pharmaceutical in Emerging Markets. *Accenture Life Sciences*. Available at https://www.accenture.com/t20161128T001148__w__/us-en/_acnmedia/Accenture/Conversion-Assets/DotCom/Documents/Global/PDF/Industries_1/Accenture-Five-Branded-Generics-Strategies-Pharmaceuticals-in-Emerging-Markets.pdf

Gilligan, C., & Lowe, R. (2018). *Marketing and Healthcare Organizations*. Academic Press.

Gopal, G., Suter-Crazzolara, C., Toldo, L., & Eberhardt, W. (2019). Beyond Adoption: A New Framework for Theorizing and Evaluating Nonadoption, Abandonment, and Challenges to the Scale-Up, Spread, and Sustainability of Health and Care Technologies. *J Med Internet Res*. doi:10.2196/jmir.8775

Gordon, I. H. (1998). *Relationship Marketing*. John Wiley & Sons.

Gough, D., Oliver, S., & Thomas, J. (2017). Introducing Systematic Reviews. In D. Gough, S. Oliver, & J. Thomas (Eds.), *An Introduction to Systematic Reviews* (3rd ed.). Sage Publications Ltd.

Grainger, C. (n.d.). *How to write a compelling LinkedIn profile summary that gets noticed*. TopCV blogpost. Available at https://www.topcv.co.uk/ career-advice/ linkedin-profile-summary

Gray, J. V., Siemsen, E., & Vasudeva, G. (2015). Colocation still matters: Conformance quality and the interdependence of R&D and manufacturing in the pharmaceutical industry. *Management Science*, *61*(11), 2760–2781. doi:10.1287/mnsc.2014.2104

Grbic, M., Stimac Grbic, D., Stimac, L., & Sostar, Z. (2019). Digital marketing in healthcare. *European Journal of Public Health*, *29*(Supplement_4), ckz186.077. Advance online publication. doi:10.1093/eurpub/ckz186.077

Greene, S. M., Tuzzio, L., & Cherkin, D. (2012). A framework for making patient-centered care front and center. *The Permanente Journal*, *16*(3), 49–53. doi:10.7812/TPP/12-025 PMID:23012599

Greenhalgh, T. (2020). Whose digital health? More-inclusive approaches to understanding and action on digital health. *BMJ (Clinical Research Ed.)*, *368*, m390. doi:10.1136/bmj.m390

Grewal, D., Hulland, J., Kopalle, P. K., & Karahanna, E. (2019). The future of technology and marketing: A multidisciplinary perspective. *Journal of the Academy of Marketing Science*, *48*(1), 1–8. doi:10.100711747-019-00711-4

Grönroos, C. (1994). Quo vadis, marketing? Toward a relationship marketing paradigm. *Journal of Marketing Management*, *10*(5), 347–360. doi:10.1080/0267257X.1994.9964283

Grönroos, C. (2000). Creating a relationship dialogue: Communication, interaction and value. *The Marketing Review*, *1*(1), 5–14. doi:10.1362/1469347002523428

Gummesson, E. (1994). Broadening and specifying relationship marketing. *Asia-Australia Marketing Journal*, *2*(1), 31–43. doi:10.1016/S1320-1646(94)70276-8

Gunjan, M., Naing, T. W., Saini, R. S., Ahmad, A., Naidu, J. R., & Kumar, I. (2015). Marketing trends & future prospects of herbal medicine in the treatment of various disease. *World Journal of Pharmaceutical Research*, *4*(9), 132–155.

Günther, L., Schleberger, S., & Pischke, C. R. (2021). Effectiveness of social media-based interventions for the promotion of physical activity: Scoping review. *International Journal of Environmental Research and Public Health*, *18*(24), 13018. doi:10.3390/ijerph182413018 PMID:34948628

Guo, C., & Li, H. (2022). Application of 5G network combined with AI robots in personalized nursing in China: A literature review. *Frontiers in Public Health*, *10*, 948303. doi:10.3389/fpubh.2022.948303 PMID:36091551

Gupta, A., Tyagi, M., & Sharma, D. (2013). Use of social media marketing in healthcare. *Journal of Health Management, 15*(2), 293–302. doi:10.1177/0972063413489058

Gupta, H., Kumar, S., Roy, S. K., & Gaud, R. S. (2010). Patent protection strategies. *Journal of Pharmacy & Bioallied Sciences, 2*(7), 2–7. doi:10.4103/0975-7406.62694 PMID:21814422

Gustavsson, E. (2014). From needs to health care needs. *Health Care Analysis, 22*(1), 22–35. doi:10.100710728-013-0241-8 PMID:23344674

Habli, I., Lawton, T., & Porter, Z. (2020). Artificial intelligence in health care: Accountability and safety. *Bulletin of the World Health Organization, 98*(4), 251–256. doi:10.2471/BLT.19.237487 PMID:32284648

Hagenaars, L.L., Klazinga, N.S., Mueller, M., Morgan, D. & Jeurissen, P. P. T. (2017). How and why do countries differ in their healthcare governance and financing-related administrative expenditure? An analysis of OECD countries by healthcare system.

Hailu, A. D., Workneh, B. D., & Kahissay, M. H. (2021). Influence of pharmaceutical marketing mix strategies on physicians' prescribing behaviors in public and private hospitals, Dessie, Ethiopia: A mixed study design. *BMC Public Health, 21*(1), 65. doi:10.118612889-020-10063-2 PMID:33413248

Hajli, N., Sims, J., Zadeh, A. H., & Richard, M. O. (2017). A social commerce investigation of the role of trust in a social networking site on purchase intentions. *Journal of Business Research, 71*, 133–141. doi:10.1016/j.jbusres.2016.10.004

Haleem, A., Javaid, M., Singh, R. P., & Suman, R. (2021). Telemedicine for healthcare: Capabilities, features, barriers, and applications. *Sensors International, 2*, 100117. doi:10.1016/j.sintl.2021.100117 PMID:34806053

Haleem, A., Javaid, M., Singh, R. P., & Suman, R. (2022). Medical 4.0 technologies for healthcare: Features, capabilities, and applications. *Internet of Things and Cyber-Physical Systems, 2*, 12–30. doi:10.1016/j.iotcps.2022.04.001

Hamel, J., Dufour, S., & Fortin, D. (1993). *Case study methods* (Vol. 32). Sage Publications. doi:10.4135/9781412983587

Han, H., & Hwang, J. (2015). Growing competition in the healthcare tourism market and customer retention in medical clinics: New and experienced travellers. *Current Issues in Tourism, 21*(6), 680–702. doi:10.1080/13683500.2015.1104292

Han, H., & Hyun, S. S. (2015). Customer retention in the medical tourism industry: Impact of quality, satisfaction, trust, and price reasonableness. *Tourism Management, 46*, 20–29. doi:10.1016/j.tourman.2014.06.003

Haristiani, R., Wahyuningsih, W., & Susaldi, S. (2022). Effect of Storytelling Therapy can Reduces Anxiety for Children with Leukemia at DR Wahidin Sudiro Husodo Hospital in Makassar. *Jurnal Ilmiah Ilmu Keperawatan Indonesia, 12*(02), 88–92. doi:10.33221/jiiki.v12i02.1877

Harrison, V. J. (2021). *Leveraging Pharma, Digital Innovation, and Partnerships to Increase Healthcare Access in China: A COVID-19 Case Study* [Doctoral dissertation]. Harvard University.

Hawe, P., & Shiell, A. (2000). Social capital and health promotion: A review. *Social Science & Medicine, 51*(6), 871–885. doi:10.1016/S0277-9536(00)00067-8 PMID:10972431

Hayes, C. J., Dawson, L., McCoy, H., Hernandez, M., Andersen, J., Ali, M. M., Bogulski, C. A., & Eswaran, H. (2023). Utilization of remote patient monitoring within the United States health care system: A scoping review. *Telemedicine Journal and e-Health, 29*(3), 384–394. doi:10.1089/tmj.2022.0111 PMID:35819861

Heale, R., & Twycross, A. (2018). What is a case study? *Evidence-Based Nursing, 21*(1), 7–8. doi:10.1136/eb-2017-102845 PMID:29146764

Health Savings Accounts in the US – Structure and Role in the System. (2023). *Health Manager – Termedia.*

Healthcare and Social Issues Committee of the Parliament of Georgia. (2017). *Vision for developing the healthcare system in Georgia by 2030*. Parliament of Georgia. Retrieved October 20, 2023, from https://georgia.un.org/sites/default/files/2020-08/Georgia%205.pdf

Henley, N., Raffin, S., & Caemmerer, B. (2011). The application of marketing principles to a social marketing campaign. *Marketing Intelligence & Planning*, *29*(7), 697–706. doi:10.1108/02634501111178712

Hennessey, E., & Mueller, J. (2020). Teaching and Learning Design Thinking (DT). *Canadian Journal of Education*, 498–521.

Henriksen, D., Richardson, C., & Mehta, R. (2017). Design thinking: A creative approach to educational problems of practice. *Thinking Skills and Creativity*, *26*, 140–153. doi:10.1016/j.tsc.2017.10.001

Herhausen, D., Miočević, D., Morgan, R. E., & Kleijnen, M. H. (2020). The digital marketing capabilities gap. *Industrial Marketing Management*, *90*, 276–290. doi:10.1016/j.indmarman.2020.07.022

Hernandez, L. M. (Ed.). (2009). *Health literacy, eHealth, and communication: putting the consumer first: workshop summary*. National Academies Press.

Herrle, J. (2018). Artificial Intelligence in Health Care. *CJO : Canadian Journal of Optometry = RCO : Revue Canadienne d'Optométrie*, *80*(4), 67–68.

Hess, J., & Litalien, S. (2004). Battle for the market: Branded drug companies' secret weapons generic drug makers must know. *Journal of Generic Medicines*, *3*(1), 20–29. doi:10.1057/palgrave.jgm.4940095

Hollebeek, L. D., Glynn, M. S., & Brodie, R. J. (2014). Consumer brand engagement in social media: Conceptualization, scale development and validation. *Journal of Interactive Marketing*, *28*(2), 149–165. doi:10.1016/j.intmar.2013.12.002

Hollebeek, L. D., Srivastava, R. K., & Chen, T. (2019). SD logic–informed customer engagement: Integrative framework, revised fundamental propositions, and application to CRM. *Journal of the Academy of Marketing Science*, *47*(1), 161–185. doi:10.100711747-016-0494-5

Holloway, D. (2012). Virtual worlds and health: Healthcare delivery and simulation opportunities. In *Virtual worlds and metaverse platforms: New communication and identity paradigms* (pp. 251–270). IGI Global. doi:10.4018/978-1-60960-854-5.ch017

Hong, I. B., & Cho, H. (2011). The impact of consumer trust on attitudinal loyalty and purchase intentions in B2C e-marketplaces: Intermediary trust vs. seller trust. *International Journal of Information Management*, *31*(5), 469–479. doi:10.1016/j.ijinfomgt.2011.02.001

Hong, Y., Wan, M., & Li, Z. (2021). Understanding the health information sharing behavior of social media users: An empirical study on WeChat. *Journal of Organizational and End User Computing*, *33*(5), 180–203. doi:10.4018/JOEUC.20210901.oa9

Hosny, A., Parmar, C., Quackenbush, J., Schwartz, L. H., & Aerts, H. J. W. L. (2018). Artificial intelligence in radiology. *Nature Reviews. Cancer*, *18*(8), 500–510. doi:10.103841568-018-0016-5 PMID:29777175

Huang, F., Blaschke, S., & Lucas, H. (2017). Beyond pilotitis: Taking digital health interventions to the national level in China and Uganda. *Globalization and Health*, *13*(1), 1–11. doi:10.118612992-017-0275-z PMID:28756767

Hung, C. L., Wu, J. H., Chen, P. Y., Xu, X., Hsu, W. L., Lin, L. M., & Hsieh, M. C. (2023). Enhancing healthcare services and brand engagement through social media marketing: Integration of Kotler's 5A framework with IDEA process. *Information Processing & Management*, *60*(4), 103379. doi:10.1016/j.ipm.2023.103379

Huntsman, J. L., & Bulaj, G. (2023). Health education via "empowerment" digital marketing of consumer products and services: Promoting therapeutic benefits of self-care for depression and chronic pain. *Frontiers in Public Health, 10*, 949518. Advance online publication. doi:10.3389/fpubh.2022.949518 PMID:36703812

Hutter, K., Hautz, J., Dennhardt, S., & Füller, J. (2013). The impact of user interactions in social media on brand awareness and purchase intention: The case of MINI on Facebook. *Journal of Product and Brand Management, 22*(5-6), 342–351. doi:10.1108/JPBM-05-2013-0299

Ibrahim, M. M., El-Khedr, S. M., & Nosek, L. J. (2013). Effective communication and job satisfaction among staff nurses working in paediatric intensive care units. *Life Science Journal, 10*(1), 2661–2669. Available at https://www.researchgate.net/publication/261359002_Effective_Communication_and_Job_Satisfaction_among_Staff_Nurses_Working_in_Pediatric_Intensive_Care_Units

Ibrahim, B., & Aljarah, A. (2018). Dataset of relationships among social media marketing activities, brand loyalty, revisit intention. Evidence from the hospitality industry in Northern Cyprus. *Data in Brief, 21*, 1823–1828. doi:10.1016/j.dib.2018.11.024 PMID:30519601

Imelda, D. C., Fenni, F., & Deveia, R. (2019). Digital marketing strategy in promoting product. *Management and Entrepreneurship: Trends of Development, 4*(10), 58–66. Advance online publication. doi:10.26661/2522-1566/2019-4/10-05

Imran, N., Zeshan, M., & Pervaiz, Z. (2020). Mental health considerations for children & adolescents in COVID-19 Pandemic. *Pakistan Journal of Medical Sciences, 36*(COVID19-S4), S67.

Invest India. (2022). *Pharma industry in India: Invest in Indian Pharma Sector.* Available at https://www.investindia.gov.in/sector/pharmaceuticals

IRS Outlines Changes to Health Care Spending Available under CARES Act. (n.d.). www.irs.gov

Jackson, M., Brennan, L., & Parker, L. (2021). The public health community's use of social media for policy advocacy: A scoping review and suggestions to advance the field. *Public Health, 198*, 146–155. doi:10.1016/j.puhe.2021.07.015 PMID:34428607

Jacobson, J., Gruzd, A., & Hernández-García, Á. (2020). Social media marketing: Who is watching the watchers? *Journal of Retailing and Consumer Services, 53*, 1–12. doi:10.1016/j.jretconser.2019.03.001

Jalali, R., & Pareek, P. (2010). Is there a need to regulate health care advertisement for lay public? *Journal of Cancer Research and Therapeutics, 6*(2), 131–133. doi:10.4103/0973-1482.65228 PMID:20622357

James, B. (2004). The new 6 Ps of pharmaceutical marketing. *Pharmaceutical Marketing, 18*(1), 1–3.

James, N. (2007). The use of email interviewing as a qualitative method of inquiry in educational research. *British Educational Research Journal, 33*(6), 963–976. doi:10.1080/01411920701657074

Jasiński, Ł. (2023). *Singapore – is it a Good Example of a Market-Based Healthcare System.* Mises Institute.

Javaid, M., Haleem, A., & Singh, R. P. (2023). ChatGPT for healthcare services: An emerging stage for an innovative perspective. *BenchCouncil Transactions on Benchmarks, Standards and Evaluations, 3*(1), 100105. doi:10.1016/j.tbench.2023.100105

Jenkinson, C., Coulter, A., Bruster, S., Richards, N., & Chandola, T. (2002). Patients' experiences and satisfaction with health care: Results of a questionnaire study of specific aspects of care. *Quality & Safety in Health Care, 11*(4), 335–339. doi:10.1136/qhc.11.4.335 PMID:12468693

Jiang, F., Jiang, Y., Zhi, H., Dong, Y., Li, H., Ma, S., Wang, Y., Dong, Q., Shen, H., & Wang, Y. (2017). Artificial intelligence in healthcare: Past, present and future. *Stroke and Vascular Neurology*, *2*(4), 230–243. doi:10.1136vn-2017-000101 PMID:29507784

Jiang, L., Wu, Z., Xu, X., Zhan, Y., Jin, X., Wang, L., & Qiu, Y. (2021). Opportunities and challenges of artificial intelligence in the medical field: Current application, emerging problems, and problem-solving strategies. *The Journal of International Medical Research*, *49*(3). doi:10.1177/03000605211000157 PMID:33771068

Jishnu, L. (2021). Big pharma and intellectual property: Why is India afraid of compulsory licenses. *Down To Earth*. Available at https://www.downtoearth.org.in/blog/health/big-pharma-and-intellectual-property-why-is-india-afraid-of-compulsory-licences--77470

Johnson, C. M., Vorderstrasse, A. A., & Shaw, R. (2009). Virtual worlds in health care higher education. *Journal of Virtual Worlds Research*, *2*(2). Advance online publication. doi:10.4101/jvwr.v2i2.699

Johnson, S. G., Speedie, S., Simon, G., Kumar, V., & Westra, B. L. (2017). Quantifying the effect of data quality on the validity of an eMeasure. *Applied Clinical Informatics*, *8*(04), 1012–1021. doi:10.4338/ACI-2017-03-RA-0042 PMID:29241241

Junusi, R. (2020). Digital Marketing During the Pandemic Period; A Study of Islamic Perspective. *Junusi*, *2*(1), 15. Advance online publication. doi:10.21580/jdmhi.2020.2.1.5717

Jurkiewicz-Świątek, I. (2014). Medical Savings Accounts as a Method of Financing Health Services. The Results of their Financing so Far in the World and the Perspective for Europe. *Public Health Management*, *12*(3), 248–257.

Kalotra, A. (2014). Marketing Strategies of Different Pharmaceutical Companies. *Journal of Drug Delivery and Therapeutics*, *4*(2), 64–71. doi:10.22270/jddt.v4i2.771

Kamarudin, Y., Low, D. F. F., Sulaiman, A., Zulhusmi, A. M., & Zakaria, N. N. (2022). Social Media Use and Marketing within the Orthodontic Practice in Malaysia. *Archives of Orofacial Science*, *17*(1), 87–100. doi:10.21315/aos2022.1701.OA05

Kamel, I. S. (2023). The role of robotics and automation in surgery: Critical review of current and emerging technologies. *Futurity Medicine*, *2*(1), 23–35. doi:10.57125/FEM.2023.03.30.03

Kang, E. Y. N., Chen, D. R., & Chen, Y. Y. (2023). Associations between literacy and attitudes toward artificial intelligence–assisted medical consultations: The mediating role of perceived distrust and efficiency of artificial intelligence. *Computers in Human Behavior*, *139*, 107529. doi:10.1016/j.chb.2022.107529

Kaplan, A., & Haenlien, M. (2009). *Users of the world, unite! The challenges and opportunities of Social Media*. Academic Press.

Kaplan, A. M., & Haenlein, M. (2012). Social media: Back to the roots and back to the future. *Journal of Systems and Information Technology*, *14*(2), 101–104. doi:10.1108/13287261211232126

Karłowska, J. (2017). *Analysis of the Polish Health Care System – a Proposal for Changes on the Example of Other Countries* [Master's thesis]. Warsaw School of Economics.

Katsikeas, C., Leonidou, L., & Zeriti, A. (2020). Revisiting international marketing strategy in a digital era: Opportunities, challenges, and research directions. *International Marketing Review*, *37*(2), 405–424. doi:10.1108/IMR-02-2019-0080

Kay, M. J. (2007). Healthcare marketing: What is salient? *International Journal of Pharmaceutical and Healthcare Marketing*, *1*(3), 247–263. doi:10.1108/17506120710818256

Keane, M., Yu, H., Zhao, E. J., & Leong, S. (2020). *Chinas digital presence in the asia-pacific: Culture, technology and platforms*. Anthem Press. doi:10.2307/j.ctv20pxxzt

Keeley, B. (2021). *On My Mind--Promoting, Protecting and Caring for Children's Mental Health.* UNICEF.

Kemper, J. A., & Ballantine, P. W. (2019). What do we mean by sustainability marketing? *Journal of Marketing Management*, *35*(3), 277–309. doi:10.1080/0267257X.2019.1573845

Kerka, S. (1997). *Developing Collaborative Partnerships*. Practice Application Brief. ERIC Clearinghouse on Adult, Career, and Vocational Education.

Keyhani, S., Diener-West, M., & Powe, N. (2006). Are development times for pharmaceuticals increasing or decreasing? *Health Affairs*, *25*(2), 461–468. doi:10.1377/hlthaff.25.2.461 PMID:16522587

Khajuria, A., & Khajuria, V. (2013). Impact of pharmaceutical marketing communication strategies on prescription practices of physicians. *Research Journal of Pharmaceutical, Biological and Chemical Sciences*, *4*(3), 882–889.

Khanal, P., Gupta, A., & Smith, M. (2016). Virtual worlds in healthcare. *Advances in Healthcare Informatics and Analytics*, 233-248.

Khan, I., Saleh, M. A., Quazi, A., & Johns, R. (2021). Health consumers' social media adoption behaviours in Australia. *Health Informatics Journal*, *27*(2), 14604582211009917. doi:10.1177/14604582211009917 PMID:33887968

Kim, Y. S., & Park, J. A. (2021). Design Thinking in the Framework of Visual Thinking and Characterization of Service Design Ideation Methods Using Visual Reasoning Model. *The Design Journal*, 931-953. doi:10.1080/14606925.2021.1977497

Kimbell, L. (2015). Rethinking Design Thinking: Part I. *Design and Culture*, *3*(3), 285–306. doi:10.2752/175470811X13071166525216

Kim, H. K., & Lee, C. W. (2021). Relationships among healthcare digitalization, social capital, and supply chain performance in the healthcare manufacturing industry. *International Journal of Environmental Research and Public Health*, *18*(4), 1417. doi:10.3390/ijerph18041417 PMID:33546393

Kim, J., Jang, S., & Lee, K. H. (2021). Evolution of digital marketing communication: Bibliometric analysis and network visualization from key articles. *Journal of Business Research*, *130*, 552–563. doi:10.1016/j.jbusres.2019.09.043

Kindig, D. A., & Isham, G. (2014). Population health improvement: A community health business model that engages partners in all sectors. *Frontiers of Health Services Management*, *30*(4), 3–20. doi:10.1097/01974520-201404000-00002 PMID:25671991

Kong, X., Yang, Y., Gong, F., & Zhao, M. (2012). Problems and the Potential Direction of Reforms for the Current Individual Medical Savings Accounts in the Chinese Health Care System. *The Journal of Medicine and Philosophy*, *37*(6), 556–567. doi:10.1093/jmp/jhs049 PMID:23192456

Korda, H., & Itani, Z. (2013). Harnessing Social Media for Health Promotion and Behavior Change. *Health Promotion Practice*, *14*(1), 15–23. doi:10.1177/1524839911405850 PMID:21558472

Kostygina, G., Tran, H., Binns, S., Szczypka, G., Emery, S., Vallone, D., & Hair, E. (2020). Boosting Health Campaign Reach and Engagement Through Use of Social Media Influencers and Memes. *Social Media + Society*, *6*(2), 1–12. doi:10.1177/2056305120912475

Kotler, M. (2020). Marketing Environment in the Digital Transformation. *Marketing Strategy in the Digital Age*, 3-45.

Kotler, Ph. (1975). *Marketing for Nonprofit Organizations*. Prentice-Hall, Inc.

Koumpouros, Y., Toulias, T. L., & Koumpouros, N. (2015). The importance of patient engagement and the use of social media marketing in healthcare. *Technology and Health Care*, *23*(4), 495–507. doi:10.3233/THC-150918 PMID:26409912

Kozierkiewicz, A., Gilewski, D. (2023). Health Savings Accounts in the USA – Structure and Role in the System. *Health Manager – Termedia.*

Kraljevic, S., Stambrook, P. J., & Pavelic, K. (2004, September). Accelerating drug discovery. *EMBO Reports*, *5*(9), 837–842. doi:10.1038j.embor.7400236 PMID:15470377

Krejcie, R. V., & Morgan, D. W. (1970). Determining sample size for research activities. *Educational and Psychological Measurement*, *30*(3), 607–610. doi:10.1177/001316447003000308

Kreps, G. L. (2006). Communication and racial inequities in health care. *The American Behavioral Scientist*, *49*(6), 760–774. doi:10.1177/0002764205283800

Kuciapiński, M. J. (2014). The therapeutic and educational properties of fairytale therapy in the early stages of children's development. *Pedagogika Rodziny*, *4*(2), 77–93. doi:10.2478/fampe-2014-0019

Kulkov, I., Tsvetkova, A., & Ivanova-Gongne, M. (2021). Identifying institutional barriers when implementing new technologies in the healthcare industry. *European Journal of Innovation Management*, *26*(4), 909–932. doi:10.1108/EJIM-02-2021-0093

Kumar, R., Sharma, K., Assaf, M., Sharma, B., & Naidu, S. (2019). Development of an Assistive Tongue Drive System for Disabled Individuals. In A. Nayak & A. Sharma (Eds.), Lecture Notes in Computer Science: Vol. 11672. *PRICAI 2019: Trends in artificial intelligence. PRICAI 2019.* Springer. doi:10.1007/978-3-030-29894-4_41

Kumar, V., & Pansari, A. (2016). Competitive advantage through engagement. *JMR, Journal of Marketing Research*, *53*(4), 497–514. doi:10.1509/jmr.15.0044

Kung, T. H., Cheatham, M., Medenilla, A., Sillos, C., De Leon, L., Elepaño, C., Madriaga, M., Aggabao, R., Diaz-Candido, G., Maningo, J., & Tseng, V. (2023). Performance of ChatGPT on USMLE: Potential for AI-assisted medical education using large language models. *PLOS Digital Health*, *2*(2), e0000198. doi:10.1371/journal.pdig.0000198 PMID:36812645

Kwortnik, R. J. Jr, & Han, X. (2011). The influence of guest perceptions of service fairness on lodging loyalty in China. *Cornell Hospitality Quarterly*, *52*(3), 321–332. doi:10.1177/1938965511409005

La República. (2019). *El déficit de la salud se financiará con deuda pública: Juan Pablo Uribe*. https://www.larepublica.co/economia/el-deficit-de-la-salud-se-financiara-con-deuda-publica-juan-pablo-uribe-2827267

Lakin, N., & Scheubel, V. (2010). *Corporate Community Involvement : The Definitive Guide to Maximizing Your Business' Societal Engagement.* Routledge.

Lamani, T. R., Sajjan, S. B., & Natekar, D. S. (2021). Effectiveness of bibliotherapy in reducing the level of anxiety among hospitalized children in selected hospital at Bagalkot. *International Journal of Research in Engineering. Science and Management*, *4*(3), 153–156.

Lasker, R. D., Weiss, E. S., & Miller, R. (2001). Partnership synergy: A practical framework for studying and strengthening the collaborative advantage. *The Milbank Quarterly*, *79*(2), 179–205. doi:10.1111/1468-0009.00203 PMID:11439464

Lattimore, C. M., Kane, W. J., Fleming, M. A., Martin, A. N., Mehaffey, J. H., Smolkin, M. E., Ratcliffe, S. J., Zaydfudim, V. M., Showalter, S. L., & Hedrick, T. L. (2021, October 08). Disparities in telemedicine utilization among surgical patients during COVID-19.[. *PLoS One*, *16*(10), e0258452. doi:10.1371/journal.pone.0258452 PMID:34624059

Lavinia, C. A. Z. A. C. U., & Elena, O. A. (2015). Healthcare Marketing-A Relational Approach. *Revista Economica, 67*(5), 59–72.

Learmonth, Y. C., Adamson, B. C., Balto, J. M., Chiu, C. Y., Molina-Guzman, I. M., Finlayson, M., Barstow, E. A., & Motl, R. W. (2018). Investigating the needs and wants of healthcare providers for promoting exercise in persons with multiple sclerosis: A qualitative study. *Disability and Rehabilitation, 40*(18), 2172–2180. doi:10.1080/09638288.2017.1327989 PMID:28524732

Lee, T. H. (2014). *The strategy that will fix health care.* Academic Press.

Lee, D., & Yoon, S. N. (2021). Application of artificial intelligence-based technologies in the healthcare industry: Opportunities and challenges. *International Journal of Environmental Research and Public Health, 18*(1), 271. doi:10.3390/ijerph18010271 PMID:33401373

Lee, S. M., & Lee, D. (2020). Healthcare wearable devices: An analysis of key factors for continuous use intention. *Service Business, 14*(4), 503–531. doi:10.100711628-020-00428-3

Legislative Herald of Georgia. (n.d.) Agreement between Georgia, on the one hand, and the European Union and the European Atomic Energy Union and their member states, on the other hand. International Treaty and Agreement of Georgia. 11. 09. 2014. https://matsne

Leowski, J. (2010). Health Policy and Public Health. CeDeWu.

Lewrick, M., Link, P., & Leifer, L. (2020). *The Design Thinking Toolbox.* Wiley. doi:10.15358/9783800657520

Liaw, S. Y., Carpio, G. A. C., Lau, Y., Tan, S. C., Lim, W. S., & Goh, P. S. (2018). Multiuser virtual worlds in healthcare education: A systematic review. *Nurse Education Today, 65*, 136–149. doi:10.1016/j.nedt.2018.01.006 PMID:29571002

Li, H., Liu, K., Gu, J., Zhang, Y., Qiao, Y., & Sun, X. (2017). The development and impact of primary health care in China from 1949 to 2015: A focused review. *The International Journal of Health Planning and Management, 32*(3), 339–350. doi:10.1002/hpm.2435 PMID:28670754

Li, J., & Wang, X. (2020). Does VAT have higher tax compliance than a turnover tax? Evidence from China. *International Tax and Public Finance, 27*(2), 280–311. doi:10.100710797-019-09567-4

Lim, A. (n.d.). *The Average Healthcare (Medical) Inflation Rate in Singapore.* https://smartwealth.sg/medical-inflation-rate-singapore

Li, R. C., Asch, S. M., & Shah, N. H. (2020). Developing a delivery science for artificial intelligence in healthcare. *npj. Digital Medicine, 3*(1), 107. doi:10.103841746-020-00318-y PMID:32885053

Liu, C. (2021). Health information systems amid COVID-19 outbreak: Lessons from China. *The HIM Journal, 50*(1-2), 99–100. doi:10.1177/1833358320947557 PMID:32806959

Liu, J. X., Goryakin, Y., Maeda, A., Bruckner, T., & Scheffler, R. (2017). Global Health Workforce Labor Market Projections for 2030. *Human Resources for Health, 15*(11), 11. Advance online publication. doi:10.118612960-017-0187-2 PMID:28159017

Liu, J. Y. W., Sorwar, G., Rahman, M. S., & Hoque, M. R. (2023). The role of trust and habit in the adoption of mHealth by older adults in Hong Kong: A healthcare technology service acceptance (HTSA) model. *BMC Geriatrics, 23*(1), 73. doi:10.118612877-023-03779-4 PMID:36737712

Liu, R., Gupta, S., & Patel, P. (2021). The application of the principles of responsible AI on social media marketing for digital health. *Information Systems Frontiers*, 1–25. PMID:34539226

Llamas, M. (2022). Selling Side Effects: Big Pharma's Marketing Machine. *Drugwatch.* Available at https://www.drugwatch.com/featured/big-pharma-marketing/

Lloveras, J., Marshall, A. P., Vandeventer, J. S., & Pansera, M. (2022). Sustainability marketing beyond sustainable development: Towards a degrowth agenda. *Journal of Marketing Management*, *38*(17), 2055–2077. doi:10.1080/0267257X.2022.2084443

Logan, A. G., McIsaac, W. J., Tisler, A., Irvine, M. J., Saunders, A., Dunai, A., Rizo, C. A., Feig, D. S., Hamill, M., Trudel, M., & Cafazzo, J. A. (2007). Mobile phone-based remote patient monitoring system for management of hypertension in diabetic patients. *American Journal of Hypertension*, *20*(9), 942–948. doi:10.1016/j.amjhyper.2007.03.020 PMID:17765133

Long, Q., Xu, L., Bekedam, H., & Tang, S. (2013). Changes in health expenditures in China in 2000s: Has the health system reform improved affordability. *International Journal for Equity in Health*, *12*(1), 1–8. doi:10.1186/1475-9276-12-40 PMID:23764104

Lorence, D. P., Park, H., & Fox, S. (2006). Racial disparities in health information access: Resilience of the digital divide. *Journal of Medical Systems*, *30*(4), 241–249. doi:10.100710916-005-9003-y PMID:16978003

Louis, D. Z., Yuen, E. J., Braga, M., Cicchetti, A., Rabinowitz, C., Laine, C., & Gonnella, J. S. (1999). Impact of a DRG-based hospital financing system on quality and outcomes of care in Italy. *Health Services Research*, *34*(1 Pt 2), 405. PMID:10199684

Lucas, C. V., & Soares, L. (2013). Bibliotherapy: A tool to promote children's psychological well-being. *Journal of Poetry Therapy*, *26*(3), 137–147. doi:10.1080/08893675.2013.823310

Ludvigsson, J. F., Svedberg, P., Olén, O., Bruze, G., & Neovius, M. (2019). The longitudinal integrated database for health insurance and labour market studies (LISA) and its use in medical research. *European Journal of Epidemiology*, *34*(4), 423–437. doi:10.100710654-019-00511-8 PMID:30929112

Lupton, M. (2018). Some ethical and legal consequences of the application of artificial intelligence in the field of medicine. *Trends Med*, *18*(4), 100147. doi:10.15761/TiM.1000147

Mac McCullough, J., Singh, S. R., & Leider, J. P. (2019). The importance of governmental and nongovernmental investments in public health and social services for improving community health outcomes. *Journal of Public Health Management and Practice*, *25*(4), 348–356. doi:10.1097/PHH.0000000000000856 PMID:31136508

MacStravic, R. E. (1977). *Marketing health care.* Aspen Systems Corporation. doi:10.1097/00004010-197702040-00017

Madanaguli, A. T., Dhir, A., Talwar, S., Singh, G., & Escobar, O. (2021). Business to business (B2B) alliances in the healthcare industry: A review of research trends and pertinent issues. *Journal of Business and Industrial Marketing*, *37*(8), 1688–1705. doi:10.1108/JBIM-01-2021-0060

Maier, E., Reimer, U., & Wickramasinghe, N. (2021). Digital healthcare services. *Electronic Markets*, 1–4. PMID:35602115

Maiolini, R., Versari, P., Rullani, F., & Seitanidi, M. M. (2022). The role of community participation in cross-sector social partnerships. *Nonprofit and Voluntary Sector Quarterly*, •••, 08997640221130696.

Malhotra, N. (2010). *Marketing research: An applied orientation* (6th ed.). Pearson Education.

Marchioli, A. (2006). Marketing social et efficacité des campagnes de prévention de santé publique: Apports et implications des récents modèles de la communication persuasive. *Market Management*, *6*(1), 17–36. doi:10.3917/mama.031.0017

Margherita, G., Martino, M. L., Recano, F., & Camera, F. (2014). Invented fairy tales in groups with onco-haematological children. *Child: Care, Health and Development, 40*(3), 426–434. doi:10.1111/cch.12076 PMID:23672257

Marilyn, J. (1996). Telemedicine: A Guide to Assessing Telecommunications in Health Care. Knowledge Management in Digital Change, 311-326. doi:10.1007/978-3-319-73546-7_19

Martin, A., & Grudziecki, J. (2006). DigEuLit: Concepts and Tools for Digital Literacy Development. *Innovation.*

Martín-Cervantes, P. A., del Carmen Valls Martínez, M., & Gigauri, I. (2022). Sustainable Marketing. In *Encyclopedia of Creativity, Invention, Innovation and Entrepreneurship* (pp. 1–8). Springer. doi:10.1007/978-1-4614-6616-1_200101-1

Martin, D., & Schouten, J. (2014). *Sustainable marketing*. Pearson.

Marzuki, S. Z., Zreik, M., Buyong, S. Z., Goyipnazarov, S., Mirzaliev, S., & Bakhramovna, I. A. (2023). An Importance Satisfaction Analysis of Hosting Events in Hangzhou, China: A Pilot Study. *Advances in Social Sciences Research Journal, 10*(6.2), 107-117.

Masood, I., Hassali, M. A., & Ahmad, M. (2009). Evolution of Marketing Techniques, Adoption In Pharmaceutical Industry And Related Issues: A Review. *Journal of Clinical and Diagnostic Research : JCDR, 3*(6), 1942–1952.

Matarín Jiménez, T.M. (2015). *Social networks in prevention and health promotion. A review of the current.* Academic Press.

Matheny, M., Israni, S. T., Ahmed, M., & Whicher, D. (2019). *Artificial intelligence in health care: The hope, the hype, the promise, the peril.* National Academy of Medicine. doi:10.17226/27111

McGahan, A. M. (1994). Industry Structure and Competitive Advantage. *Harvard Business Review*. Available at https://hbr.org/1994/11/industry-structure-and-competitive-advantage

McMillen, P. S., & Pehrsson, D. E. (2004). Bibliotherapy for hospital patients. *Journal of Hospital Librarianship, 4*(1), 73–81. doi:10.1300/J186v04n01_07

Mecklai, K., Smith, N., Stern, A., & Kramer, D. B. (2021). Remote patient monitoring—Overdue or overused? *The New England Journal of Medicine, 384*(15), 1384–1386. doi:10.1056/NEJMp2033275 PMID:33853209

Mei, C. (2020). Policy style, consistency and the effectiveness of the policy mix in China's fight against COVID-19. *Policy and Society, 39*(3), 309–325. doi:10.1080/14494035.2020.1787627 PMID:35039723

Memisoglu, M. (2018). Branding of Prescription and Non-prescription Drugs. *Acta Pharmaceutica Sciencia, 56*(1), 21. doi:10.23893/1307-2080.APS.05602

Menatti, L., Bich, L., & Saborido, C. (2022). Health and environment from adaptation to adaptivity: A situated relational account. *History and Philosophy of the Life Sciences, 44*(3), 1–28. doi:10.100740656-022-00515-w PMID:35980478

Mends-Brew, E., & Asiamah, N. (2018). Improving health workers' organisational commitment: Drawing lessons from the interaction between internal marketing and key job characteristics. *International Journal of Healthcare Management, 13*(sup1), 318–328. doi:10.1080/20479700.2018.1548152

Miao, Y. (2016). *Being middle class in China: Identity, attitudes and behaviour.* Taylor & Francis. doi:10.4324/9781315643014

Mijwil, M., Aljanabi, M., & Ali, A. H. (2023). ChatGPT: Exploring the Role of Cybersecurity in the Protection of Medical Information. *Mesopotamian Journal of CyberSecurity, 18–21*, 18–21. Advance online publication. doi:10.58496/MJCS/2023/004

Ministry of Health. (2023). The state will fully finance liver transplantation for GEL 120,000. *Surgery*, *07*, 19. https://www.moh.gov.ge/en/news/

Ministry of Health. (n.d.a) Universal Health Program. Ministry of Internally Displaced Persons from the Occupied Territories, Labour, Health and Social Affairs of Georgia. https://www.moh.gov.ge/ka/529

Ministry of Health. (n.d.b) Ministry of Internally Displaced Persons from the Occupied Territories, Labour, Health and Social Affairs of Georgia. https://www.moh.gov.ge/en/460/

Ministry of Health. (n.d.c) A brief overview of the Georgian healthcare system. https://www.moh.gov.ge/uploads/files/2018/Failebi/ 06.08.2018.pdf

Ministry of Health. (n.d.d) Georgian National Health Strategy for 2022-2030. 63-70. https://www.moh.gov.ge/uploads/publicinformation/2022/05/04/3749f20341220a6dc1ab60c0d4f3b895.pdf

Minsalud. (2022). Colombia llegó al aseguramiento universal en salud al alcanzar el 99,6%. *Minsalud.* https://www.minsalud.gov.co/Paginas/Colombia-llego-al-aseguramiento-universal-en-salud-al-alcanzar-el-99.6.aspx#:~:text=Seguidamente%2C%20la%20viceministra%20de%20Protecci%C3%B3n,839%20personas%20en%20el%20R%C3%A9gimen

Mirzaei, T., & Esmaeilzadeh, P. (2021). Engagement in online health communities: Channel expansion and social exchanges. *Information & Management*, *58*(1), 103404. doi:10.1016/j.im.2020.103404

Mladenović, D., Todua, N., & Pavlović-Höck, N. (2023). Understanding individual psychological and behavioral responses during COVID-19: Application of stimulus-organism-response model. *Telematics and Informatics*, *79*, 101966. doi:10.1016/j.tele.2023.101966 PMID:36910674

Molina-Mula, J., & Gallo-Estrada, J. (2020). Impact of nurse-patient relationship on quality of care and patient autonomy in decision-making. *International Journal of Environmental Research and Public Health*, *17*(3), 835. doi:10.3390/ijerph17030835 PMID:32013108

Möller, K., & Halinen, A. (2000). Relationship marketing theory: Its roots and direction. *Journal of Marketing Management*, *16*(1-3), 29–54. doi:10.1362/026725700785100460

Mondal, T., Jayadeva, S. M., Pani, R., Subramanian, M., & Sumana, B. (2022). E marketing strategy in health care using IoT and Machine Learning. *Materials Today: Proceedings*, *56*, 2087–2091. doi:10.1016/j.matpr.2021.11.417

Montserrat Canal, J. M., Suárez-Girón, M., Egea, C., Embid, C., Matute-Villacís, M., de Manuel Martínez, L., Orteu, Á., González-Cappa, J., Tato Cerdeiras, M., & Mediano, O. (2021). Spanish Society of Pulmonology and Thoracic Surgery positioning on the use of telemedine in sleep-disordered breathing and mechanical ventilation. Arch Bronconeumol (Engl Ed), 57(4), 281-290. doi:10.1016/j.arbr.2021.02.001

Morgan, R. M., & Hunt, S. D. (1994). The commitment-trust theory of relationship marketing. *Journal of Marketing*, *58*(3), 20–38. doi:10.1177/002224299405800302

Morley, J., & Floridi, L. (2019). Enabling digital health companionship is better than empowerment. *The Lancet. Digital Health*, *1*(4), e155–e156. doi:10.1016/S2589-7500(19)30079-2 PMID:33323183

Moro Visconti, R., & Morea, D. (2019). Big Data for the Sustainability of Healthcare Project Financing. *Sustainability (Basel)*, *11*(13), 3748. doi:10.3390u11133748

Moro, V. R., & Morea, D. (2020). Healthcare digitalization and pay-for-performance incentives in smart hospital project financing. *International Journal of Environmental Research and Public Health*, *17*(7), 2318. doi:10.3390/ijerph17072318 PMID:32235517

Morris, M. X., Song, E. Y., Rajesh, A., Asaad, M., & Phillips, B. T. (2023). Ethical, Legal, and Financial Considerations of Artificial Intelligence in Surgery. *The American Surgeon*, *89*(1), 55–60. doi:10.1177/00031348221117042 PMID:35978473

Morris, Z. S., & Clarkson, P. J. (2009). Does social marketing provide a framework for changing healthcare practice? *Health Policy (Amsterdam)*, *91*(2), 135–141. doi:10.1016/j.healthpol.2008.11.009 PMID:19147249

Mukherjee, W. (2008). Pharma pops brand-extension pill. *The Economic Times*. Available at https://economictimes.indiatimes.com/industry/healthcare/biotech/pharmaceuticals/pharma-pops-brand-extension-pill/articleshow/3173587.cms?from=mdr

Murphy, G., Corcoran, C., Tatlow-Golden, M., Boyland, E., & Rooney, B. (2020). See, Like, Share, Remember: Adolescents' Responses to Unhealthy-, Healthy- and Non-Food Advertising in Social Media. *International Journal of Environmental Research and Public Health*, *17*(7), 2181. doi:10.3390/ijerph17072181 PMID:32218252

Musielak, M. (2012). *Ethical Aspects of Health Care Management in Poland.* Nowiny Lekarskie, No. 4, OECD Health Statistics.

Naina, M., & Pooja, G. (2023). Effectiveness of Bibliothreapy in Reducing the Level of Anxiety among Hospitalised Children. *International Journal of Science and Research (Raipur, India)*, *9*(10), 15. doi:10.21275/SR23303103505

Nand, R., & Sharma, B. (2019). Meta-heuristic approaches to tackle skill based group allocation of students in project-based learning courses. In *IEEE Congress on Evolutionary Computation (CEC)* (pp. 1782–1789). 10.1109/CEC.2019.8789987

National Statistics Office of Georgia. (2023). Retrieved October 20, 2023, from https://www.geostat.ge/en

Negash, Y. T., & Sarmiento, L. S. C. (2023). Smart product-service systems in the healthcare industry: Intelligent connected products and stakeholder communication drive digital health service adoption. *Heliyon*, *9*(2), e13137. doi:10.1016/j.heliyon.2023.e13137 PMID:36820023

Neuhauser, L., & Kreps, G. L. (2003). Rethinking communication in the e-health era. *Journal of Health Psychology*, *8*(1), 7–22. doi:10.1177/1359105303008001426 PMID:22113897

NFON. (2018). *4 reasons why generation Z brings a human communication style to the workplace*. Available at https:// www.nfon.com/ en/ news/ press/ blog/ blog-detail/ 4-reasons-why-generation-z-brings-a-human-communication-style-to-the-workplace

Ng, K., Kartoun, U., Stavropoulos, H., Zambrano, J. A., & Tang, P. C. (2021). Personalized treatment options for chronic diseases using precision cohort analytics. *Scientific Reports*, *11*(1), 1139. doi:10.103841598-021-80967-5 PMID:33441956

Ng, S., & Russell-Bennett, R. (2015). The Role of Affect in Consumer Evaluation of Health Care Services. *Health Marketing Quarterly*, *32*(1), 31–47. doi:10.1080/07359683.2015.1000708 PMID:25751317

Noh, E., Begun, J. W., White, K. M., & Potthoff, S. J. (2022). US hospital engagement in cross-sector partnerships for population health improvement in socioeconomically distressed counties. *Public Health*, *205*, 55–57. doi:10.1016/j.puhe.2022.01.020 PMID:35235880

Nonis, M., Bertinato, L., Arcangeli, L., Cadeddu, C., Palinuro, A., Frattura, L., Merlino, G. L., Verdini, E., Lispi, L., & Ricciardi, W. (2018). The evolution of DRG system in Italy: The it-drg project. *European Journal of Public Health*, *28*(suppl_4), cky218–cky095. doi:10.1093/eurpub/cky218.095

Nunnally, J. C. (1967). *Psychometric Theory*. McGraw-Hill Book Company.

Nuti, S., Seghieri, C., Vainieri, M., & Zett, S. (2012). Assessment and improvement of the Italian healthcare system: First evidence from a pilot national performance evaluation system. *Journal of Healthcare Management*, *57*(3), 182–199. doi:10.1097/00115514-201205000-00008 PMID:22724376

O'Reilly, M., Dogra, N., Hughes, J., Reilly, P., George, R., & Whiteman, N. (2019). Potential of social media in promoting mental health in adolescents. *Health Promotion International*, *34*(5), 981–991. doi:10.1093/heapro/day056 PMID:30060043

Olewniczak, A. (2022). *Impact of the Coronavirus (Covid 19) Pandemic on the Financial Results and Development Prospects of the Private Medical Services Sector in Poland* [Master's thesis]. Warsaw School of Economics.

Olson, E. M., Olson, K. M., Czaplewski, A. J., & Key, T. M. (2021). Business strategy and the management of digital marketing. *Business Horizons*, *64*(2), 285–293. doi:10.1016/j.bushor.2020.12.004

Onpage. (2023). https://marketplace.connectwise.com/onpage#reviews

Oosthuizen, D., Spowart, J., & De Meyer-Heydenrych, C. F. (2015). The relationship between perceived price and consumers' purchase intentions of private label wine brands. *African Journal of Hospitality, Tourism and Leisure*, *4*(2), 1–17.

Opdenakker, R. J. G. (2006). Advantages and disadvantages of four interview techniques in qualitative research. In *Forum Qualitative Sozialforschung= Forum: Qualitative Social Research*, *7*(4), art-11.

OPS. (2022). *Salud en las Américas, perfil de Colombia.* Organización Panamericana de La Salud. https://hia.paho.org/es/paises-2022/perfil-colombia#:~:text=Para%20el%202021%20se%20estimaron,de%20los%20habitantes%20del%20pa%C3%ADs

Osei-Frimpong, K. (2017). Patient participatory behaviours in healthcare service delivery. *Journal of Service Theory and Practice*, *27*(2), 453–474. doi:10.1108/JSTP-02-2016-0038

Otani, K., Waterman, B., Faulkner, K. M., Boslaugh, S., & Dunagan, C. W. (2010). How patient reactions to hospital care attributes affect the evaluation of overall quality of care, willingness to recommend, and willingness to return. *Journal of Healthcare Management*, *55*(1), 25–38. doi:10.1097/00115514-201001000-00006 PMID:20210071

Ouzts, D. T. (1991). The emergence of bibliotherapy as a discipline. *Reading Horizons*, *31*(3), 199–206.

Paich, M., Peck, C., & Valant, J. (2011). Pharmaceutical market dynamics and strategic planning: A system dynamics perspective. *System Dynamics Review*, *27*(1), 47–63. doi:10.1002dr.458

Pande, M., & Bharathi, V. (2020). Theoretical foundations of design thinking – A constructivism learning approach to design thinking. *Thinking Skills and Creativity*, *36*, 100637. Advance online publication. doi:10.1016/j.tsc.2020.100637

Pandey, N., Nayal, P., & Rathore, A. S. (2020). Digital marketing for B2B organizations: Structured literature review and future research directions. *Journal of Business and Industrial Marketing*, *35*(7), 1191–1204. doi:10.1108/JBIM-06-2019-0283

Pandey, N., & Pal, A. (2020). Impact of digital surge during Covid-19 pandemic: A viewpoint on research and practice. *International Journal of Information Management*, *55*, 102171. doi:10.1016/j.ijinfomgt.2020.102171 PMID:32836633

Pandya, S., Thakur, A., Saxena, S., Jassal, N., Patel, C., Modi, K., Shah, P., Joshi, R., Gonge, S., Kadam, K., & Kadam, P. (2021). A Study of the Recent Trends of Immunology: Key Challenges, Domains, Applications, Datasets, and Future Directions. *Sensors (Basel)*, *21*(23), 7786. Advance online publication. doi:10.339021237786 PMID:34883787

Pansari, A., & Kumar, V. (2017). Customer engagement: The construct, antecedents, and consequences. *Journal of the Academy of Marketing Science*, *45*(3), 294–311. doi:10.100711747-016-0485-6

Paramio Pérez, G., Almagro, B. J., Hernando Gómez, Á., & Aguaded Gómez, J. I. (2015). Validación de la escala eHealth Literacy (eHEALS) en población universitaria española. *Revista Española de Salud Pública, 89*(3), 329–338. doi:10.4321/S1135-57272015000300010 PMID:26388346

Pardeck, J. T., & Pardeck, J. A. (1998). *Children in foster care and adoption: A guide to bibliotherapy*. Greenwood Press.

Park, C. W., Seo, S. W., Kang, N., Ko, B., Choi, B. W., Park, C. M., Chang, D. K., Kim, H., Kim, H., Lee, H., Jang, J., Ye, J. C., Jeon, J. H., Seo, J. B., Kim, K. J., Jung, K.-H., Kim, N., Paek, S., Shin, S.-Y., ... Yoon, H. J. (2020). Artificial intelligence in health care: Current applications and issues. *Journal of Korean Medical Science, 35*(42), e379. doi:10.3346/jkms.2020.35.e379 PMID:33140591

Park, H., Reber, B. H., & Chon, M. G. (2016). Tweeting as health communication: Health organizations' use of Twitter for health promotion and public engagement. *Journal of Health Communication, 21*(2), 188–198. doi:10.1080/10810730.2015.1058435 PMID:26716546

Parmigiani, A., & Rivera-Santos, M. (2011). Clearing a path through the forest: A meta-review of interorganizational relationships. *Journal of Management, 37*(4), 1108–1136. doi:10.1177/0149206311407507

Pascucci, F., Savelli, E., & Gistri, G. (2023). How digital technologies reshape marketing: Evidence from a qualitative investigation. *Italian Journal of Marketing, 2023*(1), 27–58. doi:10.100743039-023-00063-6

Pelet, J., Belda, S., & Arezki, D. (2023). Use of AI in Predicting Trends in Vegetation Dynamics in Africa. In J. Wang (Ed.), *Encyclopedia of Data Science and Machine Learning* (pp. 31–56). IGI Global. doi:10.4018/978-1-7998-9220-5.ch003

Pelet, J., & Ettis, S. A. (2022). Social Media Advertising Effectiveness: The Role of Perceived Originality, Liking, Credibility, Irritation, Intrusiveness, and Ad Destination. *International Journal of Technology and Human Interaction, 18*(1), 1–20. doi:10.4018/IJTHI.2022010106

Pesapane, F., Codari, M., & Sardanelli, F. (2018). Artificial intelligence in medical imaging: Threat or opportunity? Radiologists again at the forefront of innovation in medicine. *European Radiology Experimental, 2*(1), 1–10. doi:10.118641747-018-0061-6 PMID:30353365

Peter, M. K., & Vecchia, M. D. (2020). The Digital Marketing Toolkit: A Literature Review for the Identification of Digital Marketing Channels and Platforms. *New Trends in Business Information Systems and Technology*, 251-265. doi:10.1007/978-3-030-48332-6_17

Pham, C. T., Phung, D., Nguyen, T. V., & Chu, C. (2020). The effectiveness of workplace health promotion in low-and middle-income countries. *Health Promotion International, 35*(5), 1220–1229. doi:10.1093/heapro/daz091 PMID:31495871

Philips. (n.d.). *IntelliSpace discovery*. Updated 2020. Accessed August 19, 2020. https://www.usa.philips.com/healthcare/product/HC881015/intellispace-discovery

Pieh-Holder, K. L., Callahan, C., & Young, P. (2012). Qualitative needs assessment: Healthcare experiences of underserved populations in Montgomery County, Virginia, USA. *Rural and Remote Health, 12*(3), 1–11. doi:10.22605/RRH1816 PMID:22812680

Pierce, D. (2018). *Step into your new virtual office.* Wired blogpost. Available at https://www.wired.com/ story/ augmented-reality-in-the-workplace/

Piergentili, P. (2017). Monopoly and public health in the medication market: The case of sofosbuvir. *Journal of Generic Medicines, 13*(3), 131–136. doi:10.1177/1741134317705691

Pilon, L., Foster, A., Zimmerman, P. A., & Macbeth, D. (2023). The role of online marketing to engage healthcare workers with infection prevention and control information and resources: A pilot study. *Infection, Disease & Health, 28*(3), 28. doi:10.1016/j.idh.2023.02.002 PMID:36868992

Pirson, M., Martin, K., & Parmar, B. (2017). Formation of stakeholder trust in business and the role of personal values. *Journal of Business Ethics, 145*(1), 1–20. doi:10.100710551-015-2839-2

Poh, J. (2021). *Everything You Need to Know about Your MediSave Account in 2021*. Academic Press.

Poh, J. (2022). *Guide to Your MediSave Account in 2022: Its Uses*. Contributions, Limits & More.

Poly, T. N., Islam, M. M., Walther, B. A., Lin, M. C., & Li, Y. C. J. (2023). Artificial Intelligence in Diabetic Retinopathy: Bibliometric Analysis. *Computer Methods and Programs in Biomedicine*, 107358. doi:10.1016/j.cmpb.2023.107358 PMID:36731310

Popa, A. L., Ţarcă, N. N., Sasu, D. V., Bodog, S. A., Roşca, R. D., & Tarcza, T. M. (2022). Exploring Marketing Insights for Healthcare: Trends and Perspectives Based on Literature Investigation. *Sustainability (Basel), 14*(17), 10499. doi:10.3390u141710499

Popescu, C., El-Chaarani, H., El-Abiad, Z., & Gigauri, I. (2022). Implementation of Health Information Systems to Improve Patient Identification. *International Journal of Environmental Research and Public Health, 19*(22), 15236. doi:10.3390/ijerph192215236 PMID:36429954

Portafolio. (2021, June 13). *Las 10 EPS más grandes del país, según sus ingresos operacionales*. Portafolio. https://www.portafolio.co/negocios/empresas/las-10-eps-mas-grandes-del-pais-segun-sus-ingresos-en-2020-552928

Portafolio. (2022, July 27). *Panorama de seguridad alimentaria en el país mejoró en junio de 2022*. Portafolio. https://www.portafolio.co/economia/finanzas/alimentos-cuantas-comidas-al-dia-consumen-los-colombianos-segun-el-dane-568760

Porter, M. E., & Kramer, M. R. (2011). Tworzenie wartości dla biznesu i społeczeństwa. *Harvard Business Review Polska, 99*.

Prajapati, V., Tripathy, S., & Dureja, H. (2013). Product lifecycle management through patents and regulatory strategies. *Journal of Medical Marketing, 13*(3), 171–180. doi:10.1177/1745790413497388

Prater, M. A., Johnstun, M. L., Dyches, T. T., & Johnstun, M. R. (2006). Using children's books as bibliotherapy for at-risk students: A guide for teachers. *Preventing School Failure, 50*(4), 5–10. doi:10.3200/PSFL.50.4.5-10

Press Trust of India. (2019). 25 batches of drugs of 18 pharma companies found substandard since Jan 2018 by BPPI. *The Hindu Business Line*. Available at https://www.thehindubusinessline.com/news/25-batches-of-drugs-of-18-pharma-companies-found-substandard-since-jan-2018-by-bppi/article27956298.ece

Public Law No: 108-173 (08/12/2003).

Purcarea, E. V. L. (2019). The impact of marketing strategies in healthcare systems. *Journal of Medicine and Life, 12*(2), 93–96. doi:10.25122/jml-2019-1003 PMID:31406509

Purnomo, Y. J. (2023). Digital Marketing Strategy to Increase Sales Conversion on E-commerce Platforms. *Journal of Contemporary Administration and Management, 1*(2), 54–62. Advance online publication. doi:10.61100/adman.v1i2.23

Purwanto, A. (2022). How The Role of Digital Marketing and Brand Image on Food Product Purchase Decisions? An Empirical Study on Indonesian SMEs in the Digital Era. *Journal of Industrial Engineering & Management Research*.

Rahane, W., Dalvi, H., Magar, Y., Kalane, A., & Jondhale, S. (2018). *Lung Cancer Detection Using Image Processing and Machine Learning HealthCare.* Paper presented at the 2018 International Conference on Current Trends towards Converging Technologies (ICCTCT), Comibatore, India. 10.1109/ICCTCT.2018.8551008

Rahman, Z. (2017). The Impact of Social Media Engagement Metrics on Purchase Intention: A Study on Brand Fan Page Followers. *LUMEN Proceedings, 1*, 665-681.

Rathod, S. K. (2017). Compulsory licences on pharmaceutical patents in India: A short article. *Journal of Generic Medicines*, *13*(3), 108–113. doi:10.1177/1741134317691804

Rathod, S. K. (2017). The curious case of India's Bolar provision. *Journal of Generic Medicines*, *14*(1), 16–21. doi:10.1177/1741134317745351

Reardon, S. (2019). Rise of robot radiologists. *Nature*, *576*(7787), S54–S58. doi:10.1038/d41586-019-03847-z PMID:31853073

Reddy, P., Sharma, B., & Chaudhary, K. (2020). Digital literacy: A review of literature. *International Journal of Technoethics*, *11*(2), 65–94. doi:10.4018/IJT.20200701.oa1

REDMED. (n.d.) Online Clinic For Georgian Immigrants Is Now Available. https://georgians.gr/redmed-for-georgians/

Renu, N. (2021). Innovative Healthcare Marketing Strategies during COVID-19. *Journal of Marketing Management*, *9*(2), 45–49.

Restrepo-Zea, J. H., Silva-Maya, C., Andrade-Rivas, F., & Vh-Dover, R. (2014). Acceso a servicios de salud: Análisis de barreras y estrategias en el caso de Medellín, Colombia. *Revista Gerencia y Políticas de Salud*, *13*(27), 236–259. doi:10.11144/Javeriana.rgyps13-27.assa

Reubi, D., Herrick, C., & Brown, T. (2016). The politics of non-communicable diseases in the global South. *Health & Place*, *39*, 179–187. doi:10.1016/j.healthplace.2015.09.001 PMID:26365886

Reynolds, L., & McKee, M. (2011). Serve the people or close the sale? Profit-driven overuse of injections and infusions in China's market-based healthcare system. *The International Journal of Health Planning and Management*, *26*(4), 449–470. doi:10.1002/hpm.1112 PMID:22213261

Riek, L. D. (2017). Healthcare robotics. *Communications of the ACM*, *60*(11), 68–78. doi:10.1145/3127874

Riordan, R. J., & Wilson, L. S. (1989). Bibliotherapy: Does it work? *Journal of Counseling and Development*, *67*(9), 506–508. doi:10.1002/j.1556-6676.1989.tb02131.x

Rippen, H. E., & Yasnoff, W. A. (2004). Building the national health information infrastructure. *Journal of American Health Information Management Association*, *75*(5), 21–24. PMID:15141583

Rivero-Moreno, Y., Echevarria, S., Vidal-Valderrama, C., Pianetti, L., Cordova-Guilarte, J., Navarro-Gonzalez, J., ... Acero-Alvarracín, K. (2023). Robotic Surgery: A Comprehensive Review of the Literature and Current Trends. *Cureus*, *15*(7), e42370. doi:10.7759/cureus.42370 PMID:37621804

Robinson, L. (2013). Is digital health technology empowering patients? *Journal of Medical Radiation Sciences*, *60*(3), 79–80. doi:10.1002/jmrs.20 PMID:26229613

Robinson, M. N., Tansil, K. A., Elder, R. W., Soler, R. E., Labre, M. P., Mercer, S. L., Eroglu, D., Baur, C., Lyon-Daniel, K., Fridinger, F., Sokler, L. A., Green, L. W., Miller, T., Dearing, J. W., Evans, W. D., Snyder, L. B., Kasisomayajula Viswanath, K., Beistle, D. M., Chervin, D. D., ... Rimer, B. K. (2014). Mass media health communication campaigns combined with health-related product distribution: A community guide systematic review. *American Journal of Preventive Medicine*, *47*(3), 360–371. doi:10.1016/j.amepre.2014.05.034 PMID:25145620

Roca, S., Hernández, M., Sancho, J., García, J., & Alesanco, Á. (2020). *Virtual Assistant Prototype for Managing Medication Using Messaging Platforms.* Paper presented at the XV Mediterranean Conference on Medical and Biological Engineering and Computing – MEDICON 2019, Cham, Switzerland.

Rogers, M. A., Lemmen, K., Kramer, R., Mann, J., & Chopra, V. (2017). Internet-delivered health interventions that work: Systematic review of meta-analyses and evaluation of website availability. *Journal of Medical Internet Research*, *19*(3), e90. doi:10.2196/jmir.7111 PMID:28341617

Rolls, K., Hansen, M., Jackson, D., & Elliott, D. (2016). How health care professionals use social media to create virtual communities: An integrative review. *Journal of Medical Internet Research*, *18*(6), e166. doi:10.2196/jmir.5312 PMID:27328967

Rong, G., Mendez, A., Bou Assi, E., Zhao, B., & Sawan, M. (2020). Artificial Intelligence in Healthcare: Review and Prediction Case Studies. *Engineering (Beijing)*, *6*(3), 291–301. doi:10.1016/j.eng.2019.08.015

Roth-Cline, M., & Nelson, R. M. (2013). Parental permission and child assent in research on children. *The Yale Journal of Biology and Medicine*, *86*(3), 291. PMID:24058304

Royle, J., & Laing, A. (2015). The digital marketing skills gap: Developing a Digital Marketer Model for the communication industries. *International Journal of Information Management*, *34*(2), 65–73. doi:10.1016/j.ijinfomgt.2013.11.008

Rush, K. L., Seaton, C., Li, E., Oelke, N. D., & Pesut, B. (2021). Rural use of health service and telemedicine during COVID-19: The role of access and eHealth literacy. *Health Informatics Journal*, *27*(2), 14604582211020064. doi:10.1177/14604582211020064 PMID:34041936

Rusu, A., Kuokkanen, K., & Heier, A. (2011, October). Current trends in the pharmaceutical industry—A case study approach. *European Journal of Pharmaceutical Sciences*, *44*(3), 437–440. doi:10.1016/j.ejps.2011.07.008 PMID:21782941

Rycraft, S. (2018). *7 benefits of using LinkedIn.* LinkedIn blogpost. Available at https://www.linkedin.com/ pulse/ 7-benefits-using-linkedin-sarah-rycraft

Rzetecki, M. (2020). *Marketing of Medical Services – what is it?* mrzetecki.com

Sageena, G., Sharma, M., & Kapur, A. (2021). Evolution of Smart Healthcare: Telemedicine During COVID-19 Pandemic. *J. Inst. Eng. India Ser. B*, *102*(6), 1319–1324. doi:10.100740031-021-00568-8

Salcedo Aparicio, D.M., Ibarra Peña, K.A., Ceballos Muñoz, V.I., & Pazmiño Peñafiel, E.S. (2022). Digital meanings: multimodal communications and multiliteracy. *RECIMUNDO*, 147-154. .(3).junio.2022.147-154 doi:10.26820/recimundo/6

Salvini, G., Hofstede, G. J., Verdouw, C. N., Rijswijk, K., & Klerkx, L. (2022). Enhancing digital transformation towards virtual supply chains: A simulation game for Dutch floriculture. *Production Planning and Control*, *33*(13), 1252–1269. doi:10.1080/09537287.2020.1858361

Sarkar, S. (2012). The Role of Information and Communication Technology (ICT) in Higher Education for the 21st Century. *The Science Probe*, 30-41.

Sato, M., Morimoto, K., Kajihara, S., Tateishi, R., Shiina, S., Koike, K., & Yatomi, Y. (2019). Machine-learning approach for the development of a novel predictive model for the diagnosis of hepatocellular carcinoma. *Scientific Reports*, *9*(1), 7704. doi:10.103841598-019-44022-8 PMID:31147560

Saunders, M., Lewis, P., & Thornhill, A. (2019). *Research methods for business students* (8th ed.). Pearson Education Ltd.

Saura, J. R. (2021). Using Data Sciences in Digital Marketing: Framework, methods, and performance metrics. *Journal of Innovation & Knowledge*, *6*(2), 92–102. doi:10.1016/j.jik.2020.08.001

Sawa, D. (2019). Extreme loneliness or the perfect balance? How to work from home and stay healthy. *The Guardian Health & Wellbeing*. Available at https://www.theguardian.com/ lifeandstyle/ 2019/ mar/ 25/ extreme-loneliness-or-the-perfect-balance-how-to-work-from-home-and-stay-healthy

Scherer, L., Kuss, M., & Nahm, W. (2023). Review of Artificial Intelligence–Based Signal Processing in Dialysis: Challenges for Machine-Embedded and Complementary Applications. *Advances in Kidney Disease and Health*, *30*(1), 40–46. doi:10.1053/j.akdh.2022.11.002 PMID:36723281

Schillinger, D. (2002). Association of health literacy with diabetes outcomes. *Journal of the American Medical Association*, *288*(4), 475–478. doi:10.1001/jama.288.4.475 PMID:12132978

Schivinski, B., Christodoulides, G., & Dabrowski, D. (2016). Measuring consumers' engagement with brand-related social-media content: Development and validation of a scale that identifies levels of social-media engagement with brands. *Journal of Advertising Research*, *56*(1), 64–80. doi:10.2501/JAR-2016-004

Schlesinger, M., Grob, R., & Shaller, D. (2015). Using patient-reported information to improve clinical practice. *Health Services Research*, *50*(S2), 2116–2154. doi:10.1111/1475-6773.12420 PMID:26573890

Schönberger, D. (2019). Artificial intelligence in healthcare: A critical analysis of the legal and ethical implications. *International Journal of Law and Information Technology*, *27*(2), 171–203. doi:10.1093/ijlit/eaz004

Schramm, M. E., & Hu, M. Y. (2013). Perspective: The evolution of R&D conduct in the pharmaceutical industry. *Journal of Product Innovation Management*, *30*(S1), 203–213. doi:10.1111/jpim.12072

Schwartz, L. M., & Woloshin, S. (2019). Medical marketing in the United States, 1997-2016. *Journal of the American Medical Association*, *321*(1), 80–96. doi:10.1001/jama.2018.19320 PMID:30620375

Selin, E., & Graube, K. (2017). *Reading aloud to children in hospital. Bibliotherapy as a community builder.* Paper presented at IFLA WLIC 2017 – Wrocław, Poland – Libraries. Solidarity. Society. in Session 138 - Literacy and Reading, Libraries for Children and Young Adults, Public Libraries and School Libraries. https://library.ifla.org/id/eprint/1784

Selsky, J. W., & Parker, B. (2005). Cross-sector partnerships to address social issues: Challenges to theory and practice. *Journal of Management*, *31*(6), 849–873. doi:10.1177/0149206305279601

Selvaraj, M. S., Rajaprakash, S., & Mariappan, R., & RajeshKumar, M. M. (2023). An Innovation Technique Of Artificial Intelligence Enabled Doctor Assistant In Field Of Health Care. *Journal of Pharmaceutical Negative Results*, 2352–2358.

Senbekov, M., Saliev, T., Bukeyeva, Z., Almabayeva, A., Zhanaliyeva, M., Aitenova, N., Toishibekov, Y., & Fakhradiyev, I. (2020). The recent progress and applications of digital technologies in healthcare: A review. *International Journal of Telemedicine and Applications*, *2020*, 2020. doi:10.1155/2020/8830200 PMID:33343657

Serhrouchni, S., & Malmartel, A. (2021). Diagnostic agreement between telemedicine on social networks and teledermatology centers. *Annals of Family Medicine*, *19*(1), 24–29. doi:10.1370/afm.2608 PMID:33431387

Shawky, S., Kubacki, K., Dietrich, T., & Weaven, S. (2019). Using social media to create engagement: A social marketing review. *Journal of Social Marketing*, *9*(2), 204–224. doi:10.1108/JSOCM-05-2018-0046

Sheaff, R., Morando, V., Chambers, N., Exworthy, M., Mahon, A., Byng, R., & Mannion, R. (2020). Managerial workarounds in three European DRG systems. *Journal of Health Organization and Management*, *34*(3), 295–311. doi:10.1108/JHOM-10-2019-0295 PMID:32364346

Sheth, J. N., & Parvatiyar, A. (1995). The evolution of relationship marketing. *International Business Review*, *4*(4), 397–418. doi:10.1016/0969-5931(95)00018-6

Siddiq, M. (2020). ML-based Medical Image Analysis for Anomaly Detection in CT Scans, X-rays, and MRIs. *Devotion Journal of Community Service*, *2*(1), 53–64.

Simond, S. K. (1974). Health education as a social policy. *Health Education Monographs*, *2*(1_suppl), 1–25. doi:10.1177/10901981740020S102

Singh, K. (2010). Ramesh Juneja: A journey from Medical representative to meteor of India's biggest marketer of ED drugs. *The Economic Times*. Available at https://economictimes.indiatimes.com/ramesh-juneja-a-journey-from-medical-representative-to-meteor-of-indias-biggest-marketer-of-ed-drugs/articleshow/5831020.cms?from=mdr

Sinha, S., & Rajagopal, D. (2017). Max Bupa, Hospital Lobby Group spar over generic drug prescription. *The Economic Times*. Available at https://economictimes.indiatimes.com/industry/healthcare/biotech/healthcare/max-bupa-hospital-lobby-group-spar-over-generic-drug-prescription/articleshow/58634898.cms?utm_source=contentofinterest&utm_medium=text&utm_campaign=cppst

Sin, L. Y., Alan, C. B., Yau, O. H., Lee, J. S., & Chow, R. (2002). The effect of relationship marketing orientation on business performance in a service-oriented economy. *Journal of Services Marketing*, *16*(7), 656–676. doi:10.1108/08876040210447360

Sin, L. Y., Tse, A. C., Chan, H., Heung, V. C., & Yim, F. H. (2006). The effects of relationship marketing orientation on business performance in the hotel industry. *Journal of Hospitality & Tourism Research (Washington, D.C.)*, *30*(4), 407–426. doi:10.1177/1096348006287863

Smedley, T. (2013). Patent wars: has India taken on Big Pharma and won? *The Guardian*. Available at https://www.theguardian.com/sustainable-business/patent-wars-india-takes-on-big-pharma

Smith, A. C., Thomas, E., Snoswell, C. L., Haydon, H., Mehrotra, A., Clemensen, J., & Caffery, L. J. (2020). Telehealth for global emergencies: Implications for coronavirus disease 2019 (COVID-19). *Journal of Telemedicine and Telecare*, *26*(5), 309–313. doi:10.1177/1357633X20916567 PMID:32196391

Sofaer, S. (1999). Qualitative methods: What are they and why use them? *Health Services Research*, *34*(5 Pt 2), 1101. PMID:10591275

Sokoya, T., Zhou, Y., Diaz, S., Law, T., Himawan, L., Lekey, F., Shi, L., Gimbel, R. W., & Jing, X. (2022). Health Indicators as Measures of Individual Health Status and Their Public Perspectives: Cross-sectional Survey Study. *Journal of Medical Internet Research*, *24*(6), e38099. doi:10.2196/38099 PMID:35623051

Solanki, R. K., Rajawat, A. S., Gadekar, A. R., & Patil, M. E. (2023). Building a Conversational Chatbot Using Machine Learning: Towards a More Intelligent Healthcare Application. In M. B. Garcia, M. V. Lopez Cabrera, & R. P. P. de Almeida (Eds.), *Handbook of Research on Instructional Technologies in Health Education and Allied Disciplines* (pp. 285–309). IGI Global. doi:10.4018/978-1-6684-7164-7.ch013

Song, C. H., & Han, J. W. (2016). Patent cliff and strategic switch: Exploring strategic design possibilities in the pharmaceutical industry. *SpringerPlus*, *5*(1), 1–14. doi:10.118640064-016-2323-1 PMID:27347468

Song, M., Zheng, C., & Wang, J. (2022). The role of digital economy in China's sustainable development in a post-pandemic environment. *Journal of Enterprise Information Management*, *35*(1), 58–77. doi:10.1108/JEIM-03-2021-0153

Spielmans, G. I., & Parry, P. I. (2010). From evidence-based medicine to marketing-based medicine: Evidence from internal industry documents. *Journal of Bioethical Inquiry*, *7*(1), 13–29. doi:10.100711673-010-9208-8

Sreenivas, T., Srinivasarao, B., Srinivasa Rao, U., & India, A. (2013). An analysis on marketing mix in hospitals. *International Journal of Advanced Research in Management and Social Sciences*, *2*(4), 187–207.

Stanley, N., Oram, S., Jakobowitz, S., Westwood, J., Borschmann, R., Zimmerman, C., & Howard, L. M. (2016). The health needs and healthcare experiences of young people trafficked into the UK. *Child Abuse & Neglect*, *59*, 100–110. doi:10.1016/j.chiabu.2016.08.001 PMID:27552002

Stano, M. (1981, September). Individual Health Accounts: An Alternative Health Care Financing Approach. *Health Care Financing Review*, *3*(1), 117–125. PMID:10309471

Steering Committee of the Climate Change Study, Australian Academy of Science, Australian Academy of Technological Sciences, & Academy of the Social Sciences in Australia. (1995). *Climate Change Science: Current Understanding and Uncertainties*. Australian Academy of Technological Sciences and Engineering.

Strehle, E. M., & Shabde, N. (2006). One hundred years of telemedicine: Does this new technology have a place in paediatrics? *Archives of Disease in Childhood*, *91*(12), 956–959. doi:10.1136/adc.2006.099622 PMID:17119071

Sutherland, B. L., Pecanac, K., LaBorde, T. M., Bartels, C. M., & Brennan, M. B. (2022). Good working relationships: How healthcare system proximity influences trust between healthcare workers. *Journal of Interprofessional Care*, *36*(3), 331–339. doi:10.1080/13561820.2021.1920897 PMID:34126853

Swan, E. L., Dahl, A. J., & Peltier, J. W. (2019). Health-care marketing in an omni-channel environment: Exploring telemedicine and other digital touchpoints. *Journal of Research in Interactive Marketing*, *13*(4), 602–618. doi:10.1108/JRIM-03-2019-0039

Syed, M., Ahmed, F., Zahid, N., Khalid, N., & Israr, N. (2021). Essentials of Healthcare Marketing. *Asian Journal of Medicine and Health*, *19*(2), 73–79. doi:10.9734/ajmah/2021/v19i230306

Tafur, L. A., & Prada, S. (2019). El Sistema General de Seguridad Social en Salud de Colombia. *PROESA*. https://docplayer.es/142078983-Proesa-el-sistema-general-de-seguridad-social-en-salud-de-colombia-luis-alberto-tafur-calderon-md-esp-sergio-i-prada-mpa-phd.html

Taleghani, M., Gilaninia, S., & Mousavian, S. J. (2011). The role of relationship marketing in customer orientation process in the banking industry with focus on loyalty (Case study: Banking industry of Iran). *International Journal of Business and Social Science*, *2*(19).

Tan, H., Zhao, F., Hao, H., & Liu, Z. (2020). Estimate of safety impact of lane keeping assistant system on fatalities and injuries reduction for China: Scenarios through 2030. *Traffic Injury Prevention*, *21*(2), 156–162. doi:10.1080/15389588.2020.1711518 PMID:32023126

Tan, T. F., Li, Y., Lim, J. S., Gunasekeran, D. V., Teo, Z. L., Ng, W. Y., & Ting, D. S. (2022). Metaverse and virtual health care in ophthalmology: Opportunities and challenges. *Asia-Pacific Journal of Ophthalmology*, *11*(3), 237–246. doi:10.1097/APO.0000000000000537 PMID:35772084

Tan, X., Liu, X., & Shao, H. (2017). Healthy China 2030: A vision for health care. *Value in Health Regional Issues, 12*, 112–114. doi:10.1016/j.vhri.2017.04.001 PMID:28648308

Tarumi, S., Takeuchi, W., Chalkidis, G., Rodriguez-Loya, S., Kuwata, J., Flynn, M., . . . Kawamoto, K. (2021). Leveraging Artificial Intelligence to Improve Chronic Disease Care: Methods and Application to Pharmacotherapy Decision Support for Type-2 Diabetes Mellitus. *Methods Inf Med, 60*(S 01), e32-e43. doi:10.1055/s-0041-1728757

Taylor, M. J., Shikaislami, C., McNicholas, C., Taylor, D., Reed, J., & Vlaev, I. (2020). Using virtual worlds as a platform for collaborative meetings in healthcare: A feasibility study. *BMC Health Services Research, 20*(1), 1–10. doi:10.118612913-020-05290-7 PMID:32429971

Tenforde, M. W., Kim, S. S., Lindsell, C. J., Billig Rose, E., Shapiro, N. I., Files, D. C., Gibbs, K. W., Erickson, H. L., Steingrub, J. S., Smithline, H. A., Gong, M. N., Aboodi, M. S., Exline, M. C., Henning, D. J., Wilson, J. G., Khan, A., Qadir, N., Brown, S. M., Peltan, I. D., ... Feldstein, L. R.IVY Network Investigators. (2020, July 31). CDC COVID-19 Response Team; IVY Network Investigators. Symptom Duration and Risk Factors for Delayed Return to Usual Health Among Outpatients with COVID-19 in a Multistate Health Care Systems Network - United States, March-June 2020. *MMWR. Morbidity and Mortality Weekly Report, 69*(30), 993–998. doi:10.15585/mmwr.mm6930e1 PMID:32730238

Thapa, D. K., Visentin, D. C., Kornhaber, R., West, S., & Cleary, M. (2021). The influence of online health information on health decisions: A systematic review. *Patient Education and Counseling, 104*(4), 770–784. doi:10.1016/j.pec.2020.11.016 PMID:33358253

Thimbleby, H. (2013). Technology and the future of healthcare. *Journal of Public Health Research, 2*(3).

Thomas, G. (2021). How to do your case study. *How to do your case study*, 1-320.

Thomason, J. (2021). Big tech, big data and the new world of digital health. *Global Health Journal (Amsterdam, Netherlands), 5*(4), 165–168. doi:10.1016/j.glohj.2021.11.003

Thomas, R. K. (2008). *Health services marketing: A practitioner's guide*. Springer Science & Business Media. doi:10.1007/978-0-387-73606-8

Thompson, A. G., & Sunol, R. (1995). Expectations as determinants of patient satisfaction: Concepts, theory and evidence. *International Journal for Quality in Health Care : Journal of the International Society for Quality in Health Care, 7*(2), 127–141. doi:10.1093/intqhc/7.2.127 PMID:7655809

Todua, N., & Jashi, Ch. (2018). Influence of Social Marketing on the Behavior of Georgian Consumers Regarding Healthy Nutrition. *Soobshcheniia Akademii Nauk Gruzinskoi SSR, 12*(2), 183–190.

Toor, A., Husnain, M., & Hussain, T. (2017). The impact of social network marketing on consumer purchase intention in Pakistan: Consumer engagement as a mediator. *AJBA, 10*(1), 167–199.

Towe, V. L., Leviton, L., Chandra, A., Sloan, J. C., Tait, M., & Orleans, T. (2016). Cross-sector collaborations and partnerships: Essential ingredients to help shape health and well-being. *Health Affairs, 35*(11), 1964–1969. doi:10.1377/hlthaff.2016.0604 PMID:27834234

Tsitsani, P., Psyllidou, S., Batzios, S. P., Livas, S., Ouranos, M., & Cassimos, D. (2012). Fairy tales: A compass for children's healthy development–a qualitative study in a Greek island. *Child: Care, Health and Development, 38*(2), 266–272. doi:10.1111/j.1365-2214.2011.01216.x PMID:21375565

Tzokas, N., & Saren, M. (2004). Competitive advantage, knowledge and relationship marketing: Where, what and how? *Journal of Business and Industrial Marketing, 19*(2), 124–135. doi:10.1108/08858620410524007

UK VIP. (n.d.). *The four basic styles of communication.* University of Kentucky Violence Intervention and Prevention Centre. Available at https://www.uky.edu/ hr/ sites/ www.uky.edu.hr/ files/ wellness/ images/ Conf14_FourCommStyles.pdf

UN. (n.d.). *Sustainable Development Goals.* United Nations. Retrieved July 9, 2023 from https://www.un.org/sustainabledevelopment/

Urrútia, G., & Bonfill, X. (2010). Declaración PRISMA: Una propuesta para mejorar la publicación de revisiones sistemáticas y metaanálisis. *Medicina Clínica, 135*(11), 507–511. doi:10.1016/j.medcli.2010.01.015 PMID:20206945

Uzialko, A. 2019, June 9). Artificial Intelligence Will Change Healthcare as We Know it. Business News Daily.

van Esch, P., & Stewart Black, J. (2021). Artificial Intelligence (AI): Revolutionizing Digital Marketing. *Australasian Marketing Journal, 29*(3), 199–203. Advance online publication. doi:10.1177/18393349211037684

Veleva, S., & Tsvetanova, A. (2020). *Characteristics of the digital marketing advantages and disadvantages.* IOP Con. doi:10.1088/1757-899X/940/1/012065

Vélez, M. (2016). *La salud en Colombia, pasado, presente y futuro de un Sistema en crisis.* Academic Press.

Veloutsou, C., Saren, M., & Tzokas, N. (2002). Relationship marketing: What if…? *European Journal of Marketing, 36*(4), 433–449. doi:10.1108/03090560210417255

Verma, V. K., & Verma, S. (2022). Machine learning applications in healthcare sector: An overview. *Materials Today: Proceedings, 57,* 2144–2147. doi:10.1016/j.matpr.2021.12.101

Verulava, T. (2022). Factors influencing medical students' choice of family medicine. *Family Medicine & Primary Care Review, 113017.*

Verulava, T., & Jorbenadze, A. (2021). Context and issues of social health insurance introduction in Georgia. *Arch Balk Med Union., 56*(3), 349–357. doi:10.31688/ABMU.2021.56.3.09

Veseli-Kurtishi, T. (2018). Social media as a tool for the sustainability of small and medium businesses in Macedonia. *European Journal of Sustainable Development, 7*(4), 262–262. doi:10.14207/ejsd.2018.v7n4p262

Vestergaard, A., Langevang, T., Morsing, M., & Murphy, L. (2021). Partnerships for development. Assessing the impact potential of cross-sector partnerships. *World Development, 143,* 105447. doi:10.1016/j.worlddev.2021.105447

W3C. (2023). *Accessibility Fundamentals.* World Wide Web Consortium. Retrieved 5 July 2023 from https://www.w3.org/WAI/fundamentals/

Waddock, S. A. (1991). A typology of social partnership organizations. *Administration & Society, 22*(4), 480–515. doi:10.1177/009539979102200405

Wagner, H. C., Fleming, D., Mangold, W. G., & LaForge, R. W. (1994). Relationship marketing in health care. *Marketing Health Services, 14*(4), 42. PMID:10154636

Wagstaff, A. (2009). *Reforming China's rural health system.* World Bank Publications. doi:10.1596/978-0-8213-7982-0

Wang, J. (2010). *Brand new China: Advertising, media, and commercial culture.* Harvard University Press. doi:10.4159/9780674044821

Wang, J. C., & Chang, C. H. (2013). How online social ties and product-related risks influence purchase intentions: A Facebook experiment. *Electronic Commerce Research and Applications, 12*(5), 337–346. doi:10.1016/j.elerap.2013.03.003

Wang, Q., Su, M., Zhang, M., & Li, R. (2021). Integrating digital technologies and public health to fight Covid-19 pandemic: Key technologies, applications, challenges and outlook of digital healthcare. *International Journal of Environmental Research and Public Health, 18*(11), 6053. doi:10.3390/ijerph18116053 PMID:34199831

Wang, S. S., & Stefanone, M. A. (2013). Showing off? Human mobility and the interplay of traits, self-disclosure, and Facebook check-ins. *Social Science Computer Review, 31*(4), 437–457. doi:10.1177/0894439313481424

Wang, W., Sun, L., Liu, T., & Lai, T. (2022). The use of E-health during the COVID-19 pandemic: A case study in China's Hubei province. *Health Sociology Review, 31*(3), 215–231. doi:10.1080/14461242.2021.1941184 PMID:34161186

Wang, Y., Kung, L., & Byrd, T. A. (2018). Big data analytics: Understanding its capabilities and potential benefits for healthcare organizations. *Technological Forecasting and Social Change, 126*, 3–13. doi:10.1016/j.techfore.2015.12.019

Wang, Z., Xu, R., Liu, Y., & Li, Y. (2023). Licensing policy and platform models of telemedicine: A multi-case study from China. *Frontiers in Public Health, 11*, 1108621. doi:10.3389/fpubh.2023.1108621 PMID:36817879

Ward, R. (2013). The application of technology acceptance and diffusion of innovation models in healthcare informatics. *Health Policy and Technology, 2*(4), 222-228.

Waters, S., Edmondston, S. J., Yates, P. J., & Gucciardi, D. F. (2016). Identification of factors influencing patient satisfaction with orthopaedic outpatient clinic consultation: A qualitative study. *Manual Therapy, 25*, 48–55. doi:10.1016/j.math.2016.05.334 PMID:27422597

WCED. (1987). Our common future (The Brundtland Report). World Commission on Environment and Development, Oxford University Press.

Wee, C. K., Zhou, X., Sun, R., Gururajan, R., Tao, X., Li, Y., & Wee, N. (2022). Triaging Medical Referrals Based on Clinical Prioritisation Criteria Using Machine Learning Techniques. *International Journal of Environmental Research and Public Health, 19*(12), 7384. doi:10.3390/ijerph19127384 PMID:35742633

Weideman, M., & Kritzinger, W. (2017). Parallel search engine optimisation and pay-per-click campaigns: A comparison of cost per acquisition. *South African Journal of Information Management, 19*(1), 1–13.

Weinreich, N. K. (2010). *Hands-on social marketing: a step-by-step guide to designing change for good*. Sage Publications.

Wen, L. S., & Tucker, S. (2015). What do people want from their health care? A qualitative study. *Journal of Participatory Medicine, 7*, e10.

Whaley, C. M., Pera, M. F., Cantor, J., Chang, J., Velasco, J., Hagg, H. K., Sood, N., & Bravata, D. M. (2020, November 2). Changes in health services use among commercially insured US populations during the COVID-19 pandemic.[. *JAMA Network Open, 3*(11), e2024984. doi:10.1001/jamanetworkopen.2020.24984 PMID:33151319

WHO. (n.d.). *Health Promotion.* World Health Organization. Retrieved July 3, 2023 from https://www.who.int/western-pacific/about/how-we-work/programmes/health-promotion

Williamson, B. (2015). Algorithmic skin: Health-tracking technologies, personal analytics and the biopedagogies of digitized health and physical education. *Sport Education and Society, 20*(1), 133–151. doi:10.1080/13573322.2014.962494

Woodcock, E., Kier, S., & Zhao, V. (2017). Patient access metrics in the ambulatory enterprise. *Management in Healthcare, 2*(2), 153–164.

Woods, D. (2010). *Poor communication between managers and employees wastes time and impacts productivity.* HR. Available at http://www.hrmagazine.co.uk/ article-details/ poor-communication-between-managers-and-employees-wastes-time-and-impacts-productivity

World Health Organization. (2021). *Global strategy on digital health 2020-2025.* Author.

World Life Expectancy. (n.d.) World Health Rankings Live Longer, Live Better. https://www.worldlifeexpectancy.com/country-health-profile/georgia

World Ometers. (n.d.) https://www.worldometers.info/gdp/gdp per capita.

Wright, G. H., & Taylor, A. (2005). Strategic partnerships and relationship marketing in healthcare. *Public Management Review, 7*(2), 203–224. doi:10.1080/14719030500091251

Wu, C. C. (2011). The impact of hospital brand image on service quality, patient satisfaction and loyalty. *African Journal of Business Management, 5*(12), 4873.

Wu, H., Deng, Z., Wang, B., & Gupta, S. (2021). How does service price influence patients' decisions? An examination of the free-market pricing mechanism in online health communities. *Electronic Markets, 31*(4), 877–893. doi:10.100712525-020-00453-0

Yadav, M., & Rahman, Z. (2017). Measuring consumer perception of social media marketing activities in e-commerce industry: Scale development & validation. *Telematics and Informatics, 34*(7), 1294–1307. doi:10.1016/j.tele.2017.06.001

Yamashita, R., Nishio, M., Do, R. K. G., & Togashi, K. (2018). Convolutional neural networks: An overview and application in radiology. *Insights Into Imaging, 9*(4), 611–629. doi:10.100713244-018-0639-9 PMID:29934920

Yati, M., Wahyuni, S., & Islaeli, I. (2017). The effect of storytelling in a play therapy on anxiety level in pre-school children during hospitalization in the general hospital of Buton. *Public Health of Indonesia, 3*(3), 96–101. doi:10.36685/phi.v3i3.134

Yepes-Nuñez, J. J., Urrutia, G., Romero-Garcia, M., & Alonso-Fernandez, S. (2021). The PRISMA 2020 statement: An updated guideline for reporting systematic reviews. *Revista Española de Cardiología (English Ed.), 74*(9), 790–799. PMID:34446261

Yildirim, Y., Amarat, M., & Akbolat, M. (2022). Effect of relationship marketing on hospital loyalty: The mediating role of patient satisfaction. *International Journal of Pharmaceutical and Healthcare Marketing, 16*(3), 337–353. doi:10.1108/IJPHM-01-2021-0010

Yina, C., Pengcheng, L., Haomiao, N., & Yang, C. (2023). An empirical study of the impact of generic drug competition on drug prices in China. *Frontiers in Public Health, 11*, 1146531. doi:10.3389/fpubh.2023.1146531 PMID:37304112

Yin, H. S., Dreyer, B. P., Foltin, G., van Schaick, L., & Mendelsohn, A. L. (2007). Association of low caregiver health literacy with reported use of nonstandardized dosing instruments and lack of knowledge of weight-based dosing. *Ambulatory Pediatrics, 7*(4), 292–298. doi:10.1016/j.ambp.2007.04.004 PMID:17660100

Yin, R. K. (2009). *Case Study Research. Design and Methods* (4th ed.). SAGE Publications.

Yip, G. S., & McKern, B. (2016). *China's next strategic advantage: From imitation to innovation.* MIT press.

Yu, K.-H., Beam, A. L., & Kohane, I. S. (2018). Artificial intelligence in healthcare. *Nature Biomedical Engineering, 2*(10), 719–731. doi:10.103841551-018-0305-z PMID:31015651

Yu, X., Li, C., Shi, Y., & Yu, M. (2010). Pharmaceutical supply chain in China: Current issues and implications for health system reform. *Health Policy (Amsterdam), 97*(1), 8–15. doi:10.1016/j.healthpol.2010.02.010 PMID:20307912

Zamora, H. & Clingerman, E.M. (2011). *Health literacy among older adults: A systematic literature review.* Academic Press.

Zamora, H., & Clingerman, E. M. (2011, October). Health Literacy Among Older Adults: A Systematic Literature Review. *Journal of Gerontological Nursing*, *37*(10), 41–51. doi:10.3928/00989134-20110503-02 PMID:21634314

Zhou, L., Zhang, D., Yang, C. C., & Wang, Y. (2018). Harnessing social media for health information management. *Electronic Commerce Research and Applications*, *27*, 139–151. doi:10.1016/j.elerap.2017.12.003 PMID:30147636

Zhu, X., Weigel, P., Baloh, J., Nataliansyah, M., Gunn, N., & Mueller, K. (2019). Mobilising cross-sector collaborations to improve population health in US rural communities: A qualitative study. *BMJ Open*, *9*(11), e030983. doi:10.1136/bmjopen-2019-030983 PMID:31699729

Ziglio, E., Currie, C., & Rasmussen, V. B. (2004). The WHO cross-national study of health behavior in school aged children from 35 countries: Findings from 2001–2002. *The Journal of School Health*, *74*(6), 204–206. doi:10.1111/j.1746-1561.2004.tb07933.x PMID:15468523

Zineldin, M. (2006). The royalty of loyalty: CRM, quality and retention. *Journal of Consumer Marketing*, *23*(7), 430–437. doi:10.1108/07363760610712975

Zreik, M. (2022). US-China Relations in The Era of Multi-Polarism: Trade War Between the Two Economic Giants. *Eurasian Research Journal*, *4*(2), 43–65. doi:10.53277/2519-2442-2022.2-03

Zreik, M. (2023). From Boom to Bust: A Study of China's Economy in the Wake of COVID-19 Outbreak in H1 2020. *BRICS Journal of Economics*, *4*(1), 147–171. doi:10.3897/brics-econ.4.e101050

Zreik, M., & Abunamous, M. O. (2020). Human thinking at the time of Covid-19 and the role of swot analysis: A case study on the Chinese and Palestinian societies. *Psychology Research on Education and Social Sciences*, *2*(1), 31–40.

Zulman, D. M., Kirch, M., Zheng, K., & An, L. C. (2011). Trust in the internet as a health resource among older adults: Analysis of data from a nationally representative survey. *Journal of Medical Internet Research*, *13*(1), e1552. doi:10.2196/jmir.1552 PMID:21324832

About the Contributors

Kakhaber Djakeli was Fulbright Scholar at Yale University in the School of Public Health during 2006-2007. He received the Research Scholarship of German Academic Exchange Service during, 1998, 2004, 2009, 2013 and. 2016 and worked at Leibniz University of Hanover LUH, He delivered his classes in American and German Universities, during 2003-2020. He is now an associate professor at University of Georgia, in Georgia and a visiting Professor at Lublin University in Poland. Kakhaber Djakeli publish his works about Marketing, Health Economy, Health marketing, Healthcare reforming.

* * *

Mamatha A. is working as Assistant Professor in Department of Computer Science and Engineering, Ramaiah Institute of Technology. Having a total of 1.5 decade of teaching experience. She is a member of ISTE and IAENG. Her areas of interest include Image Processing, Network Security, Artificial Intelligence and Machine Learning.

Pilar Alarcón Urbistondo was born in Malaga on June 20th, 1965. Degree in Economics and Business Sciences from the University of Malaga. Doctor in Business Administration and Management from the University of Malaga and Professor of Marketing and Market Research of the University of Malaga where she also develops her teaching, research and transfer work. Her main line of work focuses on the identification and assessment of target markets and the description of the behaviors and perceptions of their consumers applied fundamentally to tourist destinations, although currently she works on these aspects in other public fields such as culture (museums) and public heath (hospitals). At the same time, she extends her work to the identification of vulnerabilities in the offer, B&B relationships and reputation in order to develope competitive intelligence (tools for obtaining and analyzing information from the environment) for decision-making by public agencies in their relations with the different stakeholders. Co-author of more than 15 book chapters, 30 articles in national, international and sectorial fields out of which 20 of them are included in magazines indexed of maximum level (Ranking JCR: Q1 y Q2) and 35 papers sent to national and international conferences. She participates as a researcher in more than 35 R & D & I international, national and regional research projects and contracts, of which in 25 she has been Responsible Investigator.

Edyta Bieliǹska-Dusza, Ph.D., is Assistant Professor in the Dept. of Strategic Analysis of the Cracow University of Economics. Her research revolves around strategy, technology, internal audit, and inter-organizational phenomena. Her lectures are dedicated to strategy management, technology audit, and technology design and forecasting, including management methods and tools. She has been a co-organizer of Scientific Conferences and has served as an expert in various projects ("Revolution 4.0. Regional Initiative of Excellence," "Innovation Brokers as a tool for effective development," "First Business - Support to start," "The Rapid Response Instrument"). She has also participated in study visits and scientific workshops (Stanford University, University of Berkeley), and has certificates (Eìcole Polytechnique Feìdeìrale de Lausanne, Switzerland; ISIS Innovation Ltd, Oxford; Strategic Business Insights, Stanford; PRINCE 1&2).

Juan Carlos Fandos-Roig is working as a Professor in Marketing and Market Research at the Department of Business Administration and Marketing of Jaume I University (Spain). He has developed his research work since 2003 at Universitat Jaume I in the fields of Relationship Marketing, Banking Marketing, Consumer Value, Purchase Motivation and Corporate Social Responsibility. Author of several marketing research articles in national and international scientific journals. He has participated in more than 40 national and international conferences.

Ioseb Gabelaia, Graceland University, USA, Doctor of Business Administration: Assoc. Professor. He is an expert in marketing, communications, and management with over 10 years of extensive experience in higher education. Enrollment Management expert. Certified Six Sigma Master Black Belt (CSSMBB). Master Scrum Accredited Certified (MSAC). A member of AMA (American Marketing Association) and EUMAS (European Marketing and Management Association). An individual committed to educating, coaching, and mentoring students/learners to achieve lifelong goals. Trainer and Mentor.

Iza Gigauri is based at St. Andrew the First-Called Georgian University. She received her PhD in Business Administration (Summa Cum Laude) from Ivane Javakhishvili Tbilisi State University (Georgia). She holds an MBA from Business School Netherlands (The Netherlands) and an MBA with the highest honors from the American University for Humanities (Georgia). She is a graduate with honors from Ilia State University (Georgia) and from Ruhr-University Bochum (Germany). She delivers lectures and teaches seminars at all three levels of higher education. She is an expert, opponent, and supervisor of doctoral dissertations and Master's theses. She won a number of international scholarships and awards in the field of her academic specialization. Her research interests include corporate responsibility, marketing, sustainability, social entrepreneurship, HRM, and leadership. She participated in 35 international scientific conferences and has published over 70 peer-reviewed papers, 2 books, and 14 book chapters. She is a scientific committee member and keynote speaker at international conferences, a guest editor, an editorial board member and a reviewer at international journals within Emerald, Springer, IGI Global, Frontiers, Taylor & Francis, Elsevier, Wiley, and Inderscience.

Gustavo Adolfo Girón-Restrepo is an Associate Professor of the Antonio José Camacho University (Colombia). Doctoral student in design, management and evaluation of public social welfare policies at the Jaume I University of Spain. Dentist, master in Public Health and specialist in health services management.

Revaz Gvelesiani, Ivane Javakhishvili Tbilisi State University, Georgia, is a full professor and head of the Department of the Politeconomy at Tbilisi State University. He has a lot of articles about economic development and studies into Economic Politics.

Irina Gogorishvili, Ivane Javakhishvili, Tbilisi State University, Georgia.

Charita Jashi graduated Foreign Language and Literature -English (Bachelor), Ivane Javakhishvili Tbilisi State University(1968), Moscow Institute of Economic and Law (1980). Doctor of Economics (1982). She is Associate Professor of Marketing Department, School of Economics and Bussiness, Ivane Javakhishvili Tbilisi State University, Tbilisi, Georgia.

Beena K. is working as Assistant professor at K S Institute of technology with 8 years of teaching experience. Her areas of Interest is Artificial intelligence,Machine Learning,Natural Language Processing

Vaneeta M. is working as an Associate Professor in Department of Artificial Intelligence and Data Science of Ramaiah Institute of Technology. Her areas of interest include Cryptography, Data Analytics, Blockchain, Machine Learning and Internet of Things.

Ashwani Panesar has a rich teaching experience of over 13 years, taking up various business management subjects at university level. Having worked closely with the sales aspect of the pharmaceutical industry (8 years), he had pursued his Doctorate in pharmaceutical marketing strategies from Jaipur National University, Rajasthan (India).

Aditya Prasad has worked in the distribution side of the pharmaceutical industry for over 9 years. Having graduated in electrical and electronics engineering, he also holds master's degrees in anthropology, management, psychology and philosophy. Presently, he is an adjunct faculty in the Department of Business Management, Osmania University, Telangana (India).

Mario Sierra Martin was born in Malaga on January 15th, 1990. Degree in Economics and Business Sciences from the University of Malaga. Degree in Marketing from the University of Malaga and Master in Digital Marketing. Doctoral student in Business Administration and Management from the University of Malaga where she also develops her teaching, research and transfer work. Her main line of behaviors and perceptions of their consumers. Digital marketing professional working in his own agency for 10 years.

Sandra Tena-Monferrer is a lecturer and researcher in the fields of Market Research and Consumer Behaviour at Universitat Jaume I (Spain). Her research focuses on shopping motives and attitudes in a retail setting. She has published in several national and international scientific marketing journals.

Nia Todua graduated with a bachelor's degree from Tbilisi State University. She obtained a master's degree at Masaryk University. Now she is a PhD student at Tbilisi State University.

Nugzar Todua graduated from Ivane Javackisvili Tbilisi State University, Faculty of Commerce (1986). He has PhD degrees in technical sciences at the Moscow State Institute of Commerce (1990) and Doctor of Economics Sciences at the Georgian Institute of Economic and Social Problems (1995). He is the Head and Full Professor of Marketing Department, School of Economics and Business, Ivane Javakhishvili Tbilisi State University, Tbilisi, Georgia.

Sangeetha V. currently working as Associate Professor in Department of Computer Science and Engineering at Ramaiah Institute of Technology, Bangalore. Has served in academia for more than a decade at various institutes. Received Ph.D from Visveswariah Technological University (VTU), Belagavi. Research specialization includes Networks and Security, Artificial Intelligence and Machine Learning, Blockchain. Published over 45 research papers in reputed National and International Conferences and Journals. Some of papers published by her enjoy good citation in Google Scholar, Scopus, Web of Science etc. She has also been the member of various professional societies including IEEE (IEEE Senior Member), IEI, ISTE (Life Member), IAENG (Member). She has served as reviewer, organizing chair for many IEEE conferences.

Agnieszka Żak is a graduate of the Cracow University of Economics (MA) and the Jagiellonian University (PhD). PhD in economics in the field of management science (2008). Assistant professor, employee of the Department of International Management at the Cracow University of Economics. Director of postgraduate studies in the field of "Enterprise management - MBA management studies" at the Cracow Business School of the Cracow University of Economics (since 2008). Research interests and article topics include: sustainable development, corporate social responsibility (CSR), corporate community involvement (CCI), cross - sector social partnerships, international management, intercultural communication. Social activities: Zaczytani.org Foundation - Coordinator in Krakow (since 2018).

Mohamad Zreik, a Postdoctoral Fellow at Sun Yat-sen University, is a recognized scholar in International Relations, specializing in China's Arab-region foreign policy. His recent work in soft power diplomacy compares China's methods in the Middle East and East Asia. His extensive knowledge spans Middle Eastern Studies, China-Arab relations, East Asian and Asian Affairs, Eurasian geopolitics, and Political Economy, providing him a unique viewpoint in his field. Dr. Zreik is a proud recipient of a PhD from Central China Normal University (Wuhan). He's written numerous acclaimed papers, many focusing on China's Belt and Road Initiative and its Arab-region impact. His groundbreaking research has established him as a leading expert in his field. Presently, he furthers his research on China's soft power diplomacy tactics at Sun Yat-sen University. His significant contributions make him a crucial figure in understanding contemporary international relations.

Index

M

N

O

P

R

S

T

V

www.ingramcontent.com/pod-product-compliance
Lightning Source LLC
LaVergne TN
LVHW060305011026
849161LV00011B/2777